635.9 F44fc
Fiala, John L.
Flowering crabapples

Flowering Crabapples
THE GENUS *Malus*

Flowering Crabapples
THE GENUS *Malus*

by

Fr. John L. Fiala

Technical Editor: Dr. Gilbert S. Daniels

TIMBER PRESS
Portland, Oregon

635.9
F44fc

Mention of a chemical product or trademark name is for information only. Always check the label before purchasing or using chemical products. Some forms of the systemic fungicide benomyl have been found harmful to ornamental plants. For all products mentioned, the manufacturer's recommendations and directions must be followed.

Copyright © 1994 by Timber Press, Inc.
All rights reserved.

ISBN 0-88192-292-7

Printed in Hong Kong

TIMBER PRESS, INC.
The Haseltine Building
133 S.W. Second Ave., Suite 450
Portland, Oregon 97204-3527, U.S.A.

Library of Congress Cataloging-in-Publication Data

Fiala, John L.
Flowering crabapples : the genus Malus / by John L. Fiala; technical editor, Gilbert S. Daniels.
p. cm.
Includes bibliographical references (p.) and index.
ISBN 0-88192-292-7
1. Flowering crabapples. I. Daniels, Gilbert S. II. Title.
SB413.C644F53 1994
635.9'773372—dc20 94-567
CIP

KENT FREE LIBRARY

Contents

Color plates follow page 112.

Grateful acknowledgment is made to the International Ornamental Crabapple Society for permission to use excerpts from numerous articles in their bulletins, and to the following individuals and organizations for use of photographs:

The Arnold Arboretum, Jamaica Plains, MA
Dr. Donald Egolf, U.S. National Arboretum, Washington, DC
Dr. Thomas Green, Morton Arboretum, Lisle, IL
Dr. Edward Hasselkus, University of Wisconsin
Roy Klehm, Klehm Nursery, South Barrington, IL
Linda Kreizer, Medina, OH
The Morton Arboretum, Lisle, IL
Dr. Stephen A. Spongberg, Arnold Arboretum, Jamaica Plain, MA
Keith Warren, J. Frank Schmidt & Son Co., Boring, OR
Michael and Lori Yanny, Johnson's Nursery, Milwaukee, WI
James Zampini, Lake County Nursery, Perry, OH

Note: All proceeds from the sale of this book accrue to the Research and Educational Fund of the International Ornamental Crabapple Society.

In grateful remembrance
and dedication to
Arie den Boer
and
Lester P. Nichols

Foreword

Father Fiala's book on crabapples fills a void in gardening and horticultural literature. With more than 900 named entities, it is a wonder that more has not been written about these splendid landscape plants.

Father Fiala has brought a welcome personal touch to the study of ornamental crabapples, inviting others to enjoy them and to learn more about them. That there is much more to be learned about crabapples is amply demonstrated by the quagmire that is the taxonomy and nomenclature of the genus *Malus.*

We applaud Father Fiala for trying to make some sense out of the confusion, but an example of the kind of nomenclatural problem that plagues the genus is demonstrated by the toringo crab. The name for this crabapple apparently must be changed from *Malus sieboldii* to *M. toringo.* Father Fiala has made that change, but his consequent proposal to apply the name *M. sieboldii* to the plant heretofore called *M.* ×*zumi* 'Calocarpa' is not in accord with the rules of nomenclature. The epithet *sieboldii* has already been used for an entirely different crabapple. The taxonomic situation involving the common apple remains confusing, also. Most of its hybrids are apparently crosses with the already hybridized *M.* ×*domestica* rather than with the wild *M. pumila,* a parent of the domestic apple that is rather rare in cultivation.

Only careful study of original descriptions, comparison with herbarium material, and the application of a range of techniques that a trained taxonomist can bring to these problems will solve them. We hope that Father Fiala's celebration of crabapples will inspire further work, and we ask that suggestions and questions be directed to the International Ornamental Crabapple Society.

Father Fiala began this project knowing his health was waning. He saw it nearly to completion, and the work very likely prolonged his life. He devoted his life to serving his Lord and his fellow humans. Father Fiala truly loved plants and tended his Lord's garden well. He left us with a more beautiful world—one enriched with new crabapples and lilacs and a botanical garden, Falconskeape. We remain grateful that he shared his knowledge about these remarkable plants with us.

International Ornamental Crabapple Society
The Morton Arboretum
Lisle, Illinois 60532

Preface and Acknowledgments

Working with flowering crabapples has been a joyful experience. Despite some disappointments, I have always been filled with the new hope of what another generation of plants would reveal. I began this adventure with simple trust in what I might be able to do in hybridization. Now I seek to share some of that life story with you.

I had wanted to write this book 50 years ago. Since then I have learned that it is not merely the writing of a book that is important; rather, an author must live the book first and then write, with conviction, the contents of his or her knowledge and heart. A book without knowledge is foolishness; a book without heart is empty and cold. I trust the reader will find this book has both knowledge and heart.

Over the past half century I have been taught many things about crabapples by wonderful teachers, a great deal of which I may have forgotten. These kind people have given me advice and taught me more than books ever could. Time with my plants, especially the time spent in hybridizing flowering crabapples, has seasoned my judgment and, I trust, added a depth of knowledge that I would never have thought possible so long ago. I stand in awe now of all that I have lived through in my study of flowering crabapples.

As I share and tell of the marvels that these trees unfold, I am mindful of those teachers who helped me live this book, especially the two men who greatly influenced my life with flowering crabapples. To one of them I wrote a simple letter, when I was but 12 years old, asking about crabapples. The six-page letter I received in answer to my question was filled with encouragement and a new vision of what could be done in hybridizing. I scarcely knew the meaning of that word when Arie den Boer of Waterworks Arboretum, Des Moines, IA, brought it to my attention, but I always admired him as a mentor who charted the course for a young farm boy. He set my feet and my resolve on firm ground by telling me that I could do something worthwhile working with crabapples, and down through the years, to his last letter from Monaco in 1962, his letters brought new visions and encouraged strength.

The other man who greatly influenced my life with crabapples was someone I met later in life. Professor Lester P. Nichols of Pennsylvania State University took time to see what I was doing with flowering crabapples and to encourage the directions of my hybridizing work. His vision, a practical application of good genetics to a wonderful experience in hybridizing, can be summed up with these words of advice:

> Trees filled with diseases will never survive, nor will you accomplish anything with them. Choose your disease-free progenitors wisely—then the challenge is to stick to the rules (no matter how beautiful the flower be). Disease resistance must be your first rule of thumb in judging your work.

Over the years we became staunch friends, evaluating and setting new goals. I have long forgotten how many beautiful flowering crabapples were felled along the way, but this professor's advice and recommendations have lasted me a lifetime.

To these two men of learning, I dedicate this book, for all that they have done for me and given to me. Without them, this book would not have been possible. I owe them more than I can repay.

And then there are a great many other men and women of vision whom I have met along life's way. They, too, have worked with me over the many years, sharing their plants and experiences, giving me vision, strength, and encouragement to finish this book. To these "life co-authors" I also am gratefully indebted:

Dr. Donald Egolf of the U.S. National Arboretum, Washington, DC, a wonderful teacher and friend in hybridizing, is a wonder-filled, living book of endless knowledge on hybridizing and plants. He has always held his book of learning open to me.

Professor Robert Clark, Meredith, NH, steadfast friend of many decades past, has patiently read the chapter on taxonomy and shared his great knowledge of plants with me. In my years of illness, he has been a comfort and strength.

Henry Ross, director of Gardenview Horticultural Park, Strongsville, OH, has been a teacher and steadfast friend for most of my life. I am grateful to him for the beauty of his crabapple introductions that grace Falconskeape Gardens and for the wisdom of his knowledge that fills my life. His garden of exotic and rare plantings is not duplicated anywhere else in the world. Together he and I, along with our crabapple introductions, have grown old with a few of our many dreams fulfilled.

Francis Nock, Perry, OH, who like Moses can take a lifeless staff, strike the ground, and make it grow, is a wonderful plantsman and propagator. Like me, he, too, sees visions and dreams whenever we walk in a garden.

Roy and Sarah Klehm, South Barrington, IL, gave me a start by promoting my introductions in their world-famous nursery. Without their patient love and help, much of my work would have gone unnoticed. These two great plantspersons have shared so much with me and lit a new lamp for me in the growing darkness.

Dr. Thomas Green of the Morton Arboretum, Lisle, IL, shared his knowledge and vision, reviewing the chapters on botanical species and crabapple names, an area in which he is an expert.

Dr. Edward Hasselkus of the University of Wisconsin, whose knowledge and ideas help fill the pages of this book, has graciously reviewed the many lists for me.

Dr. John Sabuco, Flossmoor, IL, whose landscape ideas are reflected in the chapter on landscaping, has graciously given me permission to use excerpts from his articles on crabapples in landscaping, first published in the bulletin of the International Ornamental Crabapple Society. He has also shared with me, an old man, his youthful enthusiasm and love for flowering crabapples.

Keith Warren, horticulturist for J. Frank Schmidt & Son Co., Boring, OR, has practically written the chapter on propagation and provided illustrations for it. An outstanding authority on the subject, he has been heavily involved in crabapple improvement and production at the Schmidt nursery for the past 16 years. His friendship and help in evaluating my newer crabapples are greatly appreciated.

Michael Scott of Oregon was one of the first, with Professor Les Nichols, to encourage me to introduce to the public the crabapples of my life's work. He also was among the first to propagate them.

Norbert Kinen of J. Frank Schmidt & Son Co., Boring, OR, has shared his knowledge and ideas with me.

Robert S. Lyons, Madison, OH, is another life co-author whose knowledge and ideas are shared in this book.

John H. Martens, Naperville, IL, has written knowledge-filled articles on *Malus* species from which I have gleaned much information to renew and strengthen my vision.

John den Boer, Killen, AL, has kept his father's work alive and assisted me in the listing of flowering crabapple names.

Robert Simpson, Simpson Orchard Co., Vincennes, IN, has done excellent work in introducing new and better clones of flowering crabapples, many of which fill my garden with their beauty and my life with inspiration. So many of my own introductions share their genetic background with so many of his introductions: clergyman that I am, I have been wedding our crabapple children for several decades.

Dr. Karen Murray and her husband Peter, Medina, OH, who share my love for flowering crabapples, have succeeded me as caretakers and keepers of my beloved Falconskeape Gardens. To them I entrust the legacy of my life's work and the future potential that fills the plants of that treasured garden.

Larry and Mary Eagan, friends and keepers of my Southern Garden, make possible the beautiful flowers and plants that, with these friends, are catalysts of my joy, hope, and strength.

Drs. Norman Anderson, Robert Fuller, Donald Hagan, and Charles King, all of Ocala, FL, with their great medical knowledge and skill have kept me around for yet another springtime of hybridizing and another autumn of harvesting seed. These men give me hope to finish this book despite increasing illness, difficult health, and the reckoning, fast approach of an endless winter that puts to rest forever the dreams of gardens, flowers, and many wonderful people.

All my sisters, in-laws, and relatives for whom I have named some of my finest introductions, especially my nephew LeRoy Fiala, have shared in and encouraged my crabapple work over the years and the indentured labors it entailed.

My late parents, Louis and Aloise Fiala, generously gave, over 50 years ago, to a boy of 12, five acres of land on which to plant his first orchard of trees and his endless dreams.

And now, my dear reader, I give this book to you, paraphrasing Robert Frost, who so beautifully put it, to plant, as my proxy, seeds of continuing beauty when I am long, long gone. I hope this book will kindle an environmental attitude in you and arouse your interest in planting flowering crabapples to provide beauty, fruit for birds, and an outstanding source of fall and winter food. May the flowering crabapples that have filled my life for nearly 50 years fill your hearts with their beauty, as they have mine, and may they fill our gardens, parks, and arboreta with their wonder in springtime and with their magnificent color parade in autumn.

Introduction

In the past, many articles on flowering crabapples have appeared in various horticultural and botanical journals, but only a few complete books have been written on the subject. Most of these publications were not written for the general public but are of a technical nature suitable for arboretum collectors, botanical specialists, or taxonomists.

In 1905 Professor Charles Sargent made a strong effort to improve flowering crabapples by considering, at some length, the known cultivars in his book called *Trees and Shrubs*. From 1939 to 1958 Donald Wyman wrote a number of informative articles, and in 1943 he produced a booklet entitled *Crab Apples for America*, which was the first attempt at a check list of the many crabapple species, cultivars, and clones. Many of his evaluations of the then-known species and hybrids have been superseded today, but his study was a tremendous asset in calling attention to the need for further work. Arie den Boer of the Waterworks Arboretum, Des Moines, IA, published a fairly comprehensive book in 1959 entitled *Ornamental Crabapples*, a work that stood alone for many decades as a reliable source of information.

In 1970 Roland Jefferson of the U.S. Department of Agriculture published a scholarly work entitled *History, Progeny, and Locations of Crabapples of Documented Authentic Origin* in which he carefully reviewed fundamental problems of authenticity in naming and classifying crabapples. This book brought attention to the many misnamed plants on display in arboretum collections and for sale at nurseries. Quoting Donald Wyman, horticulturist at the Arnold Arboretum, Jefferson (1970:1) wrote the following:

> Crab apples hybridize very freely, and because of this, much controversy has resulted in their proper identification. Seed has been gathered in large collections, been grown and the seedlings named after the trees from which the seed was collected. All too frequently such seed has produced plants [natural hybrids] with totally different characteristics from the parent plant, and when this has become evident, it has caused much confusion.

Jefferson's well-documented work should be consulted by all who seek authentic crabapple materials, especially those who hybridize them. It is an excellent, scientific contribution to the knowledge and progress of the location of authentic flowering crabapples, one which I do not seek to duplicate in the present volume.

In 1980 the Cooperative Extension Service of Ohio State University published a small but useful booklet entitled *The Flowering Crabapple—A Tree for All Seasons*. The compiled work of Professors James E. Brewer, Lester P. Nichols, Charles C. Powell, and Elton M. Smith, this publication should not be dismissed lightly as it was the first to present some of the selected, better, new flowering crabapples then on the market. It set standards of excellence, provided a horticultural awareness of the progress being made, and was one of the first publications to insist upon disease resistance as a leading criterion in developing modern crabapples.

It is my hope that the present volume would continue the efforts begun by these authors, all of whom, in their own way, made notable contributions to advancing flowering crabapple development.

Figure 0.1. The late Arie den Boer, father of the modern ornamental crabapple, established one of the world's greatest flowering crabapple collections, now known as the Arie den Boer Arboretum, Des Moines, IA. Through Den Boer's extensive writings and gardens, flowering crabapples gained a popularity which has continued to increase even today.

In addition to those who wrote about flowering crabapples, other individuals worked hard to develop and promote flowering crabapples. The Arie den Boer Arboretum (formerly Waterworks Arboretum) in Des Moines, IA, is dedicated to the man who first made flowering crabapples an important and national horticultural, ornamental tree. Born in Gouda, Holland, Arie den Boer served as an apprentice in 1913 in Boskoop, beginning his nursery career at Croux & Fils, Chatenay, Seine, France. From there he left for the United States where he worked for Bobbink and Atkins in Jersey and several other nurseries. A specialty in landscaping appealed to him very much, and in 1926 he was placed in charge of the extensive grounds of the Waterworks Arboretum, which he developed into what was known as the Charles Sing Denman Woods.

It was Charles Denman, the arboretum's manager, who encouraged Den Boer to establish one of the world's greatest flowering crabapple collections. To this end Den Boer accumulated every possible crabapple. His plantings attracted thousands of springtime visitors, and with them grew the popularity and planting of the crabapples he so loved. Den Boer also wrote extensively to foster public and nursery acceptance of flowering crabapples. In 1959 he published *Flowering Crabapples*, a well-known book for which he drew hundreds of detailed illustrations of flowers, leaves, and fruit for easy identification of the then-known species and hybrids. Through his efforts flowering crabapples gained popularity, a popularity that has continued to increase after his death. Truly he was one of the great crabapple pioneers and the father of modern ornamental crabapples!

Figure 0.2. The late Professor Lester P. Nichols devoted 30 years to the study of disease resistance in flowering crabapples. He was instrumental in organizing the IOCS and encouraging hybridizers to introduce smaller trees more suitable to the home gardens and trees with colorful autumn fruit.

Another tireless promoter of crabapples is the late Lester P. Nichols, professor of plant pathology extension at Pennsylvania State University, who spent a lifetime popularizing these ornamentals by his extensive studies on the disease resistance of individual clones. For more than 30 years Nichols evaluated crabapple clones for their value as ornamentals and for their disease resistance. His annual listing of disease-resistant and disease-susceptible cultivars has been a tremendous help in hybridizing newer and better clones, and his visits to my plantings at Falconskeape Gardens, his friendship, his assistance in evaluating my hybridizing efforts, and his suggestions for improvements and encouragement have been a gift to me. A welcome friend and evaluator of the many crabapple breeding programs at Falconskeape, he was also my mentor. Much of this book contains his thoughts wrapped in mine.

Nichols encouraged hybridizers to introduce smaller trees that were more adaptable to home gardens. He spoke enthusiastically of colorful autumn fruit that made the crabapple an "all seasons ornamental." More than anyone else in recent times he has advanced the flowering crabapple to its prominent position as the leading flowering tree in the United States. He was instrumental in the organization and formation of the International Ornamental Crabapple Society, bringing together crabapple notables for the first organizational meeting and giving the new organization strong leadership and direction. He wrote numerous articles on flowering crabapples, their landscape value, and diseases, and he identified the best of the modern named clones. He was a pioneer and a catalyst for the tremendous modern progress in his favorite ornamental.

I would be remiss if I did not mention the great hybridizing work done by two outstanding friends. The first, Dr. Donald Egolf of the U.S. National Arboretum, Washington, DC, is a genius in plant hybridization of many genera. His crabapple introductions, of superior quality, are only now being introduced. He has also made available to hybridizers and arboreta some authentic species material recently collected in China, Korea, and Japan. The second friend to whom I must give credit is Robert Simpson, of Simpson Orchard Company, Vincennes, IN, an outstanding evaluator of superior cultivars. He is one of the first to point out, introduce, and select some of the better, newer forms of flowering crabapples. I have used his excellent cultivars in some of my hybridization.

A summary of past and present efforts to develop and promote the newer flowering crabapples would be incomplete without mention of the excellent work being done by the International Ornamental Crabapple Society (IOCS), formed in 1985 by a small group of horticulturists under the leadership of John J. Sabuco, Michael Scott, Peter W. Bristol, Thomas L. Green, Joseph Hill, Edward Hasselkus, Michael Yanny, Norbert Kinen, William Hendricks, Robert Simpson, and Fr. John L. Fiala. In a few short years the IOCS has proven to be an outstanding organization of qualified experts whose goal is to promote and educate the public about flowering crabapples.

Mention must also be made of a few outstanding nurseries that have promoted the development of the newer cultivars: Klehm Nursery, South Barrington, IL; J. Frank Schmidt & Son Co., Boring, OR; Lake County Nursery, Perry, OH; and Simpson Orchards, Vincennes, IN. Although several other nurseries also promote crabapples, those listed have been most active in seeking out, patenting, introducing, and promoting the newer flowering crabapples clones.

Well-deserved recognition must be given to the large arboreta, botanical gardens, and parks that have maintained collections of flowering crabapples for public viewing and as source materials for hybridization and evaluation. The value of these collections cannot be measured in financial terms, for without them many outstanding species and clones would have disappeared long ago. The longevity of these collections is a national treasure.

Special recognition belongs to the Arnold Arboretum of Harvard University, which has been the "mother arboretum" for flowering crabapples as well as for much of North America's horticultural acquisitions. The arboretum's kindness to me over the years has been deeply appreciated as has its sharing of plant materials, archival data, and information. To the Arnold Arboretum's great crabapple collection must be added the ever-growing and impressive collection at the U.S. National Arboretum, Washington, DC. Not only do these two institutions maintain some of the finest crabapple collections, but in the past—and most recently via their plant explorations in China, Korea, and the islands of Japan—they have been responsible for many newly gathered crabapple species, seeds, and plants of authentic origin. The work of these institutions is richly deserving of endowment.

Other outstanding crabapple collections worthy of praise and recommendation are found at the Morton Arboretum, Lisle, IL; Boerner Botanical Gardens, Hales Corners, WI; Secrest Arboretum, Wooster, OH; and the increasingly important collections being planted at the University of Washington, Mount Vernon, WA; Kansas State University, Manhattan, KS; Holden Arboretum, Mentor, OH; and the University of Michigan, Ann Arbor, MI. Together they constitute a national horticultural treasure not found anywhere else in the world.

CHAPTER 1

Development of the Modern Flowering Crabapple

From the discovery of various crabapple species around the world to the emergence of the newest polyploid clones, the magnificent flowering crabapple has been treasured for its fruit and as an ornamental. I cannot think of any other major ornamental tree, except perhaps the lilac, that has so many new, outstanding, and really different forms. Today, flowering crabapples have reached a new zenith of popularity commensurate with their great variety in tree form, flower color, and fruit color.

SPECIES OF ASIA, NORTH AMERICA, AND EUROPE

The first phase of flowering crabapple development involved the discovery and popularization of the species. Plant explorers, such as Ernest H. Wilson, who worked first for Veitch & Sons, England, and then for the Arnold Arboretum; William Purdom, Charles Sargent, and J. F. Rock of the Arnold Arboretum; and several others, actively sought out new *Malus* species in Siberia, China, Tibet, Korea, and Japan. Other pioneers, such as Niels E. Hansen of the South Dakota Agricultural Experiment Station in Brookings and several enterprising nurseries in the Midwest, sought out native crabapples in the United States.

As new crabapple species were discovered by plant explorers abroad and at home, they were quickly introduced into arboretum plantings, public parks, and large private estates. No horticultural institution did as much for introducing and discovering new species, varieties, or special clones as did the Arnold Arboretum, Jamaica Plain, MA. As a center for crabapples, this arboretum distributed seed collected by plant explorers, seed from Kew Gardens in England, and seed or scions of many of the Siberian crabapples collected originally by Russian plant explorers for the great arboretum at St. Petersburg. Especially under Professor Charles Sargent, who took an active interest in crabapples, the Arnold Arboretum not only sought out new crabapple materials in Siberia and Japan, but it also energetically promoted any new crabapple found in its gardens or elsewhere.

Many of the newly discovered plants were too large for the smaller home garden but found their way to large estates, parks, and arboretum collections where they could be viewed in bloom by thousands of admiring visitors each spring. Although it was vogue at the time for large arboreta to plant every variation classified by taxonomists as a species or subspecies, with the rapidity of new discoveries also came some confusion as to the proper naming of these plants. Many clones suddenly received species or subspecies status, and, in the clamor for new garden material, factors like size, form, and disease resistance were mostly overlooked. Numerous inferior species and clones that would not be planted today were touted by garden writers as "exotic." Hybridizers and so-called seed planters hurriedly embraced the species in a race for breeding new hybrids and naming new plants, so that cultivars (i.e., related groups of similar seedlings) were given clonal names whereas in reality each was different from the other.

Nonetheless, the gardens, parks, and arboreta of the day were filled with magnificent springtime beauty. People stood in awe of both native and nonnative species, each with its own beauty. Many trees were large and spreading, up to 40 ft (12.2 m) high and wider in spread, and even more bore worthless fruit; only a few crabapples were truly exotic. Yet, in bloom, all the flowering crabapples managed, somehow, to be truly magnificent.

INTERSPECIFIC HYBRIDS

Following the discovery and popularization of crabapples came the period of interspecific hybrids. As various crabapple species were crossed with the newly discovered species, a series of interspecific clones emerged. Many of these clones outdid their parents in beauty. Most of them were random seedlings found under a tree in some arboretum; very few were the results of careful hybridizing. With the naming of a great number of these interspecific hybrids also came some taxonomic confusion as to what these plants were: were they cultivars (i.e., families of similar, cultivated seedlings), or were they selected individual clones that could be propagated only by asexual means?

The confusion between clone and cultivar still rages today. For some people, every named plant becomes a cultivar, even though it is a selected plant and not a member of a group of cultivated seedlings. For others, however, every named plant becomes a clone since it must be asexually propagated and is a single, selected, named plant.

I do not choose to settle this nomenclature problem in the present volume. Instead, I have chosen a middle-of-the-road position: if a plant is specially selected for certain unique characteristics, I designate it a *clone*, since to retain these characteristics it must be asexually propagated (i.e., cloned), whether it is a wild species or a cultivated plant. If a plant is a member of a group of unselected, cultivated seedlings or hybrids, I designate it a *cultivar*. By the latter term I include groups of unnamed seedlings or groups of similar seedlings of the same hybrid background (e.g., Rosybloom hybrids). For further discussion of this problem, see "A Confusing Problem of Nomenclature" in Chapter 10.

ROSYBLOOM HYBRIDS

With the discovery of *Malus pumila* 'Niedzwetzkyana' in Siberia, a new race of crabapples with dark, deep rose, red, and purple flowers became prominent: the Rosybloom hybrids. What a handsome lot they were!

Malus pumila 'Niedzwetzkyana' was discovered, named, and introduced by Niels

Hansen of the South Dakota Agricultural Experiment Station, Brookings, who obtained a plant from Mr. Niedzwetzky, of Alma Ata, Turkestan, in 1897 while on a plant expedition. Crossing this plant with *M. baccata*, Hansen named his first hybrid *M.* 'Hopa' in 1920, but the name Rosybloom was first given to hybrids and open pollinated seedlings of *M. pumila* 'Niedzwetzkyana' by William T. Macoun of the Central Experiment Farm, Ottawa, Canada, before 1920.

After World War I, efforts were made in Canada to improve and develop plants suitable for that area. Isabella Preston, also of the Central Experiment Station, was charged with this program. She later used *Malus pumila* 'Niedzwetzkyana'—mostly as open pollinated seedlings but, at times, crossed with *M. baccata*—to develop the many clones she introduced under her Lake Series of Rosyblooms. These open pollinated seedlings of *M. pumila* 'Niedzwetzkyana' are not real Rosyblooms (i.e., not hybrids with *M. baccata*), although several have very similar characteristics (e.g., red-bronze leaves, red-purple flowers, and larger red-purple fruit). They are simply open pollinated seedlings.

The general characteristics of Rosyblooms (a group of crosses with *Malus pumila* 'Niedzwetzkyana' × *M. baccata*) are reddish green to bronze leaves; red buds opening to large, dark, red-purple flowers fading to dull pink; mostly, but not always, large red-purple fruit; generally highly susceptible to apple scab and fire blight but leaf diseases not defoliating the tree. All the Rosyblooms seem to be very hardy, but most are not recommended because of their large size, fading flower color, and especially their lack of disease resistance. Despite these faults some excellent hybrids are had in second and third generations using *M. pumila* 'Niedzwetzkyana' (e.g., *M.* ×*purpurea* 'Lemoinei', *M.* 'Liset'). These selected progeny should be used for hybridization rather than the Rosyblooms.

Nonetheless, from hybridizers such as Niels Hansen to Isabella Preston (who is herself a gift to the plant world), W. R. Leslie, William Sim, Frank Skinner, and others, the handsome Rosyblooms marched forward. Adding their splendor to crabapples in bloom—rich pinks, deep rose, bright reds, and reds flushed with purple—the Rosybloom parade grounds stretched from the agricultural stations of midwestern United States and Canada to the prestigious plantings of the Arnold Arboretum, Kew Botanical Gardens, Morton Arboretum, and various university horticultural plantings. It did not seem to matter that along with their beautiful flowers the Rosybloom hybrids also produced large-sized dark red and purple fruit that was prone to many diseases. Apple scab, which not only disfigured the fruit but defoliated the trees by midsummer, and fire blight were accepted as part of the price for springtime grandeur, and spraying for disease became a necessary routine. Eventually, however, selected clones not subject to fire blight were recognized. As second-generation hybrids proved to be more resistant to disease, the bright-hued Rosyblooms paraded on.

ZUMI HYBRIDS AND MULTIBRIDS

The discovery by hybridizers of the tremendous importance of a species once called *Malus sieboldii* var. *zumi* by some or *M.* ×*zumi* by others brought into being a new race of crabapple known as the *Zumi* hybrids. The species, called *M. sieboldii* in this volume, is pure *zumi* and has none of the old *sieboldii*, which has since been renamed *M. toringo*. Two of the clones of *M. sieboldii*—'Calocarpa' and 'Wooster'—have much smaller, abundant, colorful fruit and great disease resistance. Today there are so many single, red-budded, abundant, white-flowering, disease-resistant crabapples with every color of mini, small, and medium fruit that one wonders if there could be any room for more disease-resistant hybrids of this class. How many of these splendid clones can nurseries continue to carry? It would seem that their introductions are at an end, yet more are named each day with nuances of differences.

To complicate things even more, the *Zumi* hybrids were married to the interspecific hybrids and the Rosybloom hybrids. Naturally, they begot and begot magnificent hybrids of every stature, blossom color, and wonderful fruit. The resulting multibrids (plants with many species in their makeup) are so completely intercrossed that they cannot rightfully identify their progenitors. Soon their number was so great that multibrids could find no room in the gardens, parks, and arboreta because nurseries did not have enough room to carry all the variations. Many multibrids became recluses in only one garden or arboretum, where their loveliness was soon forgotten by all.

MINI-FRUITED HYBRIDS

Out of the multibrids came the magnificent mini-fruits. Loved by birds and wonderfully handsome, these miniature crabapple trees bear fruit so small that to find any smaller fruit seems impossible. Although the mini-fruited crabapples have been tailored to so small a space that every home garden may grow them, few nurseries carry them. Many nurseries are still in the species or interspecific or Rosybloom stage of crabapple development and have not kept up with progress in hybridizing flowering crabapples. Only a few far-seeing, progressive nurseries have forged ahead and added these newest introductions.

GLORIOUS WEEPING CRABAPPLES

To the race of mini-fruited multibrids are now added the weeping crabapples. These modern weepers come in a variety of forms: some are dainty and graceful, very Oriental looking, while others are heavily branched. There are graceful semiweepers, umbrella-like or airy and carefree in form, even very low ground-covering weepers. Many of these delicate weepers are especially adapted to Japanese gardens, rock gardens, and smaller landscapes in city gardens. They will even grow well in a pot on a penthouse roof.

Add to these various forms the color of their autumn fruit and one creates rivers of molten reds, orange, or gold. What an outstanding group of cascading mountains of bloom or colorful fruit are these weepers and semiweepers suitable for every and any landscape need. What more could one ask of any flowering tree? Surely with these the hybridists have outdone themselves. Can there possibly be more? Indeed there is.

EXCLUSIVE POLYPLOIDS

The newest phase of flowering crabapples appears to be the emergence of the tetraploid and octoploid introductions. These polyploid crabapples are filled with such a rich chromosome inheritance that it is impossible to know what their fourth-generation children will look like. (With tetraploids, it takes about four generations of cross breeding to really see explosive results in genetic wonders.) The polyploids are smaller, tailored, often very rounded, heavily twigged trees or bushes with heavy-textured, leathery leaves. They are totally disease free and often brilliant in autumn color, characterized by colors that defy an artist's pallet in their variety of hues and combinations of tones. The polyploids have fragrant, large-flowered, Oriental blossoms, some with the spicy air of Old Cathay. Above all, these elegant clones are magnificent in abundant, persistent fruit.

What more beauty is yet to come from the hybridization of flowering crabapples? We do not know. But the next decade will be an exciting one for crabapple hybridizers. The progressive groundwork has been laid through the discovery of the species, the alliance of the interspecific hybrids, the grand entrance of the Rosyblooms, the debut of the *Zumi* dynasty and the multibrids, and more recently, the emerging reign of the polyploids. Selective hybridization and new developments with tetraploid crabapples have revolutionized this magnificent flowering tree, producing lower, smaller forms from 8 to 15 ft (2.4 to 4.6 m) at maturity that are entirely or mostly disease resistant, and that have unbelievable flower forms and colors, with an abundance of autumn fruit in every size and nearly every shade of color. The flowering crabapple has become an outstanding tree for all places and all seasons in any garden.

CHAPTER 2

Flowering Crabapples as Ornamental Trees

Flowering crabapples are best known in the landscape for their outstanding displays of magnificent springtime bloom and colorful autumn fruit. They are also highly prized for their disease-resistant summer foliage and varied tree form (growth habit). If crabapples were known only for their colorful fruit in autumn or their burst of bloom in spring, people would consider them exotic landscape trees. But the flowering crabapple offers much more. Year-round the regal flowering crabapple dominates our gardens and parks as THE ORNAMENTAL TREE.

MAGNIFICENT SPRINGTIME BLOOM

In the springtime crabapples unfold their deep carmine, red, pink, or white buds and explode into a truly magnificent display of clouds of white, cream, shades of pink, magenta, red, burgundy, red-orange, and orange-coral. Often the combination of bright carmine-red buds opening to white blossoms adds to the sheer beauty of color. Along with the many color possibilities, crabapple blossoms also come in several forms—single, semidouble, and double. Some of the semidouble and double blossoms look like miniature roses, others have fringed or cupped petals; some are a single color, others are a combination of two or more colors or shades.

Bloom Sequence

The bloom time of flowering crabapples extends from very early bloomers to late blooming types such as the North American species and their hybrids. Typically this period covers about 4 weeks, or, in ideal weather conditions, 5 weeks, but with the proper selection of trees according to their sequence of bloom, this period can be drawn out to nearly 6 weeks.

Figure 2.1. Diversity of fruit and leaf in *Malus*. No other ornamental equals the crabapple in diversity of fruit (color, size, persistence), blossom, leaf (shape, size, texture), and tree form. This diversity exists among the species as well as among the interspecific hybrids, multibrids, Rosyblooms, and polyploids. Photo courtesy of Michael and Lori Yanny.

Among the crabapple species the general pattern of sequence of bloom is fairly dependable, but with the large number of introduced clones it is impossible to list all of them according to their sequence of bloom. In general, most of the multibrids are mid-season bloomers. With careful selection a sequence of bloom can be had that extends probably no more than 3–4 weeks.

Peak crabapple bloom time is generally from the beginning of May in the prairie states of the Midwest to mid-May in Illinois, Indiana, Michigan, and Ohio, to the 3rd week in May for Pennsylvania and New York, to late May for the Eastern and New England states. Since springtime begins in the southern and lower areas of the Midwest, and extends westward and eastward as well as from lower altitudes to higher altitudes, each person must determine the exact dates of spring bloom in his or her geographic conditions. Once peak bloom time is determined, crabapples are fairly dependable year after year. There are, of course, especially in recent years, times of extraordinarily early and warm spring weather that force plants, including crabapples, to bloom well in advance of the normal season. For example, in 1988 the crabapples at Falconskeape Gardens in Ohio bloomed, for the first time in memory, in mid-April rather than in their usual 2nd week of May, and the late frosts that came at the end of April were disastrous. While such fickleness of weather is not uncommon in the Midwest, the blooming timetable in the Eastern and New England states is much more stable.

The average flowering period for crabapples, from bud opening to petal fall, is about 10 days, although very hot days or windy conditions with rain can cut this down dramatically to 5 or 6. Double-flowering crabapples generally have a longer period of bloom, perhaps to 12 days.

Crabapples can be divided broadly into four groups according to their blooming periods. In the earliest group, *Malus baccata*, together with its varieties and clones, is always the first to bloom. Among its varieties and clones, variety *mandshurica* always blooms first, followed by 'Jackii', 'Dolgo', 'Halward', and hybrids such as *M.* ×*robusta* and *M.* ×*arnoldiana*. This group generally blooms with the early magnolias and spring bulbs such as daffodils.

The second group of crabapples is led by *Malus* ×*purpurea* and such clones as 'Lemoinei', 'Liset', 'Orange Crush', 'Profusion', and their related hybrids. Also blooming at this time are *M. floribunda*, *M. halliana*, *M. hupehensis*, *M.* ×*magdeburgensis*, *M. micromalus*, *M. prunifolia*, the later clones of *M.* ×*robusta*, *M. sieboldii*, *M. spectabilis*, *M. toringo*, and hybrids of the above. This second group of crabapples blooms with flowering cherries, later tulips, and the early hybrid lilacs—*Syringa* ×*hyacinthiflora*—which are excellent companions.

The third group of crabapples includes *Malus florentina, M. kansuensis, M. sikkimensis, M. toringoides, M. transitoria, M. tschonoskii,* and *M. yunnanensis*. This group is in bloom with *Syringa vulgaris*, the common lilac, and peonies.

The latest blooming crabapples generally are *Malus coronaria* and *M. ioensis*. This group blooms with the tree lilacs *Syringa reticulata* and *S. pekinensis*.

Fragrance

Many crabapple blossoms are delightfully fragrant. The North American species (*Malus coronaria* and *M. ioensis* with their named clones) have that wonderful fragrance known as apple blossom. Others have an exotic Oriental fragrance resembling cinnamon or cloves. Flowering crabapples could be planted for their fragrance alone that fills the garden with a mystique equalled by few plants.

The fragrance most associated with flowering crabapples is that of the native American species, *Malus coronaria* and *M. ioensis* and their selected clones. Those who are wont to poking their noses into flowers claim that *M. ioensis* is more fragrant than *M. coronaria*. To me they both offer intoxicating fragrances that no garden should be without. Years ago, as a farm boy walking the meadows, I would stop, when the wild crabs were in late bloom, to breathe in deeply their fragrance.

What the common lilac and its readily recognizable fragrance is to all the lilacs, so these American species give meaning to fragrance in crabapples. It is a fragrance that should not be lost. Hybridizers need to incorporate it into their newer hybrids. Unfortunately, native American species do not hybridize well with their Asian cousins. Then, too, the Asian cousins at times have a fragrance all their own very unlike the fragrance of the American species. We need to preserve them all.

I have always planted a few of the most fragrant *Malus ioensis* and *M. coronaria* on the western side of my gardens so that the prevailing southwesterly winds would carry their fragrance to the house and the rest of the garden. That is where the most fragrant species belong—crabapples and lilacs as well—on the southwestern side. I have never been disappointed. Visitors frequently ask, "What is that delightful fragrance?" For shame! Many Americans and most Europeans and Asians have never smelled the wonderful fragrance of crabapples in bloom.

Because they have been so heavily planted in parks and arboreta, the species of crabapples have received the most attention from those who ferret out fragrances in gardens. Nonetheless, several of the new hybrids have delightful perfumes of their own making. A few of the modern hybrids, such as the multibrids and some of the polyploids, have a very pronounced fragrance all their own. Professor Nichols would often remark to me how he enjoyed the special crabapple fragrances. We both agreed that the native American species have the strongest and most pleasing fragrance of all.

In hybridizing the multibrids I have found fragrance to be an elusive factor. It does not always appear to be a family treasure passed from one generation to another, except in the *Malus ioensis* and *M. coronaria* groups. The following list groups crabapples according to their fragrance. In most cases, the cultivars are not as strongly fragrant as the species.

The Most Fragrant Crabapples
- *M. coronaria* group
  - *M. angustifolia*
  - *M. angustifolia* 'Prince Georges'
  - *M. bracteata*
  - *M. coronaria* var. *dasycalyx* 'Charlottae'
  - *M. dasycalyx*
  - *M. lancifolia*
  - *M.* 'Elk River' and most of its progeny, including *M.* 'Chinook', *M.* 'Cranberry', *M.* 'Kola', *M.* 'Redflesh', *M.* 'Red Tip', and *M.* 'Shoko'
  - *M.* 'Nieuwlandiana'
- *M. ioensis* group
  - *M.* 'Boone Park'
  - *M.* 'Brandywine'—excellent fragrance
  - *M.* 'Fimbriata'
  - *M.* 'Fiore's Improved'
  - *M.* 'Klehm's Improved Bechtel'
  - *M.* 'Nevis'
  - *M.* 'Nova'
  - *M.* 'Palmeri'
  - *M.* 'Plena'
  - *M.* 'Prairie Rose'—delightfully fragrant
- Multibrids
  - *M.* 'Burgandy'—grapelike fragrance, of burgundy wine
  - *M.* 'Huron'—a Rosybloom hybrid
  - *M.* 'Madonna'—delightful fragrance of jasmine and gardenia
  - *M.* 'Satin Cloud'—very strong fragrance of Oriental cinnamon or cloves

Moderately Fragrant Crabapples
- Species
  - *M.* ×*arnoldiana*
  - *M. baccata*
  - *M. floribunda*
  - *M. hupehensis*
  - *M.* ×*robusta*
  - *M. sargentii*
  - *M. sieboldii* 'Calocarpa'—most of the selected clones of what was once called *M. sieboldii* var. *zumi* have a very mild fragrance
  - *M. toringo* 'Arborescens'
- Hybrids
  - *M.* 'Bob White'—mildly fragrant
  - *M.* 'Coralglow'
  - *M.* 'Dolgo'
  - *M.* 'Lisa'
  - *M.* 'Pink Pearl'
  - *M.* 'Tanner'

COLORFUL AUTUMN FRUIT

From autumn into winter, flowering crabapples put on what is, perhaps, their greatest display, namely, that of colorful fruit. Beginning in September through November, and often into the snows of December and January, the color parade continues—unless the hungry birds put an abrupt end to the fruit. A few clones begin to color as early as late August. To many people this horticultural color parade of ripening fruit is the crowning jewel of flowering crabapples.

Fall crabapple fruit comes in a most wonderful range of colors—from pale lime, to chartreuse with bright yellow highlights, to clear lemon-yellows, to many shades of gold often rouged with pink, orange, or bright red cheeks, to bright orange, crimson, lacquered Chinese red, carmine, deep claret, burgundy, and purple-red, to bishop's purple, at times with a blue blush making the trees appear blue fruited. No other fruiting tree or shrub provides such a wide array of color. When planted side by side in masses of color in the landscape, the colored fruit of crabapple makes possible a veritable color shock of contrasts, a landscape feature that must not be lost by those who plan and design modern gardens.

The presence of two-colored fruit on crabapple clones is another design feature that should not escape the alert landscaper. Many crabapples present an array of changing fruit color as they ripen, turning often from yellow to gold to deep orange or orange-cheeked. In many clones freezing enhances the color of fruit. *Malus* 'Serenade' and *M.* 'Shaker Gold' are excellent examples of two-colored fruit enhanced by freezing. Lemon-colored and light gold-colored clones are often deepened to rich golds and coppers with recurring frosts, and their colorful fruit frequently persists into the snows of December and January and, in a few clones, even through the awakening winds of March.

The power of so many color combinations is only now being realized by a few landscape designers as one of the highlights of modern horticulture with flowering crabapples. But to be effective, autumn color in fruit must be thoughtfully conceived, planned with special cultivars, and then carefully planted. It is an art in modern garden design—a mass of magnificent springtime bloom of contrasting blossom colors followed in autumn with another massive display of magnificently contrasting colored fruit. The selection of the properly colored fruit clones thus goes far beyond tree form, height, or availability.

Size

Traditionally, any apple tree that produced fruit less than 2 in (5 cm) in diameter was considered a crabapple. Today, however, finer distinctions are made and we refer to crabapple fruit from l to 2 in (2.5–5 cm) as large-fruited; from 0.5 to 1 in (1.3–2.5 cm) as medium sized; from 0.25 to 0.5 in (0.6–1.3 cm) as small fruited; and below 0.25 in (0.6 cm) as mini-fruited.

Figure 2.2. The very small fruit of *M.* 'Elfin Magic'—only 0.4–0.5 in (1–1.2 cm) in diameter—puts this clone into the newer class of mini-fruits, so-called because their fruit is less than 0.25 in (0.6 cm) in diameter. These tiny fruits are most eagerly sought after by smaller birds.

As spectacular as flowering crabapples have always been, the newer cultivars outdo the older species. Through hybridization and selection, the fruit of these newer clones has been improved and greatly reduced in size to as small as 0.25 to 0.5 in (62.5–125 mm). These smaller fruits, which are greatly relished by many species of birds, are an asset in landscaping since they do not fall, rot, or pose other undesirable problems. Thus, smaller-fruited trees are ideal street trees if the proper form is chosen.

It is my belief that crabapples whose fruit is 0.25–0.6 in (0.6–1.6 cm) in diameter provide the showiest display of fruiting surface. Smaller trees, such as the mini-fruits, must be

Figure 2.3. The small fruit of *M.* 'Arch McKean', measuring 0.4 in (1 cm) in diameter, is typical of small-fruited crabapples that bear fruit 0.25–0.5 in (0.6–1.3 cm) in diameter.

Figure 2.4. The fruit of *M.* 'Centurion', measuring 0.6 in (1.6 cm) in diameter, is typical of medium-fruited crabapples that bear fruit 0.5–1 in (1.6–2.5 cm) in diameter.

Figure 2.5. The large fruit of *M.* 'Centennial', measuring 1.9 in (4.8 cm) in diameter, is typical of large-fruited crabapples that bear fruit 1–2 in (2.5–5 cm) in diameter.

extremely heavily fruited to be showy, and the larger fruited trees can be too heavy and messy.

Weeping Crabapples in Autumn Fruit

The newer, weeping flowering crabapples, with their great variety in types of form, are especially attractive in autumn fruit. Many are extremely heavily fruited and display spilling fountains of glowing lava in red, orange, or gold colors. They are particularly suitable for smaller gardens or for Japanese gardens, where they are like explosive orbs of color in the autumn landscape. I believe the orange-reds and brilliant, bright red fruited weepers are the most attractive crabapples in fall color. The yellow fruited are also beautiful but not quite as showy.

Too few of these modern crabapples are available, although several nurseries, seeing the trend of the future, have mostly discarded the older, disease-prone, messy, large-fruited cultivars and are making the newer ones available, mostly as patented named varieties. Although they may be more expensive initially and harder to find, most gardeners plant flowering crabapples only once, so it is worth the extra trouble and cost to search out the best varieties. Unless gardeners demand the newer cultivars, however, retail nurseries will continue to propagate the old standbys, such as *Malus* 'Almey', *M.* 'Hopa', and *M.* 'Pink Weeper' (*M.* 'Oekonomierat Echtermeyer'), and large trees like the disease-carrying Rosyblooms. A number of the Rosybloom hybrids are totally or reasonably disease resistant and are wonderful trees that have a definite and rightful place in estate gardens, parks, and arboretum collections, but they are not suitable for smaller home gardens. Since most people rarely plant framework trees in their gardens, why settle for planting outcasts when for a few dollars more and a little extra time, you can have a garden treasure of the very best for a lifetime?

DISEASE-RESISTANT SUMMER FOLIAGE

During the summer months the newer flowering crabapples remain almost entirely disease free, retaining healthy green or reddish green leaves with fruit free of scab or rot. These trees require no spraying. With their resistance to disease, they make attractive backgrounds or more formal trees that can be used for any purpose in landscape design. This is a tremendous advantage over the older, earlier hybrids, which were often very large trees and required many sprayings to keep them from being defoliated in summer and somewhat free from disease.

With time, diseases and viruses produce mutations within their own structure so that although a given crabapple may be resistant to one particular form of a disease, it may not be resistant to the mutant form of that disease. Some propagators are concerned that tissue culture may, perhaps, leave a cultured plant more vulnerable to some plant diseases, but this remains to be seen. Much more study needs to be done about the various layers of plant tissue to understand their exact work and influence upon the total plant and genetic inheritance. These problems are being worked out now and, I feel certain, will all be solved with time.

Disease resistance is of primary importance in the production of new hybrids. Furthermore, it is important that new clones that claim to be disease resistant not be tested solely under nursery conditions where routine spraying is conducted to maintain disease-free stock. In such situations it may be the effective spraying program rather than the clone itself that results in a disease-free condition. As more and more scientific hybridization with disease-resistant progenitors is conducted, modern clones are proving to show outstanding disease resistance compared to earlier hybrids. Today's newer hybrid crabapples are, indeed, a sturdy stock. More information on diseases and pests of flowering crabapples is presented in Chapter 5.

CHAPTER 3

Tree Form

One of the chief assets of the flowering crabapple, an asset that contributes to the crabapple's rating as the number-one flowering tree, is the great variety of tree forms that makes it suitable for any landscape need. Most crabapples are round and spreading in form. Only a few are small and shrublike to bushlike in form. The number of columnar, vase-shaped, and fan-shaped forms was, only a few decades ago, limited to just a very few named clones, but today hybridizers have increased the number to more than two dozen good varieties. The most surprising modern form with, perhaps, the greatest changes is the weeping crabapples. Thirty years ago only two fair weepers were available; today there are more than 50 with several subdivisions in the weeping types. The various forms can be summed up as follows:

Rounded and spreading forms	
Large trees	To 40 ft (12.2 m) high and as wide; includes several species and some of the Rosyblooms, perhaps two dozen really good plants
Medium trees	From 15 to 25 ft (4.6 to 7.6 m) high and as wide; includes the majority of named crabapples, more than 100 good selections
Small trees	From 10 to 15 ft (3.2 to 4.6 m) high and as wide; includes a good number of the newer multibrids, *Zumi* hybrids, and polyploids, perhaps 75–100 fine clones
Columnar forms	A small group of perhaps a dozen
Vase-shaped	Not more than a half-dozen good ones
Fan-shaped	Not more than a dozen really fine clones
Weeping forms	Includes about 50 very good selections, whether heavily limbed, fountainlike or umbrella, refined cascading, refined free-form, and semiweeper
Shrub or bush forms	Only about a dozen good ones available

ROUNDED AND SPREADING FORMS

The majority of named crabapples have an upright form that is rounded and spreading. This form is natural to crabapples and very pleasing in landscaping. The rounded and spreading trees go well when grouped in masses, especially when interspersed with an occasional smaller group of columnar forms to break the evenness of the rounded forms. One of the best sites for the rounded and spreading forms is on a hillside; the display is even better if it can be viewed from an adjacent hill or from across a lake. No other form is better for massed effect.

The rounded and spreading form can be broken down into three groups according to size. Large rounded and spreading trees, which include some of the species and many of the Rosyblooms, exceed 20 ft (6.1 m) in height and width, often reaching 40 ft (12.2 m) high. Specimens this large are best used as background trees on larger properties. It would be difficult to include them in any medium-to-smaller garden.

The medium-sized forms grow from 15 to 20 ft (4.6 to 6.1 m) in height and equally as wide. They are far better than the larger forms, being more adapted to smaller areas. With proper space, they are more easily worked into very effective masses or smaller groups. There are any number of outstanding clones in this group, which allow for a wide range of color in blossom as well as in fruit.

The smallest of the rounded and spreading forms are undoubtedly the most useful of all the flowering crabapples. The trees do not exceed 15 ft (4.6 m) in height and width, fitting into almost any reasonable space. Several trees of this size can make up a bed that has color harmony both in blossom and fruit. This size is ideal for specimen plantings and, for massed effect, many smaller trees can be used in the space that would accommodate only one of the largest kinds. These small forms are also ideal for all home plantings, patio and pot trees, and street plantings. Some of the finest, newest multibrids and polyploids are in this class. Here, also, can be found the best heavily fruited trees and the brightest colored fruits. A great number of the outstanding crabapples belong to this smaller form. Because trees of this form are so useful to gardeners, this group should be the one carried most by nurseries.

Among upright to spreading forms are some smaller clones such as *Malus* 'Coralburst', which is lovely in bloom and form if grafted on smaller rootstock or on its own roots; *M.* 'Doubloons', a petite white double with golden fruit; the lovely *M.* 'Jewelberry'; and *M.* 'Leprechaun', a dainty grower with very small red fruit. *Malus* 'Adirondack' is an outstanding vase-shaped rounded clone that is wonderful in bloom and perfect for any garden. *Malus* 'Autumn Glory', *M.* 'Harvest Gold', *M.* 'Indian Magic', and the outstanding *M.* 'Win-

Figure 3.1. *Malus* 'David' is typical of rounded, smaller tree forms.

Figure 3.2. *Malus* 'Golf Course' is an upright to rounded tree with ascending branching.

ter Gold' are smaller rounded trees, as are the newer mini-fruits *M.* 'Elfin Magic', *M.* 'Little Troll', or *M.* 'Tiny Tim'. One must search the lists carefully as many new cultivars are being introduced rapidly.

Many flowering crabapples are small-to-medium ornamental trees that in a few years after planting cannot be readily transplanted. One must give considerable attention and thought as to where they are to be planted and what they will look like when mature. Choose any side of a house, except the north side, and keep the trees a good distance—20 ft (6.1 m) or more—from the building. A small tree is most attractive when planted at least 15–20 ft (4.6–6.1 m) from the corner of a house; there it serves as a landscape focal point around which the garden can be designed. Never, never plant flowering crabapples against any house or building, or, perish the thought, in front of a window. They will grow and spread to block the windows or architectural design of the building completely and, in time, will have to be cut down.

COLUMNAR, VASE-SHAPED, AND FAN-SHAPED FORMS

Where only one or a few flowering trees are possible, flowering crabapples are ideal. The newer ones, with their smaller height and graceful forms, fit very well into modern home landscaping. The smaller, narrow forms fit well in narrow places and small gardens without looking the least bit overcrowded or requiring a great amount of pruning to keep them in form. These narrow, columnar trees are wonderful accents to any garden design, rising skyward in the landscape like pillars of bloom in spring and again as pillars of fruit in fall. Among these cultivars are *Malus* 'Ann Marie', *M.* 'Ballerina', *M.* 'Burgandy', *M.* 'Centurion', *M.* 'Cranberry Lace', *M.* 'Golden Candles', *M.* 'Karen', *M.* 'Lenore', *M.* 'Madonna', *M.* 'Maysong', *M.* 'Robert Clark', *M.* 'Sentinel', *M.* 'Showboat', *M.* 'Silver Moon', *M.* 'Velvet Pillar', and *M.* 'Van Eseltine', among others. *Malus* 'Red Barron' has reddish leaves and is singularly upright. All these cultivars are narrow growers, although with age they tend to spread, as does any tree. Heavy fruiting year after year tends to open a tree and make it more spreading, but some pruning will delay this march of spreading time.

Upright columnar trees, whether vase-shaped or fan-shaped in form, have outstanding value in crabapple landscaping: they are ideal for narrow places, they are excellent as a single specimen along a garden walk, they break the monotony of level horizons, and they are ideal street trees. Every gardener must find a place for one or two of these crabapples.

Double or semidouble flowers are rare in columnar, vase-shaped, or fan-shaped forms,

Figure 3.3. *Malus* 'Red Jewel' is an upright and pyramidal tree, to 18 ft (5.5 m) high and 12 ft (3.7 m) wide.

and good-to-excellent columnar clones with double flowers are even more rare; not many of them are on the market. Some of the best come from Robert Simpson's work: *Malus* 'Burgandy', *M.* 'Centurion', *M.* 'Sentinel', and the late-flowering *M.* 'Silver Moon' (one of my top ten favorites). A beautiful crabapple called *M.* 'Ballerina' has masses of large, white cupped blossoms, but alas, they come on rather sharp spurs. An excellent white double is *M.* 'Madonna'; it has fruit but its spring glory alone is sufficient to recommend it.

Excellent progress has been made in the introduction of several columnar crabapples of low-to-medium height, including *Malus* 'Adirondack'. This type of crabapple is always useful for smaller areas, tight places, and in street plantings, and it is excellent for the smaller home garden. Many smaller columnar crabapples are outstanding in blossom as well as in colorful autumn fruit.

WEEPING FORMS

Some 35 years ago the only weeping crabapples were the older *Malus* 'Exzellenz Thiel' (Späth), *M.* 'Oekonomierat Echtermeyer' (Späth), and the then-new *M.* 'Red Jade' (Reed). Since that time a great number of very fine weeping crabapples has been introduced. Many of the newest weepers and semiweepers originated at Falconskeape Gardens where one of the goals, for 50 years, was to work for better weeping forms. Today weepers are divided into classes: rough-limbed weepers, slender cascading weepers, fountainlike weepers, and free-form weepers. What a handsome group they are!

One of the first weepers, *Malus* 'Oekonomierat Echtermeyer', was a coarse-limbed tree with reddish leaves. This older tree was much too disease prone for today's gardens, so hybridizers have all but eliminated this type. A number of graceful, fountainlike weepers are currently available and make excellent garden plants. One of the first really fine fountainlike weepers was *M.* 'Red Jade' with its wonderful display of slightly large red fruit. Unfortunately, this fine plant tends to spread rather wide with age—to 35 ft (10.7 m) wide and 15 ft (4.6 m) high. It has since been surpassed by other cultivars, including *M.* 'Candied Apple', *M.* 'Louisa', *M.* 'Lullaby', *M.* 'Luwick', and *M.* 'Molten Lava'.

In my opinion, the finest weepers are the cascading forms. Among this group are the yellow-fruited *Malus* 'Autumn Treasure', *M.* 'Fiesta', the beautifully red-fruited *M.* 'Red Swan', and *M.* 'White Cascade'. In addition to the cascading forms, graceful semiweepers, such as *M.* 'Serenade' with its changing gold-orange-red fruit, are great choices in excellent weeping forms. For a small garden, weeping flowering crabapples are one of the finest choices. (For additional information on selecting a small weeper, see "Own Root Versus Grafted and Budded Trees" in Chapter 4.)

Weepers are mostly loners; that is, they do not like other performers in the spotlight to upstage them. Do not plant groups of weepers, but rather plant a single weeper as a focal point in the garden. As a center-stage performer, weeping crabapples can parade their magnificent cascading or fountainlike form.

The finest weepers in my opinion are *Malus* 'White Cascade' (Henry Ross) and my own *M.* 'Red Swan' (once called *M.* 'Red Snows', now renamed in deference to an unknown previous baptism). Totally different in form—*M.* 'White Cascade' is a finely branched cascading weeper, *M.* 'Red Swan' is a finely branched but exotic free-form weeper—these two crabapples, along with *M.* 'Molten Lava', are excellent choices for a Japanese-style garden.

A few weepers are tetraploids and one, *Malus* 'Fountain', is an octoploid. The latter actually is a hybridizer's plant and much too slow growing for most gardens. Its leaves are so small and heavy they appear diseased with some virus even though they are perfectly healthy.

Many nurseries do not like weeping crabapples because it takes extra work to provide a central trunk. To assist the progress of the weeping crabapples, the following list trumpets the worth of all known weeping crabapples to date:

M. coronaria var. *angustifolia* 'Pendula'—Never been able to find one
M. prunifolia 'Pendula'—Not of much value
M. ×*magdeburgensis* 'Elise Rathke'—Heavily limbed
M. 'Aloise' (Fiala)—Reddish leaves, red blossoms, a fountain weeper
M. 'Anne E' (Manbeck) (syn. 'Manbeck Weeper')—Spreading, white-flowered weeper with small red fruit, very good
M. 'Autumn Treasure' (Fiala)—Very fine, small cascading weeper, small gold fruit
M. 'Blanche Ames' (K. Sax)—Semiweeper to 20 ft (6.1 m), semidouble flowers, small gold fruit, excellent
M. 'Candied Apple' or *M.* 'Weeping Candied Apple' (Zampini)—Horizontal branching, free-form weeper, red fruit

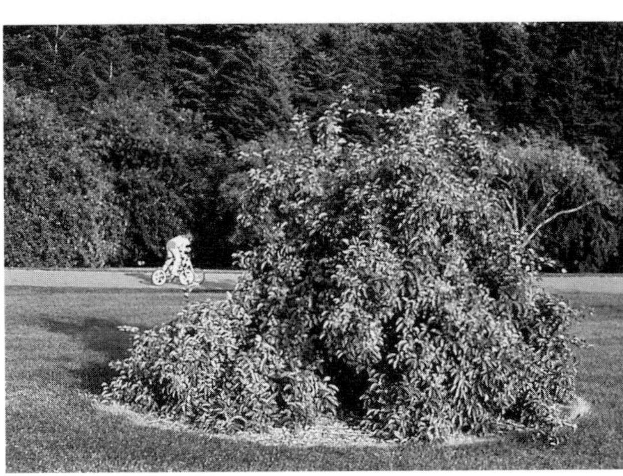

Figure 3.4. *Malus* 'Ralph Shay', pictured here in fruit, is a vigorous, sturdy, horizontally branched tree, broader than high.

M. 'Color Parade' (Fiala)—An excellent semiweeper, fruit coral with red cheeks, heavy annual fruiting

M. 'Coral Cascade' (Henry Ross)—Semiweeper, coral fruit color unique, one of the best

M. 'Dancing Elf' (Fiala/Murray)—Very refined, smaller weeper, small fruited

M. 'Dream River' (Fiala/Murray)—Heavily branched, pink buds, white blossoms, reverse petals pink, fringed

M. 'Egret' (Fiala)—Very refined long-branched fountain weeper, an octoploid, semidouble to double blossoms, red fruit; the only semidouble weeper

M. 'Elise Rathke' (Arnold Arboretum)—A heavily limbed *M.* ×*magdeburgensis* seedling; the clone not much propagated today

M. 'Exzellenz Thiel' (Späth)—An old form that produced 'Red Jade'

M. 'Fiesta' (Fiala)—A very fine, new semiweeper, unique fruit color is a combination of gold, orange, and coral red

M. 'Firecloud' (Fiala)—Semiweeper, very bright red-orange, showy fruit, very new and outstanding

M. 'Firecracker' (Fiala)—Excellent, very small fountain weeper, very red fruit

M. 'Firedance' (Fiala)—Spreading weeper, horizontal branching, troubled with some apple scab on leaves but never defoliated; should be discontinued

M. 'Flamingo' (Fiala)—Small, classic fountain weeper with red leaves, pink blossoms, dark red fruit; a fourth-generation Rosybloom weeper

M. 'Flaming Star' (Fiala)—Red-flowering graceful fountain weeper

M. 'Fountain' (Fiala)—An octoploid, classic fountain weeper, very slow growing, huge white blossoms, leaves very leathery, very small; a hybridizer's "must" parent for octoploid weepers

M. 'Girard's Weeping Dwarf' (Girard)—An older clone no longer available

M. 'Goldilocks' (Fiala)—Refined semiweeper to full weeper with bright yellow fruit, almost a mini-fruit

M. 'Henry Ross' (Fiala)—Graceful fountain weeper with gold-yellow fruit; an excellent white-flowered clone

M. 'Little Troll' (Fiala)—A new mini-fruit, graceful, small weeper, very bright fruit less than 0.25 in (0.6 cm) in diameter

M. 'Louisa' (Polly Hill)—A fountain or umbrella weeper, good pink blossoms, yellow fruit; very fine plant

M. 'Lullaby' (Fiala)—Graceful fountain to free-form weeper, small yellow fruit

M. 'Luwick' (Fiala)—Very refined, elegant fountain to free-form weeper with large pale pink blossoms, red fruit

M. 'Maria' (Fiala)—Free-form semiweeper, outstanding reddish, leathery foliage, rose red blossoms, dark red-purple fruit, very heavy annual bloomer

M. 'Ming Dynasty' (Fiala)—Heavy to free-form weeper with good reddish foliage, rose-red blossoms, and abundant, annual, dark, larger fruit

M. 'Mollie Ann' (Fiala)—A very unusual weeping octoploid with racemelike branches, in branchlet clusters of 4–7; very leathery smaller, narrow leaves; white blossoms, red fruit; should be used in hybridizing octoploids as it contains outstanding genes

M. 'Molten Lava' (Fiala)—Excellent, very heavily fruited annual, free-form weeper of great beauty, bright orange-red fruit; one of the finest

M. 'Oekonomierat Echtermeyer' (Späth)—Graceful semiweeper, bronze red foliage, rose pink blossoms, dark fruit; susceptible to most diseases

Figure 3.5. *Malus* 'Red Swan', an exotic fountainlike weeper of refined cascading form. A medium-size tree, it grows to 12 ft (3.7 m) high and has fine, pendulous branching.

M. 'Pagoda' (Fiala)—A new mini-fruit, small, dainty, slow-growing fountain weeper, white blossoms, orange-red fruit colors early

M. 'Pixie' (Den Boer)—Semiweeper, white flowers, red fruit

M. 'Red Jade' (Reed)—Classic heavily limbed weeper, outstanding in medium-size red fruit, spreads to 15 ft (4.6 m) high and 30 ft (9.1 m) wide; an excellent weeper where there is ample space; subject to fire blight in some localities

M. 'Red Peacock' (Fiala)—Smaller semiweeper to fan-shaped weeper, brilliant orange-red smaller fruit; very fine

M. 'Red Swan' (Fiala)—Very refined, delicately branched free-form weeper of elegance; fall leaves golden yellow; fruit small, oval, brilliant red, persistent; one of the very finest weepers; heavy annual bloomer; formerly called *M.* 'Red Snows'; one of the finest crabapples developed at Falconskeape

M. 'Rhapsody' (Fiala)—Smaller semiweeper, large white blossoms, small bright red fruit; a substitute for *M.* 'Red Jade'

M. 'Royal Splendor' (Fiala)—Excellent, small, refined fountain weeper, outstanding bright red fruit; very showy and select

M. 'Seafoam' (Den Boer)—Fine semiweeper, pink flowers and small yellow fruit; not very well known or much grown; difficult to find a source plant

M. 'Sensation' (Fiala)—Graceful, smaller semiweeper, heavily fruited annually,

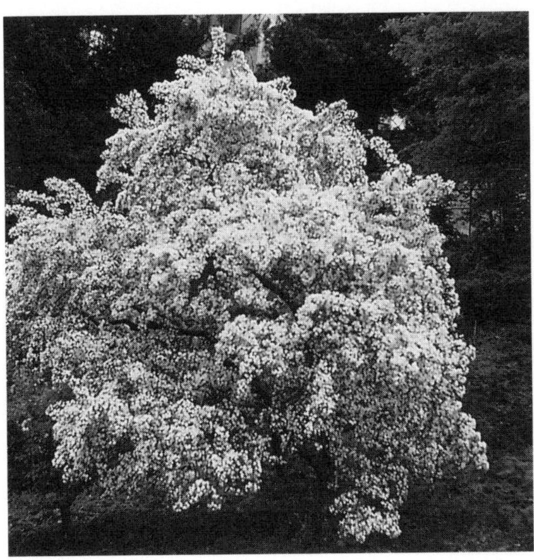

Figure 3.6. *Malus* 'Blanche Ames' is a medium, spreading to semisweeping tree to 20 ft (6.1 m) high and as wide.

fruit small, orange with red cheek; very fine and outstanding

M. 'Serenade' (Fiala)—An excellent semiweeper with outstanding orange-to-coral fruit; a showy, annual bloomer, heavily fruited; one of a very few in its fruit color class

M. 'Sinai Fire' (Fiala)—An excellent heavy weeper, horizontal-to-downward branching; very fine green leaves and bright red fruit

M. 'Snow Ballerina' (Fiala)—Formerly called *M.* 'Cascade', small weeper, white flowers, abundant red fruit

M. 'Spring Beauty' (Fiala/Murray)—Free-form weeper with pale pink blossoms; very showy

M. 'Springtime' (Fiala)—Refined red-leaf weeper, orchid blossoms are unique, hybridizers only, scab

M. 'True Love' (Fiala/Murray)—Graceful, fountain weeper; white flowers in abundance, bright red smaller fruit; showy

M. 'Waltztime' (Fiala/Murray)—Fountain weeper, large green leaves, white blossoms, orange-red fruit

M. 'White Cascade' (Henry Ross)—One of the finest introductions, a refined, graceful, cascading weeper of outstanding beauty; buds pale pink opening to faintly tinted pink-white blossoms, fruit greenish yellow; very heavy annual bloomer

M. 'Wildfire' (Fiala)—Semiweeper, pink blossoms, brilliant red fruit, very persistent and showy

M. 'Woven Gold' (Fiala)—Refined, semiweeper with small gold fruit

Among weepers, the need exists for really good bright pink and dark red flowering weepers with bright fruit. There is also a need for good double-flowered weepers. To my knowledge *Malus* 'Egret' is the only semidouble flowering weeper. Developing double-flowered weepers will be very difficult since all double-flowered crabapple trees have far less fruit than single or semidouble forms—usually the fruit is very sparse or altogether absent because on double-flowered trees the stamens are often fused as extra petals and the pistils, if they exist, are twisted and buried in the mass of petals, making the flowers rarely fertile. One of the finest attractions of weeping crabapples is their wonderful display of cascading colorful fruit, so it will not be easy to develop a weeper with double blossoms and abundant, colorful fruit.

SHRUB OR BUSH FORMS

Of the four basic crabapple forms, the small shrub or bush form has the least number of offerings. For a time *Malus sargentii* and *M. halliana* 'Parkmanii' stood out as the only candidates. Today a few more have been added, but I am not convinced that such small forms are greatly needed or useful as they are not able to put on a good showing of blossoms and fruit as well as the smaller tree forms can. I regret that in the half century of hybridizing at Falconskeape Gardens the shrub form has not been given more attention. Instead, hybridizing at Falconskeape focused on producing small tree forms that do not grow much higher than 10–12 ft (3–3.7 m), only a few feet taller than a bush or shrub form.

Really low bush forms that do not exceed 6 ft (1.8 m) are very rare. The very complicated octoploid *Malus* 'Fountain' is perhaps the smallest crabapple grown. The original tree, now

40 years old, is only about 4 ft (1.2 m) tall, and as wide, unless top grafted on a taller stem. The only other real shrub form developed at Falconskeape is *M.* 'Pink Feathers', which, at 25 years old, is only 5 ft (1.5 m) tall and 10 ft (3 m) wide. Some octoploid second- and third-generation seedlings appear to be very dwarf, but none have as yet been named. In the hands of a younger, energetic hybridizer it would not be too difficult to develop a larger group of these shrub or bush forms.

CHAPTER 4

Flowering Crabapple Culture

Flowering crabapples are very easy to grow as they make few demands and seem to accept a wide range of growing conditions that other trees and shrubs do not tolerate. With minimal care they will lavishly repay gardeners with two seasons of beauty—springtime bloom and wonderful autumn fruit.

GOOD SOIL AND DRAINAGE

Crabapple trees luxuriate in full sunlight in deep rich soils that are well drained. Soils with a pH range of 5.0 to 7.5 suit crabapples well, but the ideal pH range is from 5.5 to 6.5. Even if gardeners are fortunate to have ideal soil conditions, they may not be able to allocate the best part of the garden to crabapples. Flowering crabapples, however, are not greedy and will accept almost any soil that is not waterlogged or overly dry. As long as the soil has a reasonable amount of nutrients and water, crabapples manage to do very well.

Like most plants, crabapples prefer rich sandy loams, but even in heavier clay soils they do better than many other trees and shrubs and seem to bloom well once they are established. They will accept slightly wetter soils than lilacs, for example, but in these heavier soils they should have excellent drainage as they will not grow in waterlogged, swampy areas nor in soils inundated for long periods of time.

PURCHASING THE PLANTS

Shop around at the specialty nurseries that sell crabapples by their true (i.e., scientific) name; avoid garden stores that sell ready-to-plant pots merely by blossom color. Good, named crabapples also come in take-home pots, but many nurseries carry only the older named plants. Generally these trees are much, much cheaper than the patented, newer varieties, but there is a great deal of difference between carefully named and patented clones that are disease resistant and the larger specimens that are sold by color but with no guarantee of true excellence. Once the latter are grown and aging in your garden, you will wish you had paid a little more.

Most garden retail nurseries do an extremely poor job marketing flowering crabapples. Their clerks rarely have the knowledge needed to make a proper selection. A reliable nursery, even if you buy by mail order, usually gives you a better, guaranteed-true-to-name plant than does the local retail garden store that sells by color and no name guarantee. But as always, there are exceptional retail garden nurseries that have excellent and very knowledgeable clerks. (I once found one where the young college-aged sales person could name all the plants by their Latin names. You never forget such a person. Today he is a taxonomist at a very large arboretum.) *Caveat emptor!* Let the buyer beware!

OWN-ROOT VERSUS GRAFTED AND BUDDED TREES

The newer weeping crabapples are ideal for smaller gardens and, if they come on their own roots or grafted and budded on dwarf rootstock, they will remain small for many years. Most of the new cultivars are best on their own roots; when they are grafted on common apple rootstock they are much larger than they should be. Hopefully nursery professionals will resort to tissue-cultured plants or to budding on very dwarf stock. Keith Warren, an expert on the propagation of crabapples, assures me that good nursery professionals use the best, disease-resistant, dwarf or lower-growing rootstock that can be had. Often it may provide a better root than the own-root clone might have. Nonetheless, there will always be the unscrupulous few who will graft naturally low crabapples on common apple rootstock to create a larger, saleable plant in one year's time.

Weeping crabapples are not as rapidly produced as upright, columnar forms. They must be trained to a central leader or top grafted. Hence they command a higher price and rightfully so. They are priceless garden treasures when several years old. Many nurseries prefer not to grow the weeping cultivars simply because of the extra years of growth and special care and handling needed to bring them to marketable size.

PLANTING FLOWERING CRABAPPLES

Crabapple trees usually come from the nursery bare root. Thus it is important to keep the roots in water or covered with a wet bag until the tree is planted. Do not let the roots dry out at any time.

Dig an ample hole for the tree so the roots are not twisted or crowded under but spread out well in all directions. Place some very good soil under and over the roots to give them a good start. Fill in the hole, but leave a depression for holding water around the tree. Always plant the tree as deep as it was in the nursery—no deeper and, above all, not any shallower or the top roots will suddenly send up an army of suckers. These suckers must never be permitted to grow as they come from the understock upon which the desired clone was grafted or budded. If they are not removed, they will soon outgrow the graft or bud and the tree will be lost to undergrowth rootstock.

Crabapples are sturdy little trees, and the newer varieties can withstand rather long periods of summer drought when established. Newly planted trees, however, require care and watering during their first few years. During the first critical year, as they seek to establish themselves, they must be watered frequently. Never let them completely dry out, especially in sandy and clay soils.

Ideally, crabapples prefer well-drained, loose, organic soils with sufficient moisture and in direct sunlight. They delight in a good, deep mulch around the trunk for at least a 4–5 ft (1.2–1.5 m) radius. Adaptable as they are, crabapples bloom rather well even in partial shade, but in full shade they become long limbed and rangy, as does any tree. Once established crabapples can take care of themselves in competition with many aggressive plants, although this should not be the ideal or even ordinary case in a garden. Give them a sod free area around their trunk, fertilize on occasion, and prune only when necessary.

PRUNING

All root suckers should be removed immediately. Also remove rampant sucker growth, called water sprouts, from the branches and trunk. Never use water sprout suckers for grafting or budding; they delay the bloom time of young trees considerably.

I like to prune my flowering crabapples to two or three trunks that sometimes intertwine and give a most interesting pattern to their form as they grow older and especially when viewed in the winter landscape. (Of course, those who mow my lawn do not think as highly of my intertwined, artistic trunks, beautiful as they are, when they have to work around them.) Nothing is as beautiful as an older tree with multiple stems artistically pruned.

Choice trees should be entrusted only to professionals for pruning. Often a maintenance crew of inexperienced pruners leaves stubs of removed branches so long they can never be healed over by cambium growth. These stubs then become entrances for rot and disease into the heartwood of the tree.

Good pruning of branches, especially the larger ones, requires skill and knowledge. The branch to be removed must be shortened first, then the remaining stub cut a second time close enough to the main trunk so that it can be overgrown in time and completely healed by the new growth. A stub a few inches long will never be overgrown by new bark before rot sets in to damage the heartwood. To avoid making a rotted hole in a tree for disease or nesting birds, heavy branches must first be undercut before the final uppercut is made. If not, the weight of the removed branch will rip off the bark below the cut as it falls, damaging the entire area below the cut.

For a small one- or two-tree job, homeowners are more prone to prune the trees themselves than they are to hire a professional. Most often these trees bear the marks of this dollar-saving pruning all their lives, whether a rotting hole or a large debarked area around the removed branch that never was able to heal itself. If a tree is worth planting and is of ornamental value, it merits the relatively insignificant cost of hiring a professional pruner. But remember, not every person who hangs out a shingle knows the profession. In the tree removal business, many so-called professionals know nothing outside of cutting down and removing trees. Fred Lape of the Landis Arboretum once told me about a local person he hired to prune some choice conifers. When asked by Mr. Lape if he knew how to prune trees, the man answered, "I can cut down most any tree but I don't haul barn manure. That prunin' work has to be done by someone who has cows."

PREVENTING DAMAGE TO TREES

Although flowering crabapples are easy to grow and maintain, considerable damage is often done to trees by their human caretakers. Examples are found in every arboretum or home garden.

Lawn Mowers

Put a riding mower in the hands of a horticulturally uneducated operator and you have one of the greatest threats to the trunks of young and old trees. I once visited a large arboretum where nearly all the trees showed evidence of mower damage. I brought this to the attention of the grounds supervisor who complained, "That is because they give me all these summertime college cowboys for help."

Mower operators should not try to see how close to a tree they can maneuver the machine, but rather how wide a grass-free area they can make around the trunk. These grass-free areas are worth whatever time it takes to maintain them, if they do nothing other than reduce mower damage! Never let careless or untrained mower operators in your garden. Just because a person can cut grass with a mower is no indication the individual qualifies for garden and arboretum work.

I was once shown a planting by an arboretum superintendent, where the day before an untrained college student had completely eliminated a 2-acre (0.8-ha) planting of newly set out crabapple whips. When older trees are debarked at ground level, they are rarely able to overgrow the damage, which becomes an entrance for disease and decay. More small trees are killed by careless mowers than by rabbits or mice combined! The late Fred Lape, founder and director of the Landis Arboretum, Esperance, NY, was once asked by a visitor why he planted three trees of the same kind in all plantings. "Two for the mowers, and one to survive," came his ready reply.

Flowering crabapples ask only for reasonable care in return for a bounty of blossoms and colorful autumn fruit year after year. Mark smaller, newly planted trees with tall, white stakes that can be easily seen by tractor operators, well above the highest grass.

Chemical Weed Killers

Despite their great advantages, chemical weed killers are highly toxic materials. Several have proven to build up in the soil and, though they control weeds as if by magic during their first years, they eventually build up to lethal levels, killing the very trees and shrubs they were designed to protect. The first indication of trouble is poor, dwarfed, curly leaf development, followed by pale and yellowing leaves. Eventually the tree dies.

Today all good garden superintendents are aware of herbicide build-up. Since many chemical weed killers follow the cycle of soil build-up described above, they must be used selectively, for short and specific periods, never as a general program for an entire area. Rotating use of chemical weed killers is of no value as most of them contain similar, if not identical, components that build up in the soil with constant use. This same warning must be given for chemical sprays that eliminate root suckering.

Soil build-up toxicity often does not become apparent for a few years, and by then the trees are dying and nothing can undo the damage. Whole plantings can be killed almost at once when the soil level reaches lethal toxicity. Frequently when a planting or orchard begins to fail and die, viral infections or disease are suspected. After the trees have died, on closer examination, the constant, yearly build-up of chemical weed killers is determined to be the cause of death. Once the soil is so contaminated, it cannot be used for replanting. How long the chemical build-up remains is still unknown, but it appears to last for several years.

In conclusion, short cuts and time-saving spraying programs are not always what they appear to be initially. At times chemical weed and brush killers become a necessity (e.g., to get rid of wild grapes or multiflora rose, poison ivy, etc.), but the best gardens are generally chemical free, if possible.

Salt Spray Drift

One of the dangers to street plantings of trees and shrubs in areas that receive snow is the great damage caused by sprays of salt and other chemicals used to clear roads of ice. A classic example of salt and chemical road spray damage is found at the Morton Arboretum, Lisle, IL, where acres of choice arboretum plants and whole collections have been destroyed in the attempt to keep roads clear. On stormy, winter days with high winds, drift from road sprays goes a long way. It is not sufficient to simply avoid planting trees within 50 ft (15.4 m) of highways, for on the wind drift side, killing sprays can reach as far as 200–500 ft (61–154 m) away. Thus, when planning an arboretum, large estate, or home planting close to roadways in northern areas, chemical spray drift must be a serious, important consideration.

One year a careless road spraying crew at Falconskeape Gardens, by a single chemical spraying, completely destroyed a whole planting of lilacs and flowering crabapples 50 ft (15.4 m) from the road, despite posted signs. Even 15-year-old trees were killed. For whatever reason, road spraying crews seem unable to read signs or work around roadside plantings. Fortunately, some communities are beginning to outlaw the use of these extremely dangerous, high-powered chemicals, but for all practical purposes, choice plant materials should not be planted along sprayed highways, no matter how beautiful these plantings may be. In southern areas, where salt and chemical sprays are not common, roadsides can be made beautiful with all kinds of excellent plantings.

CHAPTER 5

Diseases and Pests of Flowering Crabapples

Flowering crabapples need very little care. Occasionally, however, when things are not going well, they may need a little attention to keep them looking and growing at their best.

Some of the worst problems for crabapples come from ordinary apple diseases, such as apple scab, various leaf diseases, fire blight, and cedar-apple rust. Hybridizers seeking to eliminate these problems have worked wonders by breeding disease resistance into the newer crabapple clones. Even if a garden is small, gardeners cannot afford to spend a lot of time spraying their trees, such as must be done in commercial apple orchards. Thus the first thing gardeners can do to keep their crabapples healthy is to purchase none but the most disease-resistant trees. The second thing they can do is to follow good, clean cultural practices.

In rating crabapples for disease resistance, one must be aware that despite the great progress made by plant hybridizers and introducers to produce disease-resistant clones, the term *disease resistant* is somewhat relative. Most of the newer introductions are far superior in disease resistance than previous crabapples and can in all honesty be labeled disease resistant, but there are epidemic years when constant rains plague an area for weeks at a time, or viral attacks break out unexpectedly, or insect hordes appear from nowhere. Under these exceptional conditions every crabapple appears to be susceptible to disease. There are, indeed, the "Years of the Apple Scab" or the "Years of the Cedar-Apple Rust" that touch every crabapple growing in a particular area. In these extraordinary years one should not condemn a special clone that has been previously disease resistant for several years or decades. I have seen excellent crabapples condemned because of one year in which they showed scab or fire blight that was of no real disfiguring consequence but happened to be epidemic that season. Disease resistance should be judged as a general characteristic, not on the basis of a single year's performance.

Many of the best disease-free crabapples are very new to commercial growers and some, as yet, have not been propagated by nurseries. In time, only disease-resistant clones will be propagated and available in the market, but until then, one must study the lists of named

Figure 5.1. Apple chlorotic leaf spot virus.

crabapples carefully and seek out those disease-resistant clones currently on the market. They will cost more, particularly if they are patented, but the slightly higher initial cost is well worth not having to spray and not having to look at scab-fruited, defoliated trees in the garden. There is no reason for any nursery to offer today the highly disease prone clones that once were the vogue because they were a new kind of crabapple, yet thousands of flowering crabapples are sold each year to a public uneducated about disease-resistant clones. Retail garden center operators must simply demand disease resistance as the first requisite of quality!

DISEASES

Apple Scab

Apple scab (*Venturia inaequalis*) is an unsightly disease of apples in general, both commercial and ornamental. It not only disfigures the fruit, but it also defoliates the tree by the beginning of or during midsummer. To prevent this disease, trees must be sprayed before their flowers open, and once again one week to 10 days after the petals have dropped. It may be necessary to repeat sprayings every 10 days for as many as five to eight applications. Any of the several new fungicides available at garden stores are suitable for this purpose.

Spraying is a time-consuming project with lots of heavy work. It is meaningful only for

Figure 5.2. Initial stage of apple scab on *M. baccata* 'Columnaris'.

the largest collections and arboreta that seek to maintain a full collection of the crabapple species and older, once-important clones. I do not advise it for any home garden or even larger estates. The alternative to spraying is to plant only disease-resistant clones. If you plant the older crabapples, however, be prepared for a spraying program. Much of the discredit to flowering crabapples in the past is attributable to such clones as *Malus* 'Almey', *M.* 'Eleyi', *M.* 'Hopa', *M.* 'Radiant', and some of the Rosybloom hybrids, as well as to several of the once touted, disease-prone species. Defoliated crabapples in midsummer, scab-ridden fruit, and the need for spraying programs all give crabapples a bad reputation that must not be tolerated.

The first evidence of apple scab is the appearance of dull, smoky areas on new leaves, particularly at the midrib. These areas soon become olive-colored and velvety as the infection progresses and then assume a definite outline as olive-green or brown circular spots. The leaves yellow and fall, defoliating the tree often by midsummer. This fungus disease overwinters on fallen leaves, producing spores in the spring that are carried by the wind and rains to opening apple buds. Thus the cycle continues. Development, which is normally rapid, is accelerated in warm spring days. Several secondary cycles may occur in a single season, each one requiring additional sprayings. A very few crabapple clones are somehow susceptible to apple scab yet do not lose their leaves. Nonetheless, they continue to reproduce the air-borne spores.

In general, apple scab is far more prevalent in humid areas of the United States than it is in drier areas. It is rarely found in the drier areas of the Rocky Mountain States, but in some heavily misted pockets along either seacoast, all crabapples are scabby.

On rare occasions, a clone that is susceptible to apple scab may also have some truly outstanding characteristic (e.g., unique blossom shape or color) that hybridizers wish to preserve. Breeding these rare clones with a strongly disease-resistant clone may result in disease-free progeny, but the susceptible gene will be lurking somewhere in the genetic background. Because this has happened to me at times in my 50 years of hybridizing, I have learned to never trust the supposedly disease-free progeny. It is one thing to plant these suspected clones as ornamentals for the garden—many are indeed very handsome and worthwhile—but it is another thing to base the entire future of hybridizing on them.

Some crabapples, such as *Malus pumila*, are notoriously disease prone, so much so that I would advise against using any of its forms for hybridization. The one exception is the only red-flowering, naturally red-leafed crabapple, *M. pumila* 'Niedzwetzkyana'. From this remarkable Russian variety, which genetically is strongly prone to apple scab, have come all the most beautiful red-flowering crabapples, including the Rosyblooms. The first Rosy-

Figure 5.3. Scab defoliation on *M.* 'Almey' (left) versus full-leafed *M.* 'Snowdrift' (right).

bloom hybrids were a sensational revolution in flowering crabapple color with their deep pink, red, and purple-red colors, but they also kept their progenitor's proneness to apple scab. Fortunately, after only a few generations, hybridizers have been able to breed out the disease-prone gene and now we have some very beautiful red-flowering, disease-free clones.

Fire Blight

Fire blight (*Erwinia amylovora*) is a widespread bacterium that survives from year to year in the margins of cankers on susceptible, infected trees and plants (e.g., pears, apple, quince, firethorn, hawthorn, mountain ash, and serviceberry). It is by far the most damaging of all crabapple diseases. Beginning at bloom time it occurs sporadically in warm moist weather, spreading from susceptible trees, but it also occurs during warm, moist summer months. When infected, tree parts—blossoms, twigs, whole branches—and even the entire tree turn brown as though scorched by a fire or an intensely dry wind. Infected blossoms appear water-soaked, shriveled, and brown. During the growing season new terminal growth suddenly wilts and turns brown, and dead leaves remain attached to branches. Cankers occur on small or large limbs, trunks, and even roots, usually starting around the base of a blighted blossom spur or shoot. Rains help spread the bacteria, and insects, attracted by the sugar in the bacterium ooze, become contaminated carriers.

Some of the most susceptible crabapples are also very beautiful in bloom. Among this group are *Malus baccata* 'Columnaris', *M.* 'Dorothea', *M.* 'Pink Perfection', *M.* 'Red Jade', *M.* ×*scheideckeri*, *M.* 'Snowcloud', *M.* 'Snowdrift', *M. tschonoskii*, *M.* 'Van Eseltine', and several clones of *M. halliana*.

Dr. Charles Powell (pers. com.), a plant pathologist at Ohio State University, described the conditions that encourage fire blight as follows:

> Conditions favorable for fire blight infection include open blossoms or succulent new growth, temperatures above 65°F [18°C], plus rainfall or a relative humidity above 60 percent. The disease is most likely to be severe in areas where fire blight was present in the preceding year.

Professor Nichols (pers. com.) observed:

> Areas of Colorado and North Dakota may have severe fire blight infections almost every year, while in some areas of the northeastern states severe infection may not be seen for 6 to 7 years. When severe infection does occur it may be devastating, as several branches or whole trees may be killed outright.

Old neglected apples and pears harbor the cankers of fire blight over winter. Such trees should be removed from proximity to flowering crabapples. Another measure of control can be attained if blossoms are sprayed with streptomycin formulations at 100 parts per million. The spray should be applied when 20–30 percent of the blossoms are open. If bloom time lasts more than 5–7 days, spraying should be repeated. Outbreaks of the infection may appear throughout the year on growing shoots following rain accompanied by wind and prolonged high humidity. In these weather conditions, spraying seems to be the only remedy of some control.

All crabapples should be inspected within 2 weeks after petal fall to ascertain any fire blight incursion. Remove all infected areas immediately and burn them. If pruning shears are used, remember to sterilize them before using them again on healthy plants. One part liquid bleach to nine parts water is an effective disinfectant for tools. Since the bacterium is especially aggressive toward new, succulent growth, avoid late-summer fertilizing of trees. Also avoid sources of organically bound nitrogen, such as barnyard manure, since they, too, can cause epidemic infections in warm, wet springs. Another precaution is to avoid planting crabapples in heavy, poorly drained soils.

Cedar-Apple Rust

Caused by the fungus *Gymnosporangium juniperi-virginianae,* cedar-apple rust is a problem only where there are large numbers of native cedars or plantings of ornamental junipers within a mile (1.6 m) of crabapples. Dr. Powell explains how the disease develops:

> Orange areas ⅛ to ¾ inch [3 to 19 mm] in diameter appear on affected leaves. The upper surface of these areas is covered with minute black dots within a reddish circle. Later, on the underside leaf surface of the orange spots, many 1⁄16 inch [1.5 mm] cup-shaped structures with fringed edges are formed in circular clusters. In late summer, spores from the cups are blown to and infect red cedars and other juniper trees, where, after 18 to 20 months, a different type of spore is produced on galls to re-infect crabapples and apple trees.

Figure 5.4. Ripened leaf spores of cedar-apple rust.

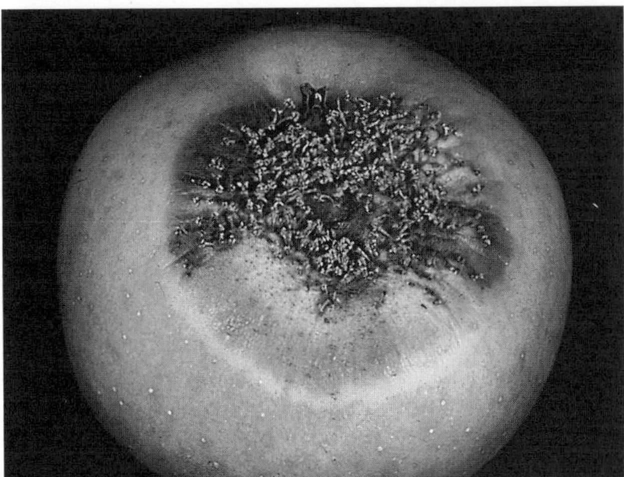

Figure 5.5. Cedar-apple rust on fruit.

Figure 5.6. Bark damage from cedar-apple rust.

Severe infection causes early leaf fall and dwarfing of infected trees. On *Malus ioensis* (Iowa or prairie crabapple), which is very susceptible, as are most of its named clones, repeated infection may cause the death not only of whole branches but of the entire tree.

Eliminating all cedar trees within a mile (1.6 m) radius of flowering crabapples provides almost complete control. When cedar trees are on neighboring properties or are a part of expensive landscaping that cannot be removed, they remain a source of constant re-infection. Three sprayings of 75 percent wettable zineb, applied at 10-day intervals starting when blossoms begin to show color, will give effective control. The most effective control is to plant completely disease-resistant crabapples.

Powdery Mildew

Caused by the fungus *Podosphaera leucotricha*, powdery mildew attacks leaves and terminal blossoms as well as fruit. Twisted, narrow, cupped terminal leaves covered with a white powdery fungus coating are the visible signs. Infected terminal growth is weakened and thus is easily killed in winter. On some highly susceptible clones such as *Malus* 'Almey', white powdery patches may be found on the fruit.

Powdery mildew is generally a problem only where air movement among trees is poor or where crabapples are growing adjacent to commercial apples such as *Malus* 'Cortland' or *M.* 'Rome'. The fungus overwinters as threads within dormant buds. High humidity and temperatures around 70°F (21°C) provide conditions ideal for disease development. Spores do not germinate from moisture on buds and leaves but rather require atmospheric moisture content approaching saturation (C. Powell, pers. com.)

To control powdery mildew, spray three times at weekly intervals with benomyl 50 percent wettable powder.

INSECT PESTS

Hardy and sturdy as they are, flowering crabapples will usually withstand minor insect attacks. When these attacks become overwhelming, however, some means of control becomes necessary. Only a very few insect pests need consideration.

Aphids

Aphids are the small sucking insects so often related to and cared for by ants, who milk them for their honey dew secretions and carry them from place to place. Ordinarily, aphids do not constitute a problem, but when they appear in great number, especially on new growth, the leaves become twisted and curled. The aphid's sticky secretions turn the foliage black due to a sooty fungus growth.

Aphids are most frequently found on new sucker growth. Thus the prompt removal of suckers helps control these pests. They are also easily controlled by a spraying of malathion, often readily available in combination with other insecticides at garden stores.

Mites

Mites, particularly red spider mites, are piercing, sucking insects so small that a hand lens is needed to see them. Ordinarily, in the northeastern states they rarely are a problem. Mites cause leaves to discolor, especially in hot, dry seasons, turning them yellow to bronze before they fall.

When mites first appear, a Kelthane™ spraying usually controls them. A second spraying may be necessary. For the most part, healthy growing trees are rarely damaged by minor insects and do not have to be sprayed.

Tent Caterpillars

Malacosoma species are a bothersome nuisance, forming unsightly silklike webs in the branch crotches of infected trees. They are becoming more and more plentiful each season as they appear to have no apparent natural enemies. Birds, fearing entanglement in the unsightly webs, refuse to eat these caterpillars.

Tent caterpillars lay their eggs in bands around small twigs in the summer or, in warmer seasons, in late fall. When the eggs hatch very early the next spring, the caterpillar larvae immediately begin eating all the leaves in the vicinity. From a silklike nest in the forks of branches, each morning they spread out on silken threads to pasture on nearby leaves, returning to their nest in the evening. When fully grown the caterpillars wander in all directions looking for a place to pupate; when they find it, they form a cocoon in late June or July, or even earlier depending on the climate. Moths soon emerge to lay their eggs in rings around twigs for the next generation. Although it is claimed there is but one generation a year, I have found these caterpillars among the trees and shrubs in my garden almost every summer month until September. I am told there is also a subspecies.

Fall Webworm

Fall webworm, *Hyphantria cunea* (Drury), exhibits the same behavior as its relative, the tent caterpillar, except that it forms its massive nest in August whereas the tent caterpillar spins its nest in early spring. The greenish gray-brown caterpillars of this species are very hairy and larger than tent caterpillars, and they spin tents that are much larger, sometimes a yard (0.9 m) long. The adults are white moths with one-inch (2.5-cm) wing spans.

Although neither caterpillar seems to permanently damage a tree, they leave unsightly, leafless branches where they have been feeding and messy webs not easily removed. If they are few and in reachable areas, the nests can be removed by hand and the caterpillars within them destroyed. It is best to destroy the nest in the evening when all the caterpillars are home for the night describing their day's foraging to one another. A paper bag is excellent for this purpose as it can later be incinerated with all the caterpillars. Destroy any egg rings if you observe them in the fall or winter when they are most easily seen on smaller branches.

If there are many fall webworms, and particularly if they cannot be reached, it is best to spray with one of the many insecticides designed for them: malathion, methoxychlor, diazinon, and other garden insect mixes where available. Spraying is most effective when feeding starts, since once the caterpillars have pupated the spray cannot reach them. When using any chemical, follow instructions strictly, wear a face mask and do not directly inhale any pesticides. Always keep pesticides away from and out of reach of children.

Apple-and-Thorn Skeletonizer

You can identify the larvae of apple-and-thorn skeletonizer, *Choreutis pariana* Clerck, when you see a small, spotted caterpillar that feeds mainly on the upper surface of leaves. The edges of leaves are rolled upward and fastened with a web. Eating all but the veins and lower surface of the leaf, the caterpillar feeds under the web. It produces two broods a year with larvae present in July and again in August-September. The adult is a small moth.

It is the second brood that seems to cause the greatest damage to trees, particularly to flowering crabapples, purple plums, and hawthorns. Ordinarily, no control is necessary but on rare occasions the brood may be so large as to disfigure a tree by defoliating large areas. Almost all garden insecticides will control these insect pests.

San Jose Scale

San Jose scale, *Quadraspidiotus perniciosus* (Comstock), usually does not infect crabapples to any large extent. When it does, however, it must be dealt with promptly as heavily infected trees or shrubs can be killed. All scale insects—oyster shell, lecanium, and San Jose—have similar life cycles. Because the insect can be reached only in the spring when the young mites or scales, looking like white fluff, are on the move, correct timing of spraying is essential. A dormant spray, such as lime sulphur, should be applied in spring before buds begin to open; after that, one of the special scalecides available at garden centers must be used in the mite or moving stage. Whatever scalecide is used, follow directions on the container carefully. Usually heavily infected branches must be removed and destroyed by burning. Heavily encrusted areas on older branches or in tree crotches must often be scraped off as no insecticide can reach them. After scraping, the areas are then thoroughly sprayed with a good scalecide.

Cicada

Cicadas (*Cicadiae* or *Magicicada septendecim*) have begun to emerge in varying cycles—every 10, 17, or 20 years, for example. In the "Year of the Locust," whichever year that may be, they greatly damage flowering crabapples, particularly young trees, for they emerge in great hordes, often by the thousands, in Ohio, Pennsylvania, and neighboring states. Their eerie droning, caused by rubbing their metalliclike wings together, can be heard for miles.

When they emerge from the pupal stage, the adult, winged cicadas do not feed on anything, but promptly begin a mating drone, which is frightening as it goes on for days at end. Upon mating, the female immediately seeks a young branch, generally a 2- or 3-year-old branch, into which she makes razorlike slits where she deposits her white eggs. She then moves below the slits and cuts a circle around the branch, thus greatly weakening it so that it falls to the ground easily when the wind blows. There the now-hatched small white grubs burrow into the ground and make their descent below the frost line, eating at roots as they grow. Fat and about 1–1.5 in (2.5–3.8 cm) in length, these grubs can devastate roots of young trees. When hatched in the thousands, as they are in the "Year of the Locust," they seriously damage the roots of even mature trees and shrubs. Moles feast upon these grubs, so if you have moles, you have grubs. The two are inseparable.

Today locusts are known to emerge in 10-, 17-, 20-, and off-year cycles. Coming clocklike to the surface to renew their life cycles, the time of their emergence can be accurately predicted by the local agricultural service, which can best inform you when not to plant young orchard trees or when to protect them with cheesecloth against the emerging hordes. If cicadas invade your territory, examine your trees and immediately cut off the egg-laden, razorslit branches, then burn them. In this way you will catch the brood before it hatches and enters the ground. You will not further damage the tree by removing these branches as infested branches will almost always die, and, should they survive, they will always have the scored-around bulge that dwarfs their growth.

No spray is effective against adult cicadas nor do they have any natural predators. Their wirelike wings and awful whir frighten even the boldest birds, who will not come near them. Some grub-killing insecticides will rid lawns of grubs, but once these pests burrow deeper, nothing reaches them. One form of digger wasp preys on cicadas but, unfortunately, in horde years the number of digger wasps is insignificant compared to the thousands of cicadas that emerge. Fortunately, the "Year of the Locust" comes rather infrequently and urbanization is somewhat diminishing the number of locusts.

Japanese Beetle

In some areas in the eastern and midwestern Great Lakes states, the Japanese beetle (*Popillia japonica*) has become a horticultural pest that must be dealt with aggressively. It loves the entire rose family of plants and has a definite preference for crabapple leaves. Eating the leaves of its host plant, the Japanese beetle, when it appears in force, can completely skeletonize a small tree.

This medium-size scarabaeid beetle has a metallic green-bronze body. Birds will not eat it, nor does it have any natural enemies, so the number of Japanese beetles increases yearly. For years we never had these beetles in Falconskeape Garden; then, suddenly, they appeared, devouring whatever suited their palate.

The most effective control for Japanese beetle seems to be sex attractive pheromone traps. Prescribed sprays designed specifically for this pest are reasonably effective, and a bacterium, commonly called milky spore disease (under the trade name Dylox and Dasanit), infects and kills the fat white grubs in the soil. Where Japanese beetle grubs are in the soil, moles will move in for they are among a mole's favorite food. Perhaps all the methods possible must be used to rid a garden of this newest scourge until far more effective means of control can be researched.

Apple Borer

The apple borer, *Synanthedon pyri*, is not a serious problem except in older trees that have been neglected and show signs of trunk decay. Should the borer problem be serious, gardeners should consult their local agricultural agent. Ordinarily, a remedy for a lone borer or two can be found in garden center preparations. Follow directions carefully.

Figure 5.7. Tree damaged by round-headed apple borer.

When an old crabapple begins to decay from within, the trouble spot has been progressing for several years. Perhaps the best remedy is to replace the old tree with a young and vigorous one. Good, careful pruning practices are necessary to prevent branch stubs from rotting into the heartwood of the tree. All cuts should be made close to the trunk, leaving only a very small bump to be overgrown by the cambium layer as soon as possible. Stubs 4 in (10.2 cm) or longer may begin to decay before they can be overgrown. These always spell trouble.

Codling Moth

Codling moths need large fruit to complete their developing cycle. Thus they are not bothersome to crabapples.

ANIMAL PESTS

Deer

Where deer are plentiful, damage to trees can be rather extensive. For one thing, deer prefer the succulent branches of last season's growth as one of their favorite winter browses. Thus a herd of 20 or more deer can heavily damage a planting of crabapples in short order. Browsing is particularly harmful as the deer destroy the fruiting buds on the outside areas of the trees. In addition to browsing, the bucks, at rutting time and also when losing their antlers, viciously attack young trees, often ripping and shredding the bark so that either the tree or its shape is so totally destroyed that it must be replaced.

Several deer repellents are available on the market, but the best repellant is a good dog. Often just walking through the garden with the dog leaves enough dog scent to ward off the deer from congregating in crabapple plantings. Where there are large herds of deer, nothing deters them.

Hunting deer is the only sure cure I know of for this difficult problem, which is far greater in public arboreta and parks than on private estates, but it often leads to a heated argument between naturalists and horticulturists. Are the gardens for plants or for animals, or for both? The more a garden is frequented by people during the winter months, the less likely deer will damage it, but one thing is sure: flowering crabapples and deer will never co-exist on peaceful terms. One will have to go.

Rabbit

Rabbits are rodents whose teeth must be kept short by constantly gnawing on wood to wear them down. If rabbits do not keep their teeth worn down and sharp, the teeth will overgrow and soon the rabbit will be unable to open its jaws because of the overlocked teeth. This, in turn, brings certain starvation.

One of the rabbit's favorite woods is crabapple. The heavy trunks of older trees are not in danger, but the bark of younger trees and their lower branches are often stripped bare up to the snow line and as high as a standing rabbit can reach. Since the snowfall varies from day to day, there is no advantage in wrapping or fencing in trees. With a snowbank and a rabbit, nothing is sacred! If a young tree is girdled all around by a rabbit, it will certainly die. Often this damage is not seen until snows have melted, but by then nothing can be done for the tree's survival.

A good licensed trapper or hunter is probably better than any other remedy. Rabbit-repellent sprays, mostly containing thiram, can be had from local garden stores, but at best they are a half measure of protection. I know of several orchardists who prune their apple trees in early winter, leaving the pruned branches strewn around the trees. Rabbits strip these first before attacking mature trees that are more difficult to reach. Most rabbits are nocturnal, debarking trees during the night hours when even a trusted rabbit dog is fast asleep. When rabbits are plentiful, expect severe damage, especially if the snowfall is heavy for then they can climb on the crusty surface to reach higher, young branchlets. In the smaller garden this is usually not a problem.

Mouse and Vole

Mice and voles can cause considerable damage as they, also, debark smaller trees. Unlike rabbits, however, these small rodents damage trees below the snow or hidden in the cover of higher grass left around the tree trunks. Since mice do not like to work in grass-free areas, one of the best preventive measures is to have a grass-free ring 3 ft (0.9 m) wide around a trunk. High grass around a trunk is an open invitation for mice to set up winter quarters. Wire or hardware cloth protection of tree trunks, particularly on very young or newly set trees, aids in reducing damage by mice, and poisoned grain baits are available from garden and farm stores. The latter must be used with care to keep pets and children from eating them.

A good barn cat, not a neutered pet but a mouser that patrols the garden, is an invaluable asset in reducing the mouse population. Patrolling in summer and late fall, "dear kitty" will be curled up in a warm hay mow or under your favorite chair in winter, not even dreaming of what the mice are doing under the heavy snow.

Where mice are plentiful, damage to trees is inevitable. Several natural predators, such as owls and hawks, once kept mice somewhat in control, but today one rarely, if ever, hears the hoot of an owl or the scream of a hunting hawk.

CHAPTER 6

Landscaping with Flowering Crabapples

Flowering crabapples are choice garden trees. You can plant a single focal specimen near the patio, using one of the smallest varieties as potted plants for the garden court, or you can plant crabapples as a central design along the garden walk, as backgrounds for flowering plants, and as flowering screens, windbreaks, or property line dividers. Many special clones are excellent street or highway trees.

Modern flowering crabapples outshine their illustrious predecessors among the species not only in bloom but also in tree form. Trees of every imaginable form exist today: beautiful upright or columnar trees; vase-shaped or fan-shaped trees; broadly spreading trees; delightful smaller, rounded, almost tailored trees; gently spreading trees; and to top it all, a whole new line of unique weepers in many shapes. More recently hybridizers have introduced shrublike and bushlike forms that are suitable for even the smallest garden. For every need and space in the garden there is an appropriate crabapple.

The effect of crabapples in the landscape is enhanced when trees are planted in odd-numbered groups (three, five, or more, where space is available) in a single color flanked by another odd-numbered group in a contrasting or complimentary color. Even in small gardens an excellent design is achieved with just a few trees, such as a white-flowering crabapple tree flanked on either side by a pink or deep red tree.

FACTORS IN SELECTING CRABAPPLES FOR THE LANDSCAPE

The successful growing of any plant, including crabapples, requires a careful consideration of the plant's characteristics as well as those of the proposed site. According to Dr. John Sabuco (1987) of Flossmoor, IL, one of North America's foremost landscape architects and a past president of the IOCS, the key factors to consider for successful crabapple plantings are as follows:

Crabapple Characteristics	Site Characteristics
Size	Area
Hardiness	Climate (micro & macro)
Fruit color & size	Background
Disease resistance	General maintenance
Fragrance	Distance from viewer
Form	Use
Food value	Ornamental/bird food

I have often gone back to Dr. Sabuco's wisdom-packed articles, not only because he has personal knowledge of the many crabapple clones, but because he also has a distinct eye for how to best use these trees to their fullest potential in different kinds of gardens, whether the desired effect is flowering beauty or magnificent fruit or both. In the lengthy quotation below, Dr. Sabuco (1987) explains the process by which he assists clients to select the right crabapple for a given site:

> When I select a crabapple for one of my clients the first order of business is to determine the size of the plant needed and in what period of time it must fulfill its role in the landscape.... In short, a tree should be able to reach its fullest capacity without need for pruning. Trees appear to grow slower as they age, when in fact they generally put on the same volume of new growth more or less, year after year. The new growth is spread out over more branch tips.... A hillside vista can be best accented with very short, wide trees. This makes the view seem more grand and does not block the view from the top of the hill. These trees are also beautifully displayed when you look up the hill or against it.
>
> Next, I take stock of my site characteristics to determine the form, flower and its color, fruit size and color; the following is a list of automatic criteria:
>
> - Close to viewer
>   - Fragrant flowers
>   - Small fruit
>   - Red fruit
>   - Persistent fruit
>   - Detailed blossoms (doubles, bicolor, etc.)
>   - Medium-to-small size (unless desired for shade)
> - Far from viewer
>   - Large fruit
>   - Yellow fruit
>   - Medium-to-large size
> - Red or dark brown stone or brick background
>   - White flowers
>   - Yellow fruit
>   - Yellow fall leaf color
> - Light brown or tan stone or brick and natural cedar
>   - White flowers
>   - Red fruit
>   - Yellow or orange fall leaf color
> - Blue sky
>   - White or red flowers

- Red fruit
- Medium-to-large size

Sunshine from behind viewer
- White flowers
- Yellow fruit

White or generally light background
- Red & rosy flowers
- Red fruit

Dark backgrounds (such as conifers)
- White flowers
- Red or yellow fruit
- Good fall leaf color

Hillsides or small slopes
- Semiweeping
- Weeping or a very wide spreader

Hanging over water, rock wall, or terraces
- Horizontal spreading
- Semiweeping
- Weeping

Near walkways
- Upright to columnar

Drives or tight corners
- Fragrant

As Dr. Sabuco would be the first to point out, these excellent observations and recommendations in no way exhaust the almost limitless combinations for effective landscape use of flowering crabapples nor do they eliminate the need for preliminary planning and knowledge of individual clones.

Figure 6.1. The twisting branches of *M. ×atrosanguinea* are often the object of artists' paintings and photographers' delight in the winter and springtime landscapes.

DESIGNING THE GARDEN

A permanent site for flowering crabapples depends on where and how they are to be used. Different considerations are given in small home gardens than are given for large estates, parks, or arboreta. Each situation requires its own unique design and special type of flowering crabapples. Choose the clone most suited to your landscape design. Be bold and lavish in using crabapples as the framework of your garden and they will never disappoint you. Do your winter homework well, determining the flower color combination, form and size of tree, and the fruit colors well before you buy your plants.

Should you be blessed with a lake or pond, plant crabapples close to the water but on higher ground so their beauty can be reflected in the water. White and light pink blossoms reflect better than do the deep reds which are also elegant mirrored next to white bloomers. Never place crabapple trees at the water's edge, where their roots are constantly in water. They will not grow, but will rot away, and, if the lake is large enough to harbor muskrats, the muskrats will tunnel under and destroy any trees planted too close to the water's edge. Find higher ground, even some short distance back from the water, where the trees can still be reflected, mirrorlike, in the lake.

Wherever crabapples are planted, they will adapt. They will delight you with billowing blossoms in springtime, with good green foliage in summer, and again in autumn with a tremendous color display of small fruit. The fruit, food for hungry birds, lasts several weeks, in some cases even into the snows of winter. If allowed to form several trunks, many crabapples develop magnificent outlines of twisting trunks and branches in the winter landscape. What more could one ask of any tree?

PATIO, POT, AND SIDEWALK CRABAPPLES

Some crabapples are ideal patio or sidewalk trees as they grow well in large pots. They must be watered and not left on their own. Also, give them sunlight or they will grow tall and rangy in their quest for light. Prune them at first only very moderately until they have formed a mature frame, then most of the lower branches can be removed.

FLOWERING CRABAPPLES FOR LARGE GARDENS AND ESTATES

Where space is not a problem, flowering crabapples can be planted to produce some of the most beautiful landscaping effects, whether through mass plantings of wide color combinations or distant vistas of color. For a magnificent show, plant three trees of the same color in a group. I believe that a triangular planting is best. Then on either side of the triangle, plant one or three trees of a contrasting color. For example, if you plant dark reds in the

Figure 6.2. The beauty of the wintertime form of exotic weepers is evident in *M.* 'Red Jade'. Photo courtesy of Michael and Lori Yanny.

center, plant white bloomers on either side, but it you plant a white bloomer in the center, plant pale pink trees on either side. Even from a distance these plantings make a wonderful display.

While planting for spring bloom, be careful to select cultivars that have equally contrasting autumn-colored fruit. Since most of the red-flowering crabapples have rather dull red to purplish fruit, they are not the best choice for the central cultivar in a group planting. Rather choose the cultivars with bright red buds that open to pure white blossoms and place red and pink blossoms next to or behind them. Those with the brightest red or orange autumn fruit should offset a central yellow-fruiting tree.

There are far more clones with fine bright red fruit than there are yellow-fruited ones. Next come a few good orange-fruited clones, then rare copper-colored and multicolored clones, and lastly, a few clones with purple fruit and one or two clones whose fruit has a bluish blush. One must plan for both the springtime and the autumn effects at the same time and not lose the impact of either one.

In larger estate gardens beautiful results can be obtained by combining smaller groups of flowering crabapples with many of the choice conifers. This combination is especially attractive using the lower growing spruces as background for the crabapples. I have seen a combination of one of the best red-flowering cultivars, *Malus* 'Liset', and the deep pink *M.* 'Dorothea' (might I jealously suggest one of my own crosses, *M.* 'Orange Crush') planted a small distance from a clump of *Acer griseum* or its magnificent hybrid (which I have seen only at Rochester, NY). The subtle tones of the maple's shiny, copper-colored bark were caught up in the orange tones of the flowering crabapple. These effects are realized only after both trees reach some degree of maturity, but they should be planned well in advance at planting time.

The color tones of some flowering crabapple blossoms are such that one must look carefully and closely to find them before selecting a companion plant. Some examples are *Malus* 'Coralglow', *M.* 'Dorothea', *M.* 'GV-19', *M.* 'Karen', *M.* 'Lonsdale', *M.* 'Louisa', *M.* 'Ross's Double Red', and *M.* 'Van Eseltine'.

GARDEN WALKS

An effective landscaping scheme for a winding "garden walk" includes a series of flowering crabapple specimens planted one-by-one or in small plantings here and there on either side of the walk (or drive), interspersed with other plantings of conifers, lilacs, shrubs, and beds of *Hemerocallis* or *Hosta*. Stagger the colors of the crabapple clones for both spring bloom and autumn fruit.

How magnificent an estate planting, arboretum, or large crabapple collection would be if it were handled in this manner! But no, most crabapples are lined up uncomplaining in orchard tree rows. Companion landscaping could make a big difference in the overall effect. For example, the excellent Lilac Walk at Ewing Park, Des Moines, IA, would be even more exciting if it were interplanted with lower-growing, newer flowering crabapples. At the Holden Arboretum, Mentor, OH, the new plantings intersperse crabapples with all kinds of companion plants in a beautifully designed garden walk. (Yes, they also have the old traditional flowering crabapple orchard and a new testing plot set out in rows.)

Hopefully a flowering crabapple-lilac combination will find favor in many large estate, park, and arboretum plantings. The two have always had a secret love affair for one another, ever since Eve was driven from paradise. In fact, an old Moravian tale claims that one angel at the gate gave Eve a spray of flowering apple blossoms to remind her of her sin, while the

Figure 6.3. A street planting of *M. sieboldii* in Medina, OH.

other angel gave her a spray of lilacs to assure her she would be forgiven. According to the legend, ever since that time crabapples bloom first and then with them, come the lilacs.

FLOWERING CRABAPPLES AS FOCAL POINTS IN A GARDEN

For a specimen or garden focal point, try one of the newest weeping crabapples, such as *Malus* 'Anne E', *M.* 'Henry Ross', *M.* 'Louisa', *M.* 'Lullaby', *M.* 'Luwick', *M.* 'Molten Lava', *M.* 'Red Swan', or *M.* 'White Cascade' in front of a small mass of blue or dark green conifers. Weeping crabapples create an outstanding effect, especially if they are chosen for heavy autumn fruiting.

Never plant weeping crabapples in groups; always plant them as single specimens of extraordinary beauty. Weepers do not look good if massed together; even three weepers in a group somehow shout out to be planted alone. If you have room, however, a short distance away from the weeper, plant a group of three slower-growing upright crabapples on either side of it. The uprights will break the horizontal form and frame the selected weeper. Although not many of these smaller upright trees are available, there are a few with no appreciable fruit, including *Malus* 'Centurion', *M.* 'Eline', *M.* 'Henning', *M.* 'Karen', *M.* 'Sentinel', and the double *M.* 'Van Eseltine'.

FLOWERING CRABAPPLES AS BACKGROUNDS AND SCREENS

As background plantings, flowering crabapples make excellent flowering/fruiting screens to hide tennis courts, laundry-drying and play areas, or any area in a backyard that needs screening. When using crabapples for screens and boundary plantings, mix upright, spreading and columnar tree forms with rounded or semiweeping forms. The variety of forms adds interest and diversity of blossom color and fruit color to the planting.

Crabapples also do well as a broad boundary line between properties, filling in with both beauty and food for migrating birds if one uses the newer small-fruited kinds that the birds love so well. At Falconskeape, the fruits of *Malus* 'Autumn Glory' and *M.* 'Leprechaun' do not last more than a month ever since the migrating cedar waxwings learned there was a favorite restaurant stop along the way. Each year they come in flocks of 20 or more and remain with us for a few days until their appetite for crabapples is sated. In the spring, robins reverse the order and can be seen flopping around after gorging themselves with the fruit of cider crabapples from cultivars that hold their fruit through winter. No other flowering tree or conifer has such versatility and adapts so well to as many uses with such minimal care.

LARGE ARBORETUM PLANTINGS

Any large planting of flowering crabapples bears with it special problems of maintenance costs, space, variability of plantings, and correct choice of materials planted. Much of what has already been said about planting, selecting appropriate clones, landscape use, and design applies equally to arboretum plantings.

The general practice, several decades ago, was to plant each genus in an area of its own, a kind of taxonomic grouping. Within these groups one could make comparison of the many species and separately named clones by passing among them, mostly in orchardlike rows. After bloom time, no one paid attention to the crabapple trees until autumn fruiting time. Although these plantings were practical, economic, and spraying-wise, they did not show what flowering crabapples could offer in conjunction with other plantings. The orchardlike setting displayed no real landscaping design of the various tree forms nor did it provide sudden vistas of landscaped beauty.

Arboreta today still need to preserve species and special clones of interest and value. Their botanical collections remain important for study, research, and hybridizing. Many of the plants can be found nowhere else and would be lost entirely if they were not kept by arboreta. The historical collections of arboreta are also important to record the horticultural

Figure 6.4. Weeping *M.* 'White Cascade' in a rock garden at Falconskeape Gardens.

progress that has been made. But in addition to these two functions, arboretum plantings are very important for educating the public about what is available in newer plants and how those plants can be used artistically in the home garden or larger estate. Rather than plant flowering crabapples in orchard rows, they are much more beautiful and educational if planted in a general landscape design in conjunction with many other species. A long, winding garden walk, landscaped on both sides with crabapples, lilacs, conifers, and a multitude of arboretum plants, is an endless delight in all seasons as something is always in flower.

Well-planned garden walks offer exciting vista openings to those who walk them. The new garden walk at the renovated Holden Arboretum, Mentor, OH, and the Long Walk at the Ewing Arboretum, Des Moines, IA, are two such plantings. Growing in beauty each year, these walks educate the public to the beauty, value, and use of a great number of horticultural specialties. They also provide the public with the opportunity to compare older trees—whether species or clones—with newer introductions. Often people are then able to re-create certain vistas of excellence in their own backyard gardens, and this, after all, is what arboreta should and could be doing.

For some arboreta, adopting this philosophy may require a total revamping of their fundamental views on arboretum plantings, but it will be certain to attract many more people to the arboretum all through the year. I challenge arboretum directors and their managing boards to give flowering crabapples, and all other genera, their rightful place: display them in their best attire—not as forgotten orchard trees.

HIGHWAY PLANTINGS

Flowering crabapple trees are excellent for highway plantings, but it is best to plant them in groups of three or more. Large massed bloom is more visible from speeding automobiles than are single trees.

Some crabapples are more effective than others in highway plantings. The shrub forms, weepers, and smaller trees to 10 ft (3 m) high should be avoided. For background, choose some of the taller species, such as *Malus baccata* or *M. tschonoskii*, with its upright form, or choose any of the disease-resistant Rosybloom hybrids, such as *M.* 'Makamik' or *M.* ×*hartwigii*, which holds its fruit until late in the winter. The upright, rounded and spreading forms are the most effective with an occasional columnar form to break the monotony of design.

The following list contains my recommendations for highway plantings:

M. 'Adams'—To 20 × 20 ft (6 × 6 m), excellent but smaller fruit
M. 'Albright'—Pink blossoms, larger fruit, second-generation Rosybloom
M. 'Amberina'—Wonderful fall fruit
M. 'Ames White'—Excellent yellow-fruited tree
M. baccata 'Jackii'—To 20 × 20 ft (6 × 6 m), very fine fall fruit
M. baccata 'Taliak'—15 × 15 ft (4.6 × 4.6 m), larger dark red fruit that lasts all winter
M. 'Ballerina'—Fine upright form for accent
M. 'Baskatong'—Pink flowering, spreading form 20 × 25 ft (6 × 7.6 m), very fine for larger red fruit, excellent disease resistance
M. 'Bob White'—Persistent fruit, green-tan to yellowish
M. 'Burgandy'—Red blossoms, upright form, excellent

Figure 6.5. *Malus* 'Coralburst' grafted on standards for a formal design.

M. 'Callaway'—Excellent white, does well even in the South
M. 'Calvary'—Fine red blossoms, dark fruit
M. 'Cardinal's Robe'—Good deep pink, red-purple fruit
M. 'Centurion'—An upright tree for accent
M. 'Dawson'—Excellent choice
M. 'Ferrill's Crimson'—Excellent choice, but difficult to find
M. 'Firebrand'—White blossoms, brilliant red fruit
M. 'Gibb's Golden Gage'—Excellent yellow-fruited tree
M. 'Gypsy Gold'—Larger gold-orange fruit very persistent, very showy
M. 'Harvest Gold'—Gold fruit persistent to winter
M. 'Henry Kohankie'—Excellent larger fruit can be seen from fast-moving vehicles
M. 'Indian Magic'—15 × 15 ft (4.6 × 4.6 m), good fruit
M. ioensis 'Klehm's Improved Bechtel'—Late bloomer, fragrant
M. 'Kirk'—15 × 15 (4.6 × 4.6 m), very showy red fruit, persistent
M. 'Lemoinei'—Plant larger trees, outstanding once it begins to bloom
M. 'Maria'—Excellent spreading to 15 ft (4.6 m), dark pink bloom, dark red fruit, very persistent
M. 'Michael'—Outstanding in its brilliant red fruit, very heavy bloomer
M. 'Ormiston Roy'—Excellent in every way
M. 'Pauline'—Very heavy, red-fruited annual bearer
M. 'Peter Pan'—Smaller fruit turns orange-rust with frost, persists to spring, very heavy bloomer
M. 'Prairifire'—An excellent tree with dark red blossoms
M. 'Ralph Shay'—Excellent in bloom and in fruit
M. 'Selkirk'—Showy, fruit colors early
M. 'Sentinel'—An upright tree, fine in all aspects
M. 'Serenade'—Vase-shaped to semiweeper, very heavy orange fruited
M. sieboldii 'Calocarpa'—Outstanding in brilliant red fruit
M. sieboldii 'Wooster'—Excellent red fruit, showy, earlier coloring than 'Calocarpa'
M. 'Sissipuk'—One of the better Rosyblooms, large background
M. 'Velvet Pillar'—Columnar, dark red foliage good for accent, few fruits
M. 'Winter Gold'—Smaller tree but the best for yellow fruit

In areas susceptible to snow and ice, highway plantings should be some distance from the pavement to escape being buried by snow plows or killed by heavy salting of icy roads.

If heavy salting is required in an area, flowering crabapples should not be planted as they are severely damaged by salt sprays. The crabapple plantings along highways in Kentucky, particularly around the Lexington area, are excellent proof of what can be achieved. Today the state would undoubtedly use newer and better varieties that were not available 20 years ago.

CHAPTER 7

Companion Plants to Flowering Crabapples

Flowering crabapples put on a display of blossoms in spring and a fruiting extravaganza in autumn that are unequalled by any other plant. Even a single crabapple with a well-kept grass-free circle around it can be a thing of great beauty: the springtime blossoms, the rich green or reddish foliage on an excellent tree form in summer, or, the magnificent fruit display in autumn. Flowering crabapples need no excuse for not having companion plants for they can very well hold center stage by themselves. Nonetheless, the singular, artistic value of any planting is increased when enhanced by selective companion plants. Correct companion plants frame and accent the beauty of crabapple trees, but are not an absolute necessity.

Today, skilled and knowledgeable landscape architects are featuring flowering crabapples as the main planting in gardens of great beauty from springtime to autumn, and, yes, even for the winter landscape. The year-round beauty of these gardens is enhanced when suitable companion plants accent crabapple floral or fruiting displays. Many plants can be used with crabapples to make a wonderful garden design. Thus each garden has its own secrets—the unique combination of companion plants that makes it a personal creation of landscaping beauty and that imprints upon its design the handiwork of its creator. The several outstanding companion plants suggested in this chapter are for those gardeners who desire a challenge and a triumph for their garden.

Which companion plants are to be included with flowering crabapples depends a great deal on what kind of garden is planned. Is yours a small home garden with miniature charm and limited space? Do you have a small, walled-in courtyard attached to a condominium? Is yours a very small roof garden on a city high-rise that has room for only a very few potted plants? Do you have greater space—perhaps a large suburban lot or even a country estate of a few or several acres? Or, are you in charge of city street plantings? Perhaps you are the director of a large city park planting, or an extensive private collection, or even an arboretum's flowering crabapple selections. Whatever your need and purpose, there are special crabapples to suit any design.

After considering the garden design, its size, purposes, use, and special features, one must determine what kind of maintenance will be provided. Are you looking for minimal or peripheral maintenance to stay within a limited budget? Or can you support the additional costs of garden beds and underplantings filled with perennials or annual bedding plants? Perhaps your budget permits the luxury of select background plants. All these factors are important considerations when beginning to plan for companion plants to flowering crabapples.

CONIFERS

When planting background conifers—whether tree or shrub forms—for flowering crabapples, one must be aware of the ultimate height and spread of the companion plantings at maturity. Background trees, especially conifers, should be at least 60–70 ft (18.2–21.4 m) behind and away from the crabapples. Otherwise, as maturity approaches, you will have an impenetrable thicket of trees and branches and be forced to remove either the crabapples or their background companions. Background or companion plantings must be allowed to develop to their fullest beauty if they are to add to the garden's total design.

At the Secrest Arboretum, Wooster, OH, an excellent collection of conifers forms a very handsome background for crabapples *Malus* 'Mary Potter', *M.* 'Lemoinei', and several of the species. The conifers are mature plantings, some 50 ft (15.2 m) high or higher, yet the landscaping design is outstanding. A visit to a conifer planting, such as the one at the Secrest Arboretum, Arnold Arboretum, Morton Arboretum, or Canada's Royal Botanic Gardens, will give an excellent indication of what conifers require as they approach maturity so as not to be crowded out, poorly shaped, or heavily pruned early in their development. In small gardens everything must be scaled down so that the smallest evergreens are used with the smaller crabapples. The resulting effect can be as pleasing as the large-scale landscaping at Secrest.

Stately conifers in combination with flowering crabapples are always appealing. The massed bloom of red buds and white flowers opening against a dark green backdrop of conifers makes viewers realize the brilliant whiteness of flowering crabs. Use selected conifers only to accent the white or pink crabapple blossoms.

The texture of the various conifers must also be taken into consideration. Pines give a heavy texture and a nature-oriented atmosphere, whereas spruces, cedars, and most other smaller growing conifers give a more delicate background appearance, suitable for the

Figure 7.1. *Malus* 'Mary Potter' with a background of spruces (*Picea* sp.) at the Secrest Arboretum, Wooster, OH.

medium and smaller growing crabapples, especially the elegant and refined fountain weepers. Specimen crabapples are in their glory with such attendants.

A massed planting of several crabapples in a single group against a conifer background is always a spectacular display. Try pale pink clones against a background of three or five blue spruces, especially the bluest cultivars *Malus* 'Moerheim' or *M.* ×*platycarpa* 'Hoopesii'. The pale pink against the blue background is most pleasing, and as time goes on, you will see that you have created a landscaping attraction that is rarely equalled. If you choose heavily fruited trees from among the pink-flowered clones, you will have an equally fantastic garden planting in autumn as well as spring. Red-, orange-, or yellow-fruited crabapples against blue conifers are outstanding. The following pink crabapples are especially pleasing with a blue background:

M. ×*atrosanguinea*
M. coronaria
M. floribunda
M. halliana 'Parkmanii'
M. 'Brandywine'
M. 'Candied Apple'
M. 'Cranberry Lace'
M. 'Dorothea'
M. 'Eline'
M. 'Indian Magic'
M. 'Joy'
M. 'Karen'
M. 'Klehm's Improved Bechtel'
M. 'Louisa'
M. 'Luwick'
M. 'Pink Princess'
M. 'Red Splendor'
M. 'Robinson'
M. 'Ross's Double Red'
M. 'Spring Song'

White-flowering crabapples are equally as impressive as the pink-flowering ones and perhaps have a wider selection of smaller, colorful fruit. *Malus* 'Liset' and *M.* 'Orange Crush', with bright red fruit tinted orange, are a bit more bold but just as delightful against a blue background. Plant either one of these beauties in a small group with white-flowering trees on both sides and the best blues of the newest spruces in the background. You can sit back and gloat over the creation you have masterfully placed in the garden.

When planting red-flowering crabapples, use a lighter-colored background. White is ideal. You can offset the red blossoms with white-flowering crabapples or a mass planting of dogwood (*Cornus florida*). A board fence painted white or a white barn also make excellent backgrounds for bright red crabapples. To subdue the bold effect of red against white, on the opposite side of a walk plant a red crabapple in the center and flank it with pale pink crabapples. Behind this group use blue spruce or any of the medium-to-lower growing conifers as a background.

A mass of blue or dark green conifers also makes an excellent background for crabapples planted as specimen plants or garden focal points.

LILACS

Early flowering lilacs are among the finest companions to flowering crabapples. The earliest lilacs—*Syringa oblata* and its hybrids *S.* ×*hyacinthiflora*—come in a wide range of colors from white, pink, blue, and lilac to deep purple. As the bright red crabapple buds explode into billowing white blossoms, the early lilacs unfurl into banners of lavender, purple, and blue. These shades, not found in crabapples, make possible a whole new array of color combinations.

Crabapples love to be attended by lilacs, but remember to use the earliest flowering lilacs only: *Syringa ×hyacinthiflora* 'The Bride' or 'Sister Justina' and the tetraploid *S. vulgaris* 'Aloise' or 'Gertrude Clark'. Common lilacs bloom a bit later, catching only the later-blooming crabapples, although there is enough overlap of buds and blossoms that they, too, go well with the crabapples if selected clones are planted. Among the red crabapples that go very well with early white lilacs are *Malus* 'Arch McKean', *M.* 'Cotton Candy', *M.* 'Debutante', *M.* 'Eline', *M.* 'Henry Kohankie', *M.* 'Indian Magic', *M.* 'Karen', *M.* 'Lemoinei', *M.* 'Liset', *M.* 'Orange Crush', *M.* 'Profusion', *M.* 'Sentinel', and *M.* 'Van Eseltine'. Any number of deep rose and bright pink flowering crabapples also go well with the excellent, newer white lilacs.

Among lavender-colored lilac species, *Syringa oblata* var. *dilatata* is a smaller, excellent, early blooming, very fragrant plant that is wonderfully suited as a companion to any of the white-flowering *Zumi* crabapples or the pale pink flowering cultivars. It is a rounded shrub to about 10 ft (3 m) tall and about as wide. Pale pink crabapples, such as *Malus* 'Debutante', *M.* 'Eline', or *M.* 'Spring Song', are also excellent when flanked with some of the best of the blue lilacs: *S.* 'Bluebird', *S.* 'Olivier de Serres', or *S.* 'Wonderblue'.

Very few late-blooming crabapples are at peak in the slightly later lilac bloom season. *Malus* 'Coralglow', a late coral pink; *M.* 'Joy', a late shell pink with dusty foliage; *M.* 'Silver Moon', a wonderful, white, late bloomer; and a very few other crabapples are at their peek when lilacs are in full bloom. The deepest purple lilacs, such as *Syringa* 'Albert F. Holden', *S.* 'Arch McKean', *S.* 'Frank Paterson', *S.* 'Sarah Sands', or *S.* 'Yankee Doodle', make an excellent background for the late-blooming *M.* 'Silver Moon'. They are also excellent when planted on either side. Thus flanked, you will have a perfection of bloom and landscape. Try using late-blooming crabapples as backgrounds to some of the fine deep purple-red, later blooming lilacs, such as *Syringa vulgaris*; *S. julianae*, a magnificent lilac species, never grows too tall, at most to 8 ft (2.4 m) high and as wide. Another cultivar of *S. vulgaris*, *S.* 'Dr. John Rankin', has violet flowers that are especially beautiful with pale pink or white crabapples.

With their pale pink to rose blossoms, the later-blooming crabapples of the *Malus coronaria* and *M. ioensis* groups, especially the roselike double forms, are excellent with the later forms of *Syringa vulgaris*. For an outstanding combination, surround some of these late-blooming crabapples with *S. julianae* or its outstanding clones, such as *S.* 'Pink Parasol' or the near-white *S.* 'Karen', or use the rare lilac species *S. reflexa*. For other later-blooming lilac hybrids, use some of the *S. ×prestoniae* like *S.* 'Ursula' (many of these are large shrubs to 18 ft/5.5 m), the beautiful *S.* 'Miss Canada', or the much smaller *S.* 'Lark Song' (to 6–8 ft/1.8–2.4 m high), *S.* 'Garden Peace', and *S.* 'Quartet'. The delightful lilac hybrids of Tibetan background also are later blooming: *S.* 'High Lama', *S.* 'Ling Tong', or *S.* 'Tong Yong'. The combinations are endless and most beautiful. Indeed the right flowering crabapples and the right lilacs are a splendid combination.

DOGWOODS

Crabapples and dogwoods were meant for each other: both bloom at the same time. Where dogwoods grow well, use them copiously with flowering crabapples. The white, pink, and red dogwoods make wonderful companions.

When merging a large planting into a woodland area, there is no better combination at the wood's edge than flowering crabapples and dogwoods. In such plantings use only the smaller forms of crabapples, those not exceeding 12–15 ft (3.7–4.7 m) in height. Some of the larger species and named clones are too tall and wide and would screen out the dogwoods, thus losing the whole effect.

A choice red- or pink-flowering dogwood surrounded on each side by some of the excellent, newer *Zumi* hybrids or the multibrids, with their masses of white flowers, is an excellent combination. Many other combinations are possible. For example, a trio of columnar or upright-growing crabapples (e.g., *Malus* 'Centurion', *M.* 'Madonna', *M.* 'Sentinel') not only gives color contrast with dogwoods, but also provides an excellent contrast in shape to the more-rounded and spreading dogwoods. The colorful autumn fruit of flowering crabapples, often cascades of rich orange-reds, goes well with the brilliantly colored and changing dogwood foliage.

MAGNOLIAS

Like conifers and lilacs, magnolias also make a splendid combination with flowering crabapples. The magnolia known as 'Dr. Merrill' is so early it can only be used with the earliest-blooming crabs. Two others magnolias, 'Elizabeth' or 'Miss Honeybee', come in shades of pale yellow that will enhance pure white or pale pink crabapples. All the pink- and purple-flowering magnolias go well with the white-flowering crabapples.

HOSTA AND *HEMEROCALLIS*

An excellent companion for crabapples is an underplanting of any one kind of hosta. Use only one variety for an underplanting; otherwise the effect will appear spotty and somewhat out of place. The newly opening leaves of hostas lend a charm to the blooming crabapples. In summer the dark green crabapple foliage not only gives needed shade to hostas, but it also provides a fine rich green canopy for their blooming. A great number of excellent, newer *Hosta* varieties are available today, so consult a hosta book or visit one of the many collections to see the wonderful choice in leaf color, texture, plant size, and flowering now available. For a formal underplanting, edge a bed of large-leafed hostas, perhaps in a blue leaf color, with a smaller gold-leafed hosta. The gold-leafed varieties also make excellent backgrounds for red-fruited weeping crabapples in autumn.

A bed of summer blooming *Hemerocallis* (daylilies) is also an excellent underplanting for crabapples. Once again, a bed of a single variety of *Hemerocallis* is far more artistic than a mixed bed of all colors and flowering scape heights. In general, it is best to not underplant weeping flowering crabapples because their long branches, which eventually reach the ground, need space for excellent weeping. The daylilies available today are truly outstanding. William Munson, a friend and one of the world's finest hybridizers, not only has produced some of the most beautiful clones available today in every array of color and ruffled excellence, but he has also written an outstanding book on the species that should be consulted by all who grow this marvelous perennial (*Hemerocallis*, published by Timber Press, 1989).

PERENNIALS AND ANNUALS

A high-maintenance companion planting of many perennials and annuals is very handsome with flowering crabapples, but, because it is difficult to maintain, it can be used only in the smaller gardens or as an occasional bed in larger state parks and arboretum plantings. Again, it is best to underplant crabapples with only one variety of perennial or annual flowers. If you mix flowers, you will get a flowering wild meadow effect. Use low-growing plants only.

If you have a greenhouse or can obtain plants in early spring that are already at the blooming stage, all sorts of combinations are possible. Some of my favorites are small violas, pansies, small very clear-blue flowering creeping veronica, creeping hardy phlox, and a host of others. One very color conscious gardener planted an enormous bed of red-purple Johnny-jump-ups (*Viola* sp.) under a clone of an older, deep red-purple blooming Rosybloom; it has remained one of the finest combinations I have ever seen. The flowers of the old crabapple were a regal purplish and not a faded magenta at all.

Generally, I avoid the bright yellows and oranges of small marigolds, although in mass plantings they could be attractive with white-flowering crabapples, and they are especially good in autumn with the bright red-fruited crabapple clones. With their brilliant colors, peonies are good companion plants where beds can be planted or along a garden walk. They are hardy and bloom early in spring.

At Gardenview Horticultural Park, Strongsville, OH, the plant genius of director Henry Ross has created, over the past 40 years, an English garden that is among the world's finest. Every imaginable choice plant is nestled somewhere in this most remarkable garden. Perhaps more choice perennials have come from this rare garden than from anywhere else in the world. Henry's underplantings are worthy of duplication, though his work and efforts could never be totally duplicated or found elsewhere. One comes away from this garden paradise each time with new ideas and garden designs.

SPRING BULBS

One of the finest displays is the combination of flowering crabapples underplanted with beds of almost any of the spring bulbs. Plant spring bulbs in masses—one kind of bulb in one color—and make your plans in autumn. Do not mix species or colors or you will get a poor, spotty effect. Some of the newer grape hyacinths, make an excellent massed bed, as do tulips.

The color tones of some flowering crabapple blossoms are so subtle that the eye does not seem to notice them until they are brought out by the color of a companion planting. Orange tones are one such example. If you plant a bed of orange-red tulips underneath *Malus* 'Orange Crush' or *M.* 'Liset', you will immediately see the orange in these crabapple flowers that you never noticed before.

Unfortunately, underplanting crabapples with bulbs presents the problem of what to do with the bulb's dying foliage. Unless allowed to dry and nourish the bulb, it becomes necessary to replace the bulbs with summer annuals and then replant the bulbs in fall. This high-maintenance underplanting probably should be discouraged as a companion planting with flowering crabapples.

SHRUBS

Most shrubs do not go well with flowering crabapples. They cannot be used as underplantings as their size and needs are too competitive for ground and nutrients, although a very few look well when planted in masses on the sides or behind the crabapples. Their need for almost annual pruning adds greatly to maintenance costs.

CHAPTER 8

Propagation

"You can have it all!" This favorite phrase aptly describes why crabapples remain the most popular flowering tree. From the city forester's perspective, a crab is a tough, adaptable tree. For the grower, it is easy to produce. For the garden center, a crab is colorful and sells itself when in bloom, while for the landscape designer, it offers great diversity in the landscape. Name your size, your tree form, or your choice of flower, fruit, or foliage color and there is a crab to fit! It is a tough plant that grows well in all but the southernmost states. Today a well-developed group of cultivars is offered for year-round color and interest, with the newest cultivars almost entirely disease resistant.

Diversity is the key to modern propagation as well. Crabs can be grafted, budded, or grown as rooted cuttings. Some can be produced via micropropagation, and a few even come relatively true to type from seed. All these methods are used by various growers. While it may seem crabapples are easy to propagate because there are so many ways to do it, this diversity creates a certain complexity. Which technique is best?

TO BUD OR NOT TO BUD

Own-root propagation (cuttings, micropropagations) versus budding or grafting has become a debated issue in modern crabapple production. Proponents of own-root trees claim protection from potential graft incompatibility, reduced suckering, root hardiness, and ease of propagation. (Also the true size of the mature tree is not regulated by the vigor of a different rootstock.) Proponents of budded and grafted plants claim reduced suckering, rootstock soil adaptability, hardiness, strong anchorage, and ease of propagation.

Keith Warren (pers. com.) of J. Frank Schmidt & Son Nursery, Boring, OR, has grown crabs by all these techniques. For a while, he was enthusiastic about the potential of own-root propagation, but, after much testing and evaluation, he has come to believe that budded crabs, on the right rootstock, offer the greatest advantage.

Most of the own-root arguments are less than persuasive. Keith Warren has never seen incompatibility with the commonly used scion/rootstock combination, although such

Figure 8.1. Keith Warren, propagator at J. Frank Schmidt & Son Co., Boring, OR, prepares scionwood for late summer and early fall budding and grafting. Keith is an outstanding crabapple authority and a founding director of IOCS.

incompatibility has been reported on *Malus baccata* rootstock. Own-root crabs generally, but not always, have reduced suckers, but suckers have not been eliminated. Suckering varies with cultivars. Most own-root crabs will probably prove to be more root hardy than those budded on domesticated rootstock, but again this will vary by cultivar and it has yet to be fully documented. The greatest problem with own-root crabs appears to be in root anchorage. Nursery trees often appear sparsely rooted and there are reports of own-root trees having been blown over in a windstorm, thus destroying landscape settings.

ROOTSTOCKS

Traditionally, most crabapples have been budded or grafted onto seedlings of domesticated apples (i.e., *Malus sylvestris* or *M. pumila*). Various understocks of *M. pumila* (also called *M. domestica* Borkhausen) are used, including the following:

M. 'Alnarp'
M. 'Anis'
M. 'Antonovka'
M. 'Budagovski'
M. 'Dolgo' seedling
M. 'Domestica'
M. 'Polish'
M. pumila clones EMLA 7, 9, 26, 27, 106, 111

The fact that the great majority of existing crabs in landscapes have been propagated via rootstocks attests to the performance and soil adaptability of these rootstocks. Domesticated rootstock, however, does have two drawbacks: it can sucker heavily, and it is not totally root hardy in the most northern areas. These drawbacks are being bypassed through use of clonal understocks. EMLA 111 (one of a series of rootstocks developed by the East Malling and Long Ashton research stations in England from Paradise stocks of Europe) virtually eliminates suckers and gives moderate improvement in root hardiness, while other clonal rootstocks developed in Poland and in the Commonwealth of Independent States are extremely hardy. Using the right clonal rootstock has the greatest potential for improving crabapple development.

In a study of crabapple suckering over a period of several years, Keith Warren was able to divide rootstocks into five groups according to the number of suckers produced per 2-year-old tree: Group I averaged 0–0.25 suckers per tree; Group II, 0.26–0.75; Group III, 0.76–2; Group IV, 2.1–4.5; and Group V, 4.6 suckers or more per tree. The five groups are as follows (K. Warren, pers. com.):

- Group I: Nearly Sucker Free
  - *M.* 'Alnarp 2'
  - *M.* 'Budagovski 490'
  - *M.* 'Budagovski 118'
  - EMLA 106
  - EMLA 111
  - 'Polish 18'
- Group II: Low Suckering
  - EMLA 7
  - EMLA 9
  - EMLA 26
  - EMLA 27
  - *M.* 'Mark'
  - 'Polish 22'
- Group III: Moderate Suckering
  - *M.* 'Dolgo' seedling
  - *M.* 'Antonovka 313'
  - *M. antonovka*
- Group IV: Heavy Suckering
  - *M.* 'Anis'
  - *M.* 'Antonovka 306'
  - *M. prunifolia*
  - *M. pumila*
- Group V: Very Heavy Suckering
  - *M. baccata*
  - *M.* 'Red Splendor' seedling

Table 1 compares the strengths and susceptibilities of three rootstocks to own-root propagations.

Table 1. A comparison of rootstock strengths and susceptibilities. Data based on research by Keith Warren at J. Frank Schmidt & Son Nursery, Boring, OR.

	M. pumila	EMLA 111	EMLA 106	Own root
Tree size	Full size	85%	65%	Varies by cultivar
Nursery vigor	Vigorous	Vigorous	Vigorous	Varies by cultivar
Soil tolerance	Widely adapted	Widely adapted	Widely adapted except in wet soils	Varies by cultivar
Root structure	Coarse	Fibrous	Coarse	Varies by cultivar
Crown gall	Susceptible	Resistant	Resistant	Mostly susceptible
Wooly apple aphid	Susceptible	Resistant	Resistant	Mostly unknown
Anchorage	Very good	Very good	Very good	Mostly unknown

CRABAPPLES FROM SEED

A few crabs will grow rather true to type from seed. *Malus sargentii* and *M. hupehensis* are sometimes produced this way. A more uniform crop and stronger growth can be expected, however, when selected clones of these species are vegetatively propagated. Crabapple seed requires a 3-month chilling period for germination to commence, after which the seed is planted in trays, kept watered and dusted with a fungicide. When plants have two or three true leaves they can be potted into peat pots or in shaded nursery raised beds. All things considered, crabapples are sturdy little plants, and if well cared for should make good growth the first year.

MICROPROPAGATION

Micropropagation of crabs has become successful. Nonetheless, laboratory grown plantlets need to be handled very cautiously to avoid shock, and carefully controlled greenhouse conditions are needed. For the first 2 weeks after removal from the flask, shade and high humidity are essential. After 3–4 weeks, plants can be moved into larger pots. When 6–8 in (15–20 cm) tall, they are hardened off and transplanted out into raised soil beds. This should be done during cool weather with frequent irrigation. At the end of the season, dormant liners can be harvested for field lining out.

SOFTWOOD CUTTINGS

Propagation by softwood cuttings is increasingly being used in crabapple production. Early July seems to be the best time to take cuttings under Oregon conditions; June is better in warmer parts of the country. Depending upon the cultivar, a basal treatment of Hormodin 2 or Hormodin 3 is best (3000 ppm IBA or 8000 ppm IBA in talc). Liquid dips in a solution of 5000–10,000 ppm IBA are also used on a few cultivars.

Cuttings are rooted in poly covered tunnel houses under intermittent mist. They are left undisturbed until late winter, at which time they are harvested bare root then held in cold storage. When the ground dries in spring, the cuttings are transplanted out into soil beds and grown to a larger size. Cuttings that have been transplanted into soil beds for a season have a higher survival rate than those that go directly from the cutting beds to final field spacing.

BUDDING CRABAPPLES

Most crabs are propagated by budding on an understock. In years past domesticated apple (*Malus pumila*) was generally used, but in recent years other *Malus* understocks have been tried. Many crabapple seedlings are root hardy and thus have been used for budding, but suckering is still a problem. The hardiest crabapple species, *M. baccata*, produces the worst suckering of any rootstock Keith Warren has tested. Clonal understocks are gaining wider acceptance. After careful testing, Warren has found that EMLA 111 has the best combination of performance characteristics and a proven record.

The majority of crabs are budded using the T-bud technique and tied with a rubber bud strip. A few species, such as *Malus floribunda* and *M. sargentii*, often give poor bud takes when T-budded; with these crabapples better results are obtained via chip budding. While T-budding generally works well on domesticated apple, chip budding is preferable on EMLA 111.

GRAFTING CRABAPPLES

Grafting is also used by some growers. Scions are bench grafted onto a chosen rootstock using a whip-and-tongue graft. The scions can be heeled into moist media, callused at moderate temperature (50–60°F/10–16°C) for 1–2 weeks, then held in cold storage until spring planting is possible.

Figure 8.2. Cuttings of *M.* 'Snowdrift' prepared with rooting compound.

Figure 8.3. Cut bud ready for insertion.

Figure 8.4. T-bud cut in understock.

Figure 8.5. Inserting bud in understock.

Figure 8.6. Chip budding.

Figure 8.7. Special bark graft used by some hybridizers to push new growth.

Grafting seems to be the only practical method of producing *Malus* 'Coralburst', *M.* 'Joy', *M.* 'Satin Cloud', and most of the tetraploid and octoploids because of their short internodes and small buds. Using a virus-free rootstock and scion, a straight stem of a crab variety with good trunk characteristics is grown as a whip to 4–6 ft (1.4–1.8 m) tall. *Malus* 'Coralburst' or other tetraploid or weeping clones (e.g., *M.* 'Red Swan') are then top grafted using a whip-and-tongue graft. It is important that the interstem be virus-free, as many crab cultivars carry viruses that are harmless to the carrier, but may be devastating to certain scion cultivars grafted onto them. With the exception of *M.* 'Coralburst' and other top-grafted clones, cultural operations involved in growing crabs by various methods become the same after a year's establishment in the field.

CULTURE OF NEWLY PROPAGATED PLANTS

Plants produced from seedling rootstocks, clonal rootstocks, cuttings, or tissue culture are all lined out when the ground dries in spring, usually in April. Rootstocks are T-budded or chip-budded in August; own-root plants are allowed to become established without training. Fields are kept weed free by cultivation and are frequently irrigated. In the fall, herbicide is applied to keep out winter germinating weeds.

Late in the winter, while plants are still dormant, all are cut down with a forage chopper to within 6 in (15.2 cm) of the ground. This removes and shreds unwanted top growth. The budded rootstocks are then neatly cut off just above the cultivar bud and own-root plants are cut off above the lowest bud within 2 in (5.1 cm) of the crown. As buds begin to grow in the spring, the strongest shoot is selected and the others rubbed off. A Grow Straight™ growth control stake is set into the ground within 0.25 in (0.6 cm) of the chosen shoot. This protects the tender shoot from hail and wind as it begins its growth toward becoming a straight trunk. Plants are fed monthly with high nitrogen fertilizers and optimum soil moisture is maintained through weekly irrigations during hot weather.

When trees reach 12–18 in (30–46 cm) in height, they are staked with a steel rod and taped with vinyl ties. Every 10 days crews walk the rows and add another tie to keep the growing trees straight. Cultivation takes place on a weekly basis.

Disease-resistant crabs have come to dominate the market. There is still a market demand for certain cultivars that are susceptible to disease, however, and these cultivars must be sprayed every 10–14 days with fungicides registered for scab and mildew. Occasionally, insect buildup will require the use of insecticides. Acephate (Orthene) should be avoided as it is phytotoxic to numerous cultivars, especially if repeated applications are made.

Through the summer any basal suckers that develop must be removed. These are pulled off or cut at their point of origin. Care must be taken as any remaining stub will resprout. Also, any limbs that develop on the lower stem are removed. These are pinched out of the leaf axil by hand while quite small, without disturbing the leaf. It is much more efficient to hand pinch than to use pruners.

Limb removal, taping, sucker removal, cultivation, spraying, and irrigation continue throughout the season. By fall, the whip or lightly branched tree should be 4–7 ft (1.2–2.1 m) in height, depending on the cultivar. Many of these will be dug and sold as one-year trees. Those that remain to be grown on to larger sizes are dormant pruned. Trees are topped at a height of 4–6 ft (1.2–1.8 m) depending on the cultivar. A new leader is established by taping the emerging shoot with masking tape.

As needed, trees are straightened and desuckered, and strong branches are pinched during the growing season to ensure an even canopy. Fertilization, irrigation, cultivation, and spraying continue throughout the season.

DIGGING AND MARKETING

Digging season begins late in the fall. Crabapples are slower to go into dormancy than most deciduous trees, so digging takes place mainly in December. Digging too early can reduce a tree's ability to survive. High clearance diggers are used to lift the trees, which are then packed by crews onto pallets for transportation to the warehouse and grading stations. Palletized trees are handled efficiently by forklift and scissorlift.

After grading, bundling, and labeling, the trees are put into humidified cold storage. Temperatures are maintained at 33–34°F (1°C), and humidity is held close to 100 percent. Regular fungicide applications are made to avoid botrytis or other disease problems. As the weather begins to warm up, the spring shipping rush is on. Orders are assembled, double checked, and carefully packed into refrigerated semitrailers. All work is finally completed when the trucks arrive at the customer's door.

Crabapples continue to be popular and in high demand. As work progresses in selective breeding, selection of new plant material, and evaluation of crabapples, this outstanding group of flowering trees is getting better and better. Efficient production means the best trees will be made quickly available in the market.

CHAPTER 9

Introducing and Hybridizing Flowering Crabapples

Of the great number of named flowering crabapples, some are outstanding plants that point to the excellent work being done both in hybridizing and in selecting superior clones, but many others are not outstanding. Arie den Boer has pointed out why there are so many mediocre crabapples:

> The vast majority of flowering crabapples, until recently, were not the results of specific hybridization, but rather, products of chance seedlings or open pollinated seed. For older cultivars up to 1930 one should be skeptical about a specific cross listing both parents.

Although several hundred crabapples have been named, fewer have been described and marketed, and a great number remain relatively unknown and unavailable. Many of them appeared to be interesting or superior clones at the time they were introduced, but, in fact, they were promising only because there was little on the market by way of genuine comparison. Perhaps 60 to 70 percent of all named crabapples—both botanical selections and named clones—should never have been introduced, albeit they show the progression from the mediocre crabapples of yesterday to the excellent crabapples on the market today.

The greatest improvements in the flowering crabapples have not been made by chance seedlings, but rather through the patient, thoughtful hybridization and selection of superior genetic materials by a relatively few individuals over the past 100 years. While the majority of new clones still appear to be open-pollinated or chance seedlings, they are coming from far better and selected seed parents. Controlled hybridization may be a newer effort, but it is proving to have excellent results.

Controlled hybridization is also a long process measured in years. The number of hybridizers today is perhaps less than five or six worldwide. Few researchers in government or private arboreta have a guarantee of the needed longevity of employment for hybridizing programs. Even fewer in private horticultural research can afford to launch a hybridization program. Because many of the pioneering hybridizers are now retired, a whole new generation of well-trained researchers is needed.

Through the long and tedious task of perfecting modern crabapples, certain individuals and organizations stand out as giants who advanced the progress of crabapple hybridization by their painstaking work. Some of them laid foundations for future hybridization, others opened new vistas of genetic creativity. In this chapter we want to identify some of the leading hybridizers, introducers, and originators of flowering crabapples both past and present. Then we will present some directions for future hybridizing efforts.

PLANT EXPLORERS AND INTRODUCERS

One must respect the labors of the early and modern plant explorers, ever searching the world for new species or outstanding variants of species already discovered. Ernest H. Wilson, William Purdom, and Charles Sargent in the past and, more recently, the members of the joint Sino-American expeditions into China have all made landmark contributions. The selective work of Karl Sax, although not as well known perhaps as is the work of others, is representative of the many important milestones along the road of progress that have given us the modern crabapple.

In Europe, Victor and Emil Lemoine of Victor Lemoine et Fils, Nancy, France, introduced the beautiful deep red clone *Malus* 'Lemoinei', while S. G. A. Doorenbos, director of the Department of Parks, The Hague, Netherlands, has produced three outstanding crabapples: *M.* 'Liset', *M.* 'Profusion', and the magnificent yellow-fruited *M.* 'Winter Gold'. Undoubtedly others outside of Canada and the United States are working with flowering crabapples, but because their introductions have not been as extensive, as popularized, or as available as have those of North American breeders and nursery professionals, they are unknown to me.

THE GREAT HORTICULTURAL INSTITUTIONS

A number of horticultural organizations, past and present, must be credited for introducing new crabapple materials, both by sending out plant explorers to distant lands and by introducing change seedlings from their own gardens.

James Veitch & Sons, Ltd., Chelsea, England, through its plant explorations in China and the Far East, brought a great number of crabapple species to Western gardens and thus greatly influenced the availability of newly discovered crabapples.

The Royal Botanic Gardens, Kew, England, has been influential in introducing, evaluating, and making new plant materials available.

The Arnold Arboretum of Harvard University, Jamaica Plain, MA, has been perhaps the foremost among horticultural institutions in introducing new crabapples and making them available. This institution's work in plant explorations has been monumental and possibly among the greatest in new crabapple selections. Its discovery of a southern growing *Malus baccata* in China promises to aid the work of hybridizing clones adapted to warmer climates.

The U.S. National Arboretum, Washington, DC, particularly in the past decade and a half, has been instrumental in introducing several botanical species from the joint Sino-American explorations in China and Korea.

The South Dakota Agricultural Experiment Station at Brookings has been outstanding, especially in the time of Niels Hansen, in developing and introducing new Rosybloom crabapples specially adapted for the harsh Western prairie conditions.

The Canada Department of Agriculture experiment stations at Beaverlodge, Alberta; Morden, Manitoba; Rosthern, Saskatchewan; Sutherland, Saskatchewan; and Ottawa, Ontario, in the times of W. R. Leslie, W. T. Macoun, and Isabella Preston, were most active in developing new Rosybloom crabapples suited to western Canada. From these sources many excellent clones were introduced, but because they did not receive marketing publicity they remain relatively unknown.

The Secrest Arboretum at the Ohio Agricultural Experiment Station, Wooster, OH, has developed an impressive number of crabapple plantings that are truly outstanding in bloom and attract thousands of visitors in spring. This collection ranks among the finest with both old and new crabapples.

The Morton Arboretum, Lisle, IL, and the Boerner Botanic Gardens, Hales Corner, WI, have impressive collections of flowering crabapples, many that are found nowhere else.

The Royal Botanic Gardens, Hamilton, Ontario, Canada, is developing an excellent collection of well-organized and carefully chosen flowering crabapples, mostly of Canadian origin.

A number of universities have excellent crabapple collections that are being upgraded and developed: University of Wisconsin, University of Michigan, University of Washington, and University of Illinois.

Several nurseries specialize in introducing newer clones of exceptional merit. Foremost in their number are Roy and Sarah Klehm of Charles Klehm and Sons Nursery, South Barrington, IL; Lake County Nursery, Perry, OH; and J. Frank Schmidt & Son Co., Boring, OR. While other nurseries also introduce new crabapple clones, none of them introduces as many new, outstanding clones as do these three nurseries and none of them is more aggressive in their efforts to seek out the finest clones. All three are to be commended, for without aggressive marketing, new clones would never be recognized or made available.

The International Ornamental Crabapple Society (IOCS) was founded by a group of dedicated crabapple enthusiasts: Peter Bristol, Fred Buscher, John den Boer, Fr. John Fiala, Thomas Green, Edward Hasselkus, William Hendricks, Francie Hill, Joseph Hill, Norbert Kinen, Robert Lyons, John Martens, Les Nichols, John Sabuco, Michael Scott, Robert Simpson, and Michael Yanny. Under the progressive leadership of the IOCS, an excellent bulletin has been published and interest in selection of new clones has been promoted. This worldwide society is open to anyone interested in flowering crabapples.

MODERN HYBRIDIZERS

Through the truly heroic efforts of a few modern hybridizers, the flowering crabapple has become the outstanding ornamental among all flowering trees. A few of the modern crabapple introducers and their general areas of work are discussed below.

Niels E. Hansen is known for his work with *Malus pumila* 'Niedzwetzkyana' at the South Dakota Agricultural Experiment Station, Brookings. From his travels to Turkestan, he brought back original material with which he began the famous crosses of red-flowering crabapples. The list of cultivars in this volume (see Chapter 12) contains many of his selections and introductions, perhaps as many as 70 or 80 clones. His work with the Rosyblooms is outstanding, as is his work with the North American species. Many more of his introductions should be grown in the largest arboreta to keep them from being lost and to maintain them for genetic breeding materials.

Figure 9.1. Roy and Sarah Klehm, Klehm Nursery, S. Barrington, IL, outstanding flowering crabapple promoters and introducers of some of the finest newer clones.

Figure 9.2. Thomas Green, Morton Arboretum, Lisle, IL, is an outstanding crabapple authority and writer, and a founding director of IOCS.

Figure 9.3. Edward Hasselkus, Department of Horticulture, University of Wisconsin, Madison, is a crabapple authority and a founding director of IOCS.

Isabella Preston and W. R. Leslie, both with the Canada Department of Agriculture, are responsible for the selection of perhaps another 50 to 60 Rosyblooms, most of them open-pollinated. These introductions have not been as widely grown and appreciated as they should have been because many are large trees and many are disease prone. Among them, however, are several outstanding clones. Some of the newest clones, developed by Thomas Machin at Devonian Botanic Garden, and those at the Canada Department of Agriculture Experiment Station, Morden, Manitoba, appear very worthwhile additions to advanced Rosyblooms.

Robert C. Simpson of Simpson Orchard Company, Vincennes, IN, was one of the first nursery professionals to plant, select, and introduce some of the heavy fruiting, smaller-fruited crabapples that today are classified among the multibrids. In his landmark work he has selected, popularized, and marketed some of the finest crabapples available today. Among his excellent introductions are *Malus* 'Burgandy', *M.* 'Indian Magic', *M.* 'Red Jewel', *M.* 'Yellow Jewel', and especially the late-blooming *M.* 'Silver Moon'. One could plant a whole garden of Simpson's excellent introductions.

Henry Ross of Gardenview Horticultural Park, Strongsville, OH, has introduced a limited number of very excellent clones, among which are some of the first polyploids: *Malus* 'Coralburst', the outstanding double-flowered *M.* 'Cotton Candy', the beautiful rosette-blossomed semiweeper *M.* 'Ross's Double Red', and the outstanding weeper *M.* 'White Cascade'. His *M.* 'Coral Cascade' remains not only one of the finest fruiting forms, but is in a coral color class of its own. Ross's introductions rank among some of the finest blooming crabapples available.

Figure 9.4. Norbert Kinen, J. Frank Schmidt & Son Co., Boring, OR, is a crabapple authority and promoter. He is also a member of the IOCS Board of Directors.

Figure 9.5. Robert Lyons, Sunleaf Nursery, Madison, OH, is a nurseryman and a crabapple authority. He is a founding director of IOCS and a member of its Executive Board.

Donald Egolf of the U.S. National Arboretum, Washington, DC, has been engaged in programs of developing superior, disease-resistant clones, and in selecting superior clones from modern plant explorations to China, Korea, and Japan. Among his named introductions are the outstanding *Malus* 'Adirondack' and *M.* 'Naragansett'. Many of his numbered selections should be named and introduced.

James Zampini of Lake County Nursery, Perry, OH, has only begun working with a number of very low growing, open-pollinated crabapples to be marketed under a series titled Round Table crabapple dwarfs. This series should have value for smaller landscaping needs.

Figure 9.6. Robert Simpson, Simpson Nursery Co., Vincennes, IN, was one of the first plant breeders to actively introduce, develop, and test the newer crabapple clones for disease resistance and autumn fruit color. Among his introductions are the beautiful *M.* 'Burgandy', *M.* 'Indian Magic', *M.* 'Silver Moon', and *M.* 'White Candle'.

Lori and Michael Yanny of Johnson's Nursery, Menomonee Falls, WI, two of the very few younger hybridizers, have undertaken a small but promising program that should show excellent results in a few years.

Fr. John L. Fiala of Falconskeape Gardens, Medina, OH, was engaged for 50 years in intensive programs (1) to produce newer multibrids, especially among the weeping crabapples; (2) to introduce small, disease-resistant trees with heavy, persistent, annual fruit in an extensive range of color; and (3) to induce polyploids. Among the 120 named clones he introduced are *Malus* 'Amberina', *M.* 'Autumn Glory', *M.* 'Molten Lava', *M.* 'Orange Crush', *M.* 'Serenade', the outstanding weeper *M.* 'Red Swan', the polyploids *M.* 'Copper King' and *M.* 'Satin Cloud', and the doubles *M.* 'Cranberry Lace', *M.* 'Doubloons', *M.* 'Eline', and *M.* 'Karen'. Falconskeape Gardens has produced more weeping and semiweeping crabapples than any other source. The first to

Figure 9.7. Donald Egolf, U.S. National Arboretum, Washington, DC, is an outstanding plant hybridizer of many genera and an Honorary Life Director of IOCS. Outstanding among his many crabapple introductions is *M.* 'Naragansett'.

Figure 9.8. James Zampini, Lake County Nursery, Perry, OH, a crabapple nurseryman and introducer of several new and better crabapples, including the Round Table Series of dwarf crabs.

Figure 9.9. Michael Yanny, Johnson Nursery, Milwaukee, WI, a crabapple authority and member of the IOCS Executive Board.

pioneer the mini-fruits with small fruit less than 0.5 in (1.3 cm) in diameter, Fr. Fiala also introduced a line of dwarf crabapples and weepers. He was a pioneer in the work with tetraploid, octoploid, and polyploid crabapples.

PRESERVING AND IDENTIFYING THE WORK OF HYBRIDIZERS

A great number of flowering crabapples, even in some of the best collections, are misnamed. While one does not wish to discard older trees that are beautiful in bloom and fruit just because they have been misnamed, their true identity needs to be researched or they should be listed as "name uncertain."

Once in my younger years I sent a large collection of my best flowering crabapples, many now patented, to one of our nation's largest arboreta because the director at that time realized these plants might have value. Twenty years later these trees were destroyed. Although they were some of the finest crabapples in the collection, because they had been carelessly left untagged, no one took time to inquire where they came from and thus they were destroyed. Had they been left, today this arboretum would have an outstanding collection of some of the newest clones already 20 years old. It seems that each time a large arboretum or public collection receives a new administration, the first order of business is to get rid of older specimens or material, beautiful though they may be, that have no apparent name or that appear to the new director to be outdated or useless. (This happens to personnel as well as to plants.)

I recall another incident in which the lifetime work of an outstanding nut tree hybridizer working at the USDA research center in Beltsville, MD, was completely destroyed in one week by a new director, who had no interest whatsoever in nut trees. Nearly 50 years of remarkable hybridization were lost forever. I was hybridizing nuts at the time and would have given anything to save those trees, and so would have the American Nut Growers Association, had we been informed of the intent to destroy a lifetime of some of the nation's best hybridizing. Not even a scion was saved!

Unfortunately, this destruction also happens to most work of individuals who do not publicize and introduce their plants while alive and able. Much of the flowering crabapple work of some of the older hybridizers is relatively unknown today, and eventually will be lost forever, because it has not been publicized and made generally available. The lifetime work of Julian Potts, which includes flowering crabapples, is one example. Much material is being lost in both public collections and, perhaps more often, in private ones.

I am not advocating that worthless, diseased clones be kept in collections simply because they are already there as older specimens. Our gardens, parks, and arboreta cannot support space for historic but valueless trees. Disease-ridden flowering crabapples whose horticultural value is very limited should be removed to make room for newer and better specimens. After all, the arboreta and larger collections are where the public goes to see and identify the "best" trees for their smaller home gardens. The public may not be aware that certain clones are disease resistant; what they see is what they believe is recommended by that institution.

INTRODUCING NEW FORMS TO THE MARKET

One of the foremost problems facing hybridizers as they work to improve crabapples is getting nurseries to accept their work. It can be almost impossible, not because the new introductions are not excellent or outstanding, but because the commercial market for crabapples is already so saturated with many excellent trees that nurseries are reluctant to add new names that they consider untried and unselected. Most nurseries want to test new crabapples for as long as 10 to 15 years, yet from experience I know that good hybridizers have already tested their selections years before they offer them to the commercial market. The original trees of most of my own introductions were 25 to 35 years old before they were considered and accepted by nurseries. During that period of waiting, three or even four new generations were growing in my garden. Unfortunately, the overwhelming majority of introductions offered by hybridizers never appear in the wings, yet alone on center stage, of the current market. Instead, these excellent crabapples are grown to cast their beauty in the introducer's garden alone. Many of them have a one-tree life span.

Many of the choicest clones are not available via nurseries, but can be acquired only by grafting a plant with a scion obtained directly from the introducer or from the arboretum collection in which it may be growing. I have always hoped for a nursery that would propagate some of every available clone, a specialty nursery where one could buy varieties not found elsewhere. Alas, dreams do not make reality. Much of nursery success depends on large sales volume. A specialty nursery, I fear, would not last long, although at one time (when giants walked the earth) two such nurseries existed: Henry Hohman Nursery, in Maryland and Julian Potts Nursery in Chesterland, OH. Today housing developments cover the acres where once grew choice flowering crabapples of every kind. Unlike Henry and Julian, nursery owners no longer walk with you through their flowering acres describing by name the merits of their crabapple children. Perhaps some day again, before many cherished but unpropagated clones pass away into forgetfulness, the Muse of Crabapple

Lovers may sing to some youthful heart and inspire it with the dedication, not for monetary gain, for there is none, but for a transcendent love of flowering crabapples to, again, recapture these special nurseries of long ago.

Another factor that greatly limits the rapid introduction of newer crabapples to the public is the general sameness of the clones offered from nursery to nursery throughout the country. The various lists of cultivar offerings constantly repeat the same tried-and-proven dozen or so names. Very few nurseries break from the old standbys and forge ahead to offer newer kinds of crabapples. What a choice gardeners and landscapers would have if every nursery offered a different list! What wonderful variety would exist in our gardens!

HYBRIDIZING POLYPLOIDS

Although the chromosome numbers of a few flowering crabapples have been counted, the data needs to be updated to include all the known species and their subspecies, and it needs to be made public (Table 2). No published records exist yet of the chromosome counts of the important subspecies and principal clones of outstanding merit. In fact, with a very few exceptions, little work has been done with the known polyploids outside the work done at Falconskeape Gardens for the past 45 years.

Ordinarily, in most species of plants, the advanced polyploids (e.g., tetraploids or above) show remarkable progress in flower size, improved petal and leaf texture, disease resistance, fruit size, more intense and newer flower patterns, and sometimes fruit color. Multiple characteristics, particularly in flower color, form, and patterns of variety, are found in a single plant, yet they are not observable in the diploid counterparts of the same species. Many of these polyploid traits are great improvements over the diploid form. Most often, if it is possible to cross the diploids with the tetraploid forms, the resultant progeny are sterile yet beautiful triploids. On occasion we find certain clones described as "sterile, produces no fruit." Are these true triploids, the result of crossing diploid and tetraploid clones? I am unaware of any research that studies this complicated polyploid breeding.

Based on the chromosome counts that have been done in *Malus*, we find natural diploids (2*x*), triploids (3*x*), several natural tetraploids (4*x*), and even one quintaploid (5*x*). From natural serendipity and laboratory conversion we may possibly have three or four octoploids (8*x*). Adding the five or six laboratory-induced tetraploids to the already existing natural polyploids, we find a solid base has been established for the tetraploid and polyploid crabapples of the future (Table 3). The initial groundwork for octoploid hybrids and advanced polyploid hybridization in flowering crabapples has also been laid. Among the octoploids are two outstanding clones, *Malus* 'Coralburst' and *M.* 'Satin Cloud', and it is possible that *M.* 'Shinto Shrine' and *M.* 'Copper King' are also octoploids. The current need then is to continue building on this knowledge by interhybridizing the existing polyploids and by adding to their number new, induced polyploids of superior clonal material.

Two or three dedicated research hybridizers, spending most of their life efforts with advanced polyploids, could revolutionize the future direction of flowering crabapples. Who will they be? It has not been given to me, so far, to see my polyploid children's children to the fourth generation. Thus I have always hoped that grants could be obtained for younger hybridizers to continue this work. The greatest results of polyploid interhybridization are not seen until at least the fourth, fifth, or sixth generations when the explosion of gene characteristics begins to work its wonders, resulting in new combinations.

Scientific hybridizers, who wish to work with advanced polyploids, stand at the threshold of advanced generations and should take advantage of the groundwork that has been

Table 2. Chromosome counts for flowering crabapples. Data based on Darlington and Wylie (1961). *Malus* $x = 17$

Name	2*n*	Source	Origin
Diploids (2*x* = 34)			
M. ×*adstringens*	34	Sax 1931a	Cultivated hybrid
M. asiatica (M. prunifolia)	34	Kobel 1927	N. Asia
M. baccata	34	Sax 1931a	Himalayas, N. Asia
M. floribunda	34	Darlington & M. 1930	China
M. fusca	34	Nebel 1929	N. America
M. halliana	34	Nebel 1929	China, Japan
M. ioensis	34	Nebel 1929	N. America
M. pumila 'Niedzwetzkyana'	34	Nebel 1929	S.W. Siberia, Caucasus
M. sieboldii var. *zumi*	34	Rybin 1926	Japan
Diploids (2*x* = 34) and triploids (3*x* = 51)			
M. prunifolia	34, 51	Nebel 1929	N.E. Asia
M. sylvestris	34, 51	Darlington & M. 1930	Afghan. cultivar
M. pumila 266 varieties	34	Einset & I. 1947, 1949	
18 varieties	51	Einset & I. 1951	
15 varieties	34–68	Einset & I. 1951	Chimaeras
Tetraploids (4*x* = 68)			
M. angustifolia	34–68	Rybin 1926	Chimaeras
	68	Sax 1931a	N. America
M. coronaria	51, 68	Dermen 1949	N. America
M. ×*platycarpa*	51	Dermen 1949	
	68	Lincoln & M. 1937	
M. hupehensis	51, 68	Dermen 1936c	China
M. lancifolia	51, 68	Dermen 1949	N. America
M. sargentii	34, 68	Nebel 1930	Japan
M. glaucescens	68	Sax 1931a	Eastern N. America
Quintaploid (5*x* = 85)			
M. toringo (M. sieboldii)	85	Olden 1945	Japan
Octoploids (8*x* = 136)			
M. 'Coralburst'	136	Fiala 1977	Cultivar
M. 'Fountain'	136	Fiala 1977	Induced cultivar
M. 'Satin Cloud'	136	Fiala 1977	Induced cultivar
M. 'Hosanna'	136	Fiala 1985	2nd generation cultivar
M. 'Egret'	136	Fiala 1977	Induced cultivar
Possible sextaploids (6*x* = 102) or octoploids (8*x* = 136)			
M. 'Shinto Shrine'	102–136*	Fiala 1977	Induced cultivar
M. 'Copper King'	102–136*	Fiala 1977	2nd generation cultivar
M. 'Arch McKean'	136	Fiala 1977	2nd generation cultivar

*Variable counts may indicate chimaeras

Table 3. Natural, induced, and second generation polyploid flowering crabapples.

Name	Introducer	Origin
Tetraploids (4*x* = 68)		
M. 'Ambergold'	Fiala	2nd generation hybrid
M. 'Ann Marie'	Fiala	2nd generation hybrid
M. 'Arch McKean'	Fiala	2nd generation hybrid
M. 'Copper King'	Fiala	2nd generation hybrid; may be octoploid
M. coronaria		Natural species
M. coronaria var. *angustifolia*		Natural variety
M. coronaria var. *dasycalyx* 'Charlottae'	E. de Wolfe	Natural selection
M. coronaria var. *glaucescens*		Natural variety
M. coronaria var. *platycarpa*		Natural variety
M. coronaria 'Coralglow'	Fiala	Induced
M. coronaria 'Nieuwland'	Slavin	Natural selection
M. 'Grandmother Louise'	Fiala	Induced
M. hupehensis		Natural species
M. hupehensis 'Donald'	Fiala	Induced
M. ioensis 'Prairie Rose'		Natural clone
M. ioensis 'Prince Georges'		Natural hybrid
M. 'Joy'	Fiala	2nd generation hybrid
M. 'Kola'	Hansen	Natural hybrid
M. 'My Bonnie'	Fiala	Induced
M. 'Peter Murray'	Fiala	2nd generation hybrid
M. 'Shinto Shrine'	Fiala	Induced
M. 'Tetragold'	Fiala	Induced
Quintaploids (5*x* = 85)		
M. toringo		Natural species
Octoploids (8*x* = 136)		
M. 'Copper King'	Fiala	2nd generation hybrid, may be a chimaera
M. 'Coralburst'	H. Ross	Natural selection
M. 'Egret'	Fiala	Induced weeper
M. 'Fountain'	Fiala	Induced weeper
M. 'Hosanna'	Fiala	2nd generation hybrid
M. 'Satin Cloud'*	Fiala	Induced
M. 'Shinto Shrine'	Fiala	Induced, may be a chimaera

*The series of *M.* 'Satin Cloud' seedlings yet to be introduced, including *M.* 'Satin Lace', *M.* 'Satin Silver', and so on, are also octoploids.

laid. We know that the North American species *Malus coronaria* and all its counted subspecies are tetraploids, that *M. toringo* appears to be a quintaploid, and that a number of very useful induced tetraploids and octoploids are now available. Could it be that these flowering crabapples do not readily hybridize with Asiatic species because of the difference in ploidy rather than because of the difference in blooming times or natural sterility? Could not a whole new race or races of flowering crabapples arise if some of the best species were converted into polyploids and then hybridized with tetraploids or advanced octoploids?

Two avenues are open to future hybridists working with the polyploids: one is to continue interhybridization of all the existing polyploid clones, the other is to increase the genetic pool by inducing new polyploids in the laboratory. Great success is predicted as the induced polyploids presently available come from a number of hybridized species and subspecies. If the natural tetraploids can be included with these induced clones, the range of newer polyploids would be considerably extended.

Although many of the existing polyploids have shortcomings in different areas, most of them are already highly resistant to diseases. Improvement needs to be made primarily in flower color and fruit color. Only a very few polyploids—induced or natural—have deep red or pink flowers, and the light pinks are mostly in the *Malus coronaria* group, which has its own breeding problems. The lone red-flowering and red-leafed clone is *M.* 'Joy', and it would need additional infusion of better red-flowering clones to support a good breeding program.

Hybridists should pursue both avenues of research: they should use the existing polyploids to their fullest potential, and at the same time, they should continue to induce new polyploids, not from seedlings, but from the very best of the already selected and proven diploid clones and species.

In selecting already proven clones for inducing polyploids, colchicine treatment has been the most effective method in the past. Those working with this alkaloid should remember that it is an extremely toxic chemical and that it should therefore be used with a mask under a hood. Careless use of this poisonous chemical can be devastating as this author can well attest.

Hybridists should also pay special attention to use only the best clones: (1) those completely resistant to all diseases, (2) those with smaller and mini-sized fruit whose color is exceptional, and (3) those with excellent, annual flowering habits and abundant bloom. Hybridists should also keep in mind the need for red, deep purple, and pink flowers, and they should try to include as many double-flowering clones as possible. When inducing new polyploids hybridists should also try to include as many different tree forms as possible—shrubs, upright, rounded, spreading, and especially weeping forms. Many of these forms are already found in existing polyploids.

The last and most important catalyst for success in the future is to find research hybridizers who will be willing to spend a lifetime in this work. A lifelong commitment to hybridizing crabapples could seem impossible for many, but to some very few it could be an exciting golden dream, as it has been for me for the past half century.

SEVEN AREAS FOR FUTURE RESEARCH

Much progressive work has already been done on flowering crabapples by hybridizers who were giants in their day. Isabella Preston, Carl and Niels Hansen, Karl Sax, Robert Simpson, H. R. and P. H. Wright, Donald Egolf, and Fr. Fiala, for example, have produced some excellent clones that are worthy foundation materials for further hybridizing. The work they have laid does not need to be repeated in the future, unless newer and better clones can be substituted, but rather future hybridists should build on it. Some areas that need further work for interested crabapple hybridizers could well include the following:

1. Expand the number of good polyploid hybrids. With the emergence of tetraploid and octoploid clones, this area of hybridization has just begun to open. From crossing polyploids in other genera, we know that it will be at least the fourth or fifth generation before we have a sufficiently large gene-chromosome pool to see remarkable results and radical breakthroughs. The existing group of polyploids needs to be expanded to include polyploids with pink and red flowers, double flowers, fragrance, and colorful autumn fruit.

2. Develop clones with better pink, red, and deep purple flowers.
3. Improve late-blooming hybrids, particularly the disease-prone North American species, to obtain disease-free, late-blooming clones with the strong fragrance and double flowers of the North American species.
4. Continue to pursue fruit of excellent color, especially in the yellow-bright gold group, that is also abundant and persistent for longer periods. The fruit of some of the newest multibrid crabapples changes color as ripening advances (e.g., from yellow to orange to brilliant red, often retaining cheeks of a previous color), a trait that is extremely attractive.
5. Continue to seek small, genetically dwarf, bushlike trees, weepers and upright forms that can be grown in very limited spaces. Already there exists an increasingly larger group of small-sized crabapples, tailored for smaller gardens, condominium complexes, commercial shopping plazas, street plantings, and planter culture.
6. Investigate the breeding potential of the lesser-used species, such as *Malus florentina, M. fusca, M. toringoides, M. tschonoskii,* and *M. yunnanensis.* Most of these species have been little touched by hybridization. Funded research to individuals or horticultural institutions working in this area could accomplish a great deal.
7. Develop a strain of flowering crabapples for southern (not tropical) climates that requires fewer hours of chilling to break dormancy and bloom. Most crabapples (and apples) require a fairly great number of chilling days to break dormancy in spring and if they do not receive these hours they never break dormancy but resprout from the root. This eventually kills the tree in a very few years. Currently, many flowering crabapples either will not grow or do very poorly in warmer climates with limited chill days. Several of the multibrids seem to indicate they could break dormancy and grow and flower well in southern gardens. I began testing a few possibilities at Ocala, FL, with measured success for selected clones (e.g., *Malus* 'Dorsett Golden'), but what is needed is testing on a larger scale by a university research program that would plant a sizeable number of selected clones for evaluation and hybridizing research.

   The warm-climate Israeli apples, such as *Malus* 'Anna' and *M.* 'Ein Shemer', for example, both clones of *M. pumila* var. *sylvestris* or *M. sylvestris,* could be used to develop crabapples suitable for southern states and warm climates where flowering crabapples have not done well in the past. These small apples or very large crabapples (fruit 2–2.5 in/5–6.3 cm across) were introduced by the Israeli Agriculture Department in 1967 and are grown in that country commercially. *Malus* 'Anna', which is carried by nearly all nurseries in the southern United States, has yellow fruit with a red blush; *M.* 'Ein Shemer' has yellow fruit. Both of these new apple clones, which require only about 300–400 hours of chilling to break dormancy in spring (versus the usual 600 hours of chilling below 45°F [7°C] required of most apples and crabapples), can be grown in northern and central Florida and may be forerunners of a new line of Southern Belle hybrids. Neither clone is recommended for ornamental value, but both are highly recommended for hybridizing with Asiatic and North American species to extend the range of flowering crabapples.

   The greatest promise for developing warm-climate crabapples appears to exist in the polyploid crabapple clones, especially those with heavy, leathery leaves, so indicative of warmer climate plants. Perhaps some southern nursery could set aside a few acres to make this kind of testing and selection, using the existing polyploids and newer multibrid clones, similar to what is being done for crabapple evaluation in the North. The funding of such research would add a whole new area of ornamental crabapples to southern horticulture. Because many selected pear clones grow and bloom very well in southern climates, it is relatively certain that strains and selected clones of flowering crabapples could also be developed. *Malus* 'Satin Cloud' appears to have promise for southern areas.

CHAPTER 10

Taxonomy of the Genus *Malus*

Flowering crabapples belong to *Malus*, a large genus comprising many species and various hybrids. While Liberty Hyde Bailey and other taxonomists considered *Malus* a subgenus of *Pyrus*, today most taxonomists follow Miller and Rehder, considering *Malus* a separate genus of its own split off from *Pyrus*. The taxonomy of *Malus* is as follows:

Order	Rosales
Family	Rosaceae
Subfamily	Pomoideae (contains 14 or more genera, including *Malus*)
Genus	*Malus*
Species	c. 24 (or 31, depending on how the varieties are classified)
Varieties	Many
Hybrid Clones, Cultivars, and Strains/Groups	Over 700, and increasing with hybridization

Rehder subdivided *Malus* into five sections, but because his is an older classification, some of the newer species and the older disputed species are not included (e.g., *M. formosana, M. toringo*). Through the efforts of the International Ornamental Crabapple Society much work is being done to clarify, sort out, and classify these crabapples of recent or complex origins. Also, with recent plant explorations in China, the islands of Japan, Korea, and Taiwan, new plant materials are being discovered and older, poorly documented forms are being reexamined or reintroduced. In time, Rehder's classification may be updated, but meanwhile it is usable for those interested in taxonomy, and I am presenting it in this volume with a few minor additions suggested by Rehder or other taxonomists, botanists, and botanical geneticists who followed him. Among the most notable changes to Rehder's classification are (1) the renaming of *M. sieboldii* (Regel) Rehder to an older, previous name *M. toringo* Siebold ex De Vriese 1848 (Wijnands 1979); (2) the elevation of Rehder's *M. sieboldii* var. *zumi* to species rank with the name *M. sieboldii*; and (3) in the North American crabapples, the reclassification by Fiala of several species to varietal standing (see under section *Chloromeles*).

BOTANICAL SUMMARY OF THE GENUS *MALUS* MILLER

Section *Eumalus* Zabel
- Series *Pumilae* Rehder—leaves convolute in bud, always undivided
  - 1. *M. pumila* Miller—common apple; Eurasia
    - var. *sylvestris* Miller—rarely cultivated
    - 'Niedzwetzkyana' (Dieck) Schneider
      - Synonym: var. *niedzwetzkyana* (Schneider) Rehder
    - × *M.* ×*atrosanguinea* (see under #7)
      - Synonym: *M.* ×*purpurea* (Barbier) Rehder
      - 'Aldenhamensis' (Gibbs) Rehder
      - 'Eleyi' (Bean) Rehder
      - 'Lemoinei' (Lemoine) Rehder
    - × *M. baccata* (see under #5)
      - Synonym: *M.* ×*adstringens* Zabel
    - × *M. coronaria* (see under #20)
      - Synonym: *M.* ×*heterophylla* Spach
    - × *M. ioensis* (see under #23)
      - Synonym: 'Red Tip'
    - × *M. ioensis* (see under #23)
      - Synonym: *M.* ×*soulardii* (L. H. Bailey) Britton
    - × *M. prunifolia*
      - Synonym: *M.* ×*astracanica* Dumont de Courset
    - × *M. spectabilis* (see under #3)
      - Synonym: *M.* ×*magdeburgensis* Schoch
  - 2. *M. prunifolia* (Willdenow) Borkhausen
    - 'Rinki' (Koidzumi) Rehder
    - × *M. baccata* (see under #5)
      - Synonym: *M.* ×*robusta* (Carrière) Rehder
    - × *M. floribunda* (see under #8)
      - Synonym: *M.* ×*scheideckeri* F. L. Späth ex Zabel
      - × *M. pumila* 'Niedzwetzkyana' (see under #8)
      - Synonym: *M.* ×*gloriosa* Lemoine
    - × *M. pumila* (see under #1)
      - Synonym: *M.* ×*astracanica* Dumont de Courset
    - × *M. toringo* (see under #10)
      - Synonym: *M.* ×*sublobata* (Zabel) Rehder
  - 3. *M. spectabilis* (Aiton) Borkhausen
    - 'Riversii' (Booth) Nash
    - × *M. baccata* (see under #4)
      - Synonym: *M.* ×*micromalus* Makino
    - × *M. pumila* (see under #1)
      - Synonym: *M.* ×*magdeburgensis* Schoch
  - 4. *M.* ×*micromalus* Makino—(*M. spectabilis* × ? *M. baccata*) of Japanese hybrid origin

Series *Baccatae* Rehder—calyx deciduous (partly so in some hybrids)
5. *M. baccata* (Linnaeus) Borkhausen
var. *himalaica* (Maximowicz) Schneider
var. *mandshurica* (Maximowicz) Schneider
'Jackii' Rehder
'Rockii' Rehder—today considered a clone
× *M. floribunda* (see under #8)
Synonym: *M.* ×*arnoldiana* (Rehder) Sargent
× *M. halliana* (see under #7)
Synonym: *M.* ×*hartwigii* Koehne
× *M. prunifolia* (see under #2)
Synonym: *M.* ×*robusta* (Carrière) Rehder
× *M. pumila*
Synonym: 'Hopa'
× *M. pumila* (see under #1)
Synonym: *M.* ×*adstringens* Zabel
× *M. sieboldii* (see under #9)
Synonym: *M.* ×*zumi* (Matsumura) Rehder—no longer considered a hybrid
M. sikkimensis (Hooker) Koehne
? × *M. spectabilis* (see under #4)
Synonym: *M.* ×*micromalus* Makino
6. *M. hupehensis* (Pampanini) Rehder (*M. theifera* Rehder)
7. *M. halliana* Koehne
var. *spontanea* (Makino) Koidzumi
'Parkmanii' Rehder
× *M. baccata* (see under #5)
Synonym: *M.* ×*hartwigii* Koehne
× *M. pumila* 'Niedzwetzkyana' (see under #1)
Synonym: *M.* ×*purpurea* (Lemoine) Rehder
× *M. toringo* (see under #10)
Synonym: *M.* ×*atrosanguinea* (F. L. Späth) Schneider
Section *Sorbomalus* Zabel—leaves folded in bud, sharply serrate
Series *Sieboldianae* Rehder
8. *M. floribunda* Siebold—cultivated in Japan
M. brevipes Rehder—related species or hybrid
× *M. baccata* (see under #3)
Synonym: *M.* ×*arnoldiana* (Rehder) Sargent
× *M. prunifolia* (see under #2)
Synonym: *M.* ×*scheideckeri* (Späth) Zabel
× *M. pumila* 'Niedzwetzkyana'
Synonym: *M.* ×*gloriosa* (Lemoine)
9. *M. sieboldii* (Asami) Fiala—formerly *M.* ×*zumi* Rehder (*M. baccata* var. *mandshurica* × *M. sieboldii*).

Note: Today *Malus sieboldii* var. *zumi* (Matsumura) Asami has been renamed as *M. sieboldii* Fiala, a separate species, and the former *M. sieboldii* (Regel) Rehder has been renamed *M. toringo* Siebold ex De Vriese (Wijnands 1979) (see under #10).

10. *M. toringo* Siebold ex De Vriese (Wijnands 1979)
 × *M. halliana* (see under #7)
  Synonym: *M.* ×*atrosanguinea* (Späth) Schneider
 × *M. prunifolia* (see under #2)
  Synonym: *M.* ×*sublobata* (Zabel) Rehder

Note: *Malus toringo* replaces *M. sieboldii* (Regel) Rehder and *M. sieboldii* var. *arborescens* Rehder; *M.* ×*zumi* 'Calocarpa' Rehder and 'Wooster' Rehder become *M. sieboldii* 'Calocarpa' (Rehder) Fiala and *M. sieboldii* 'Wooster' (Rehder) Fiala.

11. *M. sargentii* Rehder—cultivated in Japan

Series *Florentinae* Rehder—calyx and pedicels tomentose, leaves always lobed, styles 5

12. *M. florentina* (Zuccagni) Schneider

Series *Kansuenses* Rehder—styles glabrous

13. *M. fusca* (Rafinesque) Schneider
14. *M. toringoides* (Rehder) Hughes
 M. transitoria (Batalin) Schneider—closely related to *M. toringoides*
15. *M. kansuensis* (Batalin) Schneider
 M. honanensis Rehder—closely related species

Series *Yunnanenses* Rehder—fruit with cup-shaped cavity at apex of core not free, with grit cells

16. *M. prattii* (Hemsley) Schneider
17. *M. yunnanensis* (Franchet) Schneider

Section *Chloromeles* Rehder

18. *M.* ×*platycarpa* Rehder (see under revised #20)
  Synonym: *M. coronaria* var. *platycarpa* (Rehder) Fiala
19. *M. glaucescens* Rehder (see under revised #20)
  Synonym: *M. coronaria* var. *glaucescens* (Rehder) Fiala
 M. glabrata Rehder
  Synonym: *M. coronaria* var. *glabrata* (Rehder) Fiala—closely related to *M. coronaria* var. *glaucescens* (see under revised #20)
20. *M. coronaria* (Linnaeus) Miller
 var. *elongata* Rehder
 var. *dasycalyx* Rehder
  'Charlottae' Rehder
 'Nieuwlandiana'
 × *M. pumila* (see under #1)
  Synonym: *M.* ×*heterophylla* Spach
 M. bracteata Rehder (see under revised #20)
  Synonym: *M. coronaria* var. *bracteata* Fiala
21. *M. lancifolia* Rehder (see under revised #20)
  Synonym: *M. coronaria* var. *lancifolia* Fiala
22. *M. angustifolia* (Aiton) Michaux (see under revised #20)
  Synonym: *M. coronaria* var. *angustifolia* (Wenzig) Fiala
23. *M. ioensis* (A. Wood) Britton
 var. *texana* Rehder
  × *M. pumila* (see under #1)
  Synonym: *M.* ×*soulardii* (L. H. Bailey) Britton

×*M. pumila* 'Niedzwetzkyana' (see under #1)
Synonym: 'Red Tip'
'Fimbriata' A. Slavin
'Flore Plena' (Schneider) Rehder
'Palmeri' Rehder

Note: Today, taxonomists would classify only two species under section *Chloromeles* (Rehder) Fiala; the remaining "species" would be treated as varieties or clones. The two species are *Malus coronaria* and its varieties, all of which are natural tetraploids, and *M. ioensis* and its forms, all of which are diploids. Together with the morphological structures of plants, equal importance for differentiation must also be given to chromosome counts. Chromosomes, although microscopic, are also stable, observable, genetic characteristics and, I feel, should be given as much consideration in taxonomic classification as any other observable characteristic.

Revised 20. *M. coronaria* (Linnaeus) Miller—all natural tetraploids
var. *angustifolia* Fiala
var. *bracteata* Fiala
var. *dasycalyx* Fiala
var. *glaucescens* Fiala
var. *lancifolia* Fiala
var. *platycarpa* Fiala
'Charlottae'
'Nieuwlandiana'
×*M. pumila* (see under #1)
Synonym: *M.* ×*heterophylla* Späth
Revised 23 = 21. *M. ioensis*—all natural diploids
var. *texana* Rehder
'Fimbriata' A. Slavin
'Flore Plena' (Schneider) Rehder
'Palmeri' Rehder
×*M. pumila* (see under #1)
Synonym: *M.* ×*soulardii* (Bailey) Britton
×*M. pumila* 'Niedzwetzkyana' (see under #1)
Synonym: 'Red Tip'

Section *Eriolobus* Schneider—leaves deeply lobed; flowers 6–8, slender stalked, fruit 1.5 cm across
24. *M. trilobata* (Labill.) Schneider

Section *Docyniopsis* Schneider—leaves not or slightly lobed; flowers 2–5, styles villose below; fruit 3 cm across
25. *M. tschonoskii* (Maxim.) Schneider

CLASSIFICATION OF THE NORTH AMERICAN SPECIES

Although some taxonomists along with Rehder are wont to recognize many North American species, others (including this author) hold the opinion, supported by chromosome study, that there are presently three distinct, species native to North America—*Malus coronaria*, *M. ioensis*, and *M. fusca*—and that all the other North American crabapples are varieties, clonal forms, or natural hybrids between these three far-ranging species. When one grows a large number of selfed seed from these species, the progeny has considerable variation. (A third group of taxonomists-botanists, believing that *M. ioensis* is the diploid form of *M. coronaria*, would reduce the North American species to two: *M. coronaria*, with a diploid form *M. ioensis*, and *M. fusca*).

Malus coronaria is a natural tetraploid with 68 chromosomes, whereas *M. ioensis* and *M. fusca* are diploids with 34 chromosomes each. Some of the hybrids are triploid with either 51 or 68 chromosomes. The group listed under *M. coronaria* appears to be closely related, all with 68 (tetraploid) chromosomes; those under *M. ioensis* and *M. fusca*, again, group together having 34 (diploid) chromosomes.

My suggested reclassification of the North American crabapple species, varieties, and clones is as follows:

M. coronaria (Linnaeus) Miller
- var. *angustifolia* (Michaux) Fiala—68 chromosomes; one specimen has 34 chromosomes and is perhaps a hybrid seedling
- var. *bracteata* (Rehder) Fiala—chromosomes not counted
- var. *dasycalyx* (Rehder) Green, Fiala
  - 'Charlottae', a double-flowering clone of great beauty and fragrance. Some botanists would place it under *M. coronaria* but it appears, more correctly, to be a form or hybrid of var. *dasycalyx*. Rehder, and more recently, Dr. Thomas Green, Morton Arboretum, place it under var. *dasycalyx*.
- var. *glabrata* (Rehder) Fiala—possibly a hybrid or form of var. *glaucescens*
- var. *glaucescens* (Rehder) Fiala—68 chromosomes
- var. *lancifolia* (Rehder) Fiala—51 and 68 chromosomes
- ×*platycarpa* (Rehder) Fiala—synonym: *M. coronaria* × *M. pumila*; 51 and 68 chromosomes; a natural hybrid or a group of similar hybrids
  - 'Hoopesii', a hybrid cultivar
  - 'Matthews', a hybrid cultivar
  - 'Aucubeafolia' (Rehder) Fiala
  - 'Coralglow' (Fiala)
  - 'Elk River' Hansen
  - 'Nieuwland' (Slavin)
  - 'Pink Pearl' (Sax)
  - 'Thoms' (Thoms)

M. ioensis Britton—34 chromosomes, a natural diploid; its clones have not been counted
- var. *texana* (Rehder) Fiala
- 'Boone Park' (Den Boer)
- 'Brandywine'
- 'Fimbriata' (Slavin)
- 'Fiore's Improved' (Fiore)
- 'Klehm's Improved Bechtel' (Klehm)
- 'Nevis' (Arrowwood)
- 'Palmeri' Rehder
- 'Plena' Rehder—synonym: 'Bechtel Nova' (considered a lighter pink sport of 'Plena')
- 'Prairie Rose'—open-pollinated seedling of *M. ioensis*
- 'Prince Georges'—probably a hybrid, possibly with *M. coronaria* var. *angustifolia*

M. fusca Schneider—34 chromosomes, a natural diploid
var. *levipes* Schneider
×*dawsoniana* Rehder

The older classification for the native North American crabapples, accepted by Rehder and some taxonomists, disregards the chromosome relationships and recognizes the following as valid species and not as varieties:

M. angustifolia Michaux
M. bracteata Rehder
M. coronaria Miller
M. fusca Schneider
M. glabrata Rehder
M. glaucescens Rehder
M. ioensis Britton
M. lancifolia Rehder
M. platycarpa Rehder

Thus Rehder and those who agree with him recognize nine native North American species rather than three. In time taxonomists will sort out the true species from varieties, for there appears to be a central area for each of the three native species, from which point natural interspecific hybrids begin to appear, with the greatest difference at the farthest point from the main location of the given species. The climatic and geographic conditions most probably influence regional adaptations, natural mutations, and genetic variations, creating varieties rather than distinct species and allowing for a degree of interspecific natural hybridization.

Great opportunity exists for hybridization between the North American species and the best Asiatic ones, especially with the much improved, newer hybrid cultivars. The semi-double, double, and even single blooming North American species with their later blooming and strong, captivating fragrance coupled with the Asiatic species in disease resistance, better tree forms and excellent smaller, colorful, autumn fruit would greatly enhance newer crabapple hybrids. Such hybridization efforts should be greatly encouraged particularly to stabilize the strong apple-blossom fragrance.

PROPOSED CHANGE TO ELEVATE *MALUS SIEBOLDII* VAR. *ZUMI* TO SPECIES RANK

With the name change I am proposing in this classification—from *Malus sieboldii* (Regel) Rehder to *M. toringo* and reclassification of the species—some other changes become evident and necessary, specifically concerning the taxonomic place of *M. sieboldii* var. *zumi* and its clones (e.g., 'Calocarpa', 'Wooster'). Rehder considered it a hybrid of *M. baccata* var. *mandshurica* × *sieboldii* and called it *M.* ×*zumi*.

I am convinced that this crabapple is incorrectly described as a hybrid of *Malus baccata* × *M. sieboldii* (*M. toringo*). Having worked with selected clones of *M. sieboldii* var. *zumi*, especially with 'Calocarpa' for nearly 50 years, except for the leaf similarities in lobing I cannot find any indication of *M. toringo* hybridization. Thus I consider *M. sieboldii* var. *zumi* a separate species, similar in some ways (e.g., its small, bright red fruit) to *M. baccata*, yet differing in many other aspects. The description given by Rehder for *M.* ×*zumi* adequately describes *M. sieboldii* var. *zumi*, but, if not a hybrid, what is its species or origin?

Since *Malus sieboldii* is no longer an accepted name for me, being replaced by *M. toringo* (see discussion following), and, since Rehder adequately described *M.* ×*zumi*, I propose using the older name still used by many taxonomists today, but dropping the var. *zumi*. The new taxon would therefore stand as *M. sieboldii* (Rehder) Fiala, with Rehder's description for *M.* ×*zumi*. The old taxon—*M. sieboldii* (Regel) Rehder—would be replaced as *M. toringo* Siebold ex De Vriese (Wijnands 1979).

PROPOSED CHANGE TO RENAME *MALUS SIEBOLDII* (REGEL) REHDER TO *M. TORINGO*

This crabapple taxon has seen a great deal of controversy as to its real species status, its description and as to its true or valid name. It has been described by von Regel as *Pyrus sieboldii*, by Siebold as *Malus toringo* and *Pyrus toringo*, and by Rehder as *M. sieboldii* (Regel) Rehder. On the basis of research done by Dr. D. O. Wijnands, Wageningen Agricultural University, Wageningen, Netherlands, the more recent name of *M. sieboldii* (Regel) Rehder, according to taxonomic rules, must give way to the previous name *M. toringo* (Siebold) Siebold ex De Vriese.

In March 1979 Wijnands published an update and a change of name for this crabapple from *Malus sieboldii* (Regel) Rehder to the original name of *M. toringo* (Siebold) Siebold ex De Vriese (Wijnands 1979). Citing earlier sources of nomenclature and description (which Rehder apparently knew, according to private file cards on *Malus*, but did not use for some unknown reason), Wijnands, following Hara's evidence, listed the following authorities:

Sorbus toringo Siebold 1848; Siebold ex De Vriese (Wijnands 1979).
Malus toringo (Siebold) Siebold ex De Vriese, *Tuinbouw-Flora* 3:368, 1856.
Sorbus toringo Siebold, *Jaarb. Kon. Ned. Maatsch. Aanmoediging v.d. Tuinbouw*, p. 47, 1848.
Sorbus toringo (K. Koch) Siebold ex Carrière, *Rev. Hort.*, 1870–71:451, t. 63.
Pyrus sieboldii Regel, *Ind. Sem. Hort. Petrop.*, 1858:51, 1859.
Malus sieboldii (Regel) Rehder, *Plant. Wilson.*, 2:293, 1915.

Quoting an extract from page 47 of the 1848 *Cataloge on Plants from Japan, the Indes-Orientales et Occidentales Neerlandais*, a listing of plants offered by Von Siebold & Comp. á Leyde, written in Dutch, Wijnands wrote: "Six plants of a new importation from Japan of *Sorbus toringo* are for sale at 500 francs each." The description is in a footnote in French, "with white and rose flowers, leaves 3 lobed and smaller than *M. spectabilis*, with yellow fruit."

Wijnands noted that the taxon is not to be confused with the common apple used in Japan and that "the name 'toringo' in Japan is synonymous with *Malus prunifolia* var. *rinki*." Thus the new name of *M. toringo* already had some old Japanese confusion about it. Because of the Japanese use of "toringo" as a synonym for *M. prunifolia* 'Rinki', Rehder may have passed over the older taxon (i.e., *M. toringo*) in favor of *M. sieboldii*. Now that the name has been changed back to *M. toringo*, there is certain to be confusion about two uses of "toringo"!

There remains yet another problem that most taxonomists tend to ignore. Generally they describe *Malus toringo* as a species, although several voice doubts that it may be a hybrid with "red and yellow fruit." It is my opinion that genetically an original *Malus* species had one-colored fruit, most probably red, and that the yellow fruit came later as a mutational fruit color, frequently linked with the pink-flowering gene. (I am aware that a few other species are also described as having red and yellow fruit.) With time, through the introduction of mutations or through interspecific hybridization of distant ancestry in the natural state, a species may evolve to the point where the fruit has two or more colors. The primal species becomes contaminated with geographic and climatic adaptational variants. How is this conclusion reached? By observing carefully protected self-pollinated seedlings. When these seedlings bear fruit of two different colors, or a combination of colors (e.g., yellow with a reddish blush, or orange colored fruit), one should immediately suspect some distant, hybrid origin or admixture from foreign pollen—at least this is my personal view.

The problem of "red and yellow" fruit will always remain with us. I do not believe it can ever be settled. What were the early taxonomists really describing? A specimen of a true species, or a specimen that was similar to the true species but already contaminated with interspecific hybridization in the wild? When one reads many of the older species descriptions, keeping in mind genetics, a great deal of 'hybrid description' is contained in them. This leads me to conclude that some of these taxonomic descriptions are based on crabapple hybrid specimens and not on specimens of the true species.

In the case of the classic *Malus sieboldii* taxonomy controversy, it is interesting to note that in one description (i.e., of Siebold ex De Vriese), the specimen has "yellow fruit," whereas in another description (i.e., of [Regel] Rehder) it has "a red or brownish yellow fruit." In the latter description, the word *or* immediately betrays genetic impurity, possibly from a distant, natural, interspecific hybridization, or, more probably, the admixture into a species of its own color mutations. I am convinced that both men are describing different plants or at least variants of a species.

One of the problems facing previous generations of taxonomists is that they had to base their decisions on whatever specimen was given them. They had little means of knowing if a specimen was a valid new species or an interspecific natural hybrid. They knew nothing about polyploids nor were they concerned with chromosome counts. Since those days, however, taxonomists have access to additional information. From chromosome counts, we know that *Malus sieboldii* (Regel) Rehder (what is now called *M. toringo*) is a very rare, natural quintaploid, which immediately indicates that it is a very different kind of crabapple species or variant, the only one of all the crabapples that is so unique!

On the basis of chromosome counts, then, I distinguish, in this volume, between *Malus sieboldii* (Regel) Rehder, which I call *M. toringo*, and *M. sieboldii* var. *zumi*, which I call *M. sieboldii*: *M. toringo* is a quintaploid (5*x*) having yellow fruit, whereas the new *M. sieboldii* is a diploid (2*x*) having red fruit. The yellow-fruited clones in *M. sieboldii* (Regel) Rehder—what I call *M. toringo*—should be considered either as color mutations or the admixture of hybrid origins, both of which can occur in the wild state. Thus the name *M. sieboldii* is properly a red-fruited species.

PROBLEMS IN CLASSIFYING CRABAPPLES

There will be more reclassification of the species and their varietal forms as time passes. Probably not many new additions will be made from the wild as the habitat for native plants undergoes urbanization and urban sprawl. Time is fast running out for finding new plant materials, even in remote areas. There are, however, great opportunities for hybridization of many of the lesser known species, especially among the fast-disappearing North American species.

Great opportunities also exist in converting the native species, *Malus ioensis* and *M. fusca* into tetraploids. *Malus coronaria* and its varieties are already natural tetraploids. Their interspecific hybridization with the Asiatic species and many of the newer multibrids should produce an array of uniquely different crabapples. An open field exists in working with the many new multibrids (plants with several species in their parentage). We should begin using newer nomenclature in designating hybrids. I have suggested in another work on lilacs that we use the word *hybrid* for a plant of two species; *tribrid* for a plant of three species; *quatrobrid* for four; *quintobrid* for five; *sextobrid* for six; *septobrid* for seven; *octobrid* for eight; *nonobrid* for nine; and *deccabrid* for ten. With rapid advances in hybridization, these designations give precise meaning to what kind of hybrid we are referring without cumbersome wordage.

Although taxonomists differ as to the exact number of species and their classification, the species listed above and their principal varieties and clonal forms are generally accepted today. The greatest differences among taxonomists concern the classification of *Malus coronaria* and *M. ioensis*. Further study of these two may find they are one species, with *M. coronaria* being the tetraploid form and *M. ioensis* being the diploid. Taxonomists also differ over the reclassification of *M. sieboldii* to *M. toringo* with *M.* ×*zumi* being reclassified to become the species *M. sieboldii*. Thus several points of the taxonomy of *Malus* still need changes, refinement, and reclassification.

One difficulty in classifying crabapples comes from planting open-pollinated seed and then giving it a species name. Only asexual propagation by graft, cutting, or tissue culture will assure the propagation of a valid species. (Some few botanists question the clonal reliability of tissue cultured plants.) I once visited a nursery where blocks of so-called *Malus sieboldii* plants were being sold as "true species" plants. Yet all the plants were from open-pollinated seed in which there were hundreds of variants, even a red-leafed one! In time these so-called 'true species seedlings' totally distort the identification of the real species.

Another difficulty facing taxonomists is that many native crabapples are fast disappearing, if not lost, in most of their natural habitat. Some are lost to rapid urbanization and commercial farming, others to the overlapping of native species or the "natural" cross breeding of native species with commercial orchards. For example, where the native North American species *Malus ioensis* grows near orchards of the marketed apple, *M. pumila*, wind often carries pollen to the native crabapples and hybrid cultivars result. The overlapping of native species, which, as a result of environmental and climatic influences, also produces hybrids—mutations and adaptive clones with regional variations but only slight taxonomic differences. Often these are hybrids are mistaken as separate, native species, but to consider them as such would be an error. Taxonomists must consider a large number of native plants before any single individual can be classified as a species or variety.

Unfortunately, the native crabapples will soon be found only in the larger collections and as arboretum specimen plants. Before they disappear a last effort should be made to identify and preserve all that is possible. The flowering crabapples have become sophisticated inbreds of modern horticulture. Sadly, the story of the species, which begins with "Once upon a time," now ends with "the natives no longer posses the land!"

A CONFUSING PROBLEM OF NOMENCLATURE

A problem of nomenclature exists today with regard to the use of the words *clone* or *cultivar*. Many taxonomists, and most of the general public, have a problem calling a single, specified, and selected plant a *cultivar*, if that designation only means "a cultivated plant originating in cultivation" (as opposed to a plant found in the wild), for in the past the word *cultivar* has simply meant "a cultivated group of plants." The word *clone* appears to be readily understood by the overwhelming majority as a plant "exactly the same as the original one," whether its origin be in the wild or as a cultivated plant. Thus a clone is a selected plant whose unique characteristics can be retained only by asexual propagation—be that by tissue culture, rooted cuttings, budding, or grafting. To remain identical a clone cannot be reproduced by seed, for no matter how similar, seedlings are never identical (i.e., exactly the same as the seed parent plant). Let me add here that expert tissue culturists disagree on whether tissue culture *always* reproduces an identical plant. Some differences in plants stem from the layer of plant tissue being cultured; more differences are attributable to the skill of the culturists; and other differences arise because chemical hormones used in tissue culture produce mutations. These can be real problems and need to be addressed by plant propagators if plants are to remain identical clones.

Species are expected to have a certain amount of variability in their selfed seedlings; hence, when a very special seedling appears with unique characteristics (e.g., *Malus baccata* 'Jackii'), it must be named as a clone and propagated asexually to preserve those characteristics and not by seed. Group hybrids of species originating in cultivation (e.g., Rosyblooms) are considered cultivars.

In the past the International Committee on Nomenclature, which zealously guards the registry of all named plants, put forth some confusing and ambiguous directions as to what was and was not a cultivar or a clone. Recently it has issued many pages of instructions to clarify the distinctions, but it seems the ordinary public, many taxonomists, botanists, geneticists, and horticultural writers remain as confused as ever. In this book I have chosen to use the word *clone* when writing of a specially selected plant with particular characteristics which can be reproduced only by asexual propagation. On the basis of this definition, a clone could be a very select form of a species. For example, when protected, selfed seed of a species is planted, many species produce seedlings of varying characteristics. Should someone select a seedling that has some unique variation, it would have to be cloned (i.e., asexually propagated) to preserve that uniqueness, be it a native species or a cultivated plant. Any hybrid that is named for its unique characteristics is a clone—whether it originated in the wild or in cultivation—because it must be reproduced only asexually to preserve these characteristics.

The taxonomic confusion still rages. In some circles every named plant is a cultivar, even though it is a selected plant and not a member of a group cultivar, while in other circles the same plant is a clone since it must be asexually propagated and is a single, selected, named plant! I do not choose to settle, or even enter into, this nomenclature problem, which despite recent attempts at clarification, remains as confusing as ever and *cultivar* is still an ambiguous term. Does it include only one, selected, named, cultivated plant, or does it include the whole family, group, or strain of similar unselected seedlings?

In this book I have chosen a middle-of-the-road position. If a plant is specially selected for certain unique characteristics, I designate it a *clone*, since to retain its unique characteristics it must be asexually propagated (i.e., cloned). If a plant is a member of a group of unselected, cultivated seedlings, I designate it a *cultivar*. This term applies to groups of unnamed seedlings or groups of similar seedlings of the same background (e.g., the Rosybloom hybrids).

I am certain there will be a very great outcry from some nomenclature perfectionists. Perhaps some taxonomists will protest my definitions, but I write for an understanding of the named crabapples, many of which must be asexually propagated to retain their unique identity, and are therefore clones. The vast majority of the public, for whom this book is also written, are untrained in nomenclatural taxonomy, but they readily understand what the words *clone* and *cloning* mean. For most of them a clone is an identical plant in all its parts and a cultivar is a cultivated plant. I regret any problems I may cause purists of nomenclature rules, but for the countless individuals, who plant gardens, produce or buy nursery materials, and read horticultural books, the present rules of nomenclature remain extremely ambiguous, despite many pages of recent clarifications.

Plate 1. *Malus* 'Centurion', bright cherry-red fruit.

Plate 2. *Malus* 'Woven Gold', bright yellow-gold fruit.

Plate 3. *Malus* 'Molten Lava', brilliant orange-red fruit.

Plate 4. *Malus* 'Winter Gold', bright lemon-yellow fruit.

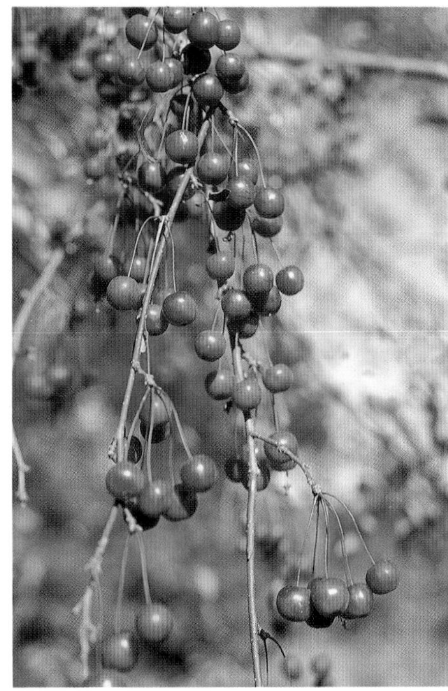

Plate 5. *Malus* 'Joy', medium purple; excellent next to yellow-fruited.

Plate 6. *Malus* 'Red Jewel', bright cherry-red fruit.

Plate 7. *Malus* 'Golden Candles', chartreuse-bright lemon fruit.

Plate 8. *Malus* 'Peter Murray', fruit a combination of gold and burnished orange.

Plate 9. *Malus* 'Coralene', fruit a showy coral and copper.

Plate 10. *Malus* 'Royalty', dark red.

Plate 11. *Malus* 'Van Eseltine'.

Plate 12. *Malus* 'Kelsey'.

Plate 13. *Malus* 'White Candle', a new, very double, upright white crabapple.

Plate 14. *Malus* 'Karen', deep carmine buds flushed with fuchsia-purple that open to double, white flowers whose petals are edged pink.

Plate 15. *Malus* in the Lagoon Area of J. Frank Schmidt & Son Co. arboretum, Boring, OR.

Plate 16. Flowering crabapples in the LH Gardens, taken from the roof of the McKay Center.

Plate 17. Blooming crabapples surround Falcon Lake, Falconskeape Gardens, Medina, OH.

Plate 18. *Malus baccata* 'Halward' and *M.* 'Liset' at Falconskeape Gardens.

Plate 19. *Malus* collection, Boerner Botanical Gardens, Hales Corner, WI.

Plate 20. *Malus* 'John Downie' at Boerner Botanical Gardens.

Plate 21. *Malus* 'Indian Magic' at Rock Springs Collection.

Plate 22. *Malus* 'Hillier' at the Arnold Arboretum, Jamaica Plains, MA.

Plate 23. Rosyblooms at a shopping plaza, Medina, OH.

Plate 25. The double, pink blossoms of *M.* 'Cotton Candy' are complimented by the white blossoms of *M.* 'Leprechaun', a very heavy annual bloomer.

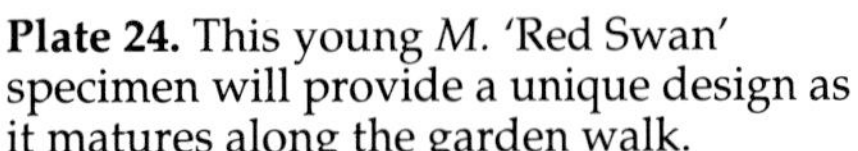

Plate 24. This young *M.* 'Red Swan' specimen will provide a unique design as it matures along the garden walk.

'late 26. *Malus halliana* 'Parkmanii', a pink-flowering crab-pple that looks good when planted in front of blue conifers.

Plate 27. *Malus* 'Silver Moon', a late-blooming white crabapple, is most effective with deep purple, later-blooming lilacs, such as *Syringa* 'Sarah Sands'.

Plate 28. Lilacs and crabapples at Falconskeape Gardens.

Plate 29. *M.* ×*arnoldiana* is a large, upright tree with spreading branches.

Plate 30. As old as it is, *M.* ×*arnoldiana* remains one of the beautiful crabapples in bloom.

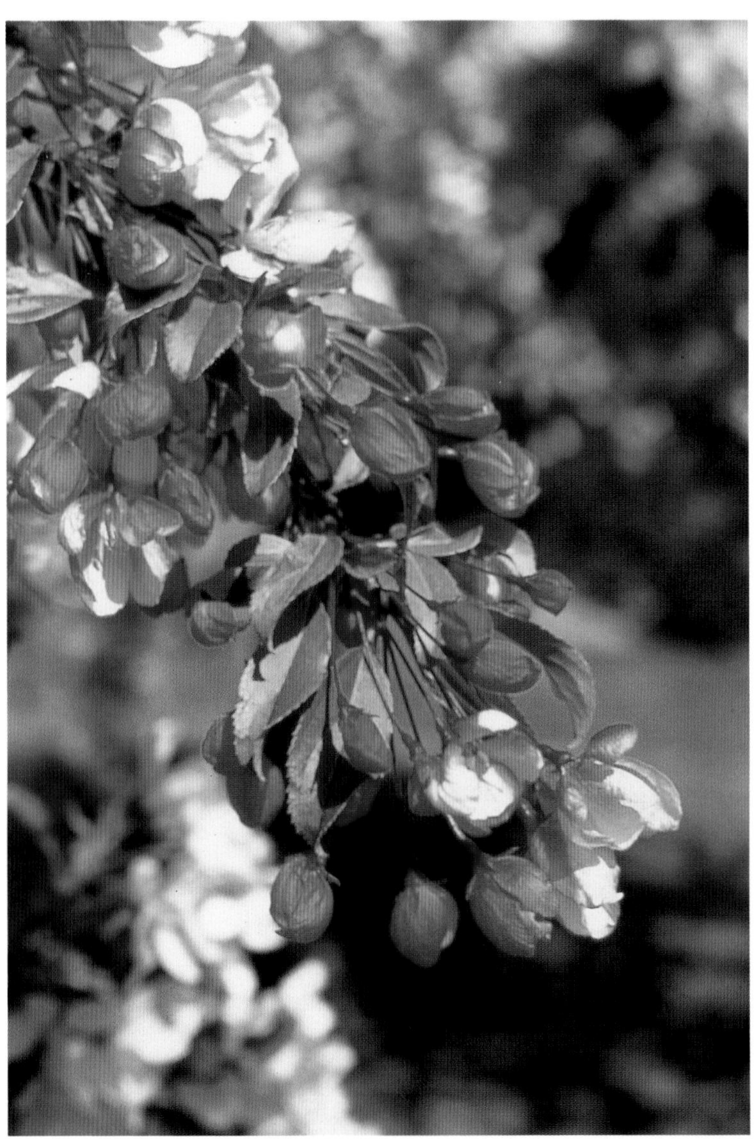

Plate 31.
Opening red buds of *M.* ×*arnoldiana*.

late 32. *Malus ×atrosanguinea* in bloom.

Plate 33. *Malus ×atrosanguinea* buds.

late 34. Closeup of *M. ×atrosanguinea* flowers showing two-oned pink-red blossoms.

Plate 35. Although the fruit of *M. ×atrosanguinea* is not showy by today's standards, its springtime show of magnificent blossoms makes it a standard as a specimen crabapple.

Plate 36. Coming from Northeast Asia and colder areas of northern China, *M. baccata* is one of the hardiest of all crabapples and among the first to bloom.

Plate 37. *Malus baccata* 'Alexander', a medium, upright multibrid that is very handsome in abundant, annual bloom.

Plate 38. *Malus baccata* 'Halward' is an excellent, white blooming crabapple with dark glossy green leaves.

Plate 39. *Malus baccata* 'Halward' flowering branches.

ate 40. *Malus baccata* 'Halward' has very small, brilliant red uit.

Plate 41. *Malus baccata* 'Jackii' grows to be a rather tall, spreading tree.

'late 42. *Malus baccata* 'Jackii' flowers.

Plate 43. *Malus baccata* 'Jackii' is an excellent clone with glossy red fruit.

Plate 44. *Malus coronaria* blossoms.

Plate 45. *Malus coronaria* var. *bracteata* tree form.

Plate 46. *Malus coronaria* var. *bracteata* blossoms.

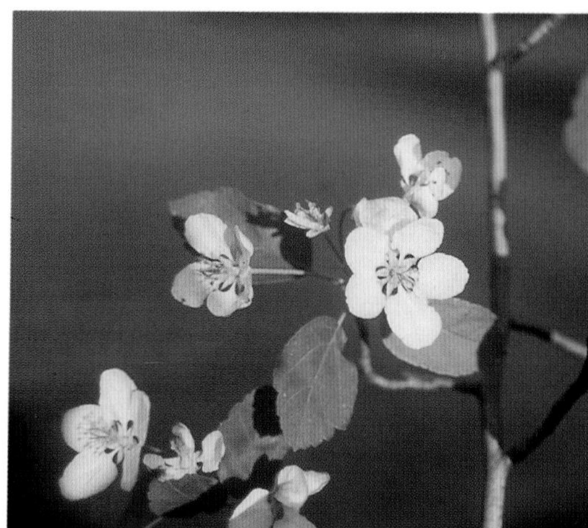

Plate 47. *Malus coronaria* var. *dasycalyx* blossoms.

Plate 48. *Malus coronaria* var. *dasycalyx* 'Charlottae' blossoms.

Plate 49. *Malus coronaria* var. *glabrata* blossoms.

Plate 50. *Malus coronaria* var. *glaucescens* leaf.

Plate 51. *Malus coronaria* var. *platycarpa* 'Hoopesii' blossoms.

Plate 52. *Malus coronaria* 'Coralglow', a late-blooming hybrid has unique coral-colored blossoms. No other crabapple has blossoms this color and very few others are late blooming.

Plate 53. *Malus coronaria* 'Elongata' is wonderfully fragrant.

Plate 54. *Malus coronaria* 'Pink Pearl' has beautiful, unique coral-colored blossoms.

Plate 55. *Malus floribunda*, introduced from Japan in 1862, is still one of the finer species for larger gardens. It has been used extensively in hybridizing.

Plate 56. *Malus floribunda* tree form.

Plate 57. *Malus floribunda* flowers.

Plate 58. *Malus floribunda* fruit.

Plate 59. *Malus halliana* var. *spontanea* is very dwarf and twiggy, vaselike, broader than tall. Recently it was surpassed by *M. halliana* National Arboretum No. 127.

Plate 60. *Malus halliana* var. *spontanea* blossoms.

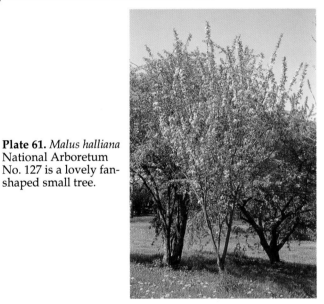

Plate 61. *Malus halliana* National Arboretum No. 127 is a lovely fan-shaped small tree.

Plate 62. *Malus halliana* National Arboreum No. 127 has bright pink, double blossoms.

Plate 63. *Malus halliana* 'Parkmanii', a small tree with elegant semidouble, pink blossoms, is one of the choicest offspring of this species.

Plate 64. The shell-pink blossoms of *M. halliana* 'Parkmanii' blossoms are among the most attractive crabapple blossoms.

Plate 65. *Malus hupehensis*—a tetraploid form.

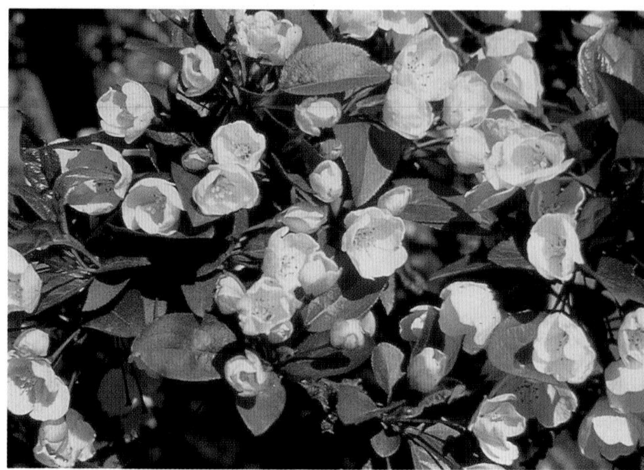

Plate 66. *Malus hupehensis* blossoms.

Plate 67. *Malus hupehensis* 'Donald', a glossy leafed, newer form.

Plate 68. *Malus hupehensis* 'Donald' blossoms.

Plate 69. *Malus hupehensis* 'Donald' fruit.

Plate 70. *Malus hupehensis* 'Wayne Douglas' has purplish, larger fruit, hinting at hybrid origin.

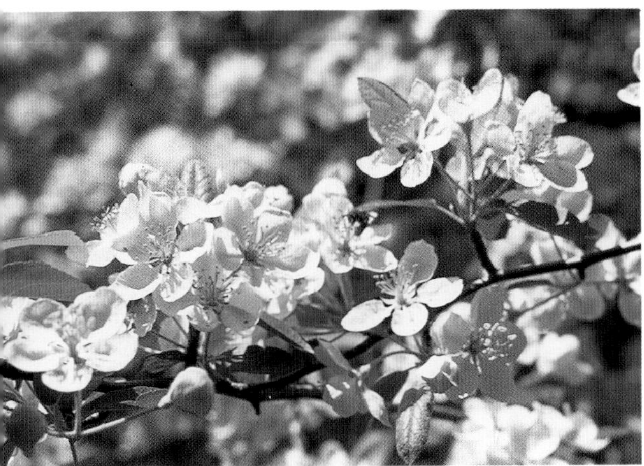

ate 71. *Malus ioensis* is perhaps the finest of the North Ameri-
n species and, although subject to cedar-apple rust, is consid-
ed by many equal to the best Asiatic species. It blooms fully 2
eeks later than other crabapples and has abundant annual
ossoms that are exceptionally fragrant. Unlike *M. coronaria* it
a natural diploid.

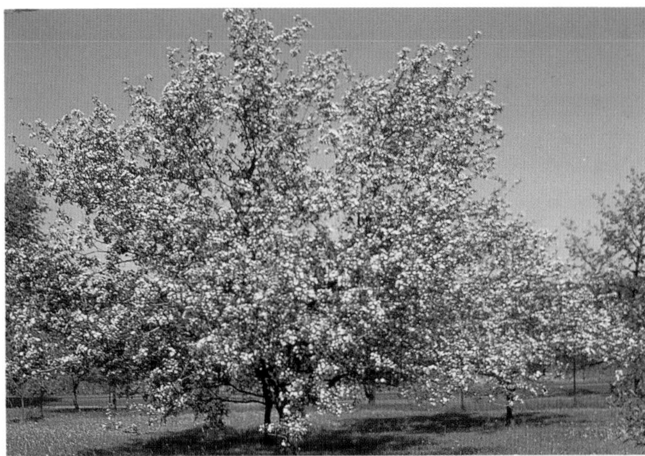

Plate 72. *Malus ioensis* 'Klehm's Improved Bechtel' tree in bloom.

Plate 73. *Malus ioensis* 'Klehm's Improved Bechtel' flower.

late 74. *Malus ioensis* 'Klehm's Improved Bechtel' fruit.

Plate 75. *Malus ioensis* 'Klehm's Improved Bechtel' autumn leaf color.

Plate 76. *Malus ioensis* 'Nova' fragrant, double flowers.

Plate 77. *Malus ioensis* 'Plena' tree in bloom.

Plate 78. *Malus ioensis* 'Plena' has wonderful double, very fragrant flowers.

Plate 79. *Malus ioensis* 'Prince Georges' is a delightfully fragrant hybrid with no fruit.

Plate 80. *Malus pumila* 'Niedzwetzkyana', a break of serendipity that led to the deep red-leafed, red-budded, and red-flowered crabapples with somewhat larger red-purple fruit. Insignificant in itself, its progeny is regal red.

late 81. *Malus pumila* 'Niedzwetzkyana' blossom.

Plate 82. *Malus pumila* 'Niedzwetzkyana' fruit.

Plate 83. *Malus* ×*purpurea* 'Lemoinei', one of the first of the magnificent red flowering multibrid crabapples. Its singular fault is the time it takes before it begins to bloom, about 7 years, but once of blooming age, it is a heavy, annual bloomer increasing with beauty each year. In regal splendor it dominates any landscape.

Plate 84. *Malus* ×*purpurea* 'Lemoinei' flower.

Plate 85. *Malus* ×*purpurea* 'Lemoinei' fruit.

Plate 86. *Malus ×robusta*, a cross of *M. baccata × M. prunifolia*, is a large tree, showy in white bloom. Selected named clones are superior to the simple cross.

Plate 87. *Malus ×robusta* blossoms.

Plate 88. *Malus ×robusta* is called the cherry crabapple because of its small red fruit.

Plate 89. *Malus ×robusta* 'Gary's Choice', a clone rarely seen.

Plate 90. *Malus ×robusta* 'Persicifolia' tree in bloom.

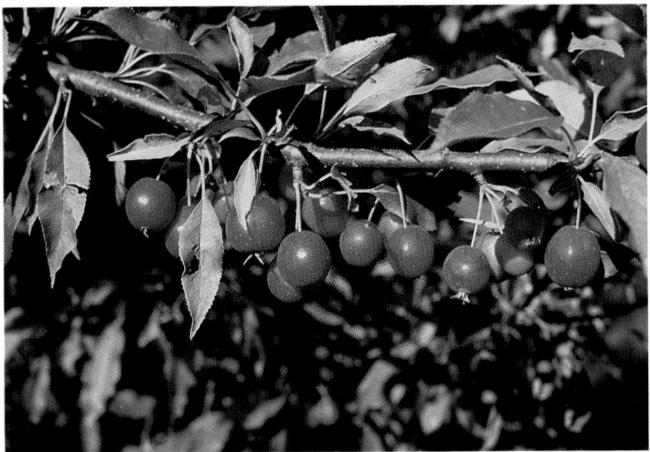

Plate 91. *Malus ×robusta* 'Persicifolia' fruit.

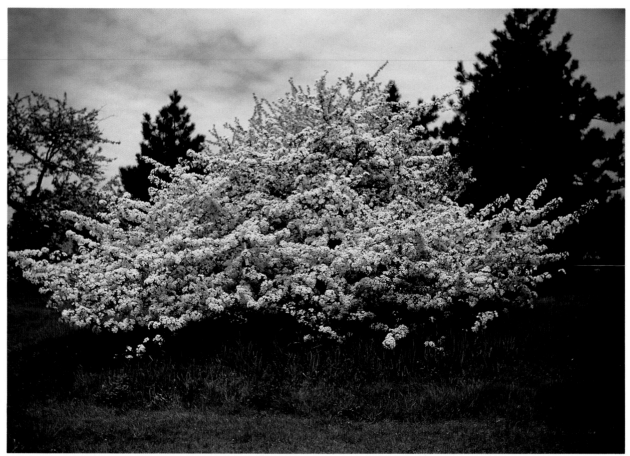

Plate 92. *Malus sargentii*, the smallest of the species crabapples, is an excellent ornamental.

Plate 93. *Malus sargentii* blossoms.

Plate 94. *Malus sargentii* fruit.

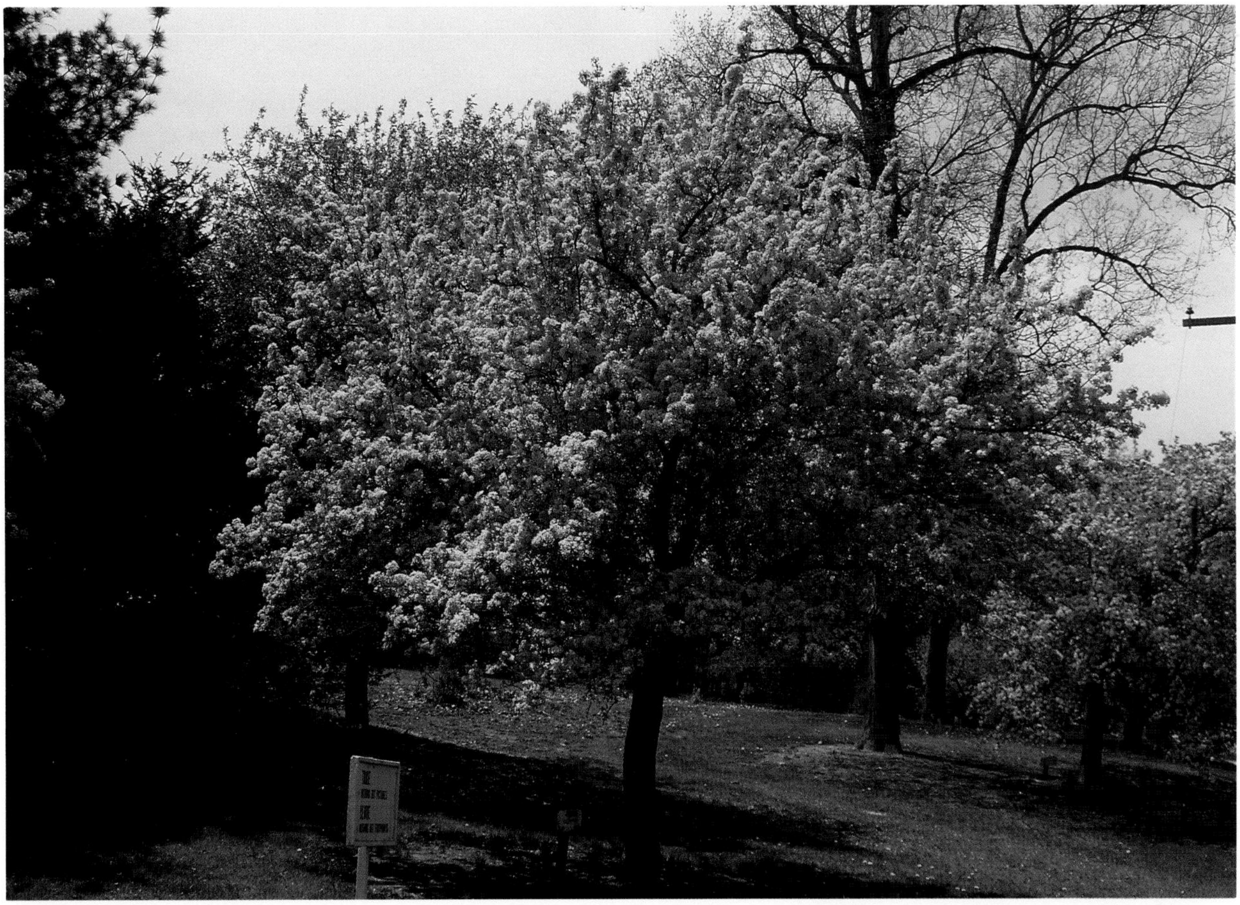

Plate 95. *Malus ×scheideckeri*, a fine semidouble hybrid of *M. floribunda* × *M. prunifolia*, is beautiful in spring bloom but lacks the luster of colorful fruit in autumn so necessary in modern flowering crabapples. Today it is seen only in the largest arboretums. Its value in hybridizing is very limited.

Plate 96. *Malus ×scheideckeri* blossoms.

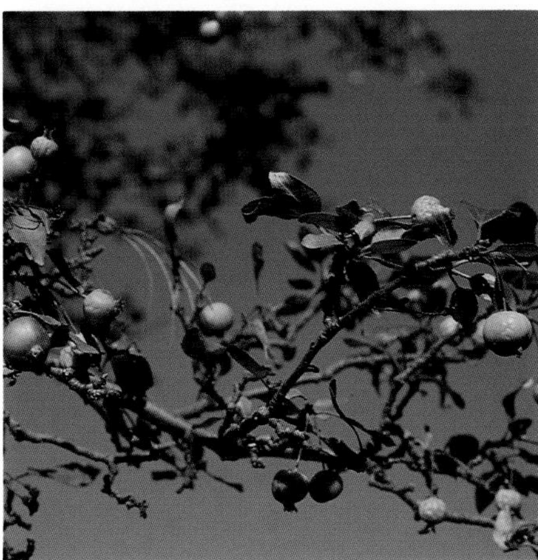

Plate 97. *Malus ×scheideckeri* fruit.

Plate 98. *Malus sieboldii* 'Calocarpa', one of the finest of all the flowering crabapples.

Plate 99. *Malus sieboldii* 'Calocarpa' blossoms.

Plate 100. *Malus sieboldii* 'Calocarpa' fruit.

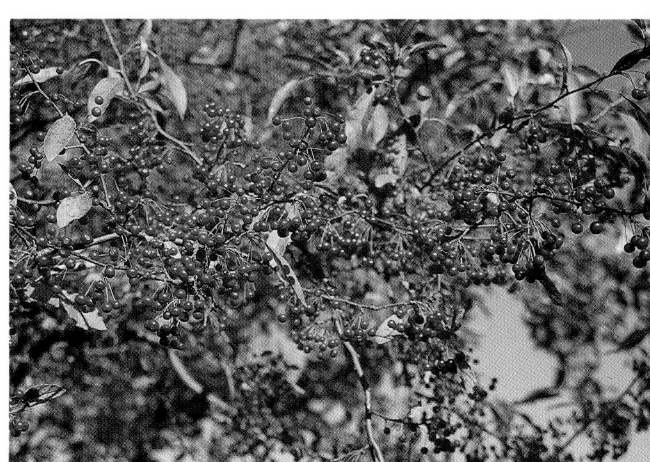

Plate 101. *Malus sieboldii* 'Wooster' fruit.

Plate 102. *Malus sikkimensis* is rarely seen today except in a few arboreta.

Plate 103. *Malus sikkimensis* flower.

Plate 104. *Malus sikkimensis* fruit.

Plate 105. *Malus spectabilis* is a species not known in the wild.

Plate 106. *Malus spectabilis* flower.

Plate 107. *Malus spectabilis* 'Plena', a double white.

Plate 108. *Malus spectabilis* 'Riversii', the finest *M. spectabilis* clone.

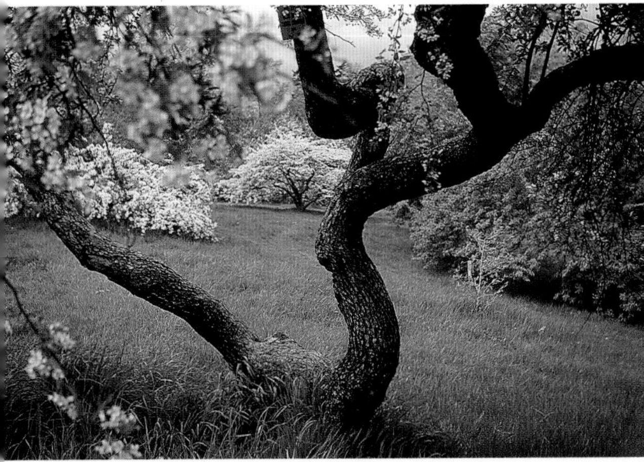

Plate 109. *Malus toringo* (once called *M. sieboldii*) with picturesque main branching.

Plate 110. *Malus toringo* blossom.

Plate 111. *Malus toringo* fruit.

Plate 112. *Malus toringo* 'Fuji' tree form.

Plate 113. *Malus toringo* 'Fuji' double flowers.

Plate 114. *Malus toringo* 'Fuji' yellow fruit.

Plate 115. *Malus tschonoskii* has a unique columnar form.

Plate 116. *Malus tschonoskii* with whitish gray leaves.

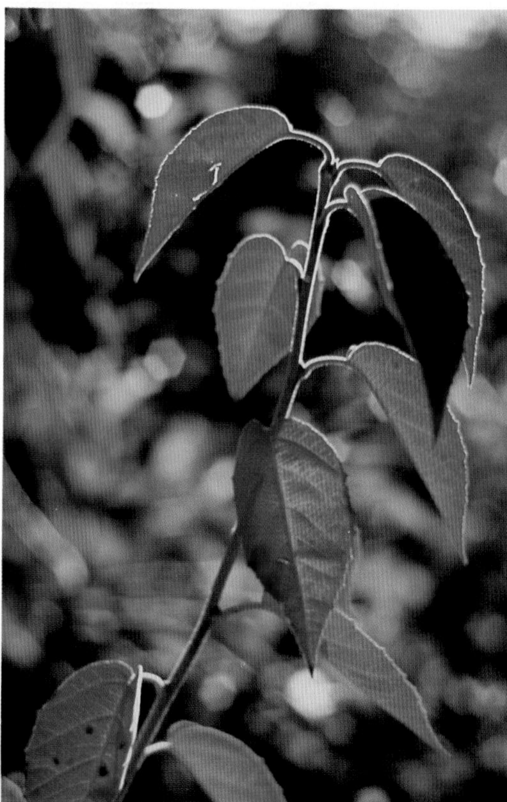

Plate 117. *Malus tschonoskii* autumn leaf color.

Plate 118. *Malus yunnanensis* fruit.

Plate 119. *Malus yunnanensis* 'Veitchii' blossom.

Plate 120. *Malus yunnanensis* 'Veitchii' blossom after petal fall.

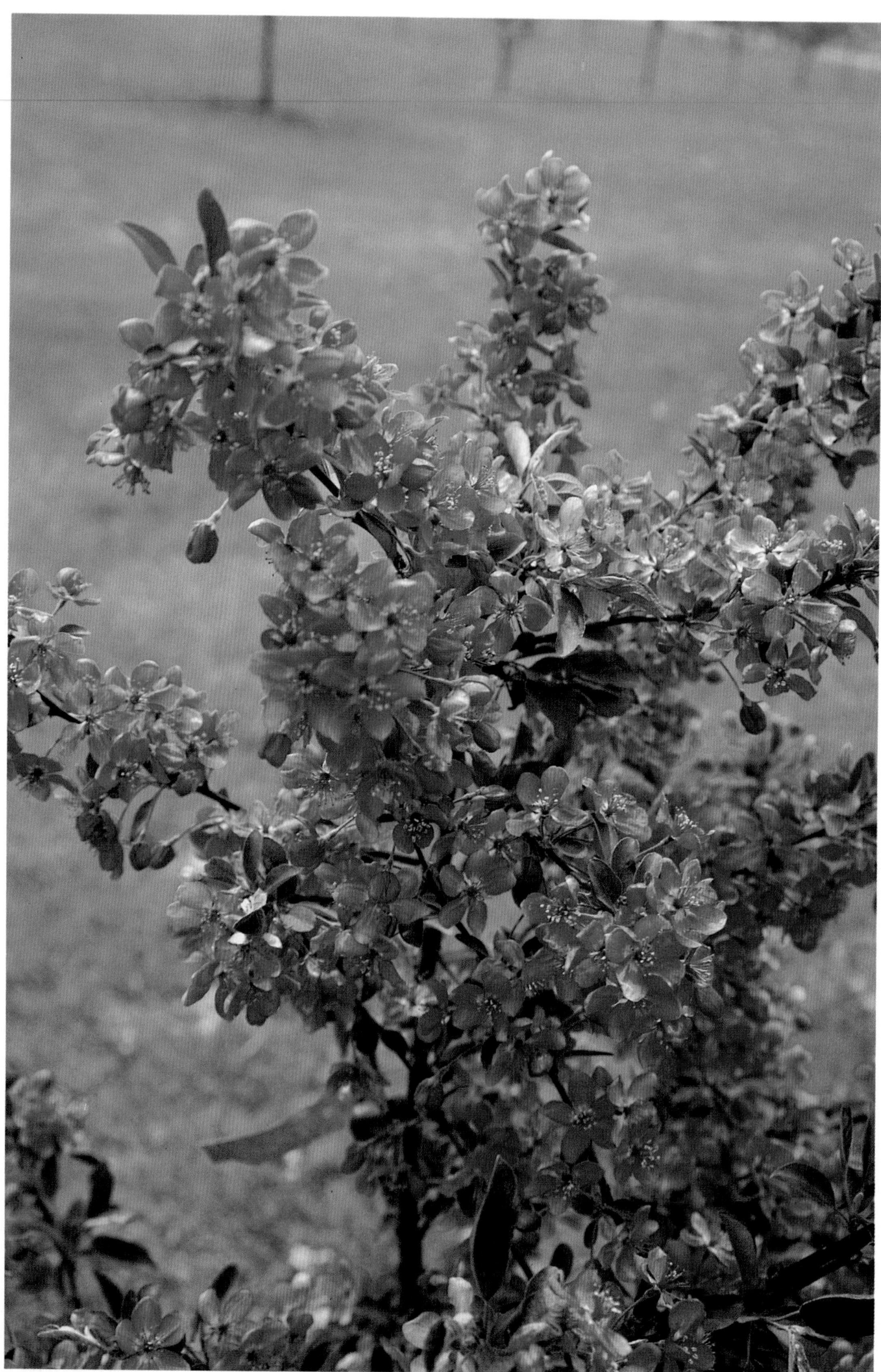

Plate 121. *Malus* 'Adams' is one of the finer red-flowering crabapples.

Malus 'Adirondack', One of the Finest Upright Crabapples

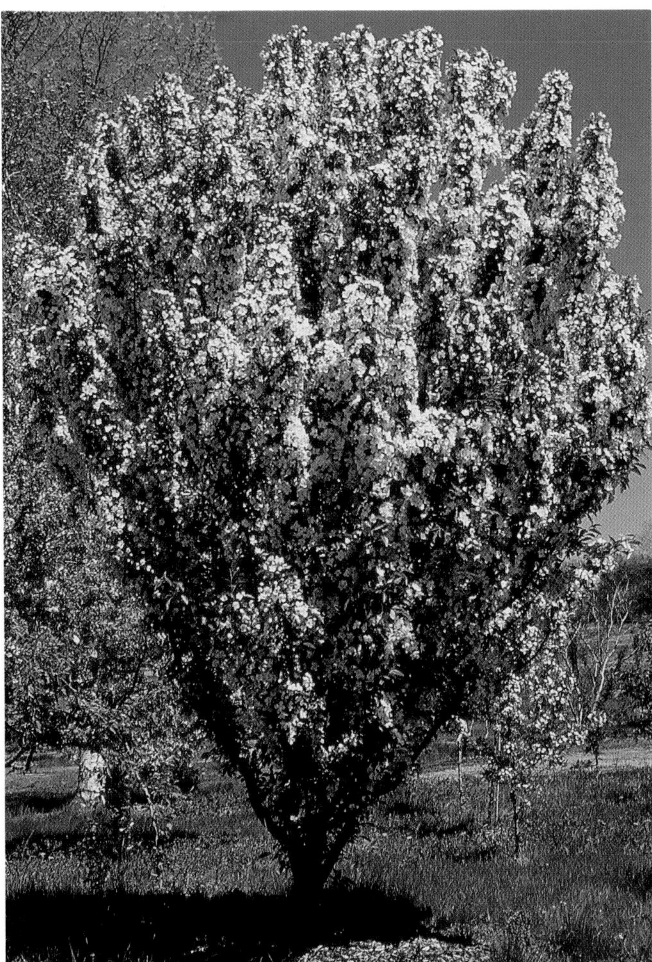

Plate 122. *Malus* 'Adirondack' is a narrow, upright tree with distinct obovate growth.

Plate 123. *Malus* 'Adirondack', an excellent annual bloomer, has heavy-textured, wide-spreading, white flower with traces of red.

Plate 124. *Malus* 'Adirondack' fruit is bright red-orange and medium to small in size.

Plate 125. *Malus* 'Aloise' is a very graceful weeper.

Plate 126. *Malus* 'Amberina' blossoms.

Plate 127. *Malus* 'Amberina' has magnificent orange-red smaller fruit that is excellent among the yellow leaves of autumn and very showy after leaf fall.

Plate 128. The bright red flowers of *M.* 'American Masterpiece', one of the Round Table Series of dwarf crabapples developed by James Zampini, show no bleaching.

Plate 129. The attractive pumpkin-orange fruit of *M.* 'American Masterpiece' is a welcome contrast in the autumn.

late 130. *Malus* 'Arch McKean', a smaller, upright multibrid
ith pale pink blossoms and deep red mini-fruit.

Plate 131. *Malus* 'Autumn Glory', an abundant annual bearer, is very showy in spring.

Plate 132. *Malus* 'Beverly' has very showy, small, bright red fruit but only in alternate years.

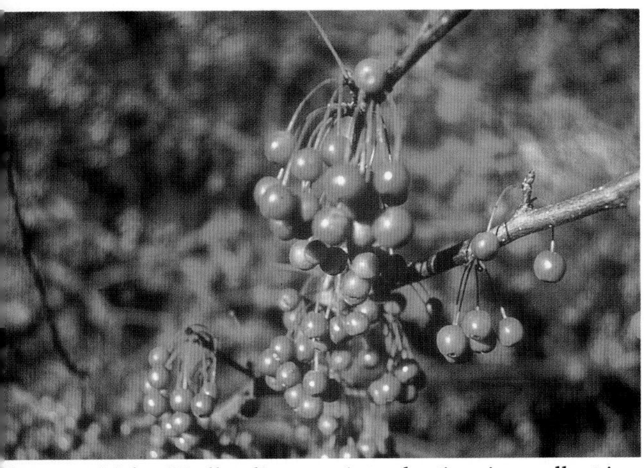

late 133. *Malus* 'Birdland', a new introduction, is excellent in
ll fruit color. Pictured here is the fruit after frost.

Plate 134. *Malus* 'Blanche Ames' bears semidouble, white flowers in great profusion annually.

Plate 135. *Malus* 'Bob White' in bloom.

Plate 136. *Malus* 'Bob White' has the good quality of an autumn change of leaf color to a bright gold which enhances the fruit.

Plate 137. *Malus* 'Bob White' was introduced for its abundant golden fruit. Frui color is a bit better after frosts.

Plate 138. In springtime bloom, *M.* 'Brandywine', one of the better, newer, double-flowering crabapples, provides an outstanding display of sheer beauty.

Plate 139. *Malus* 'Brandywine' deep rose-red buds open to very fragrant roselike blossoms.

Plate 140. The yellowish green fruit of *M.* 'Brandywine' is large, messy, and falls early—the one fault of this magnificent tree.

Plate 141. *Malus* 'Callaway', an excellent ornamental, is uniquely adapted for southern regions.

Plate 142. *Malus* 'Calvary' flowering branch.

Plate 143. *Malus* 'Calvary' fruit.

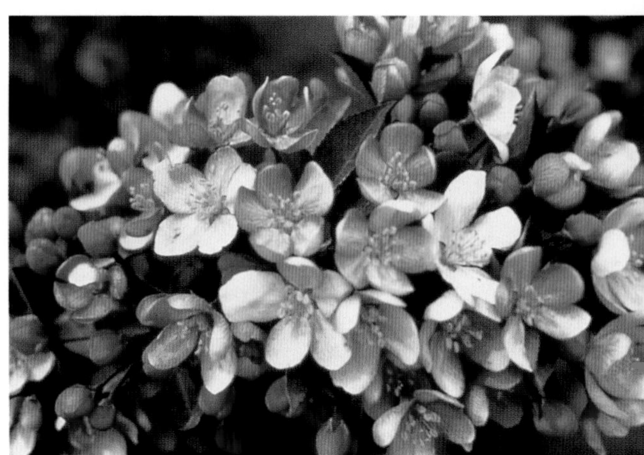

Plate 144. *Malus* 'Camelot', one of the Round Table Series of dwarf crabapples developed by James Zampini, has single flowers that are fuchsia-pink on white.

late 145. *Malus* 'Cardinal's Robe' tree in bloom.

Plate 146. *Malus* 'Cardinal's Robe' fruit.

late 147. The white blossoms of *M.* 'Christmas Holly' are very
owy in spring as are the hollylike red fruit in fall.

Plate 148. *Malus* 'Copper King' has wonderful abundant copper-gold-orange fruit.

Plate 149. *Malus* 'Coralburst', one of the first polyploid introductions to reach the commercial market, immediately became a success because of its magnificent bloom, dwarf form, and adaptability to all types of garden design.

Plate 150. *Malus* 'Coralburst' coral pink buds open to double rose flowers.

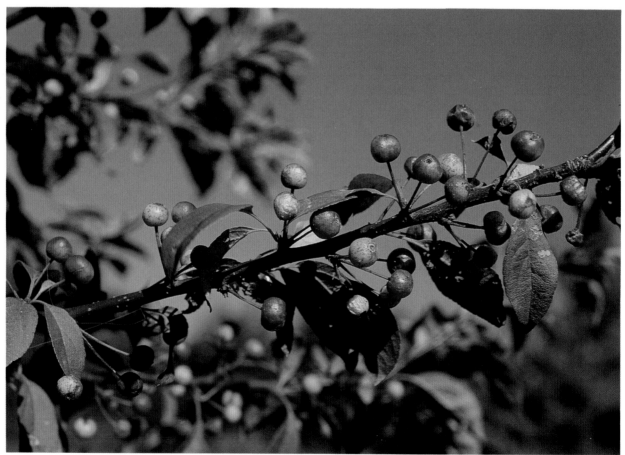

Plate 151. *Malus* 'Coralburst' fruit is a unique bronze color.

'late 152. *Malus* 'Coral Cascade', with its pink-coral-orange ruit that becomes more copper-orange after frosts and persists n beauty into January, is one of the very best in its fruit color lass.

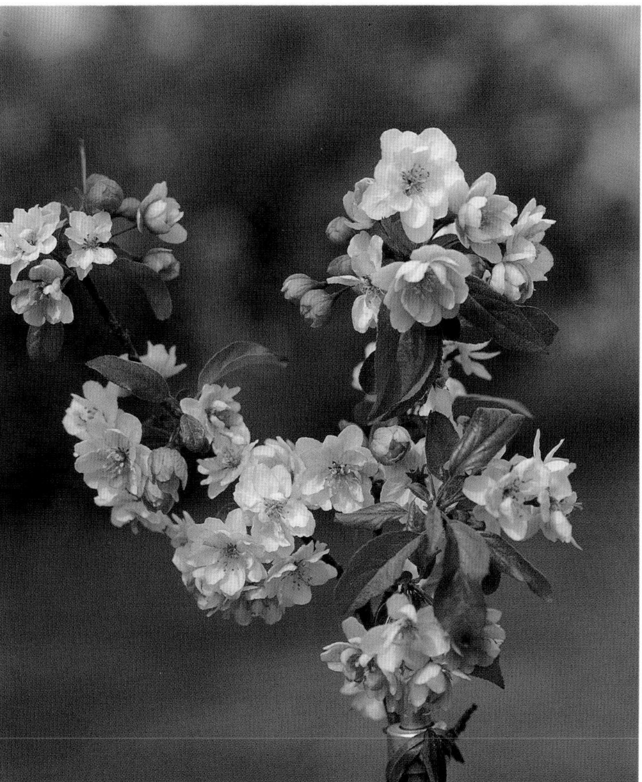

Plate 153. *Malus* 'Cranberry Lace', an upright double-flowering crabapple, is attractive in bloom and in abundant red fruit.

Plate 154. *Malus* 'David', an outstanding white-flowering clone with good red fruit.

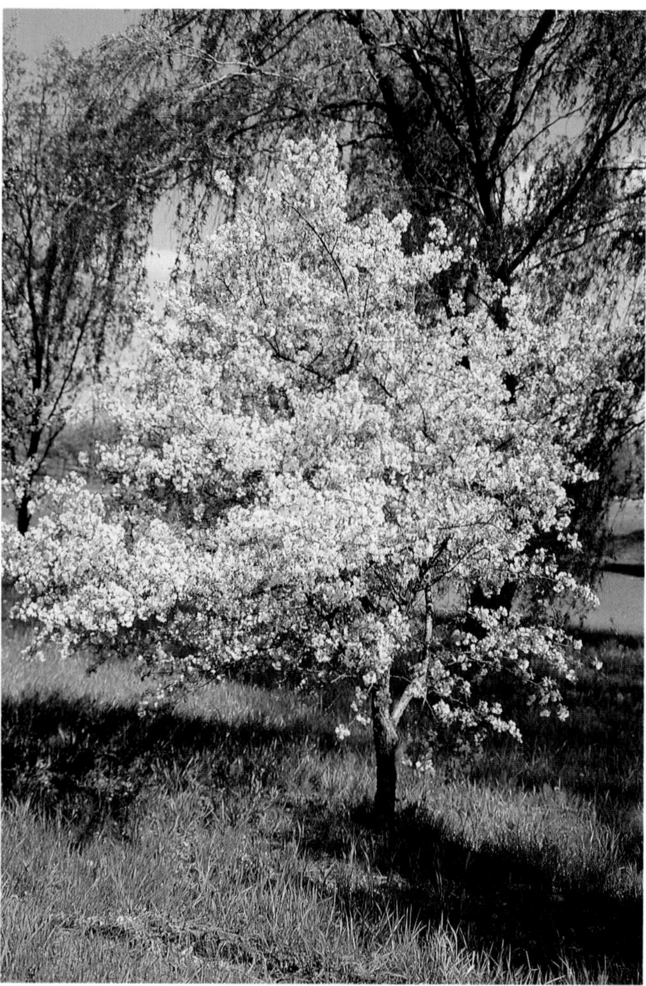

Plate 155. *Malus* 'Doubloons', a smaller tree to 12 ft (3.7 m) high, is an excellent crabapple for any garden.

Plate 156. The double to semidouble, white blossoms of *M.* 'Doubloons' open from brilliant carmine buds.

Plate 157. *Malus* 'Doubloons' fruit before frost is a bright lemon color.

Plate 158. *Malus* 'Doubloons' fruit after frost turns a deeper lemon-gold.

Plate 159. New and as yet not well known, *M.* 'Eline' is a small tree with semidouble blossoms and copper-gold fruit.

Plate 160. *Malus* 'Erie', an open-pollinated seedling of *M. pumila* 'Niedzwetzkyana', one of Isabella Preston's Lake Series.

Plate 161. *Malus* 'Fountain', an octoploid dwarf weeper, in bloom.

Plate 162. *Malus* 'Golden Galaxy', an outstanding gold-fruited multibrid, is a smaller tree with white flowers and very showy autumn fruit.

Plate 163. The magnificent *M.* 'GV-19', a heavy annual bloomer, has double rose-to-pink blossoms that appear early on the tree and last for two or three weeks.

Plate 164. *Malus* 'Hamlet', one of the Round Table Series of dwarf crabapples developed by James Zampini, has rosy-pink blossoms.

Plate 165. *Malus* 'Hopa', the first selection of *M. pumila* 'Niedzwetzkyana', is probably a cross of *M. pumila* 'Niedzwetzkyana' × *M. baccata*.

Plate 166. *Malus* 'Hopa' blossom.

Plate 167. With its heavily fruited branches, *M.* 'Indian Magic' is a very effective ornamental.

Plate 168. *Malus* 'Indian Magic' rose-colored blossoms.

Plate 169. *Malus* 'Indian Magic' autumn leaves.

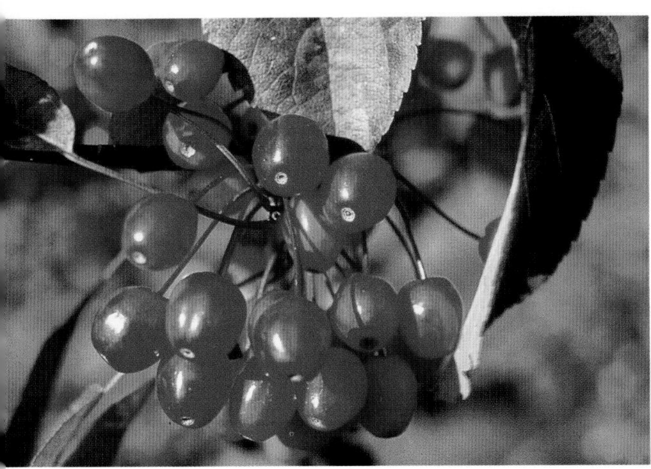

Plate 170. The elliptical glossy red fruit of *M.* 'Indian Magic' turns orange after frosts.

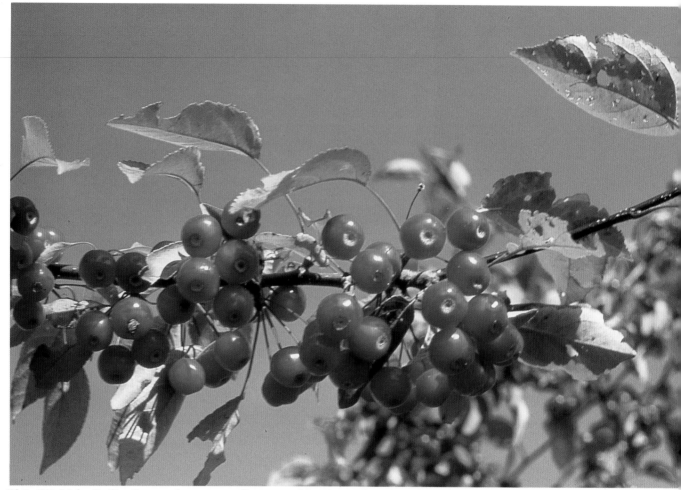

Plate 171. *Malus* 'Indian Summer', an outstanding, annual-bearing crabapple with brightly colored fruit that puts on a magnificent autumn display.

Plate 172. *Malus* 'King Arthur' is one of the Round Table Series of dwarf crabapples developed by James Zampini.

Plate 173. *Malus* 'King Arthur' has bright red fruit.

'late 174. *Malus* 'Lancelot', one of several
lwarf crabapples developed by James
:ampini, Lake County Nursery, Perry,
)H, in autumn foliage.

Plate 176. *Malus* 'Lancelot' fruit is light-to-medium gold.

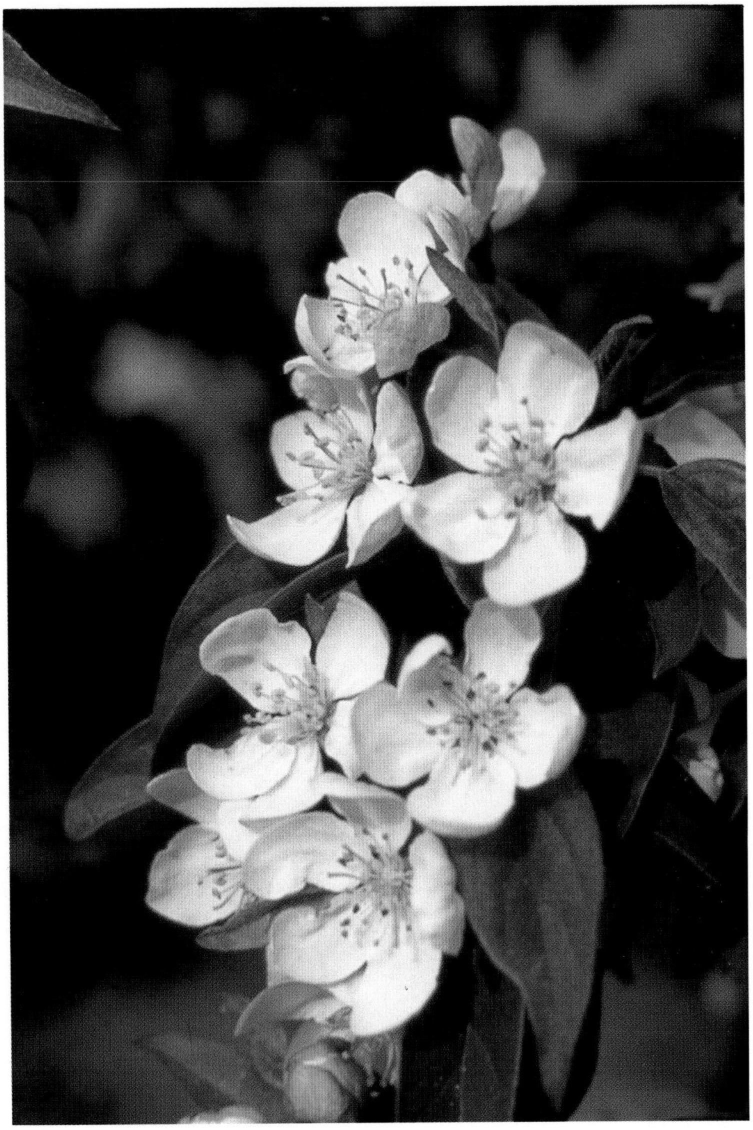

Plate 175. *Malus* 'Lancelot' blossoms.

Plate 177. *Malus* 'Leprechaun' is a very heavy annual bloomer that produces red mini-fruits.

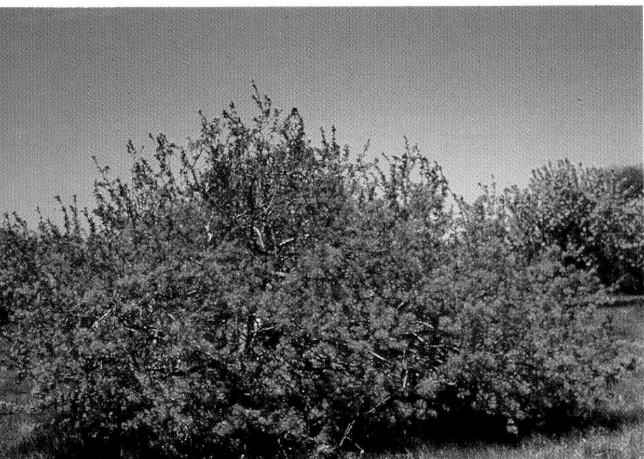

late 178. *Malus* 'Liset', a cross of *M.* ×*purpurea* 'Lemoinei' × *M.* *eboldii*, is probably the brightest orange-red crabapple.

Plate 179. *Malus* 'Liset' is excellent in bloom.

late 180. *Malus* 'Liset' is excellent in fine deep purple, smaller maroon-red fruit. The glossy fruit is too dark to be showy unless lanted next to yellow-fruited clone.

Plate 181. *Malus* 'Louisa' is one of the newer spreading, fountainlike weepers of low height.

Plate 182. *Malus* 'Louisa' has rose-colored buds and blossoms borne in great profusion annually.

Plate 183. *Malus* 'Louisa' lemon-gold fruit.

Plate 184. *Malus* 'Lullaby', a smaller, more refined version of 'Red Jade' with large white flowers and yellow fruit.

late 186. *Malus* 'Madonna', a double-flowering white crab-pple with an upright form, is excellent for narrow places in he landscape.

late 188. *Malus* 'Maria' blossoms.

Plate 185. *Malus* 'Luwick', graceful, refined weeper with excellent form, in bloom.

Plate 187. *Malus* 'Makamik', one of the few Rosyblooms that can be recommended, makes an excellent bloomer but lacks any good fall display of fruit.

Plate 189. *Malus* 'Mathews' blossoms.

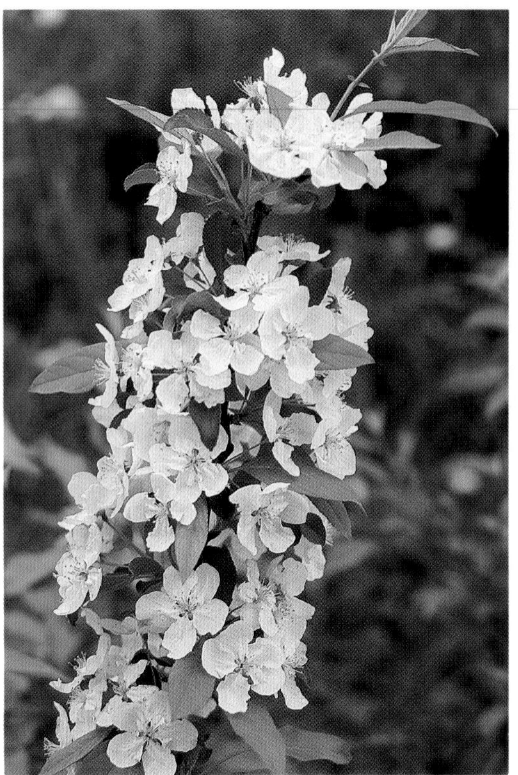

Plate 190. *Malus* 'Maysong', a very upright, narrow tree, is excellent for tight places. Its large, white, cupped blossoms are very showy.

Plate 191. *Malus* 'Michael', an extremely showy mini-fruited clone, has brilliant orange-red fruit that colors early Septembe and persists to December.

Plate 193. *Malus* 'Morning Sun', magnificent springtime bloor

Plate 192. *Malus* 'Molten Lava' is one of the showiest weepers on the market today and among the best in heavy fruiting.

Plate 194. *Malus* 'Morning Sun', colorful autumn fruit.

late 195. *Malus* 'Naragansett' in spring, an excellent white-owering tree for the smaller landscape.

Plate 196. *Malus* 'Naragansett' in autumn.

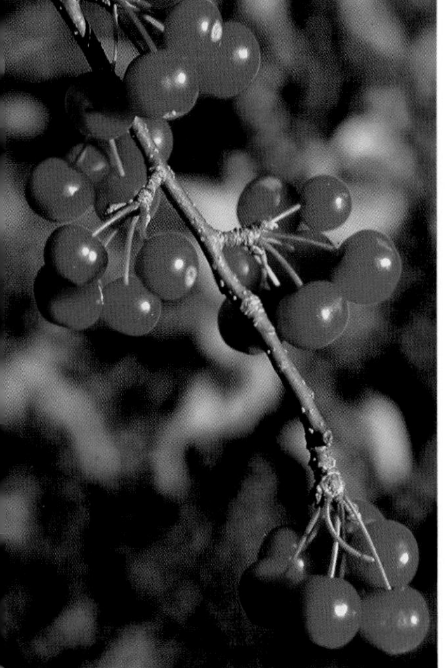

late 197. *Malus* 'Naragansett' produces xceptionally fine, brilliant red small fruit.

Plate 198. *Malus* 'Oekonomierat Echtermeyer', a cross of *M.* 'Exzellenz Thiel' × *M. pumila* 'Niedzwetzkyana'.

Plate 199. *Malus* 'Orange Crush', an exceptional red-flowering crabapple with attractive fruit.

Plate 200. With its deep purplish red fruit and its very fine blossom color, *M.* 'Prairifire' fits well into any landscape.

Plate 201. *Malus* 'Profusion' tree in bloom.

Plate 202. *Malus* 'Profusion' fruit.

lateP 203. *Malus* 'Purple Prince' tree in bloom.

Plate 204. *Malus* 'Purple Prince' fruit is bluish-purple with a fine blue bloom.

Plate 205. *Malus* 'Pygmy', a genetic dwarf, is almost a perfectly rounded tree.

late 206. *Malus* 'Radiant'

Plate 207. *Malus* 'Redbird', one of the finest early coloring crabapples, is an annual bloomer whose primary ornamental value lies in its brilliant crimson-red fruit. However, the combination of white flowers with unopened bright red buds in spring is also very ornamental.

Plate 208. *Malus* 'Red Jade' an excellent weeping crabapple, is a large tree that needs room to develop to perfection. The bright red fruit persists into winter.

Plate 209. *Malus* 'Red Peacock' blossoms.

Plate 210. *Malus* 'Red Peacock', a choice crabapple where there is space to appreciate its spreading form, is very effective in heavy fruit on cascading branchlets, similar to a peacock's tail.

late 211. *Malus* 'Red Swan', a medium-size, exotic fountain-ke weeper, ranks with *M.* 'White Cascade' as one of the finest eeping crabapples (and the author's favorite). Pictured is the riginal *M.* 'Red Swan' at Falconskeape Gardens, Medina, OH. he 30-year-old tree has not been pruned.

Plate 212. *Malus* 'Red Swan' puts on a long fall show of brilliant red fruit against the golden background of the autumn leaves.

late 213. *Malus* 'Red Swan' has unique abundant blossoms at follow rose buds.

Plate 214. *Malus* 'Red Swan' fruit is small, oblong in flowing racemes, and bright orange-red.

Plate 215. *Malus* 'Ross's Double Red' is a magnificent spreading tree with outstanding double rose-pink flowers.

Plate 216. *Malus* 'Royal Scepter', one of the Round Table Series of dwarf crabapples developed by James Zampini, has double rose-pink and white blossoms.

Plate 217. *Malus* 'Royal Scepter' fruit is bright red, very abundant, and showy.

Plate 218. *Malus* 'Sarah', with its large, semidouble blossoms, puts on a very showy annual display of both blossoms and fruit.

Plate 219. *Malus* 'Satin Cloud', the first of a series of polyploids developed at Falconskeape Gardens, Medina, OH, has abundant, pure satin white blossoms with a unique Oriental fragrance that strongly resembles cinnamon and clove.

Plate 220. *Malus* 'Satin Cloud' is disease-free and has leathery, green leaves in the summer that turn to brilliant shades of orange-red and purple in the autumn.

Plate 221. *Malus* 'Satin Cloud' fruit is small, hard, and persistent, turning from greenish-yellow to amber-yellow.

Plate 222. *Malus* 'Scugog' blossom, another of Isabella Preston's Lake Series.

Plate 223. *Malus* 'Selkirk', an excellent Rosybloom, has very showy purplish-pink blossoms.

Plate 224. *Malus* 'Selkirk' fruit is among the glossiest, brightest red fruit of any crabapple.

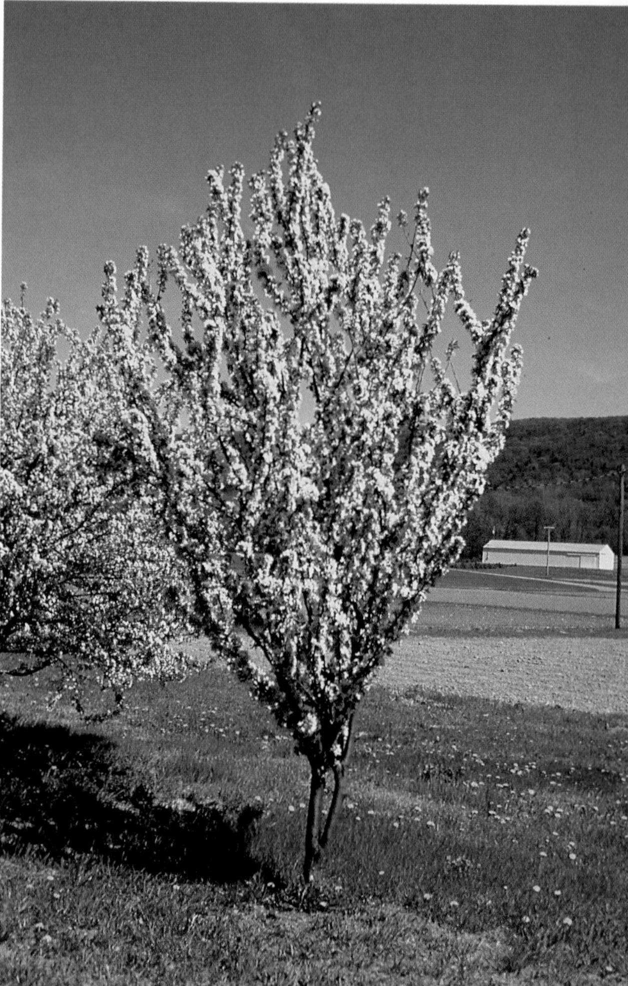

Plate 225. *Malus* 'Sentinel' is a narrow, upright tree that should be far better known and grown.

Malus 'Serenade', A Semiweeper with a Unique Fruit Color

Plate 226. *Malus* 'Serenade' branches are very fine and arching.

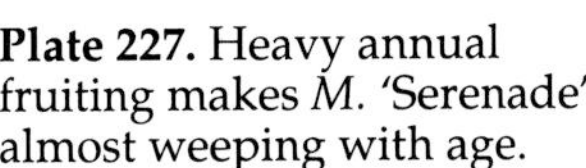

Plate 227. Heavy annual fruiting makes *M.* 'Serenade' almost weeping with age.

Plate 228. *Malus* 'Serenade' blossoms.

Plate 229. *Malus* 'Serenade' fruit is exceptionally colorful: beginning a pale coral, it becomes a deep coral-orange with amber highlights, finally turning pale orange-gold to deep burnt orange with frosts.

Plate 230. *Malus* 'Silver Moon' is strongly oval to upright in shape. It blooms fully 10 days after most crabapples have faded, making it a most welcome late-blooming addition to the landscape.

Plate 231. *Malus* 'Silver Moon' has marvelous pure white blossoms.

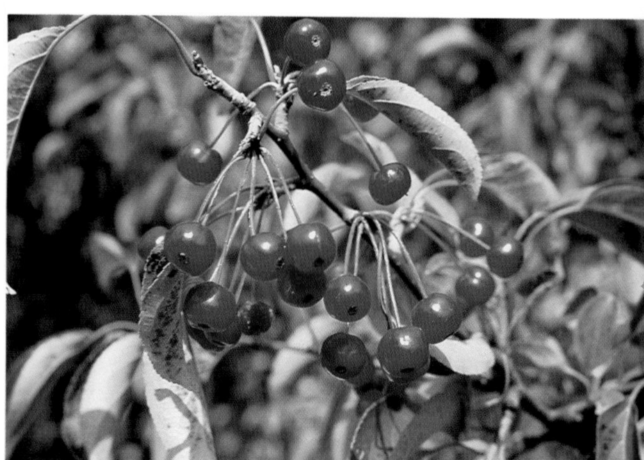

Plate 232. *Malus* 'Silver Moon' fruit is bright red fruit.

'late 233. *Malus* 'Sinai Fire', a weeper with somewhat unique, lownward branching and bright orange-red fruit.

Plate 234. *Malus* 'Sir Galahad', one of the Round Table Series of dwarf crabapples developed by James Zampini.

'late 235. *Malus* 'Snow Ballerina', an excellent small, fountain-ike weeper, has deep rose-pink buds that open to large, single, vhite blossoms in great profusion. This annual bloomer is very howy in white cascades of bloom.

Plate 236. *Malus* 'Snowdrift', a chance seedling of unknown parentage, is outstanding in bloom.

Plate 237. *Malus* 'Spring Song' is a small, gold-fruited multibrid of exceptional merit in showy, large, pink blossoms.

Plate 238. *Malus* 'Starlight' is a heavy bloomer whose starlike blossoms have prominent yellow anther centers.

Plate 239. The fragrant white blossoms of *M.* 'Sugar Tyme' are showy in spring as are the small, red fruit in fall.

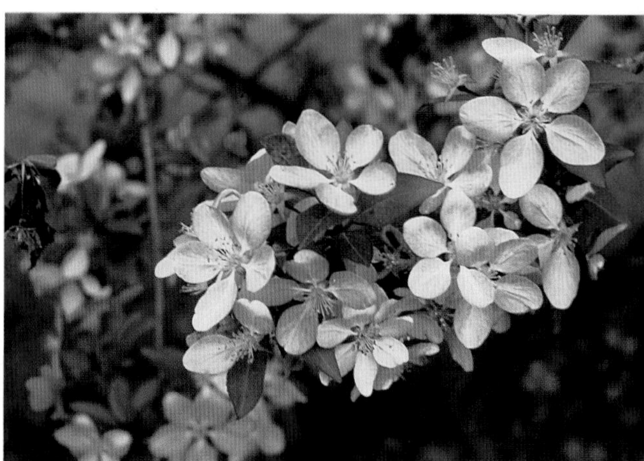

Plate 240. *Malus* 'Timiskaming' blossom, one of Isabella Preston's Lake Series.

Plate 241. *Malus* 'White Cascade', one of the finest of the new fountainlike weeping crabapples, in white bloom.

Plate 242. *Malus* 'White Cascade' is truly magnificent in pink buds.

Plate 243. *Malus* 'White Cascade' fruit.

Plate 244. *Malus* 'Wildfire', an attractive semiweeper, has bright red buds that open to pink flowers. The fruit also is red.

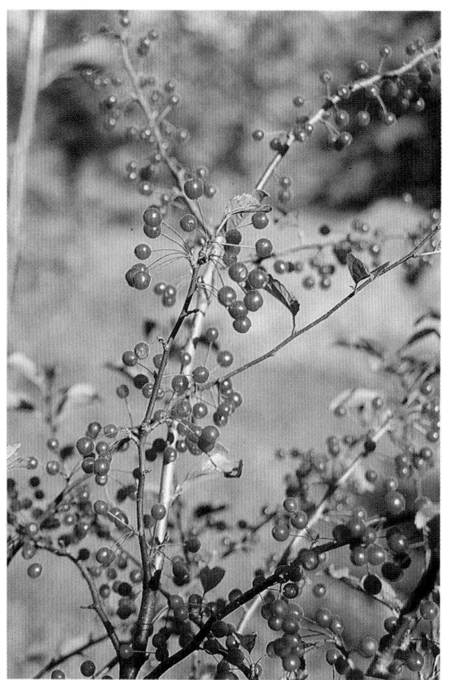

Plate 245. *Malus* 'Yuletide', one of the finest mini-fruited trees, will be popular with landscapers for its spring bloom, fall fruit, and small size.

CHAPTER 11

Botanical List of Crabapple Species

The following list of crabapples presents the accepted botanical species with their related varieties, hybrids, and named clones. Each of the crabapples described in this chapter is of documented authentic origin; that is, the original type plant or the parent plants are known. Named clones of documented authentic origin are listed in this chapter with the appropriate parent species and some of the more important clones are described in this chapter. Most named clones, however, are described in Chapter 12, which lists all the named clones, whether their origin is known or not, in alphabetical order.

Names and Descriptions. Over the years much consideration has been given to naming new species and to reclassifying older names and variants. Today, most members of the scientific community accept the classification of the genus *Malus* presented by Alfred Rehder, with some differences as to groups and individual species. It is my opinion, together with several taxonomists and botanists, that Rehder may have been too ready to name every variation, giving many of them species or subspecies rank. Thus, the list of accepted species presented in this chapter departs from Rehder in the number and classification of valid species and subspecies, particularly in the North American species, relegating some of Rehder's taxa to varietal or clonal rank.

The reader will quickly note that some of the species and clones described in this chapter have conflicting descriptions. Unless, as Donald Wyman and Roland Jefferson pointed out, a plant is propagated by asexual means, seedlings can vary considerably from desirable horticultural plants to discards, yet all of them bear the same name. Because crabapples so readily hybridize by wind-borne and insect-borne pollen, it is often impossible even for experts to determine the exact classification of a plant, not to mention its exact parentage.

Great abuse has arisen by nurseries planting random, open-pollinated seed of a given species, then treating all seedlings as equal. In fact, it is still common practice in some nurseries to plant open-pollinated species seed. One then sees why a given species grown from seed is outstanding in one location while at another, a mile away, it may be quite inferior and even different. Professor Lester Nichols once told me that in his study of crabapple diseases he found at least five different clones bearing the name *Malus* 'Winter Gold', all asexually propagated. He never determined which was the real clone! Professor Nichols added that he had come across this same situation many times with other named clones as well as with seed-sown species and subspecies.

Much of taxonomy is dependent on the examination and careful description of herbarium specimens. But what plant of a species did the first collector gather? Was it a typical specimen generally representative of the whole species, or was it a particular variant that struck the plant explorer's eye? Was it truly typical—a valid sample—or was it merely one of several possible variations within the species?

Some years ago I made a study of selfed species seed. To ascertain how much variation exists in a species, I planted three separate seedling beds, each one containing approximately 1000 seedlings of *Malus sieboldii*. Much more variation existed than what I expected. At least 112 of the 3000 seedlings were notable variations from the taxonomic description of the species, and another 25 seedlings were mutations. These same variants exist in nature. Since the taxonomic description of a species often rests on the first specimen prepared by a collector, one must realize that a number of variants exist for that species, all of which still fit the general species description. Only in the asexually propagated, named clones is there real stability.

There exists today a new field of plant selection in which selfed species seed is planted on a large scale, then the best horticultural plants are selected, not necessarily representative of the species type. These specially selected plants with outstanding characteristics should be given a clonal name; they should not be offered as the typical specimen.

Those who hybridize for any length of time (over 50 years in my case) come to evaluate the particular clone used in hybridizing rather than the description for the species. Minor variations, such as individual disease resistance, become very important in gene transmission for better or poorer plant progeny. In-depth study of a species points to a common geographical center for that species from which radiates, in widening circles, the number of variations, especially those produced by geographic and climatic influences. Often a chromosome count of the variation shows a difference of one or more chromosomes, or their parts, that account for the deviation from the species. In *Paeonia brownii*, for example, the chromosome number increases as one sees the species in its native California slowly spread northward, but are these variants therefore a different species?

Today the chromosome count of individual plants and species is an observable factor. It should be included in the taxonomic description of every species and its variants. At present, only a general counting of the chromosomes of the flowering crabapples in the genus *Malus* has been made. Yet, comparing the North American species with close, supposedly related species or their subspecies shows an interesting relationship between some of them (see reclassification of *M. coronaria* in Chapter 10). These variations attest to the adaptability of the species and may be given subspecies rank, but they fall short of being separate, independent species.

In the North American crabapple species, and in some Asiatic species as well, too much importance has sometimes been given to minor botanical variants. Many of these variants have been graced with unnecessary botanical names when they should have received varietal or cultivar status. Realizing the difference of opinions among taxonomists, botanists, and geneticists, the present volume gives both classifications—Rehder's standard classification of the genus *Malus* and a new reclassification by the author. The reclassification does not intend to settle any taxonomic arguments but rather to present an accepted, although not unanimously, presentation of flowering crabapples that is practical, scientific, and understandable. Some of the academic classifications do not have verifiable, living counterparts, but exist only as herbarium specimens or, at times, only as written descriptions of long-lost herbarium specimens. The following list simply presents all the names, accepted and rejected, with as much pertinent information as was available at the time of writing.

After more scientific research and thoughtful study, hopefully taxonomists, together with botanists and plant geneticists, will agree on a final order or proper species, subspecies, varieties, and clonal names for the genus *Malus*. Then may all the true crabapples live happily ever after! Until then, the following botanical list is given with all its inherent flaws but counting all the botanical members as present, at least as many as could be ascertained as being legitimate.

The description accompanying a botanical name is the one accepted by the person who first described the plant correctly according to the rule of international nomenclature. I have not listed all the variant names by succeeding taxonomists or botanists, interesting though they may be. Since only the first adequately described name is the valid name, I have felt it an encumbrance to list all the scientific names subsequently added to that species. For such historical nomenclature the reader is referred to the works of Alfred Rehder, L. H. Bailey, and others. What the species was once called matters very little, except to taxonomists; what it is called today is of importance.

Evaluations and Recommendations. Some crabapples, especially those that no longer exist or those that are grown only as a single plant in a given collection, are listed with no description or, at best, a minimal description. Others, the better-known crabapples, are described and evaluated for beauty of bloom and autumn fruit. When known, a rating for disease resistance is given. Faults, such as proneness to disease, overly large fruit size, and alternate blooming, are noted as are suggestions for landscape value and/or hybridization. The ratings are as follows:

Excellent	Superior in every way: flowering annually, good fruit color, disease resistant
Recommended	Superior for a special reason (e.g., double flowers, very rare, exceptional hybridizing value) or outstanding in bloom, fruiting, or autumn leaf color despite minor disease susceptibility
Good	Satisfactory in flowering and fruit color but slightly susceptible to apple disease
Not recommended	Having too many negative factors to be continued in commerce or for landscaping use
Name only	Known by name only; no, or very limited, information available

Throughout the descriptions, "excellent" crabapples are marked with an asterisk (*) and "recommended" crabapples are marked with a plus sign (+).

At times a crabapple is designated "excellent" for a very special reason: it may be unusual in double flowers or very rare. It may have slightly larger fruit (making it excellent for highway planting since small fruit cannot be seen by fast-traveling vehicles), or it may be so outstanding in bloom, fruiting, or autumn leaf color that it merits recommendation despite minor disease susceptibility. Some crabapples are recommended solely because they have outstanding hybridizing value. A few are so unique that one could build a whole new race of flowering crabapples using them as foundation breeders. Other crabapples are recommended because they are representative of advanced, induced polyploids that have only very recently been created and introduced.

A few crabapples designated "good" will be acceptable because of outstanding annual bloom, although they may have poor or no fruit (e.g., some of the double-flowering crabapples) or be slightly susceptible to minor diseases (e.g., may have some leaf spot but are not injured or defoliated by it). Plants subject to considerable defoliation, fire blight, large fruit, early fruit rot, and alternate-year blooming are placed on the "not recommended" list.

In recommending or evaluating a species or a clone I have combined the recommendations of many experts from the past and the present, although they do not always agree in their opinions and evaluations. Included in this group are crabapple pioneers such as Arie den Boer, Roland Jefferson, Alfred Rehder, Charles Sargent, and Wheelock Wilson; crabapple authorities of today such as Robert Clark, John den Boer, Thomas Green, Ed Hasselkus, Robert Lyons, Henry Ross, and John Sabuco; and crabapple hybridizers such as Donald Egolf, Carl Hansen, Niels Hansen, Isabella Preston, and Robert Simpson. Naturally I also have included my own observations over the past 50 years.

Disease Ratings. Disease-resistance ratings are taken mostly from the many annual reports published by the late Professor Lester Nichols. Titled *Disease Resistant Crabapples*, this work is undoubtedly one of the monumental studies on the susceptibility to disease of various clones. Not only did Nichols' study examine a large number of crabapples in many different locations, but it covered several years. The disease-resistance ratings of newer clones not rated by Nichols are based on information supplied by the plant introducer and the nursery propagating the clone.

It is important to remember that not all crabapples do well in every location. A concern that Professor Nichols and I often discussed was the variability of many crabapples that are completely disease resistant in the drier midwestern and eastern United States but show some disease susceptibility when planted in areas of greater moisture or heavy rainfalls. It would be wrong to list a crabapple as susceptible to some or all diseases simply because in one geographic area it does not perform well. To be fair to any given plant introduction, eventually crabapples will have to be rated by specific areas of the country. Until then, all ratings remain rather subjective and of limited use. They do, however, help weed out the most offending clones and point out those that appear to be superior. A crabapple's performance in local arboretum collections, propagating nurseries, and large private plantings is the best indicator of disease susceptibility and general evaluation of that crabapple.

Where nursery ratings for disease are given, the question arises as to the validity of these ratings since spraying programs are a general rule because of the nursery's need to produce healthy stock. The resistance or susceptibility to disease, under more or less sterile nursery conditions, cannot validly determine the real disease resistance of any crabapple for the home owner who never sprays ornamental landscaping. This was a continuing problem Professor Nichols faced in his ratings. A few nurseries maintain a special "no spray" testing plot to determine the susceptibility of their plants to disease, but most nurseries use extensive, routine sprayings and are as disease sterile as a hospital ward because of fear of any contaminating diseases.

In addition to leaning very heavily on the studies of the late Professor Nichols, I also have relied on Charles Powell and on the judgment of crabapple growers and outstanding nursery professionals like Norbert Kinen, Roy and Sarah Klehm, Michael Scott, Keith Warren, Michael Yanny, and James Zampini. Their combined observations have been an education in evaluation, since they see flowering crabapples from so many different viewpoints.

Locations. Many descriptions include numbers corresponding to locations where specimen trees can be found. For a list of these numbers and the places they represent, see "Key to Crabapple Locations" (Appendix 5).

M. ×adstringens Zabel ex Rehder
Parentage: *M. baccata* × *M. pumila*
Introduced in 1910 from China. Leaves pubescent; flowers mostly pink to pinkish, on short stalks, with villous calyx; fruit usually subglobose, to 2 in (5 cm) in diameter, red, yellow, or green, with rather short stalks. Particularly susceptible to most apple diseases. Has a number of clones in culture, including *M.* 'Hopa', *M.* 'Hyslop', *M.* 'Martha', and *M.* 'Transcendent'.

Hybrids of *M. baccata* with *M. pumila* (such as *M. ×adstringens*) are large trees with considerable spread. Although their bloom time may be somewhat outstanding, the leaf blights, scab, rusts, and other diseases that mostly disfigure the leaves of these hybrids in summer and their rather large fruit prohibit recommending most of the hybrid progeny, either for ornamental use or for hybridization. The large, fallen, diseased fruit causes problems especially when trees are planted close to houses or along the street. The need for routine spraying to keep the trees from being defoliated in summer militates against recommendation of their continued propagation. Newer cultivars, highly resistant to diseases, have already supplanted these older hybrids for all landscaping uses.

M. angustifolia
See *M. coronaria* var. *angustifolia*.

***M. angustifolia* 'Pendula'**
See *M. coronaria* var. *angustifolia* 'Pendula'.

***M. angustifolia* 'Plena'**
See *M. ioensis* 'Prince Georges'.

M. apetela Schneider
Parentage: A clone of *M. pumila*
A petalless apple of no value. A worthless clone that never should have been named. A biological deformation or a mutant.

*****M. ×arnoldiana*** (Rehder) Sargent
Plates 29, 30, 31
Synonym: *M. floribunda* var. *arnoldiana* Rehder
Trade name: Arnold crabapple
Parentage: *M. baccata* × *M. floribunda*
Originated as a chance seedling at the Arnold Arboretum circa 1883. Introduced by the arboretum as No. 139-1. Originally named *M. floribunda* var. *arnoldiana* by Alfred Rehder in 1909; renamed *M. ×arnoldiana* by Charles Sargent in 1920.

A large, upright, spreading tree to 25 ft (8 m) high and 35 ft (11 m) wide, with long, pendulous branches; leaf edges have a very slight wave; buds dark red, on long stems, opening to large, abundant flowers 2 in (5 cm) across, pink fading to white-pink, single; fruit oval, yellow with a faint pink or red blush, 0.4–0.6 in (1–1.5 cm) wide and 0.5–0.6 in (1.2–1.5 cm) long, with a flattened calyx end.

Because this is an alternate bloomer and subject to diseases, Lester Nichols believed it should be phased out, but I would find this difficult to do for it is very floriferous. If I had a large estate or arboretum, I would find a corner to keep this venerable matriarch that has been used extensively in hybridization. Many of its progeny are outstanding (see list below), but when one carefully examines these cultivars, their good points are attributable to the other crabapple involved in the cross and not to *M. ×arnoldiana*. Although at one time this hybrid was a popular clone, it is no longer recommended for continued propagation because it is too large, an alternate bearer, and subject to disease. As a historic crabapple it might be carried by the larger arboreta, but it is not for the smaller garden or for any landscape design today. Loc. 4, 8, 10, 12, 13, 14, 18, 24, 26, 31, 32, 41, 43, 55, 61, 68, 69, 73, 79, 85.

Progeny of *M. ×arnoldiana* include the following:

- *M.* 'Barbara Ann' Wyman
- *M.* 'Cardinal' Wellington
- *M.* 'Dorothea' Wyman
- *M.* 'Henrietta Crosby' Sax
- *M.* 'Henry F. Dupont' Sax
- *M.* 'Linda' A. den Boer
- *M.* 'Van Eseltine' New York Experiment Station—Geneva

M. asiatica
See *M. prunifolia* var. *rinki*.

M. ×astracanica Dumont de Courset
Synonym: *M.* 'Astrachan'
Parentage: *M. pumila* × *M. prunifolia*
Known in Europe since 1700s. Leaves sharper and more serrate than those of *M.*

pumila; fruit bright red. Of no ornamental value or any horticultural importance. Subject to severe scab. Loc. 12, 32, 35, 54.

M. atropurpurea
See *M.* 'Jay Darling' in Chapter 12.

M. ×atrosanguinea (Späth) Schneider Plates 32, 33, 34, 35, Fig. 6.1
Trade name: Carmine crabapple
Parentage: *M. halliana* × *M. toringo*
An elegant natural hybrid with deep carmine buds, spreading form, and deep pink-rose blossoms. One of the cherished older crabapples. Introduced into the United States by the Arnold Arboretum in 1889.

A medium-sized, spreading tree 15–18 ft (4.6–5.5 m) high and 25 ft (8 m) wide, with very picturesque branching if allowed multiple trunks; leaves very dark green; buds deep carmine, opening to single, rose-to-light pink flowers, abundant, 1 in (2.5. cm) across; fruit small, red-yellow (or green-yellow, according to another source), not particularly showy.

Although the fruit of this hybrid is insignificant by modern standards, the carmine buds are an effective contrast to the pink flowers, and the springtime show of magnificent blossoms makes this tree a standard specimen crabapple. It is a dependable annual bloomer and resistant to most diseases, except moderate scab. This fine ornamental should be used for springtime background color. It is not suitable for the small garden. It makes an excellent multitrunked specimen in the winter landscape and probably could be used effectively in hybridizing programs. Loc. 2, 14, 15, 18, 20, 22, 26, 31, 35, 40, 43, 47, 53, 54, 55, 61, 68, 69, 71, 79, 80, 81, 86, 89.

M. aurea
See *M. pumila* 'Aurea' in Chapter 12.

*+***M. baccata*** (Linnaeus) Borkhausen Plate 36
Trade name: Siberian crabapple
Named by Carl Linnaeus in 1767. Introduced into Europe from Siberia in 1784 by the Royal Botanic Gardens, Kew, England. Seed was sent from the vicinity of Hailar, Manchuria, by H. G. MacMillan and J. L. Stephens to the Plant Industry, USDA, on 23 November 1934. USDA plant introduction No. 1076683.

One of the first crabapples to come into springtime bloom. Bears some of the smallest fruit. A rounded, upright tree with spreading branches and slender branchlets, up to 40 ft (12 m) high and equally as wide, extremely hardy, with a strong root system; leaves good; buds creamy pink to pinkish, opening in a great profusion of single, pure white, delightfully fragrant flowers on abundant fruiting spurs, 1.2–1.6 in (3–4 cm) across; fruit red (in some forms yellow to yellow-brown), 0.4 in (1 cm) in diameter, borne in great quantities on long, thin stems.

Native to northern parts of eastern Siberia, southward into Mongolia and northern China, this species is the most northerly flowering crabapple. It is undoubtedly the hardiest of all species in the genus *Malus*, an excellent annual bloomer with abundant autumn fruit, and highly resistant to most apple diseases, except for moderate scab. It has played an important role in modern hybridization programs.

When grown from seed, *M. baccata* is quite variable so the best clones should be named and propagated asexually. Donald Wyman noted, "Many plants growing in America were introduced as seed from abroad, hence their trueness to name is subject to question." Some confusion has been caused because of the many varietal forms and hybrids associated with this species. In a few collections, trees labeled *M. baccata* have no *M. baccata* blood in them (A. den Boer, pers. com.). In general, true Siberian crabapples are characterized by entirely smooth young shoots and smooth leaves (on both sides) with no incisions. The only exception is *M. baccata* var. *mandshurica*, which shows a slight hairiness on its leaves, especially on young shoots.

Many of the newer flowering crabapples that have some *M. baccata* blood in them are hybrids of great beauty with abundant annual fruiting. In general, *M. baccata* has limited usefulness in modern landscaping because the tree is too large for small gardens. Some of its selected clones (e.g., *M. baccata* 'Halward'), however, are smaller trees suitable for any garden. The species has value to modern hybridizers because of its extreme hardiness, its very early bloom untouched by early frosts, and its fine, colorful, small fruit. In the past, *M. baccata* was used considerably by hybridizers, including P. H. S. Brooks, N. E. Hansen, W. L. Kerr, W. L. Leslie, W. T. Macoun, I. Preston, and F. L. Skinner. Crossed with *M. pumila* 'Niedzwetzkyana', it has produced a great number of red-flowering, red-purple fruiting crabapples known as the Rosyblooms, one of the largest groups of any hybrid cross except for the modern multibrids (see *M. pumila* 'Niedzwetzkyana' for more information about the Rosyblooms). Loc. 2, 3, 8, 9, 10, 14, 15, 24, 26, 31, 35, 37, 47, 61, 81.

Over the years botanists and taxonomists have differed greatly as to the exact name and number of forms of *Malus baccata*. For example, in his card file notes on flowering crabapples at the Arnold Arboretum, Alfred Rehder listed "*M. baccata* var. *microcarpa*—sent to the Arnold Arboretum from Russia in 1889," synonym *M. baccata*. Rehder also noted that "seed collected as *M. baccata* by F. Meyer = *M. sieboldii* var. *zumi*." Today, the clones of *M. baccata* described below generally are accepted.

Species crosses of *M. baccata* include the following:

M. ×*adstringens* (*M. baccata* × *M. pumila*)
M. ×*arnoldiana* (*M. baccata* × *M. floribunda*)
M. ×*hartwigii* (*M. baccata* × *M. halliana*)
M. ×*micromalus* (*M. baccata* × *M. spectabilis*)
M. ×*robusta* (*M. baccata* × *M. prunifolia*)
M. sieboldii (formerly *M.* ×*zumi*) (*M. baccata* × *M. toringo*)

Named clones of *M. baccata* include the following:

M. 'Adam'
M. 'Alberta'
M. 'Albright'
M. 'Alexis'
M. 'Almey'
M. 'Alred'
M. 'Altagold'
M. 'Amsib'
M. 'Amur'
M. 'Ann Trio'
M. 'Arctic Dawn'
M. 'Athabasca'
M. 'Babine'
M. 'Barbara Ann'
M. 'Baskatong'
M. 'Beauty'
M. 'Big River'
M. 'Boom'
M. 'Brier'
M. 'Caputa'
M. 'Cardinal'
M. 'Carleton'
M. 'Centennial'
M. 'Columbia'
M. 'Columnaris'
M. 'Cranberry'
M. 'Crimson Brilliant'
M. 'Currant'
M. 'Dan Trio'
M. 'David Nairn'
M. 'Dolgo'
M. 'Dorothea'
M. 'Elsa'
M. 'Elsie Burgess'
M. 'Erl Trio'
M. 'Fairy'
M. 'Fay Trio'
M. 'Foxley'
M. 'Gibb'
M. 'Goldfinch'
M. 'Goolsbey'
M. 'Gracilis'
M. 'Halward'
M. 'Hampton's Siberian'
M. 'Hans Trio'
M. 'Heart River'
M. 'Helen'
M. 'Henrietta Crosby'
M. 'Henry F. DuPont'
M. 'Hopa'
M. 'Huron'
M. 'Irene'
M. 'Ivan'
M. 'Jackii'
M. 'Jay Darling'
M. 'Jewell'
M. 'Joan'
M. 'Joe Trio'
M. 'Jubilee'
M. 'Katherine'
M. 'Keo'
M. 'Kerr'
M. 'Lady Northcliffe'
M. 'Lee Trio'
M. 'Linda'
M. 'Martha'
M. 'Martha-Dolgo'
M. 'McPrince'
M. 'Mecca'
M. 'Mecca-Dolgo'
M. 'Midnight'
M. 'Milo'
M. 'Mount Arbor Special'
M. 'Muskoka'
M. 'Namew'
M. 'Nipissing'
M. 'Northland'
M. 'Olga'
M. 'Osman'
M. 'Patricia'
M. 'Paul Imperial'
M. 'Pink Beauty'
M. 'Pink Giant'
M. 'Prince'
M. 'Printosh'
M. 'Purple Wave'
M. 'Radiant'
M. 'Redflesh'
M. 'Red Heart'
M. 'Red River'
M. 'Red Silver'
M. 'Red Splendor'
M. 'Robert Nairn'
M. 'Robin'
M. ×*robusta* No. 5
M. ×*robusta* 'Gary's Choice'
M. ×*robusta* 'Persicifolia'
M. 'Rosilda'
M. 'Royalty'
M. 'Rudolph'
M. 'Sapina'
M. 'Saska'
M. 'Selkirk'
M. 'September'
M. 'Shaker Gold'
M. 'Silvia'
M. 'Simcoe'
M. 'Sissipuk'
M. 'Snowcap'
M. 'South Dakota Ben'
M. 'South Dakota Bison'
M. 'South Dakota Eda'
M. 'South Dakota Jonsib'
M. 'South Dakota Macata'
M. 'Spring Snow'
M. 'Sundog'
M. 'Taliak'
M. 'Tanner'
M. 'Timiskaming'
M. 'Toba'
M. 'Tolsteme'
M. 'Toshprince'
M. 'University'
M. 'Van Eseltine'
M. 'Vanguard'
M. 'Wabiskaw'
M. 'Walters'
M. 'White Fox River'
M. 'Whitney'
M. 'Yellow Siberian'
M. 'Zaza'
M. 'Zelma'
M. 'Zita'

Varietal names of *Malus baccata* no longer accepted include the following:

M. baccata aurantiaca Regel—A plant exists at the Morton Arboretum differing from others. A clone that has not been described.
M. baccata cerasifera (Spach) Koidzumi—A plant exists at the Morton Arboretum differing from others. A clone that has not been described.
M. baccata cerasiformis Borkhausen
M. baccata ceratocarpa Borkhausen
M. baccata conocarpa
M. baccata costata Borkhausen
M. baccata domestica (Spach) Likh.
M. baccata edulis Borkhausen
M. baccata flava Borkhausen—Synonym: *M. baccata* 'Yellow Siberian'
M. baccata flavescens Borkhausen
M. baccata fructu-lutea Borkhausen
M. baccata lasiostyla Borkhausen

M. baccata latiofolia Matsumura
M. baccata latiostyla Borkhausen
M. baccata lutea
M. baccata macrocarpa
M. baccata microcarpa Borkhausen
M. baccata obconoides Regel
M. baccata oblonga Borkhausen
M. baccata praecox Borkhausen
M. baccata pruniformis Borkhausen
M. baccata sanguinea
M. baccata siberica Borkhausen
M. baccata striata Borkhausen

M. baccata var. ***himalaica*** (Maximowicz) Schneider

Synonyms: *M. himalaica, M.* 'Himalaica'

Trade name: Himalayan crabapple

Introduced circa 1917. Native of western Himalayas and southeastern China. Wild seed collected by Joseph Rock, 1933, in Yetsi Valley, Muli territory, Szechwan, China. USDA plant introduction No. 103288.

A pyramidal tree when young, becoming rounded with age; "showy white blossoms; attractive berrylike red or yellow fruit" (Alfred Rehder). One of the best forms of *M. baccata* for disease resistance. Loc. 31, 35, 37, 47, 54.

M. baccata* var. ***mandshurica*** (Maximowicz) Schneider

Synonym: *M. mandshurica*

Trade name: Manchurian crabapple

An excellent showy crabapple, perhaps the earliest to bloom. Introduced from China to England in 1824 and to the Arnold Arboretum in 1882. Introduced to the United States in 1910.

Flowers white, to 0.5 in (1.2 cm) across, fragrant; fruit very small, to 0.5 in (1.2 cm) in diameter, deep red, although a yellow form is reputed. Subject to moderate scab and mildew (Nichols).

Since this variety was introduced, the Sino-American plant explorations in 1980–1981 have brought back new forms of *M. baccata*, some from extremely southern locations in China. Among these new plants are the beautiful *M. baccata* 'Alexander' and *M. baccata* 'Spongberg'. Both are outstanding in blossom and fruit and are now being used by hybridizers to add genetic vigor to the newer crabapples.

In the same Sino-American plant explorations, seed of variety *mandshurica* was brought from China to the United States, where is was grown by Donald Egolf at the National Arboretum, Washington, DC. Several very interesting seedlings were selected by Egolf, some of which were sent to the Falconskeape Gardens, Medina, OH, to enhance the author's breeding material. Many of these selections of variety *mandshurica* are showing considerable promise with smaller, brilliant red fruit, excellent growth habit, and disease resistance. They should soon be showing some outstanding progeny by hybridization. All the very best clones should be named, asexually propagated, and identified so their particularly fine characteristics might be retained. When they are unnamed, they soon become a seedling lot and are propagated by seed, thus their unique properties are lost. Loc. 9, 14, 18, 26, 31, 35, 37, 47, 54, 69, 79.

M. baccata var. ***mandshurica*** **'Midwest'**

See *M.* 'Midwest' in Chapter 12.

*+***M. baccata*** **'Alexander'** Fiala Plate 37

A seedling selected at Falconskeape Gardens, Medina, OH, from a group of seedlings obtained from the Arnold Arboretum's Sino-American botanical expedition (SABE) to China in 1980. One plant of Arnold Arboretum No. 1843-80, the same group from which *M. baccata* 'Spongberg' was selected; this seed was collected from the southernmost region of China where *M. baccata* had not been known to be native—the Shennongjia Forest District—specifically, the south end of the Loyang Riber Gorge near Pingquan, 4265 ft (1300 m), 31°30′ N, 110°30′ E, SABE No. 1298, 14 September 1980. This seed could belong to a different species because of its most southern origin, but it appears to belong to *M. baccata*. Similar seedlings at the Arnold Arboretum also have superior clones from the same seedling group (as yet unnamed).

A small, upright to slightly rounded tree to 12 ft (3.5 m) high in 10 years; leaves green, excellent, disease free; buds white, opening to large, single, somewhat cupped flowers 1 in (2.5. cm) across, very handsome in abundant, annual bloom; fruit 0.6–0.8 in (1.5–2 cm) in diameter, bright red, persistent.

According to Stephen Spongberg of the Arnold Arboretum, this excellent clone "may have much to offer since it comes from the most southern region where *M. baccata* had not previously been found to be native." The clone was named to honor John H. Alexander III, propagator at the Arnold Arboretum who germinated the seed. Loc. 47, 86, 100.

M. baccata **'Alexis'**

Name only. Loc. 16.

***M. baccata* 'Aspiration'**
Name only. Disease free. Loc. 87.

***M. baccata* 'Aurantiaca'**
Name only. Disease free (Nichols). Loc. 31, 32.

***M. baccata* 'Cerasifera'**
Name only. Disease free (Nichols). Loc. 31, 81, 89.

***M. baccata* 'Columnaris'** Rehder Fig. 5.2
Trade name: Column Siberian crabapple
One of the most columnar of all the flowering crabapples. Flowers white; fruit yellow cheeked with red. Highly susceptible to fire blight; thus should be discarded and little used in hybridization. Subject to moderate to severe scab (Nichols). A large botanical collection or arboretum could carry this crabapple to maintain its existence. In reality it has little to offer; many newer hybrids are similar in form and far superior in blossom, fruit, and especially in disease resistance. Loc. 9, 13, 14, 18, 24, 26, 31, 32, 35, 37, 40, 54, 69, 77, 79, 80.

***M. baccata* 'Costata'**
Name only. Subject to moderate scab. Loc. 12, 35, 37, 54.

***M. baccata* 'Flavescens'**
Synonyms: *M. baccata* 'Fructu Flava', *M. baccata flava*
A yellow-fruited clone. Disease resistant (Nichols). Loc. 16, 31, 32.

***M. baccata* 'Flexilis'**
Similar to *M. baccata* 'Gracilis' but larger. A tree to 25 ft (8 m) high, somewhat pendulous; flowers white, abundant; an annual bloomer; fruit medium-sized, red, persistent. Good disease resistance; subject to mild scab and very mild fire blight. A very showy form of *M. baccata*. Loc. 26, 32, 54, 61.

***M. baccata* 'Fructu Flava'**
See *M. baccata* 'Flavescens'

***M. baccata* 'Gracilis'**
Trade name: Dwarf Siberian clone
Plant sent to the Arnold Arboretum in 1913 by James Veitch & Sons, Chelsea, England, from seed No. 329 collected by William Purdom in 1910 in northern China. One of the better clones of *M. baccata*.
A graceful, semiweeping tree; buds rose-pink, opening to white, starlike flowers 1.7 in (4.3 cm) across; fruit 0.3 in (0.8 cm) in diameter, dark red to red-brown. Apart from its smaller form, this obsolete clone has little to offer, and many newer hybrids are far superior in form, fruit color, and disease resistance. Loc. 9, 11, 31, 32, 54, 61, 79, 81.

*+***M. baccata* 'Halward'** Fiala 1984
Plates 18, 38, 39, 40
An outstanding clone raised from seed by Ray Halward, former plant propagator at the Royal Botanic Gardens, Hamilton, Ontario, Canada, in 1948; scions sent to Falconskeape Gardens, Medina, OH, in 1958.
A rounded tree to 15 ft (4.6 m) high by 15 ft (4.6 m) wide, rather slender but heavily branched; leaves very dark green, glossy, disease resistant; buds white, opening to single, pure white flowers in great abundance; fruit very small, 0.4 in (1 cm) in diameter, bright red, very showy, persistent. Completely disease resistant and worthy of being marketed commercially (Nichols).
An excellent, annual flowering crabapple of great beauty as it matures. It also is outstanding in small, bright red autumn fruit and glossy green disease-free foliage. One of the finest clones of *M. baccata*. Loc. 47, 100, and Royal Botanic Gardens, Hamilton, Ontario, Canada.

*+***M. baccata* 'Jackii'** Plates 41, 42, 43
Grown from scions collected in Seoul, Korea, and sent to the Arnold Arboretum by J. G. Jack in 1905. One of the better clones of *M. baccata*. Outstanding for landscape use.
A broad, upright, rounded tree to 20 ft (6 m) high and as wide; leaves longer than those of the species; buds white tinged pink, opening to excellent flowers 1.6 in (4 cm) across, larger than flowers of the species, white fragrant; fruit long-stemmed, deep red-purple or maroon-red, shaded tan on one side, small, 0.5 in (1.2 cm) in diameter. Excellent disease resistance after 10 years of testing (Nichols).
This crabapple makes a good background tree for smaller hybrids, but it is too large for the average gardener. Named for Professor Jack of the Arnold Arboretum. Loc. 5, 9, 11, 14, 18, 24, 26, 31, 37, 47, 54, 61, 69, 71, 79, 81, 86.

***M. baccata* 'Lady Northcliffe'** Aldenham House Gardens before 1929
Roland Jefferson claimed this clone was of unknown parentage, while Arie den Boer claimed it was a "selected *M. baccata* clone, introduced into the United States by the Mor-

ton Arboretum, Lisle, IL." With pink blossoms, it probably is an open-pollinated seedling of *M. baccata*.

An upright, rounded tree to 20 ft (6 m) high and as wide; buds rose-red, opening to pale pink flowers that fade to white, 1.1 in (2.7 cm) across, single; fruit yellow-orange, 0.6 in (1.5 cm) in diameter. Disease resistant after 6 years of testing (Nichols). After all the years, however, this clone remains unknown in North America. Loc. 12, 35, 81.

***M. baccata* 'Odorata'**

Name only. Extremely fragrant. Disease resistant. Loc. 31, 32.

*****M. baccata* 'Spongberg'** Fiala

A seedling selected at Falconskeape Gardens, Medina, OH, from a group of seedlings obtained from the Arnold Arboretum's Sino-American botanical expedition (SABE) to China in 1980. One plant of Arnold Arboretum No. 1843-80, the same group from which *M. baccata* 'Alexander' was selected; this seed was collected from the southernmost region of China where *M. baccata* had not been known to be native—the Shennongjia Forest District—specifically, the south end of the Loyang Riber Gorge near Pingquan, 4265 ft (1300 m), 31°30′ N, 110°30′ E, SABE No. 1298, 14 September 1980. This seed could belong to a different species because of its most southern origin, but it appears to belong to *M. baccata*. Similar seedlings at the Arnold Arboretum also have superior clones from the same seedling group (as yet unnamed).

A tree with open form; leaves bright green, glossy; buds white, opening to large, single flowers 1 in (2.5 cm) across, less cupped than the species, very showy, heavy annual bloomer; fruit bright red with slight orange tint, very showy, persistent, 0.5 in (1.2 cm) in diameter. Appears to be disease resistant.

An excellent tree that should be of interest in both landscaping and hybridizing as seed was collected from the southernmost region of China where *M. baccata* had not been known to be native. Should be used in hybridization. Named to honor Stephen Spongberg, research taxonomist and editor of the Arnold Arboretum journal. Loc. 32, 47, 86, 100.

*****M. baccata* 'Taliak'** Ross

A chance seedling of *M. baccata* discovered by Henry Ross, Gardenview Horticulture Park, Strongsville, OH. Named by the author for a prominent doctor in Strongsville, OH, on whose property the plant was originally discovered.

A tree to 15 ft (4.6 m) high and about 18 ft (5.5 m) wide, upright to rounded when young but soon spreading with the very heavy crop of somewhat larger fruit, heavily branched; leaves dark green, disease free; buds pale pink-white, opening to single, pure white flowers; fruit somewhat larger, 0.5–0.6 in (1.2–1.5 cm) in diameter, dull red to red-brown or purple-red, persistent. Completely disease free (Nichols).

This annual bearer produces extremely heavy blooms in alternate years and a light crop in off years. It is a dual purpose crabapple—its fruit is good for jellies and the tree form is very picturesque in fall and winter landscapes. Although the fruit is too large to make this excellent tree suitable for small home gardens, the tree is an excellent ornamental for backgrounds in large parks and for highway plantings. It is best after leaf fall. We were reluctant to introduce it, but were urged to do so by many who saw it in fruit. Fruiting is so heavy as to make the tree a weeper after a few years of bearing. The abundant oxblood-colored fruit is excellent if planted in front of yellow-fruiting crabapples. Loc. 31, 47, 86.

***M. baccata* 'Walters'** Flemmer

An open-pollinated seedling of *M. baccata* grown at Princeton Nurseries, Princeton, NJ. Selected as a street tree in Maplewood, NJ, for its upright habit and vigor, which exceed that of the species. Named for Richard Walters, former city arborist, Maplewood, NJ.

Leaves dark green, disease free; buds pink, opening to white, single flowers; fruit 0.4 in (1 cm) in diameter, bright red, persistent. Moller's Nursery, Gresham, OR, sold a clone by the name *M.* 'Walters' to Johnson's Nursery, Menomonee Falls, WI. It is either a form of *M. toringo* or a hybrid with yellow fruit. Since *M. baccata* 'Walters' has nomenclatural precedence, I have listed this second *M.* 'Walters' as *M.* 'Johnson's Walters' (which see).

***M. baccata* 'Yellow Siberian'** N. E. Hansen

Synonyms: *M.* 'Argentea', *M. baccata flava*, *M.* 'Flava'

A clone or most probably a hybrid of *M. baccata*. Fruit gold. Subject to severe scab (Nichols). Loc. 54.

Progeny of *M. baccata* 'Yellow Siberian' include *M. baccata* 'Hans Trio' N. E. Hansen.

M. bracteata Rehder

See *M. coronaria* var. *bracteata*.

***M. brevipes* Rehder Fig. 11.1

Trade name: Nippon crabapple

A species or, most probably, a hybrid of unknown origin, closely related to or a variety of *M. floribunda*. Introduced into cultivation in 1883. A small or medium-sized tree or shrub of lower and denser habit than *M. floribunda*; leaves smaller, more closely serrate, with shorter, spreading teeth; flowers single, nearly white on glabrous pedicels, about 0.4 in (1 cm) long, petals oval; fruit subglobose, 0.4 in (1 cm) in diameter, slightly ribbed, bright red, not pulpy at maturity, on stiff, upright stalks (based on Alfred Rehder's description). According to Arie den Boer, this crabapple forms "a stiffly branched compact bush or a very small tree." Should be phased out because of too much disease (Nichols).

This species is not commonly grown or available except as scions from the collection of a larger arboretum. It could well be used by hybridizers to produce smaller, shrublike cultivars. It deserves more attention because of its small size and small, very bright red fruit. Loc. 16, 24, 32, 79, 87.

M. cerasifera

See *M.* ×*robusta*.

M. coronaria (Linnaeus) Miller Plate 44

Synonym: *Pyrus coronaria* Linnaeus

Trade names: American crabapple, Wild sweet crabapple

Widely distributed over the eastern half of the United States, from New York to Alabama and westward to eastern Indiana. Has a number of subspecies or varieties. Often becomes a rather large, widely limbed tree, mostly found in small thickets. Alone it may grow to 30 ft (9 m) high or more and equally as broad. It is somewhat difficult to transplant as it gets older and, like all crabapples, is best grown on its own roots or medium-growing rootstock. (It is the author's opinion that *M. pumila* should never be used as a rootstock because of the many diseases it transmits.)

"Bracts tomentose at first; leaves ovate to ovate-long, acute, usually rounded at the base, 5–10 cm long, irregularly serrate and usually slightly lobed . . . floccose-tomentose when young, finally glabrous, green beneath" (Alfred Rehder). Buds deep pink, opening to single flowers that are light pink to pink-white or even salmon-pink, delightfully fragrant, one of the strongest fragrances of all crabapples. "Fruit is depressed-globose, about 3 cm across, ribbed at apex, greenish" (Rehder). Highly susceptible to scab and cedar-apple rust (as are all its forms).

Figure 11.1. *Malus brevipes* (Nippon crabapple), a smaller, spreading tree rarely seen except in larger collections, is closely related to *M. floribunda*.

Although this species and its forms are not recommended for home planting because of their susceptibility to disease, they are a truly unique and beautiful group of crabapples, especially the double-flowering clones, which are among the most beautiful flowering and the most strongly fragrant crabapples. Late bloomers, they have a unique, strong fragrance not found in any other species. Much should be done to preserve them and seek out more disease-resistant clones (e.g., *M. coronaria* 'Coralglow'). Research should be directed to improving and saving this truly unique North American species, which is fast disappearing from the countryside and is found only in the largest arboretum collections. The species and its varietal forms are not offered by any nurseries we could find. Few arboreta carry any of the single forms. Most of them can be found only at the Morton Arboretum and the Boerner Botanical Gardens. Loc. 14, 31, 35.

The best of the *M. coronaria* group would be the following: *M. coronaria* var. *dasycalyx* 'Charlottae', *M. coronaria* var. *glaucescens*, *M. coronaria* var. *lancifolia*, *M. coronaria* 'Coralglow', *M. coronaria* 'Elk River', and *M. coronaria* 'Nieuwland'. Considerable hybridization is needed in this group and would have great promise.

Species crosses of *M. coronaria* include the following:

M. coronaria var. *platycarpa* (*M. coronaria* var. *lancifolia* × *M. pumila*)

M. ×*heterophylla* (*M. coronaria* × *M. pumila*)

M. coronaria* var. *angustifolia (Wenzig) Fiala

Synonym: *M. angustifolia* (Aiton) Michaux

Trade name: Southern crabapple

A southern form of *M. coronaria* with 68 chromosomes and extremely fragrant flowers. Native of southeastern United States, from Virginia to Florida and westward into Mississippi. It was classified by Nathaniel Britton as *M. coronaria*.

André Michaux described it thus:

> A tree rarely 30 feet high with a short trunk 8″ to 10″ in diameter, rigid, spreading, rarely slender and pendulous . . . Flowers about 1″ in diameter, very fragrant on slender glabrous or rarely puberulous pedicels, ¾ to 1″ long, in mostly 3–5 flowered clusters; . . . petals oblong-ovate, gradually narrowed below into a long claw, rose colored about ¼″ wide; stamens shorter than petals; styles 5 united at base, villous below the middle; fruit depressed-globose, pale yellow-green, ¾″ to 1″ in diameter.

Alfred Rehder described it thus:

> Shrub or tree to 10 m. with slender branches; lvs. ovate-oblong, oblong or lance-oblong, obtuse or acutish, usually broad-cuneate, 3–7 cm. long, coarsely crenate-serrate or sometimes nearly entire, rarely more sharply serrate, glabrous and light green beneath, usually turning brown in drying . . . under favorable conditions half-evergreen; flowers 2.5 cm. across (single, pink); fruit subglobose or sometimes higher than broad, 1.5–2.5 cm. across, greenish.

Should be phase out—susceptible to both scab and fire blight (Nichols). Loc. 35, 68.

M. coronaria var. ***angustifolia* 'Pendula'** Rehder

Synonym: *M. angustifolia* 'Pendula'

"With slender, pendulous branches." This pendulous form is very difficult to find in cultivation and is most probably a lost clone.

M. coronaria var. ***angustifolia* 'Plena'**

See *M. ioensis* 'Prince Georges'.

M. coronaria var. ***angustifolia* 'Prince Georges'**

See *M. ioensis* 'Prince Georges'.

M. coronaria var. ***bracteata*** Fiala Plates 45, 46

Synonyms: *M. bracteata*, *M.* 'Buncombe'

A natural tetraploid with 68 chromosomes. Very similar to *M. coronaria*. Most probably *M. bracteata* is not a true species but a varietal form of *M. coronaria*. The great similarities to and wide distribution of *M. coronaria* argue well for one or two native species with regional climatic and natural hybrid variations. Alfred Rehder (quoted in Sargent 1926) described the tree's history:

> Syn. *Pyrus bracteata* (Rehd.) Bailey, a native American crabapple found wild from Missouri south to Georgia, also called the 'Buncombe Crab', grown from seed sent in 1912 to the Arnold Arboretum by B. F. Bush and C. P. Sargent from Campbell, MO.

A medium-sized tree, widely branched; buds flesh pink, opening to pale pink flowers about 1.2–1.6 in (3–4 cm) across, single, fragrant. Rehder further described the variety thus:

> Leaves less lobed (than *M. coronaria*), those of flowering bracts elliptic-ovate to oblong, abruptly acute or obtusish, sparingly serrate or sometimes entire, those of shoots slightly lobed, pubescent when young, soon glabrous, green or pale beneath.

Because this late-blooming crabapple is susceptible to rust disease, moderate scab, and fire blight, it is not recommended for smaller (i.e., home) gardens. Loc. 14, 31, 32, 54.

M. coronaria var. ***dasycalyx*** (Rehder) Fernald Plate 47

Synonym: *M. dasycalyx*

Trade name: Great Lakes crabapple

Found from southern Ontario to Ohio and Indiana. Introduced into cultivation about 1920. Leaves paler beneath, those of shoots sometimes pubescent on the veins; calyx villous; flowers rose-pink, single, 1.4 in (3.5 cm) across, very fragrant, but otherwise much like the species. No horticultural value; too much disease. Loc. 18, 31, 54.

M. coronaria var. ***dasycalyx* 'Charlottae'** (Rehder) Fiala Plate 48

An excellent form of *M. coronaria* var. *dasycalyx* with large, semidouble flowers. Similar to the species. Discovered by E. de Wolf as a natural seedling near Waukegan, IL, in 1902, and named to honor his wife.

A tree becoming broad-branched with age; buds buff-apricot, opening to light pink flowers 2 in (5 cm) in diameter, semidouble to double, with 12–20 petals (half as many as *M.* 'Bechtel'); fruit green to green-yellow, with a slight bluish bloom, 0.25–1.25 in (0.6–3 cm) in diameter. Subject to rusts and fire blight (as are all the clones of *M. coronaria* and most of its varieties. Should be phased out—too much disease (Nichols).

Although beautiful, fragrant, and late blooming, *M. coronaria* var. *dasycalyx* 'Charlottae' remains a one-season tree with unattractive autumn fruit. For this reason, and because of its susceptibility to diseases, this crabapple is only questionably recommended for home landscaping. In a large arboretum collection or a large estate planting it certainly has a place, if only for its fragrance and late flowering. Certainly hybridizers should seek to improve it.

Some botanists would place *M.* 'Charlottae' as a clone of *M. coronaria;* others like Alfred Rehder and the author feel it is more rightfully a clone of variety *dasycalyx* or even a hybrid of a form of *M. coronaria* × *M. ioensis.* It has some similarities with double forms of *M. ioensis,* yet it most resembles variety *dasycalyx.* Someone pointed out that it is an intermediate form between *M. coronaria* and *M. ioensis,* and its location is closer to *M. ioensis* and *M. dasycalyx.* Loc. 3, 10, 14, 24, 26, 31, 35, 54, 68, 79, 81.

M. coronaria var. ***glabrata*** (Rehder) Fiala
Plate 49

Synonym: *M. glabrata* Rehder
Trade name: Biltmore crabapple

Native from North Carolina to Alabama, this variety differs only slightly from *M. coronaria* var. *glaucescens* and is probably a poorer form of it with single, pink flowers. Grown from seed collected in the wild by Charles S. Sargent. Introduced in 1912 by the Arnold Arboretum; first recorded as Sargent's *Malus* Seedling No. 7. A natural tetraploid with 68 chromosomes. Because it is not particularly ornamental, it should not be used in landscaping, but hybridizers seeking to extend flowering crabapples farther south may find some value. Subject to mild scab and moderate cedar-apple rust (Nichols). Loc. 14, 31, 54, 61, 81.

M. coronaria var. ***glaucescens*** (Rehder) Fiala
Plate 50

Synonym: *M. glaucescens* Rehder

Native from New York to North Carolina and westward into Alabama. A natural tetraploid with 68 chromosomes.

A shrub or small, round-headed tree with spiny branches; leaves quite glabrous at maturity, dark green above, glaucous beneath, turning yellow and dark purple in autumn; buds pink, opening to single, pink flowers 1.4–1.6 in (3.5–4 cm) across, fragrant; fruit depressed-globose, yellow-green turning brown-yellow and waxy, fragrant, 1.4 in (3.5 cm) in diameter. Subject to cedar-apple rust.

This variety is of no particular horticultural value; however, in the hands of hybridizers it could be used to extend new hybrid ranges southward, as it has a wide southern range of adaptation, fragrant blossoms, good fruit, and a desirable autumn leaf color. It should be crossed with the newer, disease-resistant, lower-growing, autumn-colored, small-fruited Asiatic hybrids.

M. coronaria var. ***glaucescens*** **'Dunbar'**
B. Slavin

Synonym: *M. coronaria* var. *glaucescens*
Trade name: Dunbar crabapple

A selected open-pollinated seedling grown by Bernard Slavin, Monroe County Parks, Rochester, NY. Named to honor John Dunbar, Monroe County Parks Department, Rochester, NY. Only slightly different from *M. coronaria* var. *glaucescens.* Subject to severe cedar-apple rust and mild scab (Nichols). Loc. 12, 15, 24, 31, 66, 81, 89.

****M. coronaria*** var. ***lancifolia*** (Rehder) Fiala

Synonym: *M. lancifolia* Rehder
Trade name: Allegheny crabapple

Native from Pennsylvania and Virginia to Alabama. A natural tetraploid with 68 chromosomes, although one count, which may be an error, indicates a diploid with 34 chromosomes.

A tree to about 24 ft (7.5 m) high, with spreading, often spiny branches; leaves ovate-lanceolate to oblong-lanceolate, acute or acuminate, rounded or broad-cuneate, 1.6–3.1 in (4–8 cm) long, coarsely serrate, those of shoots oblong-ovate, incisely serrate and slightly lobed, pubescent when young, glabrous at maturity; flowers very fragrant, single, 1.2–1.4 in (3–3.5 cm) across, pink; fruit subglobose, about 1 in (2.5 cm) across, waxy-green. Subject to moderate scab, mild cedar-apple rust, and fire blight; thus, should be phased out (Nichols).

Because it is an annual bearer, this variety has more value in landscaping woody and forest margins. It has rarely been used in hybridization, though it should be used to extend the southern and warmer ranges of crabapples. Crossed with the best, newer Asiatic hybrids, this variety could well be pivotal in the development of a new race of southern flowering crabapples with fine fragrance and small, colorful autumn fruit. Loc. 24, 26, 31, 32, 54, 61, 68.

M. coronaria var. ***platycarpa*** Fiala

Synonyms: *M. ×platycarpa* Rehder, *M. platycarpa* Rehder
Trade name: Georgia crabapple

Introduced in 1912. Native from North Carolina through Georgia. Once considered a species, later a hybrid group, and most recently, a variety of *M. coronaria.* Has a natural tetraploid form with 68 chromosomes and also a diploid form with 34 chromosomes. It could well be a southern form of *M. coronaria*, perhaps a cross of *M. coronaria* var. *lancifolia* × *M. pumila* or of *M. coronaria* var. *angustifolia* × *M. pumila*. Arie den Boer pointed out the following:

> A considerable number of hybrids between *lancifolia* and an orchard apple, found in a grove of *lancifolia* trees, all showed the characteristic lance shape of the species in the leaves of the spurs. In the case of the Georgia crab (×*platycarpa*) the spur leaves point to *M. coronaria* (var. *lancifolia*) as one parent.

A medium-sized tree to 19.6 ft (6 m) high, with rather spreading, thornless branches; leaves ovate to elliptic, rounded at base and at apex, but with short acute point, sharply and usually doubly serrate, larger than the species; pink buds followed by white flowers 1.2–1.6 in (3–4 cm) across, single; fruit depressed-globose, deeply impressed at ends, about 2 in (5 cm) in diameter, yellow-green. Subject to moderate scab and severe cedar-apple rust; thus, should be phased out (Nichols).

This crabapple never gained much popularity as an ornamental, although it is sometimes used for that purpose. The fruit is often used in the South for preserves. Found only in the largest collections and hence not readily available to hybridizers, this crabapple should be made available as it could be used to extend the hybrid range southward. Loc. 10, 14, 31, 35, 73.

Seedlings of *Malus coronaria* var. *platycarpa* vary considerably in type, leaf variations, and vigor; only the best (e.g., *M. platycarpa* 'Hoopesii') should be propagated, the rest can be discarded. Just because natural seedlings have been named and described, even mistakenly given species rank, as in the case of *M.* ×*platycarpa*, does not mean they should be perpetuated. So many new, disease-resistant and beautiful hybrids are now available that we must learn to discard many of the older crabs, especially those of unknown parentage with no horticultural or genetic value. We must not clutter our gardens, parks, and arboreta with nondescripts.

M. coronaria var. ***platycarpa* 'Hoopesii'** (Rehder) Fiala Plate 51

Synonym: *M.* ×*platycarpa* var. *hoopesii* Rehder
Trade name: Hoopes crabapple

Known only as a cultivated plant since 1876. Not different from the variety. Definitely a clone and not a subspecies. Leaves slightly or not lobed; calyx and pedicels pubescent; buds pink, opening to single, white flowers 1.6 in (4 cm) across; fruit green, 2 in (5 cm) in diameter, sometimes used for jellies; an annual bearer. Subject to moderate scab and severe cedar-apple rust (Nichols). Loc. 4, 15, 16, 31, 32, 54, 89.

M. coronaria Arnold Arboretum No. 33340
See *M. coronaria* 'Pink Pearl'.

***M. coronaria* 'Aucubaefolia'** (Rehder) Fiala

Same as the species but with variegated leaves. This form is very difficult to find, and perhaps is now lost to cultivation.

***M. coronaria* 'Coralglow'** Fiala 1987 Plate 52

A hybrid of *M. coronaria* 'Pink Pearl' (Arnold Arboretum No. 33340) that retains the same unique bud and blossom color (in a somewhat lighter shade) but is resistant to leaf diseases and has much smaller red-green fruit. This unique tree has deep coral, single, very late flowers that are mildly fragrant and bloom annually.

A tree to 12 ft (3.5 m) high by 14 ft (4.3 m) wide, with branches twisted and horizontal at odd angles, very picturesque, especially in winter landscape, similar in shape to the parent tree; leaves dark green; buds bright rose-coral, opening to single, pale coral flowers, fading to light coral-pink; fruit red with a bright green cheek, somewhat large to 0.75 in (1.9 cm) in diameter, persistent, showy. Disease resistant despite its parentage.

Despite its larger fruit, this clone is highly recommended for two reasons: there are no other crabapples in this color class, and very few crabapples are as late blooming. It is an excellent background tree, especially in massed plantings on large estates, in parks, and arboreta when it is planted for its late blooming feature (after all the other crabapples have faded), but it is not suitable for close-in landscaping, where the fruit might be a problem. Could well be used by hybridizers for the blossom color and late bloom. Very superior to its parent *M. coronaria* 'Pink Pearl' in several ways: the leaves have far better disease resistance and never defoliate; the fruit is smaller and has better color (is red rather than pale green); and the tree is disease resistant and an annual bloomer. Loc. 47, 100.

***M. coronaria* 'Elk River'** N. E. Hansen

Discovered by A. W. Keays growing near Elk River, 40 mi (60 km) north of Minneapolis, MN. Introduced in 1930 by Niels E. Hansen, South Dakota Agriculture Experiment Station, Brookings.

A spreading tree to 18 ft (5.5 m) high. Roland

Jefferson (1970, p. 13) described the buds as pink to rose-red with carmine veins; the flowers as single, pink with a rose-pink flush on the back of petals, 1.6 in (4 cm) across; and the fruit as dark green and 1.2 in (3 cm) in diameter. Subject to mild scab and cedar-apple rust (Nichols). Should be used more in landscaping large gardens, parks, and arboreta, as well as for hybridizing. Loc. 79, 81.

A large number of the progeny of *M. coronaria* 'Elk River' were introduced by Hansen. Many of them should be used far more in background landscaping, either in clumps or as single specimens. Today they are extremely difficult to find, except in one or two Western arboretums. They also should be used in advanced hybridization, especially with the newer Asiatic cultivars. The fine work of Hansen certainly deserves to be continued, not repeated, in advanced hybrids that use some of his introductions as basic materials.

Progeny of *M. coronaria* 'Elk River' include the following:

- *M.* 'Chinook' N. E. Hansen
- *M.* 'Cranberry' Wodarz
- *M.* 'Kola' N. E. Hansen
- *M.* 'Redflesh' N. E. Hansen
- *M.* 'Redflesh Winter' N. E. Hansen
- *M.* 'Red Tip' (open pollinated) N. E. Hansen
- *M.* 'Shoko' N. E. Hansen
- *M.* 'Tipi' N. E. Hansen
- *M.* 'Wamdessa' N. E. Hansen

***M. coronaria* 'Elongata'** (Rehder) Fiala Plate 53

Synonyms: *M. fragrans attenuata*, *M.* 'Rehder Sweet'

A cultivar of no added value to the species. Native from New York to North Carolina and Alabama. Leaves narrowly triangular-ovate or oblong-ovate, more deeply lobed and incisely serrate, sometimes cuneate. Loc. 10, 31, 35, 54.

***M. coronaria* 'Nieuwland'** A. D. Slavin

Synonym: *M.* 'Nieuwlandiana' Slavin

Selected by Bernard Slavin, Parks System, Rochester, NY, from a group of seedlings of *M. coronaria*. Named in 1931 by Slavin's son, Arthur, to honor the Rev. J. A. Nieuwland, professor of botany at the University of Notre Dame.

Buds rose-red, opening to pink flowers 2.1 in (5.5 cm) across, fragrant, double; fruit yellow-green, about 1.6 in (4 cm) in diameter.

A selection that should be grown more, especially in large parks. A fine clone for hybridizers seeking to incorporate the fragrance and double blossoms into new hybrids with Asiatic species and modern disease-resistant clones. Loc. 4, 14, 18, 24, 68.

***M. coronaria* 'Pink Pearl'** Sax Plate 54

Synonym: Arnold Arboretum No. 33340

Once considered a seedling of *M. sargentii* × *M.* ×*astracanica*, now considered an open-pollinated chance seedling of *M. coronaria*. One of the latest-blooming crabapples, it begins with a magnificent display of coral bloom unique in flowering crabapples and ends covered with large green apples.

A medium-sized tree with twisted branches growing horizontally in irregular form; leaves subject to every apple disease, defoliating by July; buds deep coral-pink, opening to single, fragrant, coral-pink flowers; fruit green, to 1.4 in (3.5 cm) in diameter. Should be phased out—highly susceptible to all diseases, especially extreme scab (Nichols).

The thin, multiple branches sucker abundantly on the limbs of this tree, making some pruning necessary. Because of its unusual tree form, this crabapple is suitable for a Japanese garden or as a focal tree, especially in a winter landscape where there is lots of snow. The tree is also attractive for the shrinking color of its annual blossoming. Loc. 18, 31, 47.

Attempts have been made at Falconskeape Gardens, Medina, OH, over the past 20 years to hybridize this clone to retain its unique blossom color and form but to obtain a disease-resistant tree that does not lose its leaves. Good success has been achieved with five seedlings, which are more disease resistant than the parent and better plants. One of them, such as *M. coronaria* 'Coralglow', which is entirely disease resistant and has smaller, red-cheeked, green fruit, but still retains the late blooming and the unique coral blossom, should replace *M. coronaria* 'Pink Pearl' in future hybridizing programs.

***M. coronaria* 'Thoms'** Thoms

Discovered as a spontaneous seedling by Louis Thoms on his farm near Franklin, OH, in 1920. Introduced by the Siebenthaler Nursery in 1927. John Wister believed this clone was probably identical to *M. coronaria* and appeared spontaneously in Pennsylvania. A hybridizer's crabapple.

Flowers single, pink, 1.6 in (4 cm) across (slightly larger than species); fruit green-yellow, about 1 in (2.5 cm) in diameter.

M. dasycalyx

See *M. coronaria* var. *dasycalyx*.

M.* ×*dawsoniana Rehder
Synonym: *M.* 'Dawson'
Trade name: Dawson crabapple
Parentage: *M. fusca* × *M. pumila*

Introduced by the Arnold Arboretum from seed collected in Oregon by Cyrus G. Pringle in 1881. Named at the arboretum for Jackson Dawson, one of its former propagators. Type plant (now dead) No. 5407; grafts from type plant now No. 5407-2. Not of particular ornamental value, but may be of limited value to hybridizers.

An upright, densely twigged, rather narrow tree with a rounded head; leaves elliptic to elliptic-oblong, 1.6–3.5 in (4–9 cm) long, not lobed; buds white, opening to single, white flowers on slender stalks with 3–5 glabrous styles, 1–1.4 in (2.5–3.5 cm) across; fruit elliptic-oblong, 1.6 in (4 cm) long, 1 in (2.5 cm) wide, yellow-green and red, excellent autumn color. Excellent disease resistance (Nichols).

A unique tree for its long fruit, which is twice as long as wide, and for its autumn foliage—two features that may be of interest to hybridizers. Also of interest to hybridizers for its excellent disease resistance, annual bearing, and late blooming. Best suited for larger estate and park plantings. Loc. 9, 12, 14, 26, 31, 81, 86.

M. florentina (Zuccagni) Schneider Fig. 11.2
Trade name: Italian crabapple

An upright to vase-shaped tree to 20 ft (6 m) high. Not showy in bloom nor abundant in fruit. Severely subject to fire blight (Nichols).

About this crabapple, J. Martens (1986, 3ff) wrote the following:

> This crabapple is a taxon of considerable controversy as to its classification. It has leaves that resemble the English Hawthorn (*Crataegus oxyacantha* syn. *C. laevigata*). Its white flowers grow in bunches in the form of a corymb (flat-topped cluster). Similarly, the fruits, yellow, ripening to a rich red, grow in clusters.

Figure 11.2. *Malus florentina* (Italian crabapple) is a species from the mountains of Italy that has confused botanists.

Arie den Boer added, "It has a compact, upright or pyramidal form, but in a location to its liking, sometimes becomes a broad bush." Alfred Rehder described it thus:

> A small round-headed tree with upright branches; young bracts villous; leaves broad-ovate, usually truncate at base, 3–6 cm. long, all incisely lobed and serrate with several lobes on each side, tomentose beneath; petioles 1–2.5 cm. long, pubescent; flowers 6–8, white, (single), 1.5–2 cm. across . . . fruit, broad-ellipsoid, 1½ cm. long, red. In cultivation 1877; habitat Italy. . . . leaves turning orange and scarlet.

Pizzetti (translated by Henry Crocker) described its autumn foliage as having "magnificent orange-scarlet shades." Arie den Boer stated, "In Iowa this plant has not given evidence of being completely hardy." Whereas Pizzetti and Crocker claimed that *M. florentina* is a "beautiful, hardy plant, thriving at Kew, England, from plants introduced from Florence in 1886," they noted that it is native to northern Italy and very rare both in the wild and in cultivation.

K. Browicz gave the crabapple's range from Italy to the Balkans and called it the Balkan crab. In *Fragmenta Floristica et Geobotanica* (Browicz 1970), he appeared to consider *M. florentina* an intergeneric hybrid of *M. sylvestris* × *Sorbus torminalis* and thus proposed a new name, *Malosorbus florentina*. According to Browicz, *M. florentina* was mentioned by Tilli under the name *Crataegus italica* in 1723, although numerous classifications had been made in the past (e.g., *Crataegus florentina*, *Sorbus florentina*, *Pyrus florentina*, *Malus crataegifolia*, *Torminaria florentina*, *Cormus florentina*, and *Pyrus crataegifolia*). Browicz then systematically narrowed the choice to two: *Sorbus* and *Malus*.

In 1874 Wenzig first proposed that the plant was a cross between *Sorbus torminali* and *Pyrus malus* (synonym *Malus pumila* var. *sylvestris*). Later, in 1883, he changed his mind saying the classification should be *Sorbus crataegifolia*. Subsequent authorities have argued for and against the hybrid origin. Browicz, evaluating all the evidence, came to the tentative conclusion that it is a hybrid and that the question has not yet been definitively settled.

Huckins (1972) concluded that *Malus florentina* should remain in *Malus*, largely as a result of Browicz's work. Specifically he proposed that Section II, *Sorbomalus*, consist only of *Florentinae* Rehder and that it be a monotypic section: "This assignment is not meant to negate an affinity with *Sorbus* or other pomoid genera nor to exclude the eventual possibility of treating this taxon as a monotypic genus or even as a member of *Sorbus*."

Despite the taxonomic difficulties, *Malus florentina* proves to be a somewhat difficult grower in the North but might profit by hybridizing research in a more southerly location and perhaps beget a new southern hybrid race in *Malus*. It is unavailable in nurseries and, to my knowledge, the Boerner Botanic Gardens near Milwaukee, WI, and the Morton Arboretum, Lisle, IL, may have the only living specimens in the United States. It would be interesting research in *Malus*. It has not yet been used in hybridizing. Loc. 10, 14, 26, 31, 81, 87.

*__M. floribunda__ Siebold Plates 55, 56, 57, 58

Trade name: Japanese flowering crabapple

One of the most beautiful of the flowering crabapple species, also one of the oldest in cultivation. Its origin—when, where, and how—remains unknown. Many taxonomists and botanists believe it originated in Japan and was introduced to Western horticulture about 1862. Because its seedlings show considerable variation and it has never been found in the wild, some authorities question its species status, believing it to be a hybrid of unknown parentage. It is one of the finest flowering crabapples in its annual flowering display, disease resistance, tree form, and fruit attractiveness. No other species has produced so many outstanding hybrids or achieved an equal level of landscaping excellence. It is indeed a crabapple for all seasons!

A small, spreading tree 12 ft (3.5 m) high and 18 ft (5.5 m) wide; buds deep pink to red, opening to single, white flowers; blooms while young; fruit yellow and red, 0.4 in (1 cm) in diameter. Resistant to foliar and fruit diseases, but slightly susceptible to powdery mildew and moderately susceptible to fire blight (Nichols).

Alfred Rehder described it thus:

> A shrub or tree to 10 m with wide spreading branches; leaves elliptic-ovate or ovate to oblong-ovate, acuminate, usually cuneate, 4–8 cm long, sharply serrate . . . finally nearly glabrous; flowers deep carmine in bud, changing to pale pink or finally nearly white, 2.5–3 cm across; pedicels pubescent, purple 2.5–3.4 cm long, petals 4; fruit globose, 6–8 mm across, red.

Arie den Boer, describing the fruit, said, "The small, yellow, round fruit, which sometimes has a reddish blush is eagerly eaten by several species of birds." Donald Wyman claimed the fruit was "yellow, sometimes brownish." All the trees I have seen have yellowish fruit 0.4 in (1 cm) in diameter, sometimes with a pale red or rusty flush.

If the tree is to be faulted at all, it would be because of the poor fruit color and because mature trees, with their broad spread, are not suitable for smaller city gardens. Despite its poor fruit color, the tree is very showy because of the heavy fruiting quality and its small size—"relished by birds!" It remains a spectacular specimen tree for a landscaping focal point! Where space allows, it makes an outstanding show for it is extremely floriferous, an annual heavy bearer, and quite resistant to most apple diseases.

Malus floribunda is often seen as a shrubby tree, but it is most spectacular when pruned to tree form with spreading branches artistically trained from near ground level. Pruned in this manner it is a work of art in the winter landscape. It should not be planted against or too close to buildings as it needs room to display its beauty. For a large park, arboretum, or estate it is excellent planted in a group of three trees massed on a hillside, or reflecting its pale pink-white mass of bloom on a slight rise at the waterside!

Nurseries should continue to offer and encourage the planting of this fine crabapple. Hybridizers should continue to use it, preserving its pollen for crosses with the very fragrant, later-blooming *M. coronaria* and *M. ioensis* to produce newer strains of small-fruited, disease-resistant, late-blooming cultivars. Loc. 4, 5, 13, 14, 18, 19, 22, 26, 31, 32, 35, 41, 43, 44, 46, 47, 54, 61, 68, 69, 71, 79, 80, 81, 86, 88, 91, 100.

Species crosses of *M. floribunda* include the following:

- *M. ×arnoldiana* (*M. floribunda* × *M. baccata*)
- *M. ×scheideckeri* (*M. floribunda* × *M. prunifolia*)

M. floribunda var. ***arnoldiana***

See *M. ×arnoldiana*.

M. floribunda **'Ellwangeriana'** Ellwanger and Barry Nursery

Trade name: Ellwanger crabapple

A spreading tree to 18 ft (5.5 m) high and 25 ft (8 m) wide; buds pink, opening to single, pink and white flowers; fruit green-yellow with red cheek, not particularly showy, 0.6 in (1.5 cm) in diameter; alternate bearer. Subject to mild fire blight and slight mildew (Nichols). Possibly a hybrid. Listed by Gibbs as very ornamental. Loc. 12, 31, 35, 37, 54, 79, 81, 89.

***M. floribunda* 'Exzellenz Thiel'** Späth 1909
Parentage: *M. prunifolia* 'Pendula' × *M. floribunda*

Introduced to the United States by the Arnold Arboretum in 1912. One of the first weeping crabapples.

A small, weeping tree with pendulous branches; buds rose-red, opening to white-pink flowers 1.8 in (4.5 cm) across; fruit orange-yellow with red cheek, slightly more than 0.5 in (1.2 cm) in diameter. Alternate bearer. Subject to very severe scab and mild fire blight.

A fairly good weeper that produced *M.* 'Red Jade' but cannot compare with newer, weeping clones, most of which trace back, some generations, to this clone. When crossed with *M. pumila* 'Niedzwetzkyana', this clone produced *M.* 'Oekonomierat Echtermeyer' Späth, a rather poor, disease-ridden weeper that should be discarded. Loc. 9, 26, 31, 35, 37, 81.

Progeny of *M. floribunda* 'Exzellenz Thiel', all weepers, include the following:

> *M.* 'Oekonomierat Echtermeyer' Späth
> *M.* 'Pixie' A. den Boer
> *M.* 'Red Jade' Reed
> *M.* 'Seafoam' A. den Boer

***M. floribunda* 'Hilleri'**
See *M.* 'Hillier' in Chapter 12.

M. formosana Kawakami
Trade names: Formosan crabapple, Taiwan crabapple

This species is extremely rare in the United States. The only known plants are at the Germ Plasm Repositories in Corvallis, OR, and Geneva, NY, from seed obtained by Melvin Westwood, Corvallis, OR, collected directly from trees he had marked in Taiwan. Arie den Boer, who in 1940 obtained seed from the Japanese government then in Taiwan, recounted the following history:

> Attempts to raise this plant in the U.S. have been made several times. I tried it also. After several years of correspondence with various organizations in Japan, governmental and commercial, I succeeded in obtaining about 15 grams of seed. I was informed by consular officials in Taiwan that it had been necessary to send an armed expedition into the mountains to collect that small amount of seed. After so much trouble this was going to be an experiment worth watching. However, with the best of care, including shading and timely watering, the seeds did not germinate. It then occurred to me that in the virgin forests on the mountain slopes of Taiwan there would probably be a heavy layer of humus. At least I considered it possible, and I decided to imitate that condition covering the seed box with some partly decayed leaves and some sphagnum moss. It is difficult to say that this was exactly what the seeds needed for germination, but germinate they did. Unfortunately the terrific drop in temperature on Nov. 11, 1940, killed all the seedlings!

Malus formosana grows in the mountains of central Taiwan in a very limited area at the altitude of 7000–8000 ft (2100–2400 m), in the vicinity of Mt. Ali. Although it appears that the species exists from the southern mainland of China to Hainan, it is from Taiwan that the North American seed came. Westwood noted that some of the trees he saw in the mountains appeared to be 100 or more years old. If true, such a life span would make *M. formosana* a very unusual crab. Arie den Boer affirmed that among crabapple species, *M. formosana* grew closest to the equator.

The taxonomy for this crabapple is by no means certain as various names are found in botanical works, including *M. melliana* (Handel-Mazzetti) Rehder and *M. doumeri* (Bois) A. Chevalier.

Martens described *M. formosana* thus:

> A deciduous tree over 30 m tall, stems often spiny when young; buds glabrous, branchlets grayish pubescent; leaves chartaceous (yellow-green), pubescent when young, soon glabrous, oblong or elliptic to ovate, 5–15 cm long, 2.5–6 cm wide, apex acute, base rounded or obtuse, irregularly serrate, 8–11 lateral veins per side and slightly tinged with rose; petioles to 3.5 cm long; flowers 3–6 in a terminal corymb; pedicels 1–2.5 cm long; calyx 5 lobed, the lobes ovate-lanceolate, 6–7 mm long, 2.5–3.5 cm wide, white-grey pubescence on both surfaces; petals 5, white tinged with yellow, obovate, 1–1.3 cm long, 7–9 mm wide, the apex emarginate or rounded; stamens numerous; ovary 5-celled, each with 2 ovules, 4–5 styles; pome globose, 4–5 cm in diameter with persistent calyx, yellowish-red.

Efforts should be made to preserve this species so it is not lost. It would be of interest to hybridize it with North American and Asiatic species.

M. fusca (Rafinesque) Schneider Fig. 11.3

Trade name: Oregon crabapple

The only North American species native west of the Rocky Mountains, with a range from coastal central Alaska, through southern British Columbia, Washington, Oregon, and northern California. Archibald Menzies is believed to have been the first European to encounter this species circa 1793, but David Douglas collected specimens circa 1823. The oblong fruit makes this species unique among crabapples.

Malus fusca is found in moist, deep, rich soil, often shrubby with numerous slender branches, at times forming large impenetrable thickets. The largest specimens grow to 40 ft (12 m) high with trunks 12–18 in (30–45 cm) in diameter in the valleys of western Washington and Oregon. The species is very hardy and disease resistant; it tolerates moist soils more so than other crabapples. It has withstood temperatures of –70°F (–57°C) in Fairbanks, AK, and –50°F (–46°C) in British Columbia. Although seldom used as an ornamental, *M. fusca* may have some limited potential for hybridization because of its high disease resistance.

Young shoots clothed with white-gray hairs that become glabrous, purple-brown the second season; leaves deciduous, ovate to ovate-lanceolate, acute or acuminate, usually round or cuneate at the base, sometimes obscurely lobed above the middle, finely sharply serrate, 1.5–3.5 in (3.8–9 cm) long, 0.75–1.25 in (1.9–3 cm) wide, dark dull green, at first puberulous above, finally glabrous, paler pubescent beneath; flowers white to pink-white, single, 0.75–1 in (1.9–2.5 cm) across, terminal or produced in the axils of terminal leaves, 8–12 forming a corymb 2–3 in (5–7.6 cm) wide; petals 5, orbicular with a short claw and a few jagged teeth near the base, 0.6 in (1.5 cm) long, creamy white; stamens 16–20; fruit ellipsoid, attractive, medium-sized, about 0.6 in (1.5 cm) long, pendulous, glabrous, yellow tinged with pink or red on the sunny side and green in the shade, ripens in October, usually contains 3 pale brown seeds; calyx falls away leaving a small pit at the apex. Highly resistant to scab and fire blight after 20 years of testing (Nichols).

There is considerable variation in this species: not only are the leaves lobed, but in some trees, there is practically no lobing; some trees have elliptical fruit that is longer than wide, while others have round fruit. The skin of the fruit is not fragrant or waxy like the other North American species. One fault of this species is that it is an alternate bloomer.

Malus fusca is found in most larger arboreta

Figure 11.3. *Malus fusca* (Oregon crabapple), a little known North American species, is white flowering.

and university collections (e.g., Arnold Arboretum; Morton Arboretum; Michigan State University campus; University of Alaska in Fairbanks; University of Oregon; Butchard Gardens in Victoria, British Columbia; University of Minnesota Landscape Arboretum; and a native plant on the grounds of the University of Washington). It has not yet been used in hybridizing. Loc. 12, 15, 26, 31, 89.

Species crosses of *M. fusca* include *M.* ×*dawsoniana* (*M. fusca* × *M. pumila*).

M. fusca var. ***levipes***

Flowers single, pink-white, 1 in (2.5 cm) across; fruit 0.4 in (1 cm) in diameter, red or yellow-red. An alternate bearer.

***M. fusca* 'Wagener'**

A selected clone. Very resistant to disease (Nichols). Should be used in hybridizing because of excellent disease resistance. Loc. 10, 15.

M. glabrata Rehder

See *M. coronaria* var. *glabrata*.

M. glaucescens Rehder

See *M. coronaria* var. *glaucescens*.

M.* ×*gloriosa Lemoine before 1931

Synonym: *M.* 'Gloriosa'

Parentage: *M.* ×*scheideckeri* × *M. pumila* 'Niedzwetzkyana'

Named prior to 1931, but introduced to the United States by the Arnold Arboretum in 1936. A medium-sized, round to spreading tree; leaves red-green; buds red-purple, opening to purple, single flowers 1.6 in (4 cm) across; fruit brown-red to red, 1.2 in (3 cm) in diameter. Subject to severe scab (Nichols). An alternate, light bloomer. Should be discarded. Loc. 9, 14, 15, 24, 26, 31, 54, 61, 79, 81, 87.

M. halliana Koehne

A diploid with 34 chromosomes. A smaller-growing species. Cultivated in Japan and China. Introduced into the United States from Japan in 1863 by G. R. Hall, for whom the species was named. Alfred Rehder described the species thus:

> It is a small tree or shrub to 5 m with a rather loose open head; young bracts soon glabrous, purple; leaves ovate or elliptic to oblong-ovate, 3–5 cm long, acuminate, crenate-serrulate, quite glabrous, except the midrib above, dark green and lustrous above and often purple-tinted; petioles 5–20 mm long; flowers 4–7, bright rose, 3–3.5 cm across; pedicels slender, nodding; styles 4–5; terminal flowers usually without pistils; petals usually more than 5; fruit obovoid, 6–8 mm across, purplish, ripening very late.

The fruit of this species is not ornamental. Varietal forms much more important than the species. Fine disease resistance (Nichols). Loc. 4, 16, 24, 26, 35, 47, 54.

Species crosses of *M. halliana* include the following:

M. ×atrosanguinea (*M. halliana* × *M. toringo*)
M. ×hartwigii (*M. halliana* × *M. baccata*)

M. halliana var. ***spontanea*** (Makino) Koidzumi Plates 59, 60

Introduced into the United States by the Arnold Arboretum in 1919 from a plant collected by E. H. Wilson in the mountains of Kyushu Island, Japan. Alfred Rehder described it thus: "Leaves smaller (than species), elliptic or elliptic-obovate; flowers smaller nearly white, single; young foliage purple when unfolding." A very dwarf, twiggy, vase-shaped tree broader than tall; blooms well only in alternate years. Completely disease resistant (Nichols). Not of meaningful value as an ornamental but should be retained in large arboretum collections. Best used by hybridizers seeking bushlike, smaller flowering crabapples. Probably a hybrid. Loc. 4, 13, 14, 31, 32, 47, 54.

***M. halliana National Arboretum No. 127** Egolf Plates 61, 62

Collected in China and introduced in 1978 by Donald Egolf of National Arboretum, Washington, DC. A selection of seedlings of *M. halliana*. An excellent form. Much taller than *M. halliana* 'Parkmanii' with much better fruit.

An upright, somewhat fan-shaped or vase-shaped tree to about 12 ft (3.5 m) high and half as broad; leaves deep green; buds deep rose, opening to medium rose, semidouble to double, mildly fragrant flowers in long clusters; fruit small, red, 0.4 in (1 cm) in diameter, quite attractive, but not as abundantly fruited as flowered. (All semidouble- or double-flowering crabapples have more flowers than fruit as many double flowers are sterile.) An annual bearer. Subject to mild fire blight, but still worthy of being grown. It merits inclusion in all larger collections because of its better qualities and its vaselike form can well be used by homeowners and landscapers in smaller gardens. Excellent also for hybridizers seeking double-flowering crabapples and fine form. Loc. 35, 47.

***M. halliana 'Parkmanii'** Rehder Plates 26, 63, 64

Synonyms: *M.* 'Parkman', *M.* 'Parkmanii'

Introduced into the United States in 1861 from cultivated plants in Japan. Named by G. R. Hall in 1863 for a friend, historian Francis Parkman. One of the shortest crabapple species.

A round tree to 15 ft (4.6 m) high and as wide, with slender, twiggy branches; leaves bronze green, glossy, leathery, relatively small, thus adding to the texture of the delicate tree; buds bright rose, unique in that they hang in pendulous clusters on long, deep crimson pedicels; flowers semidouble to double, with 15 petals, a pleasing shell pink color—one of the most attractive of the crabapples and the best low-growing pink; fruit, long stemmed, very small, 0.25 in (0.6 cm) in diameter, red to red-purple, unimportant, sparse, and not particularly attractive. Subject to moderate cedar-apple rust and mild fire blight.

This is one of the most difficult crabapples to grow well, yet it is prized for its springtime bloom. Growing slowly, it reaches small bush size only after several years. It is an excellent plant for forcing bloom. Although it is not as hardy as most crabapples, it is well worth using in hybridizing because of its lovely spring blossoms, fine leathery leaves, small form, and very small fruit. As a landscaping plant its value is in its small stature and double blossoms. It should not be overlooked by modern landscapers. Loc. 4, 16, 18, 24, 31, 35, 39, 47, 54, 58, 61, 79, 80, 81, 89.

Progeny of *M. halliana* 'Parkmanii' include *M.* 'Dorothea' Wyman.

***M. ×hartwigii** Koehne Fig. 11.4

Synonym: *M.* 'Hartwigi'

Parentage: *M. halliana* × *M. baccata*

Intermediate between the parents. Cultivated since 1906. An upright, globe-topped tree with excellent habit; leaves dark

Figure 11.4. *Malus ×hartwigii* puts out annual cascades of white bloom. A high percentage of the blossoms are semidouble.

green; buds pink, opening to semidouble pink flowers that change to white, 1.6 in (4 cm) across, produced in great abundance; pedicels and calyx red; fruit small, 0.6 in (1.5 cm) in diameter, yellow-green blushed red, persistent to midwinter, abundant. Disease resistant. An annual bearer. A good semidouble-flowering hybrid that has been overlooked. Excellent for landscapers and hybridizers. Loc. 14, 15, 24, 31, 54, 79, 81, 87.

M. ×heterophylla Spach

Parentage: *M. coronaria* × *M. pumila*

Malus ×heterophylla is often classified under *M. ×soulardii* because the two hybrids are so similar, but this practice should be discouraged as the hybrids represent two distinct crosses: *M. ×heterophylla* is a cross of *M. coronaria* × *M. pumila*, and *M. ×soulardii* is a cross of *M. ioensis* × *M. pumila*. It is possible that *M. ioensis* is a diploid form of *M. coronaria*. If so, this could account for why the two hybrids are so very similar. Taxonomically, however, the strict cross name should be adhered to without confusing the two. No diseases (Nichols). *Malus* 'Mathews' is a clone of *M. ×heterophylla*. Loc. 54.

M. himalaica

See *M. baccata* var. *himalaica*.

M. honanensis Rehder

Trade name: Honan crabapple

A species closely related to or a variety of *M. kansuensis*. Introduced into the United States in 1921 from seed No. 1691 sent to the Arnold Arboretum by J. Hers from northeastern China.

Leaves broad-ovate, rarely oblong-ovate, with 2–5 pairs of broad-ovate serrulate lobes, pubescent beneath; inflorescence glabrous; buds white, opening to single, white flowers 0.8 in (2 cm) across, in clusters of 10 or more; flowers produced when plants are very young; styles 3–4; fruit subglobose, about 0.3 in (0.8 cm) in diameter, dotted, yellow-green with rosy cheeks. No disease (Nichols).

This crabapple is seldom seen outside botanic gardens. It is very much like *M. kansuensis* but smaller and with small, more deeply lobed or incised leaves. Not particularly ornamental but the leaves do change to a brilliant red in autumn. Arie den Boer noted that in flower this crabapple could easily be mistaken for a variety of *Cotoneaster*. Loc. 54, 73.

M. *hupehensis (Pampanini) Rehder
Plates 65, 66

Synonym: *M. theifera* Rehder

Trade name: Tea crabapple

Known since 1900 in China and the Himalaya Mountains. Introduced into the United States by the Arnold Arboretum through seed collected by E. H. Wilson in 1908 in Ichang, western Hupei, China. Called *M. theifera* for many years until reclassification returned the species to its first description by Renato Pampanini in 1910 as *M. hupehensis* (*Pyrus hupehensis*). In nature, both a triploid (51 chromosomes) and a tetraploid (68 chromosomes) form exist—the latter being the slightly better form. *Malus hupehensis* 'Donald' may be an induced octoploid (136 chromosomes) of the species.

An open, irregular, spreading tree to 16 ft (5 m) high and 25 ft (8 m) wide, with straight, upright, spreading limbs, studded from the short trunk to the tips with countless, very short, lateral twigs of equal length on which flower spurs are formed; buds pink, opening to single, white, fragrant flowers; fruit green-yellow with slight red cheek, 0.4 in (1 cm) in diameter, not too showy. Good to excellent disease resistance.

Because of its unique branches, this tree appears to have a widely spreading vase-shaped form. Each season it reaches out in spread. It is extremely picturesque in the landscape, especially in wintertime, and a mature tree is a splendid focal point when used as a single specimen in the landscape. In Old China the long branches, which can extend as far as 40 ft (12 m) from the trunk if left undisturbed and unpruned, were propped up by supports and the spreading canopy used as shade for tea tables.

Trees of this species should not be pruned, as each pruning produces double-branched growth that spoils the attractive vase form of the tree. The species should be used far more on larger estates, parks, and arboretum collections. It is a heavy but somewhat alternate bloomer.

Pollen of this species appears to be reasonably fertile and could be used by hybridizers, but because the species is apomictic, it has not been used much in hybridizing programs. Naturally fertilized, most of its seedlings are identical to the parent plant, although on occasion slight variations (e.g., in leaf texture, slight pink-white in blossoms, and sometimes redder fruit) are found. One form has white buds and smaller white flowers; another has pink buds and larger pink bloom. All forms have the same leaf structure, tree form, and mostly green fruit blushed red. Loc. 4, 12, 14, 18, 24, 26, 31, 35, 37, 47, 55, 61, 68, 73, 79, 81, 85, 86, 89.

M. hupehensis **'Donald'** Fiala 1950 — Plates 67, 68, 69

A tetraploid clone that may be an induced octoploid with 136 chromosomes. A superior form of *M. hupehensis* developed at Falconskeape Gardens, Medina, OH, by using colchicine. Named to honor the introducer's nephew, Donald Kozak, a horticulturist.

Leaves very heavy, glossy, dark green; flowers tinted pink, fragrant, abundant; fruit green with red cheek. An excellent, annual bloomer. Excellent disease resistance (Nichols). Recommended as slightly better than the species in tree form, leaf characteristics, and redder fruit. Loc. 31, 47, 100.

***M. hupehensis* 'Rosea'**

Same as species but with pale pink flowers instead of white. This form has been described but appears to be lost as clones so named are not the true form. Loc. 12, 18.

***M. hupehensis* 'Wayne Douglas'** Hill — Plate 70

A seedling selected by Polly Hill, Martha's Vineyard, MA. The tree form, type of blossoms, leaves, and fruit indicate that this crabapple may be a unique hybrid of unknown parentage.

A medium-sized, upright but somewhat spreading tree with a rounded form, not like the long-branched form of the species; buds pale pink, opening to white, single flowers; fruit purple (rusty-purple), borne in small clusters, somewhat larger than the species, 0.5 in (1.2 cm) in diameter, not particularly showy. Appears to be disease resistant.

A worthy addition to the progeny of *M. hupehensis*. Could be interesting for hybridizing.

M. ioensis (A. Wood) Britton — Plate 71

Trade names: Iowa crabapple, Prairie crabapple, Midwest crabapple

A natural diploid with 34 chromosomes. Some taxonomists consider it a diploid form of the tetraploid *M. coronaria*. One of the most beautiful North American crabapple species. Native to Iowa and the neighboring states of Minnesota, Wisconsin, Nebraska, and Kansas, extending to parts of upper Texas and Louisiana. J. Martens said of it:

> Then came the settlers, and, with them, the European crabs favored for their larger fruits and customary taste. What with the clearing of the woodlands and the introduction of competition, *M. ioensis* lost its area of monopoly and dominance as THE crabapple of the upper Mississippi Valley. Gradually it became an arboretum and nursery tree, rather than a wild one. Regarding its wild occurrence (30 years ago), "There are isolated trees and small groups near Chicago, and the plant has been found near Milwaukee, Wisconsin. A large native mass was found in northwestern Indiana." Now with extreme urbanization, the question arises, "Are there any more specimens of *M. ioensis* existing in a truly wild state?"

What a pity that state parks have not taken it upon themselves to plant and preserve this fine native tree!

Most of Alfred Rehder's subspecies of *M. ioensis* have been classified as clones. As single plants they do not meet the requirements of a subspecies.

Like *M. coronaria* and its clones, *M. ioensis* and its forms are highly susceptible to scab and cedar-apple rust. Judged on susceptibility to cedar-apple rust, both species and their clones would have to be phased out (Nichols). Although they are not recommended for home planting for this reason, they are a truly unique and beautiful group of crabapples, especially the double-flowering clones, which are among some of the most beautiful flowering and strongly fragrant of all crabapples. Late bloomers, they have a unique, strong fragrance not found in any other species. Thus, they are recommended for their late bloom, double flowers (in some clones), and especially for their fragrance. Large arboretum collections should continue to carry *M. ioensis*, and hybridizers should use the species in every attempt to produce disease-resistant hybrids. Much should be done to preserve and improve all the North American species. Loc. 10, 14, 26, 31, 32, 54, 68, 79.

Species crosses of *M. ioensis* include the following:

M. 'Evelyn' (*M. ioensis* × *M.* ×*purpurea*)
M. ×*soulardii* (*M. ioensis* × *M. pumila*)

M. ioensis **var. *texana*** Rehder
Synonym: *M.* 'Texana'
Most probably a variant form of a southern *M. ioensis*. No disease (Nichols). Loc. 35.

M. ioensis **'Amsib'** N. E. Hansen 1932
Parentage: *M. ioensis* × *M. baccata*
The name "Amsib" represents the origins of the two parents: *Am* from American crabapple (*M. ioensis*) and *sib* from Siberian crabapple (*M. baccata*). The form of *M. ioensis* used in this cross was a wild, red-fruited selection. An upright tree; flowers pink; fruit green with dull red blush, about 1.4 in (3.5 cm) in diameter. No disease (Nichols). Loc. 35, 37.

***M. ioensis 'Boone Park'**
Discovered by Arie den Boer and Clyde Heard in Boone Park, Boone, IA, and introduced by them. Flowers single, light pink, 1.6 in (4 cm) across; fruit dull green to dull yellow, 1.2 in (3 cm) in diameter. Subject to moderate scab and cedar-apple rust (Nichols). Loc. 54, 61, 68, 81.

***M. ioensis 'Fimbriata'** A. D. Slavin 1931
Trade name: Fringe petal crabapple
A seedling discovered by Bernard Slavin, Rochester Park, Rochester, NY. Named in 1931 by Slavin's son, Arthur, for the finely fringed edges of the petals.

Expanding buds brown-red to red, opening to shell-pink, double flowers 2 in (5 cm) across, very fragrant, and with 34 petals. Seldom does this clone produce fruit. Perhaps a hybridizer will find some fertile pollen and use this excellent crabapple for newer plants. Loc. 31, 79.

***M. ioensis 'Fiore's Improved'** Fiore 1964
Selected from a seedling bed at Charles Fiore Nurseries, Prairie View, IL, before 1964. Better than the species.

Bark very smooth, light gray, fragrant; flowers single or occasionally semidouble, deep rose pink, twice the size of the species; fruit one-third larger than the species.

Should be used for hybridization despite the usual susceptibility of *M. ioensis* and related crabapples to disease. More native seed needs to be planted before all the stands of *M. ioensis* disappear to urbanization, and the best of these seedlings should be selected for hybridization. Loc. 89.

***+M. ioensis 'Klehm's Improved Bechtel'**
Plates 72, 73, 74, 75
Synonym: *M.* 'Klemi' Klehm (a Latinized name that should not be used for a clone)
A selection by Clyde Klehm, which he found growing in a Chicago park. According to Roy Klehm (pers. com.), his Uncle Clyde was sitting on a park bench with the young lady he was dating when he saw this unique plant blossoming in a group of native crabapples. Having no way to mark the plant, the young lady tore a piece of the lace from her petticoat. Thus marked, Clyde returned to the tree in the fall for scionwood. Although the plant was named after the Klehms, not the young lady, years later Roy Klehm memorialized the unknown young lady by naming a *Hemerocallis* 'Pink Petticoat'.

A vase-shaped tree to 20 ft (6 m) high and 18 ft (5.5 m) wide; leaves soft green covered with a silky tomentum; flowers double, large, pink, very fragrant, blooms late; very few fruit, 1 in (2.5 cm) in diameter, green inconspicuous. Subject to moderate scab and cedar-apple rust as well as to mild fire blight (Nichols).

A fine tree for blossoms and fragrance, despite some disease susceptibility. Probably one of the best clones of the *M. ioensis* group. Should be planted in larger gardens, parks, and arboretum collections. Also should be the one most offered and used in hybridizing for all its fine qualities. Hybridizers should attempt to improve its disease resistance (e.g., *M.* 'Klehm's Improved Bechtel' × *M. coronaria* 'Coralglow'). Loc. 15, 18, 24, 31, 79, 81, 86, 100.

***M. ioensis 'Nevis'** Arrowwood
Discovered in 1930 by James Arrowwood near Nevis, MN. Introduced by Niels E. Hansen, South Dakota Agriculture Experiment Station, Brookings. This dwarf seedling of *M. ioensis* bears flowers when only 4 ft (1.2 m) high.

Flowers single, pink, about 1.6 in (4 cm) across; fruit green, 1.2 in (3 cm) in diameter. Mostly disease resistant, but subject to severe scab (Nichols). Rather outstanding for a clone of *M. ioensis*. Should be used in landscaping and hybridizing. Loc. 31, 79.

All the progeny of *M. ioensis* 'Nevis' have been selected by N. E. Hansen. Despite the disease susceptibility of *M. ioensis*, Hansen's selections should be far more available in nurseries and they should be used by hybridizers for the many fine qualities they possess (e.g., smaller form). Arboreta should also have them at least for their genetic value, if not to make them available to hybridizers. A complete collection in the Midwest (where *M. ioensis* and *M. coro-*

naria are native) would make an interesting educational study in hybridization and a source for scionwood. Perhaps an arboretum could take on this project. It would be a misfortune if the great work of N. E. Hansen with this group of crabapples were to be lost. No one should have to repeat his work. Hopefully, some larger arboretum will make such a planting and young hybridizers will take up where Hansen's work left off.

Progeny of *M. ioensis* 'Nevis' include the following:

M. 'Wakonda' N. E. Hansen
M. 'Wecota' N. E. Hansen
M. 'Wetonka' N. E. Hansen
M. 'Wiyuta' N. E. Hansen
M. 'Wotanda' N. E. Hansen

***M. ioensis 'Nova'** Augustine Nursery 1928 Plate 76

Received in 1928 by the Morton Arboretum, Lisle, IL, as *M. ioensis* 'Flore Plena Nova'. Later the name was changed to *M. ioensis* 'Nova'. Arie den Boer considered this plant a sport of *M. ioensis* 'Plena' that differed only in having a deeper pink flower. Flowers double, with 18–35 petals, rose-pink, 1.8 in (4.5 cm) across; fruit few, green to green-yellow, 1.3 in (3.2 cm) in diameter. This form is another native selection that should be hybridized with the newest Asiatic hybrids. Loc. 31, 54, 89.

***M. ioensis* 'Palmeri'** Palmer

Introduced in 1910 from seed sent to the Arnold Arboretum by E. J. Palmer, Webb City, MO. This form differs from the species in having smaller, oblong, more thinly pubescent leaves, rounded at the apex. It is an insignificant difference that only clutters up the botanical listings. Should be phased out because of severe scab and cedar-apple rust (Nichols). Loc. 31, 61.

***M. ioensis 'Plena'** Bechtel 1888 Plates 77, 78

Synonyms: *M.* 'Bechtel', *M.* 'Flore Plena'

Trade name: Bechtel crabapple

Discovered in Staunton, IL, by E. A. Bechtel. Introduced between 1840–1850. An annual bearer, it is one of the most beautiful native crabapples when in bloom and a very fine double pink form.

Flowers pink, double, with 30–33 petals; fruit green. Subject to cedar-apple rust and fire blight. Should be phased out because of too many diseases (Nichols). Should be used in hybridizing for its rose-colored double blossoms and its excellent fragrance. Also, some arboreta should keep this beautiful crabapple. Loc. 5, 14, 40, 43, 72, 73, 79, 81, 88.

***M. ioensis 'Prairie Rose'**

An open-pollinated seedling of *M. ioensis*. Introduced before 1959 by the Agriculture Experiment Station, University of Illinois, No. OPS 825. Similar to *M. ioensis* 'Plena', but with flowers that are deeper pink, very fragrant, and double. In the 45 years this sterile clone has grown in my garden, it has never produced fruit. Its pollen may be fertile. Although it is subject to severe cedar-apple rust, I would not be without this clone because of its fragrance. Loc. 16, 19, 24, 31, 46, 47, 61, 73, 79.

***M. ioensis 'Prince Georges'** Plate 79

Synonyms: *M. coronaria* var. *angustifolia* 'Prince Georges', *M. angustifolia* 'Plena', *M. coronaria* var. *angustifolia* 'Plena'

Parentage: *M. ioensis* × *M. coronaria* var. *angustifolia* (?)

To some it is most probably a sterile hybrid of *M. ioensis* × *M. coronaria* var. *angustifolia*, but others doubt that a diploid in nature can cross with a tetraploid. This hybrid of uncertain parentage originated from open-pollinated seed collected in 1919 for the Arnold Arboretum by a plant explorer from the USDA. It is one of the best hybrids of the group. The original plant was grown at the Plant Introduction Station, Glenn Dale, MD; scionwood from it was then sent to the Arnold Arboretum in 1930. The arboretum introduced the crabapple in 1943 and named it after Prince Georges County, MD, where the Glenn Dale station is located.

A medium-sized to small tree; expanding buds deep rose-pink, opening to double, light rose-pink flowers 2 in (5 cm) across, with 53–61 petals, wonderfully fragrant; not known to produce fruit. Late blooming but a heavy, annual bloomer. Mildly subject to scab and cedar-apple rust, neither of which have been found at Falconskeape Gardens, Medina, OH, on our 50-year-old tree. It appears to be more resistant to scab and fire blight than most members of the *M. ioensis* and *M. coronaria* groups.

This magnificent crabapple is a wonderful tree for naturalizing woodland edges and as a specimen tree, even for smaller gardens. To the author it is one of the most beautiful crabapples. Nursery professionals should become more acquainted with it. For its springtime beauty it should be planted more as a specimen tree. Loc. 3, 4, 12, 13, 18, 24, 26, 31, 32, 35, 47, 54, 68, 69, 79, 80, 87.

***M. ioensis* 'Red Seedling No. 1'**
See *M.* 'Evelyn' in Chapter 12.

***M. ioensis* 'Spinosa'**
Of no horticultural value, this thorny form should not have been named. Subject to moderate scab and mild cedar-apple rust (Nichols). Loc. 31.

M. kansuensis (Batalin) Schneider Fig. 11.5
Synonyms: *Pyrus kansuensis* Batalin, *Eriolobus kansuensis* (Batalin) Schneider
Introduced by the Arnold Arboretum from seed collected in 1911 by E. H. Wilson in Tachien-Lu, western Szechwan, China. Native of Kansu, Hupei, and Szechwan provinces in China. Alfred Rehder described it thus:

> A small tree to 8 m.; young brts. pubescent; leaves ovate, truncate, rounded or broad-cuneate at base, 5–8 cm long, 3 or sometimes 5-lobed, with triangular-ovate acute closely serrate lobes, pubescent beneath, at least on the veins; petioles 1.5 cm long; flowers 4–10, white,. 1.5 cm across; pedicels 1.5–2.5 cm long . . . fruit ellipsoid, about 1 cm long, yellow or red.

Not particularly ornamental; flowers single. Subject to severe scab in some locations, disease free in others (Nichols). This crabapple is very rare and found only in a few of the largest arboretums. It has not yet been used much in hybridizing. Loc. 10, 12, 31, 61.

M. kansuensis* var. *calva Rehder
A handsome, small tree, not particularly showy; leaves beneath, calyx, and pedicels glabrous, even when young. Subject to moderate scab (Nichols). A little known and seldom seen species, even in the larger collections. To my knowledge it has never been used in hybridization. Loc. 37.

Figure 11.5. The rare *M. kansuensis* in bloom.

M. lancifolia
See *M. coronaria* var. *lancifolia.*

M. leucocarpa
See *M.* ×*robusta* 'Leucocarpa'.

M. macrocarpa
See *M. toringoides* 'Macrocarpa'

M.* ×*magdeburgensis Schoch Fig. 11.6
Synonym: *M.* 'Magdeburg'
Parentage: *M. spectabilis* × *M. pumila*
Very showy in bloom. Buds pink, opening to single and semidouble, pink flowers with 7–15 petals, 1.6 in (4 cm) across; fruit 1.2 in (3 cm) in diameter, yellow-green often blushed red, not ornamental; heavy annual bloomer. Good disease resistance; subject to mild scab (Nichols). Loc. 10, 12, 18, 26, 31, 35, 54, 81, 87.

Figure 11.6. *Malus* ×*magdeburgensis* at the Arnold Arboretum, Jamaica Plain, MA.

M. mandshurica
See *M. baccata* var. *mandshurica.*

***M. mandshurica* 'Midwest'**
See *M.* 'Midwest' in Chapter 12.

M.* ×*micromalus* Makino Fig. 11.7
Trade names: Kaido crabapple, Midget crabapple
Parentage: *M. spectabilis* × ? *M. baccata*
Introduced into the United States circa 1856. Native to North Korea and the islands of Japan. A handsome, upright, pink ornamental, very

Figure 11.7. *Malus* ×*micromalus* at the Secrest Arboretum, Wooster, OH.

showy in white bloom. One of the earliest crabapples to bloom.

An upright bush or small tree to 12 or 15 ft (4–4.6 m) high and 8–10 ft (2.5–3 m) wide; leaves elliptic-oblong, acuminate, cuneate, 2–3.9 in (5–10 cm) long and 0.8–1.6 in (2–4 cm) broad, serrulate; pedicels slender, 0.8–1.2 in (2–3 cm) long; flowers pink (not fading as do many other crabapples), single, 1.6 in (4 cm) across, rather large, and showy; fruit subglobose, 0.4–0.6 in (1–1.5 cm) in diameter, light green-yellow and somewhat ribbed, red with cavity at base, calyx persistent. An alternate bloomer. Subject to mild scab (Nichols).

While the fruit of this hybrid could be mistaken for the fruit of *M.* ×*scheideckeri*, the leaves are different: those of *M.* ×*micromalus* are evenly toothed while those of *M.* ×*scheideckeri* are irregularly toothed. Also, the fruits of *M.* ×*micromalus* lose the calyx segments, and the flowers are single and not semidouble.

Although outstanding in flower, this crabapple is not recommended for home landscaping or even for parks because so many new hybrids are far superior. Loc. 12, 13, 14, 18, 24, 26, 31, 32, 35, 37, 39, 54, 87, 89.

M.* ×*moerlandsii Doorenbos

This name was given by S. G. A. Doorenbos, The Hague, Netherlands, to a group cross of *M.* ×*purpurea* 'Lemoinei' × *M. toringo* (formerly *M. sieboldii)* made prior to 1938 and including *M.* 'Liset' and *M.* 'Profusion'. Without a clone name, the group name is meaningless, although there is a crabapple listed simply as "×*moerlandsii* (Loc. 15, 54)." Using a group name in a hybrid cross for a single clone should not be done as group names are reserved for species.

M. orientalis

Grown from seed collected in Armenia, 2 mi (3 km) below Haghartsin, at 5900–6200 ft (1800–1900 m) elevation. Seed collected by T. Elias in September 1976 for the Arnold Arboretum. Loc. 16.

M.* ×*platycarpa

See *M. coronaria* var. *platycarpa.*

M.* ×*platycarpa var. ***hoopesii***

See *M. coronaria* var. *platycarpa* 'Hoopesii'

M. prattii (Hemsley) Schneider

Synonyms: *Pyrus prattii* Hemsley, *Docyniopsis prattii* (Hemsley) Koidzumi

Trade name: Pratt's crabapple

Discovered by and named for A. E. Pratt, from *Malus* seed No. 1107 collected by E. H. Wilson in Wa-Shan, western Szechwan, China, in 1904. Introduced by the Arnold Arboretum in 1909. Alfred Rehder described it thus:

> A tree to 10 m; leaves ovate or elliptic to ovate-oblong, acuminate, usually rounded at base, 6–15 cm long, and 3.5–7.5 cm broad, finely and doubly serrate, with callous-pointed teeth and with 8–10 pairs of veins sparingly pubescent beneath; petioles 1.5–3 cm long; flowers white, 2 cm across in many flower clusters, petals suborbicular; styles 5, glabrous; fruit globose-ovoid or subglobose, 1–1.5 cm across, red or yellow, punctate, on stout stalks, calyx persistent. Handsome tree with large leaves but with neither flowers nor fruit conspicuous.

Although it appears disease resistant (Nichols), it is not a tree for horticultural beauty and it has little to offer hybridizers, so it should be retained only in the largest collections. In England it is said to have good autumn color but this feature alone is insufficient to recommend it. Loc. 10, 16, 31, 32, 81, 87.

M. prunifolia (Willdenow) Borkhausen

Trade names: Pearleaf crabapple, Plumleaf crabapple

Introduced before 1831 from northeast Asia. An alternate bloomer that produces great quantities of fruit. Because there are several forms of this crabapple which differ in size, shape, and color of the fruit, it is believed this crabapple is a hybrid. The fruit may be red, yellow, or orange and, according to the clones, 0.8 in (2 cm) or more across. Specimens found in many botanic collections are not always true to description. Alfred Rehder described it thus:

A small tree, young brts. pubescent; leaves ovate or elliptic, 5–10 cm long, acute or short-acuminate, rounded or cuneate at base, sharply serrate, pubescent on the veins beneath, finally glabrous; petioles slender, 1.5–5 cm long; buds pinkish, opening flowers white, single, about 3 cm across; pedicels 2–3.5 cm long; fruit subglobose or ovoid about 2 cm across, yellow or red with a cavity at the base; calyx not impressed.

Subject to moderate scab (Nichols). Most clones of *M. prunifolia* are susceptible to diseases and should be avoided.

Many of the varietal forms of *M. prunifolia* are of doubtful validity. Although Rehder treats this crabapple as a species, many authorities do not accept it as a true species since it has never been found in the wild. Instead, it is viewed as a hybrid of unknown parentage, which is the most that can be said of it. Arie den Boer believed there was no reason to prefer this crabapple over others. Loc. 10, 14, 26, 31, 32, 54, 68.

Species crosses of *M. prunifolia* include the following:

- *M. ×astracanica* (*M. prunifolia* × *M. pumila*)
- *M. ×robusta* (*M. prunifolia* × *M. baccata*)
- *M. ×scheideckeri* (*M. prunifolia* × *M. floribunda*)
- *M. ×sublobata* (*M. prunifolia* × *M. toringo*)

M. prunifolia **var. rinki** (Koidzumi) Rehder

Synonym: *M. asiatica*

Trade name: Chinese pearleaf crabapple

Introduced into the United States about 1850. Cultivated as an ornamental because of its growth habit and colorful, persistent fruit.

An upright, narrow tree; buds single, pink, opening to white flowers about 2 in (5 cm) across; fruit green and red, 0.6–1.2 in (1.5–3 cm) in diameter, abundant, persisting 3–4 months. An alternate bloomer. Should be phased out—subject to very severe scab (Nichols). It could be a background tree on large estates and parks, but with so many excellent newer crabapples, there is no reason to grow it.

Both "rinki" and "ringo" are derived from the Chinese name for this apple, *linkum*. In Japan, the word *to-ringo*, meaning Chinese apple, is used for the same plant, but do not confuse this use of the word with the newly renamed species *M. toringo* (formerly *M. sieboldii*). Loc. 10, 12, 14, 24, 31, 54, 79, 80, 81.

M. prunifolia **'Fastigata'**

Received by the USDA before 1906. This form fastigiates only when young; as increasingly heavier fruit crops are borne, it becomes more downward and spreading, with the branches remaining in that position.

Flowers single, white, 1.8 in (4.5 cm) across; fruit yellow or red, 0.8 in (2 cm) in diameter. An alternate bearer, yet its fruit is impressive although a bit large. Subject to very mild scab. Loc. 10, 26, 31, 32, 54, 79, 81.

M. prunifolia **'Pendula'**

Trade name: Pendent crabapple

Similar to the species, but with pendulous branches. Better weeping cultivars on the market today are more refined. Subject to severe scab (Nichols). Loc. 18, 31, 32, 54, 61, 81.

M. pumila Miller

Trade name: Common apple

Cultivated in Europe and West Asia from ancient times. Together with its numerous clones has become the commercial fruit apple of the world. Although most of its fruit is over 2 in (5 cm) in diameter and thus it cannot be classified as a crabapple, this species has played a major role in the development of modern crabapples. Over the years great strides have been made in improving its size, taste, and quality as an eating apple.

A tree to 49 ft (15 m) high, with a short trunk and rounded head; leaves broad-elliptic to elliptic or ovate, 1.8–3.9 in (4.5–10 cm) long and 1.2–2.1 in (3–5.5 cm) broad; buds pink, opening to white flowers suffused pink; fruit subglobose, 0.8 in (2 cm) and much larger. Subject to mild scab (Nichols).

Because *M. pumila* is subject to all the apple diseases and insect infestations, it therefore must be sprayed several times in the growing season. It has been used in hybridizing with extremely limited success, although some varieties have been of great use in hybridizing the smaller flowering crabapples. Because of its proneness to disease, this species should not be used in hybridizing new flowering crabapple cultivars. Loc. 14, 15, 31.

Species crosses of *M. pumila* include the following:

- *M. ×adstringens* (*M. pumila* × *M. baccata*)
- *M. ×astracanica* (*M. pumila* × *M. prunifolia*)
- *M. ×dawsoniana* (*M. pumila* × *M. fusca*)
- *M. ×heterophylla* (*M. pumila* × *M. coronaria*)
- *M. ×magdeburgensis* (*M. pumila* × *M. spectabilis*)
- *M. ×platycarpa* (*M. pumila* × *M. coronaria* var. *lancifolia*) (see *M. coronaria* var. *platycarpa*)

M. ×*soulardii* (*M. pumila* × *M. ioensis*)
M. 'Hopa' (*M. pumila* × *M.* ×*robusta*)

M. pumila var. ***sylvestris*** (Linnaeus) Miller
Synonym: *M. sylvestris* Miller
Trade name: European wild apple
Differs from the species chiefly in the nearly glabrous or slightly pubescent leaves; the glabrous pedicels and glabrous or slightly villous calyx; and the styles, which are also usually glabrous (Rehder). Some taxonomists consider it to be the European counterpart of the far-ranging *M. pumila* and thus prefer to list it as a separate species (namely, *M. sylvestris*).

Whether variant or species, this apple is rarely cultivated and it is little known today. It may have hybridized with other species in developing the modern commercial eating apple. It is an annual bearer. A double form, *M. pumila* var. *sylvestris* 'Flore Plena', fits exactly the description of *M. spectabilis* 'Alba Plena' in flower, fruit, leaves, and tree form. Whatever difficulties in names, *M. pumila* var. *sylvestris* is a fine ornamental with small, tasty, yellow-red fruit. It is subject to mild scab (Nichols). Loc. 14, 31, 35, 37, 54, 73, 81.

M. pumila var. ***sylvestris* 'Flore Plena'**
A double form of *M. pumila* var. *sylvestris*, which fits exactly the description of *M. spectabilis* 'Alba Plena' in flower, fruit, leaves, and tree form.

M. pumila var. ***sylvestris* 'Plena'** Fig. 11.8
Synonym: *M. sylvestris* 'Plena'
A group of similar seedlings with double flowers. A small, spreading to rounded tree to 15 ft (4.6 m) high and as wide; buds pale pink to white, opening to clusters of lovely pure white flowers 1.6 in (4 cm) across, double, with 13–15 petals; fruit 1.6 in (4 cm) in diameter, yellow with red cheeks, very sweet, good eating. Subject to mild scab and fire blight (Nichols).

Figure 11.8. *Malus pumila* var. *sylvestris* 'Plena' tree in bloom.

Although this crabapple is not suitable for home gardens because of the large fruit, it may have some use in hybridizing for double-flowering clones. The author has used it in hybridizing for doubleness, despite its disease susceptibility. Very often it has been confused with *M. spectabilis* 'Alba Plena'. Arie den Boer noted that some confusion exists regarding this variety because of a double, white-flowered apple with smaller, sweet-tasting fruit on short stems. Loc. 26, 31, 35, 37, 54, 68.

M. pumila var. ***translucens***
Synonyms: *M. pumila* 'Plena', *M. pumila* 'Translucens', *M. spectabilis* 'Alba Plena'
Subject to mild scab (Nichols). Loc. 4, 12, 18, 24, 31, 32, 37, 47, 54, 79.

***M. pumila* 'Niedzwetzkyana'** (Dieck) Schneider Plates 80, 81, 82
Synonym: *M.* 'Almata' N. E. Hansen
Trade name: Red Vein crabapple
This clone of *M. pumila* has brought about the greatest change in modern crabapples. Because of its unique color—its young leaves, buds, blossoms, fruit (including the flesh), bark, and wood of the branches are red—it has been used a great deal in hybridizing. There is still much to be gained by continued use of the true form and some of its best seedlings, especially in hybridizing with the newest multibrid clones.

Buds red, opening to single, red flowers 1.8 in (4.5 cm) across; fruit red-purple, with red flesh, 2–2.4 in (5–6 cm) in diameter, larger than the fruit of *M.* ×*purpurea*. An alternate bearer, but some progeny bloom annually. Subject to severe scab (Nichols).

Two accounts are given of the introduction of this red-colored Asian mountain apple. Vick (1990) stated:

> In his 1897 journey through Turkestan, Russia, and west China in search of plants suitable for the Northern Great Plains, Niels Hansen, State Agri. Stat., Brookings, South Dakota, visited a Mr. Niedzwetzky, who had located a red-fleshed apple in the Tian-Shan Mountains separating Turkestan and China. A shrub of 12′ high with reddish leaves, red blossoms, bark and wood, frt. a deep red-purple inside and out, (giving it the common name of 'Red Vein Crab'), Hansen noted that the fruit measured 2″ and described it as "good juicy, subacid, eating apple." Hansen

named the find *Pyrus malus niedzwetzkyana* to honor Mr. Niedzwetzky. Today it is known as *M. pumila* 'Niedzwetzkyana'. Hansen also gave the new apple a cultivar name, 'Almata', after the city of Alma Ata in that region. He grew open pollinated seedlings of this new apple and also crossed it with *M. baccata*, thus beginning what is known today as the Rosybloom crabapple strain.

In an earlier account of the history of *M. pumila* 'Niedzwetzkyana', Donald Wyman (1955) stated that it "was introduced into the U.S. by the Arnold Arboretum in 1896. Found in Siberia in 1891 by George Dieck, Zoeschen, Germany. The true 'Niedzwetzkyana' is very rare in the trade."

Are both accounts true? If so, it appears this apple was found in different places by two different individuals some years apart. Or, perhaps the two plants are one and the same? If Hansen originally named his plant *M. pumila* 'Niedzwetzkyana', what was the plant introduced by Dieck called 6 years earlier at the Arnold Arboretum? I have not been able to ascertain if the two plants, Hansen's and the one at the Arnold Arboretum, are identical, nor have I been able to ascertain the introduction number of the latter.

The plant brought back by Hansen appears to be the one most used in hybridizing. One of Hansen's first selections (probably pollinated by a form of *M. baccata*), was selected in 1920 for hardiness and attractive red flowers. It was known as *M.* 'Hansen's Red Leaf Crabapple', although its official name is *M.* 'Hopa' and it has also been called *M.* 'Hoppi', *M.* 'Sunburst', and *M.* 'Pink Sunburst'—different names but the same clone. In the same year Isabella Preston, Department of Agriculture, Ottawa, Canada, made a number of crosses between *M. pumila* 'Niedzwetzkyana' and some forms of the Siberian crabapple, *M. baccata*. She, too, planted a large number of open-pollinated seeds. These seedlings of *M. pumila* 'Niedzwetzkyana', which Hansen, Preston, and others developed, were called "Rosybloom Crabapples" by William T. Macoun before 1920. The group includes open-pollinated seedlings of *M. pumila* 'Niedzwetzkyana' and crosses of *M. pumila* 'Niedzwetzkyana' × *M. baccata*. Most Rosyblooms are open-pollinated seedlings. The goal of these hybridizers was to produce hardy crabapples that could withstand the harsh winters of the Canadian and U.S. prairie.

After 10 years of growing and evaluating the seedlings, Preston selected a number that appeared to be particularly attractive ornamentals and of a hardy nature. Collectively called Rosybloom crabapples because of their deep pink, rose, or purple-rose blossoms, these seedlings plants were introduced circa 1930. Most of them, although quite showy in springtime bloom, are rather coarse, large trees. Many are susceptible to leaf diseases and many are alternate bloomers, but their most negative aspect is the somewhat larger fruit that often is scabby and falls quite early. To be at their best, they require several sprayings.

The original group of Rosyblooms, raised by Preston, were known as the Lakes Series, all named for Canadian lakes. Many of these seedlings are not true Rosyblooms (i.e., they are not crosses of *M. pumila* 'Niedzwetzkyana' × *M. baccata*). A considerable number are open-pollinated seedlings of *M. pumila* 'Niedzwetzkyana', and a few may be better in hybridization than *M. pumila* 'Niedzwetzkyana'. Most of them are not suitable for the smaller home garden or landscapes. They do have some value for their massed bloom in large parks, but, even here, there are better-colored, disease-resistant, smaller, bright fruited crabapples that should be planted in their stead.

All the Rosyblooms are outstanding in their large flowers, which are deep rose-red, pink, rose with lavender, or magenta-purple fading quickly to a washed mauve. As a group, they are rather large trees, often reaching 35–40 ft (11–12 m) high and as wide. Their fruits are large, mostly 1.6 in (4 cm) wide and 1.5 in (3.8 cm) long, carmine-red with a yellow-brown spot on the shaded side or a dull red. The great fault of the Rosyblooms is that most are leafless or heavily defoliated with apple scab by midsummer, if not sprayed. Today many of the older clones should be discarded as ornamentals as there are newer hybrids of superior form and disease resistance. A few of the older Rosybloom introductions, however, might benefit from advanced hybridizing.

Although several of the Rosyblooms are excellent crabapples, they are seldom propagated or offered as ornamentals by nurseries. Those with larger fruit could be used for jellies as well as some ornamental color. It would be interesting if some hybridizer would attempt another series with *M. pumila* 'Niedzwetzkyana' using some of the more refined species or hybrids, such as *M.* ×*arnoldiana*, or crossing some of the better Rosyblooms with more recent multibrids rather than with *M. baccata*. The best of the Rosyblooms have fine genetic potential, especially the later introductions not of Preston origin. In their time the Rosyblooms were a great color addition to flowering crabapples and became very popular despite their proneness to apple scab. Today many of them have been supplanted by the multibrids of much smaller stature, particularly those with some *M. ×purpurea* breeding. Among the finest red-budded, crimson-flowering clones of *M. pumila* 'Niedzwetzkyana' are *M. ×purpurea* 'Lemoinei', *M.* 'Liset', and *M.* 'Orange Crush'. Loc. 8, 10, 13, 14, 15, 24, 31, 32, 54, 79, 81, 87.

Species crosses of *M. pumila* 'Niedzwetzkyana' include the following:

- *M. ×gloriosa* (*M. pumila* 'Niedzwetzkyana' × *M. ×scheideckeri*)
- *M. ×purpurea* (*M. pumila* 'Niedzwetzkyana' × *M. ×atrosanguinea*)
- *M. ×purpurea* 'Lemoinei' (*M. pumila* 'Niedzwetzkyana' × *M. ×atrosanguinea*)

Progeny of *M. pumila* 'Niedzwetzkyana', better known as the Rosybloom crabapples, are listed here with their introducers; descriptions are given in Chapter 12. In general, the Hansen hybrids are far better than the Preston crosses. The Rosyblooms of W. R. Leslie, Dominion Experiment Farm, Morden, Manitoba, Canada, like Hansen's introductions, are the best of this group. Carl Hansen also introduced a few Rosyblooms.

- *M.* 'Amisk' Preston
- *M.* 'Arrow' Preston
- *M.* 'Athabasca' Preston
- *M.* 'Babine' Preston
- **M.* 'Baskatong' Preston
- *M.* 'Chilko' Preston
- *M.* 'Cowichan' Preston
- *M.* 'Dauphin' Preston
- *M.* 'Erie' Preston
- *M.* 'Geneva' Preston
- *M.* 'Hopa' N. E. Hansen
- *M.* 'Jay Darling'
- **M.* 'Kingsmere' Preston
- *M.* 'Leslie' Northwest Nursery
- **M.* 'Makamik' Preston
- *M.* 'Meach' Preston
- *M.* 'Muskoka' Preston
- *M.* 'Namew' Preston
- *M.* 'Neville Copeman' Copeman
- *M.* 'Nipissing' Preston
- **M.* 'Pink Beauty' CDA—Morden
- **M.* 'Pink Giant' C. Hansen
- *M.* 'Redfield' New York State Experiment Station—Geneva
- *M.* 'Redford' New York State Agriculture Station—Geneva
- *M.* 'Red Silver' C. Hansen
- **M.* 'Red Splendor' Bergeson
- *M.* 'Red Tip' N. E. Hansen
- *M.* 'Rondo' CDA—Ottawa
- *M.* 'Rosseau' Preston
- *M.* 'Rudolph' F. L. Skinner
- *M.* 'Scugog' Preston
- **M.* 'Selkirk' CDA—Morden
- *M.* 'Simcoe' Preston
- **M.* 'Sissipuk' Preston
- **M.* 'Strathmore' W. R. Leslie
- **M.* 'Sundog' W. R. Leslie
- *M.* 'Timiskaming' Preston
- **M.* 'Tomiko' CDA—Ottawa
- **M.* 'Wabiskaw' Preston
- **M.* 'Wakpala' N. E. Hansen
- *M.* 'Zaza' N. E. Hansen
- *M.* 'Zita' N. E. Hansen

***M. pumila* 'Paradisiaca'** Schneider
A dwarf form not of horticultural significance. Subject to severe fire blight. Loc. 35.

***M. pumila* 'Pendula'**
Synonym: *M.* 'Elise Rathke' Späth? 1886
With large heavy pendulous branches and larger fruit, this form is of no ornamental value today except as an oddity, although it is still found in some older collections. The only good thing that can be said of it is that it is picturesque in the winter landscape because of heavy branching. Today there are far better weeping crabapples. Flowers single, white, 1.8 in (4.5 cm) across; fruit green, 2 in (5 cm) in diameter. Subject to severe scab and mild fire blight. Loc. 14, 18, 24, 26, 31, 81.

***M. pumila* 'Plena'**
See *M. pumila* var. *translucens.*

***M. pumila* 'Translucens'**
See *M. pumila* var. *translucens.*

M. ×purpurea (Barbier) Rehder
Parentage: *M. ×atrosanguinea* × *M. pumila* 'Niedzwetzkyana'
This famous cross originated at A. Barbier Nursery, Orleans, France, before 1900. It is one of the earliest crabs to flower and an annual bloomer, but its flowers quickly fade to a poor washed-out mauve color. A medium-sized tree, it is far better known through its many progeny, which have taken its place as some of the finest deep red-purple clones available today. Alfred Rehder described it thus:

> Young leaves and brts. purple; leaves smaller, lustrous on shoots occasionally slightly lobed; pedicels longer; petals oblong; styles often 4; flowers single, purplish-red, 4 cm. across; fruit 1.5–2.5 cm. across, dark purple in color.

Subject to very severe scab (Nichols). It would be safe to say that almost all modern red-flowering crabapples can be traced back to *M. ×purpurea*. Loc. 3, 8, 14, 15, 24, 26, 31, 35, 47, 54, 79, 87.

Progeny of *M. ×purpurea* include *M.* 'Evelyn' A. den Boer (*M. ×purpurea* × *M. ioensis*).

***M. ×purpurea* 'Aldenhamensis'** (Gibbs) Rehder

Originated as a chance seedling in 1920 in the garden of the Honorable Vicary Gibbs, Aldenham House, Elstree, Hertfordshire, England. Introduced to the United States in 1923 by the Arnold Arboretum. After blooming in spring, this form blooms intermittently, often a second or even a third time.

A medium-sized, rounded to spreading tree to 15 ft (4.6 m) high and as wide; leaves red-green to bronze-green; buds bright carmine-red, opening to single and semidouble, vinous-red flowers 1–1.2 in (2.5–3 cm) across; fruit subglobose, deep purple-red, shaded side green to bronze, 0.6–1 in (1.5–2.5 cm) in diameter. Subject to severe scab and mild fire blight (Nichols).

This clone should not be confused with the Aldenham eating apple, which is 2.6 in (6.5 cm) in diameter. Today it is not used often as better red-flowering clones are in commerce. Loc. 9, 13, 14, 15, 18, 24, 26, 31, 35, 37, 54, 79, 81, 89.

***M. ×purpurea* 'Barbier'**

See *M.* 'Barbier' in Chapter 12.

***M. ×purpurea* 'Dakeri'**

Name only.

***M. ×purpurea* 'Eleyi'** (Bean) Hesse 1904

Raised and named before 1920 for Charles Eley, East Bergholt, Suffolk, England. Introduced to the United States one year later by the Arnold Arboretum. Compared to *M. ×purpurea*, this clone's flowers are slightly darker and its foliage considerably darker. The form is thought by some to be an unstable variety of what is now called *M.* 'Jay Darling'. Arie den Boer, however, studied the two and concluded they were different names for the same plant that grows differently in different locations (see *M.* 'Jay Darling' in Chapter 12 for further discussion of the problem). Often an alternate bloomer, *M. ×purpurea* 'Eleyi' is subject to leaf diseases and has declined in popularity so that it is no longer considered horticulturally valuable. Lester Nichols recommended phasing it out as it is subject to very severe scab. Newer clones are superior to this red-flowering, purple-fruited clone, which should therefore be discarded. Loc. 5, 8, 15, 18, 24, 26, 31, 39, 40, 41, 43, 44, 54, 74, 79, 80, 81.

***M. ×purpurea* 'Eleyi Compacta'**

Originated from seed by S. G. A. Doorenbos, Department of Public Parks, The Hague, Netherlands. Introduced in 1952. A very compact and dense tree; leaves dull purple-red; flowers single, vinous-red. It is valued for its young plant which flowers well. It may have some value to hybridizers for its compact growth, although other superior clones are available today.

***M. ×purpurea* 'Kornicensis'**

Synonym: *M.* 'Kornik'

Received at the Arnold Arboretum from Kornik Arboretum, Kornik, Poland, in 1939. Buds dark red, opening to single, light purple-red flowers 1.6 in (4 cm) across; fruit dark purple-red, lighter on shaded side, 0.6 in (1.5 cm) in diameter. Subject to moderate scab (Nichols). Not well known nor readily found, except at the Arnold Arboretum. It has nothing new to offer and other clones are superior. Loc. 15, 31, 41, 81, 89.

M. ×purpurea* 'Lemoinei' (Lemoine) Rehder

Plates 83, 84, 85

Parentage: *M. pumila* 'Niedzwetzkyana' × *M. ×atrosanguinea*

Undoubtedly the finest of the progeny of *M. ×purpurea* to be named so far. Originated at the famous nursery, Victor Lemoine et Fils, Nancy, France, in 1922, probably as a chance seedling. Named by Emil Lemoine. Introduced into the United States in 1925 by the Arnold Arboretum. It probably is the most popular of all the red-flowering crabapples.

A medium-sized, upright to spreading tree to 18 ft (5.5 m) high and as wide; leaves glossy, purple on new shoots, turning a deep purple-green with maturity; expanding buds dark red, opening to single and semidouble flowers 1.6 in (4 cm) across, red-purple to crimson, fading to a slightly lighter shade that does not fade to mauve as readily as other cultivars but holds its color well; fruit dark red, turning bronze on the shaded side, about 0.7 in (1.8 cm) in diameter, generally too dark to be effective. Excellent disease resistance. In some locations longitudinal cracks appear in the bark of scaffold branches. These seem to heal over the same year they appear and do not detract from the appearance of the tree.

Older trees are showpieces in the landscape as they bloom heavily and annually. Planted in groups of three or as a single specimen among white-flowering crabs, this crabapple has no equal! The one detracting quality that causes nurseries to reject it is that young plants do not begin blooming until they have attained some size, about their 5th or 6th year. Once the tree begins to bloom, however, it does so regularly and with increasing beauty. It is much sought after in bloom for it outstanding color.

Most of the newer red-flowering clones are descendants of *M.* ×*purpurea* 'Lemoinei'. Two exceptional clones among its progeny are *M.* 'Liset' by Doorenbos and the newest, *M.* 'Orange Crush', by Fiala. Both bloom when young and, because of their brighter bud and blossom color, are perhaps superior, both in blossom and in attractive fruit. *Malus* ×*purpurea* 'Lemoinei' should still be used in hybridizing as it has much to offer. It should be crossed with the new *M. halliana* National Arboretum No. 127 with its double, pink flowers, and some hybridizer should save its pollen for some of the later-flowering species of *M. coronaria* and *M. ioensis*, which could produce some outstanding hybrids! In all aspects, despite the years it takes to come into bloom, it is a magnificent tree well worth the time in waiting! Loc. 3, 4, 11, 15, 18, 24, 26, 31, 32, 35, 43, 47, 54, 68, 79, 80, 81, 87.

Species crosses of *M.* ×*purpurea* include *M.* ×*moerlandsii* (*M.* ×*purpurea* 'Lemoinei' × *M. toringo*).

Progeny of *M.* ×*purpurea* 'Lemoinei' from first to third generations include the following:

- *M.* 'Brandywine' Simpson
- *M.* 'Buccaneer' Fiala
- *M.* 'Calvary' Fiala
- *M.* 'Cardinal's Robe' Fiala
- *M.* 'Cranberry Lace' Fiala
- *M.* 'Firecracker' Fiala
- *M.* 'Liset' Doorenbos
- *M.* 'Maria' Fiala
- *M.* 'Orange Crush' Fiala
- *M.* 'Profusion' Doorenbos
- *M.* 'Purple Prince' Fiala
- *M.* 'Wildfire' Fiala

M.* ×*robusta (Carrière) Rehder Plates 86, 87, 88

Synonym: *M. cerasifera* Schneider

Trade name: Cherry crabapple

Parentage: *M. baccata* × *M. prunifolia*

A group of hybrid crabapples mostly with cherrylike fruit from small to fairly large. Alfred Rehder described *M.* ×*robusta* thus:

> Lvs. glabrescent or pubescent beneath: flowers slender stalked, white or pinkish: calyx usually glabrous: fruit subglobose or ellipsoid, red or yellow, slender stalked, up to 2 cm across, usually partly with and partly without calyx.

This usually medium-sized tree is one of the first to bloom, but an alternate bloomer and hence not used much for landscape value. Subject to very mild traces of scab (Nichols). Loc. 8, 10, 12, 14, 15, 24, 26, 31, 35, 47, 61, 81.

Species crosses of *M.* ×*robusta* include *M.* 'Hopa' (*M.* ×*robusta* × *M. pumila*).

***M.* ×*robusta* 'Arnold-Canada'**

Synonyms: *M.* 'Arnold-Canada No. 5', *M.* ×*robusta* No. 5, *M.* Ottawa No. 524

Parentage: *M. baccata* × *M. prunifolia*

Listed by Roland Jefferson as a crabapple of documented authentic origin. Grown from seed obtained through the Arnold Arboretum from Russia in 1927. Budded plant from William Purdom. Original plant collected near Peking, China, on the road to Wutai Shan, for the Arnold Arboretum. Introduced in 1947 by Canada Department of Agriculture, Ottawa, Ontario. It differs from *M.* ×*robusta* by having a wider, spreading habit; slightly larger, bright red and yellow fruit; and much larger, broad, oval leaves that turn bright yellow in autumn. Jefferson (1970, p. 20) judged it to be of value because of its bright fruit and fine fall leaf color. It should be investigated by hybridizers seeking to incorporate fall color as an added attraction to the colorful fruit. Flowers and fruit are similar to those of *M.* ×*robusta*. I have designated this clone as *M.* 'Arnold-Canada No. 5' to honor its places of introduction and so that its identity will not be lost. It is better known in Canada than in the United States. Loc. 16.

***M.* ×*robusta* 'Costata'**

Obsolete. Name only.

***M.* ×*robusta* 'Cowles House'**

Name only. Disease resistant (Nichols). Loc. 61, 86.

***M.* ×*robusta* 'Erecta'** (Carrière) Rehder

Synonym: *M.* ×*robusta fastigiata*

Name only. Grown from seed sent by C. S. Sargent from Beijing, China, in 1904 to the Arnold Arboretum. An upright tree; expanding buds white traced with pink; flowers white, 1.6 in (4 cm) across, single and double; fruit yellow and red to deep crimson, 0.9 in (2.3 cm) in diameter; an alternate bloomer hence not recommended for general propagation. Subject to mild scab and fire blight (Nichols). Loc. 10, 12, 24, 26, 31, 32, 54, 81.

***M.* ×*robusta* 'Gary's Choice'** Gary Plate 89

An upright tree to 25–30 ft (8–9 m) high and 20 ft (6 m) wide, with many thin branchlets that give it a weeping effect; buds white, opening to masses of single, white flowers; fruit 0.4 in

(1 cm), medium red, persistent. An annual bloomer. Disease resistant. A finer tree than *M.* ×*robusta* with more class in form. Excellent where space permits, especially in larger estates, parks, and arboretum plantings. This crabapple is no longer readily available and there is some question whether it may not be the same as *M. baccata* 'Flexilis'.

***M.* ×*robusta* 'J. L. Pierce'**
Name only. Disease free (Nichols). Loc. 61.

***M.* ×*robusta* 'Leucocarpa'**
Synonym: *M. leucocarpa*
Name only. A pale yellow fruiting clone. No disease (Nichols). Better clones are available today. Loc. 24, 35.

****M.* ×*robusta*** No. 5 CDA—Ottawa
See *M.* ×*robusta* 'Arnold-Canada'.

****M.* ×*robusta* 'Persicifolia'** Rehder
Plates 90, 91
Trade name: Peachleaf crabapple
A much better clone of *M.* ×*robusta* in that it is more shrublike, sending up several slender branches from the base. Hardy and handsome. Introduced in 1910 from seed collected by William Purdom on the Road to Wutai Shan, near Peking, China. Plants received in 1913 at the Arnold Arboretum from J. Veitch & Sons (Purdom No. 179).

A shrublike tree; leaves, narrow, dark green, lightly glossy, 3 in (7.6 cm) long, fine-toothed, resembling peach leaves; buds rose-pink, opening to pure white masses of single flowers 1.6 in (4 cm) across; fruit bright red, shaded side sometimes yellow-green or brown-green, elliptical, 0.75 in (1.9 cm) across, persistent often until February or March. An annual, abundant bearer. High disease resistance; subject to slight scab and mild fire blight (Nichols).

This clone is one of the finest two-season crabapples as it is very showy in spring bloom and in fall fruit. It should be used more by hybridizers for its low, interesting form and fine horticultural qualities. It is fine for large estates and parks as a background tree, but much too large for smaller gardens. Loc. 5, 14, 18, 24, 26, 31, 32, 37, 54, 79, 81.

***M.* ×*robusta* 'Red Siberian'**
Name only. Red-fruited clone with showy fruit to 0.75 in (1.9 cm) in diameter. Other named clones are better. Subject to mild scab (Nichols). Loc. 35.

***M.* ×*robusta* 'Yellow Fruited'**
Name only. Subject to mild scab and cedar-apple rust (Nichols). Loc. 10, 11, 12, 18.

***M.* ×*robusta* 'Yellow Siberian'**
Name only. No diseases (Nichols). Loc. 35.

***M.* ×*robusta* 'Xanthocarpa'**
Arnold Arboretum No. 116-46 SD, Rock No. 23380. Similar to *M.* ×*robusta* 'Yellow Fruited' or *M.* ×*robusta* 'Yellow Siberian', but more disease resistant. Name only. Loc. 16.

M. rockii Rehder
A botanical name referring to *M.* 'Rockii', a doubtful species or subspecies. Seed No. 2380 was sent by Joseph Rock from China to the Arnold Arboretum in 1922. Buds pink, opening to single, white flowers; fruit about 0.4 in (1 cm) across, bright red, persistent. Disease resistant. Subject to mild powdery mildew (Nichols). Loc. 15, 31, 32, 54, 81.

*+***M. sargentii*** Rehder Plates 92, 93, 94
Trade name: Sargent's crabapple
Introduced into the United States from Japan in 1892 by the Arnold Arboretum. Grown from seed No. 4681 collected near Mororan in Hokkaido, Japan, by C. S. Sargent in 1892. Valued because it is the smallest species.

A shrub, growing only to about 6–8 ft (1.8–2.5 m) high, spreading 8–15 ft (2.5–4.6 m) or about twice as wide as high, densely branched, with branches growing from the base and no attempt to form a leader; laterals grow at nearly right angles from the branches; leaves similar to those of *M. sieboldii* 'Calocarpa' but much heavier, a darker green, and with one pair of large lobes at the base; flowers profuse, pure white, fragrant, single; fruit dark red to purple, 0.25–0.3 in (0.6–0.8 cm) in diameter, persistent. Very fine disease resistance (Nichols). Alfred Rehder described it thus:

> It is a low shrub with horizontally spreading branches, often spinescent; young brts. tomentose; leaves ovate, acuminate, rounded or subcordate at the base, acuminate, 5–8 cm long, sharply serrate, villous when young, finally nearly glabrous, those of shoots usually broad-ovate, mostly 3-lobed; petioles 2–3 cm long, pubescent; flowers pure white, single, 2.5 cm across; pedicels 2–3 cm long, like the calyx glabrous, petals oval, broad at base, overlapping; styles usually 4 (3–5); fruit subglobose about 1 cm across, dark red, slightly bloomy.

Although this species is attractive as a low

shrub with very small showy fruit, a negative feature is that it is an alternate bloomer and hence not generally recommended for the average home garden that cannot afford off seasons of flowering. It should be used in large estate, park, and arboretum collections. It also is of value to hybridizers looking to produce bush-size crabapples with miniature fruits. An excellent smaller crabapple that is always outstanding with a great variety of landscape uses—for smaller city lots, small gardens, patios, in front of larger plantings, and wherever a smaller shrub-tree is needed. Loc. 3, 5, 13, 14, 18, 19, 22, 24, 26, 31, 32, 35, 37, 38, 39, 40, 43, 46, 47, 54, 55, 68, 71, 73, 79, 80, 81, 86, 100.

***M. sargentii* 'Rosea'**

Synonym: *M.* 'Scanlon's Pink Bud Sargent'

Selected at the Arnold Arboretum from a group of seedlings numbered 1 B.H.S. received in 1921 from the Rochester Parks Department, Rochester, NY. An excellent shrub form, it differs from the species by having red-pink buds that open to white flowers 1.4 in (3.5 cm) across; fruit dark red, 0.4 in (1 cm) in diameter. Subject to moderate scab. Loc. 4, 14, 18, 31, 35, 39, 55, 73, 79, 81.

Progeny of *M. sargentii* 'Rosea' include *M.* 'Mary Potter' Sax.

***M. sargentii* 'Roselow'**

This is not a clone but rather a strain of greatly variable seedlings sent out by USDA Soil Conservation Service. As with all strains, the cultivar or strain name becomes associated with every variable seedling, many of which are not worthy of any introduction, and thus we have many plants—some good, most inferior—all named *M. sargentii* 'Roselow'. Loc. 81.

***M. *sargentii* 'Tina'** Hook's Nursery, Lake Zurich, IL

A dwarf form of the species. Selected by William McReynolds, of Hook's Nursery, Lake Zurich, IL, from open-pollinated seed obtained from Japan. Named for McReynolds' granddaughter. A tree to 5 ft (1.5 m) high; buds red, opening to single, white flowers; fruit small, red. No disease (Nichols). Excellent for smaller landscapes and as a specimen plant. Also excellent in hybridizing for dwarf plants. Loc. 5, 31, 61, 79.

M. ×scheideckeri Späth ex Zabel 1889 Plates 95, 96, 97

Parentage: *M. floribunda* × *M. prunifolia*

Originated before 1888 in Scheidecker Nursery, Munich, Germany. Introduced to the United States by the Arnold Arboretum in 1889. Sometimes confused for *M. spectabilis* 'Riversii' (which see).

A small, upright tree; leaves ovate, 2–3.9 in (5–10 cm) long, sharply and coarsely serrate; flowers pale rose pink, usually semidouble, 10 petals, 1.2–1.4 in (3–3.5 cm) across; fruit slightly ribbed or angular, yellow-orange, 0.6 in (1.5 cm) in diameter, persistent calyx. Should be phased out—moderately susceptible to scab and fire blight (Nichols).

Because the flowers are produced in dense clusters all along the slender branches, this smaller tree is especially suitable for gardens where space is limited. It tolerates pruning well and can be easily trained to a standard form. It should be used much more in landscaping, offered by more nurseries, and used far more in hybridizing, especially for its semidouble blossoms and small fruit. Loc. 12, 18, 24, 26, 31, 35, 37, 39, 40, 41, 43, 54, 55, 79, 80, 81.

Species crosses of *M. ×scheideckeri* include *M. ×gloriosa* (*M. ×scheideckeri* × *M. pumila* 'Niedzwetzkyana').

M. sieboldii (Rehder) Fiala 1990 Fig. 6.3

Author's proposed name for the crabapple known as *M. ×zumi* Rehder or *M. sieboldii* var. *zumi* (Matsumura) Asami, but now upgraded to a species. For further discussion of the reason for the name change, see "Proposed Change to Elevate *Malus sieboldii* var. *zumi* to Species Rank" in Chapter 10.

Introduced into the United States by the Arnold Arboretum from seed collected in 1892 by C. S. Sargent in Honshu, Japan, where it is rare. A small to medium-sized, rounded tree to 12 or 15 ft (4 or 4.6 m) high and 10 ft (3 m) wide, somewhat bushy, slow growing; buds red to carmine, opening to abundant, single, white flowers; fruit red, very small, 0.4-0.6 in (1–1.5 cm) in diameter, very showy, abundant. An annual bearer. Disease resistant (Nichols). Alfred Rehder described it thus:

> Leaves ovate to ovate-oblong or oblong, acuminate, 4–9 cm long, those of flowering brts. entire or crenate-serrulate, of shoots serrate or occasionally slightly lobed, pubescent beneath, when young becoming glabrous; flower buds deep pink (to carmine), opening to single, white blossoms, 2.5–3 cm across; fruit about 1.2 cm across, red (or yellow).

I believe the true species has only red fruit; the yellow is a later hybridization or mutational addition. Loc. 3, 12, 14, 24, 26, 31, 32, 35, 47, 54, 81, 86.

Two forms of *M. sieboldii* have been used in recent decades by hybridizers: *M. sieboldii* 'Calocarpa' and *M. sieboldii* 'Wooster'. These clones were especially important in the author's beginning hybridizations at Falconskeape Gardens, Medina, OH: they were chosen in 1940, with other species and selected clones, as foundation material for the author's hybridization programs. Crossed and recrossed with other species and selected named clones, they have produced a whole array of multibrids (plants with many species in their makeup), many of which have been induced into tetraploids. The success of the hybridization program at Falconskeape rests heavily on these select clones. In 50 years nearly 12 generations of hybridization have been accomplished (often grafting 1-year-old hybrids into mature trees to provide rapid growth and earlier blooming to obtain pollen for hybridizing.

In recent years seed has been collected in the wild in China, Korea, and Tibet by the USDA and sent to the National Arboretum under the names of *M. mandshurica* and *M. sieboldii*, where Donald Egolf has made several selections from the many seedlings. Among some of the seedlings growing there and at Falconskeape Gardens, are some with outstanding bright red, small fruit, excellent tree form, and disease resistance. I consider *M. mandshurica* to be *M. baccata* var. *mandshurica* and propose renaming *M. ×zumi* as *M. sieboldii*. It is these selections that appear to have considerable merit, both in themselves and as new materials for hybridizers.

The best of these newer seedlings should be named as specific clones and selected for breeding use. They should not be propagated by seed, as has been the custom in the past (witness the confusion by calling all seedlings of *M. sieboldii* 'Calocarpa' by the clone name *M. sieboldii* 'Calocarpa' rather than propagating the clone asexually). I do not believe these plants are hybrids but, more correctly, could be labeled as seedlings (i.e., named clones of *M. sieboldii* (Rehder) Fiala).

This is a species whose possibilities have not yet been exhausted by hybridizers. It is just now being appreciated as one of the finest, perhaps the best, of all the crabapple species. Its relationship as a hybrid should be severed once and for all!

*+***M. sieboldii* 'Calocarpa'** (Rehder) Fiala
Plates 98, 99, 100

Trade name: Redbud crabapple

Author's proposed name for the crabapple known as *M. ×zumi* 'Calocarpa' Rehder. For further discussion of the reason for the name change, see "Proposed Change to Elevate *Malus sieboldii* var. *zumi* to Species Rank" in Chapter 10.

A selected seedling clone introduced into the United States by the Arnold Arboretum from seed sent from Japan in 1890 by William S. Bigelow. A dense, upright to spreading tree, 15 ft (4.6 m) high and as wide, smaller than the species; leaves scarcely lobed, those of shoots more deeply lobed; buds deep red, opening to single, white to pink-white flowers 1.4 in (3.5 cm) across; fruit 0.4 in (1 cm) in diameter, bright red to red-orange, often lighter on the shaded side. A reliable, abundant, annual bloomer. Subject to slight scab, mild fire blight, and slight powdery mildew (Nichols), but at Falconskeape Gardens, Medina, OH, this clone has been disease free for 50 years.

One of the most beautiful of all the ornamental crabapples both in bloom and in fruit. Excellent as a single specimen, a patio tree, or massed with variously colored fruiting clones, giving marvelous color contrasts. Also excellent smaller gardens, especially where a small tree with abundant blossoms, good healthy leaves, and a splendid parade of very small, colorful fruit is needed. Virtually disease-free. Birds relish the small fruit, which never is messy. This clone has also been used very heavily by hybridizers and is the parent of many of the newer, highly disease resistant hybrids.

Unfortunately the real *M. sieboldii* 'Calocarpa' is difficult to find. Nursery professionals have been planting the seed of supposed *M. sieboldii* 'Calocarpa' for decades, but the real plant is a clone that cannot be obtained by seed. It must be asexually propagated. Among its seedlings are a great variety of good specimens that are not as fine as the parent, although they are all sold with the label *M. sieboldii* 'Calocarpa'. I would accept only those plants that are asexually propagated from an authentic arboretum plant. Because it is such an outstanding clone, it is unfortunate that any red-fruited specimen of *M. sieboldii* slightly resembling it is immediately labeled *M. sieboldii* 'Calocarpa'. Loc. 4, 5, 14, 18, 22, 24, 26, 31, 32, 35, 37, 39, 40, 41, 43, 46, 47, 54, 55, 58, 61, 68, 69, 71, 73, 74, 76, 77, 79, 81, 82, 84, 86, 100.

***M. sieboldii* 'Wooster'** (Rehder) Fiala 1954
Plate 101

Synonym: *M.* 'Slansky's Red Fruited'

Author's proposed name for the crabapple known as *M. ×zumi* 'Wooster' Rehder. For further discussion of the reason for the name change, see "Proposed Change to Elevate *Malus sieboldii* var. *zumi* to Species Rank" in Chapter 10.

Grown from open-pollinated seed of *M. sieboldii* collected at the Ohio State Agriculture Experiment Station, Wooster, OH, by Fr. John Fiala in 1949. Selected from a group of seedlings grown at Falconskeape Gardens, Medina, OH. An outstanding clone selected for its early orange-red fruit and excellent disease resistance.

A small tree to 12 ft (3.5 m) high and 10 ft (3 m) wide; leaves very dark green, disease free; buds bright carmine red, opening to single, white flowers; fruit 0.6 in (1.5 cm) in diameter, brilliant orange-red, coloring very early in late August, persistent through October when migrating birds finish its fruiting season. Completely disease resistant after 21 years of testing (Nichols).

Because of its disease resistance, this clone was chosen as one of the foundation clones for crabapple breeding at Falconskeape Gardens; it has continued to be a superior progenitor of disease-resistant hybrids. Many scions of this clone have been disseminated to nursery professionals and hybridizers. It has appeared at times in a few nursery catalogues under different names. It has been an important parent for the *Zumi* hybrids and many of the newer multibrids developed over the past decades at Falconskeape Gardens. Genetically it imparts both its disease resistance and bright, small, orange-red fruits to its progeny. An outstanding clone but outdone by many of its offspring.

Malus sieboldii 'Wooster' differs from *M. sieboldii* 'Calocarpa' in that it colors three weeks sooner and has slightly smaller fruit that is bright orange-red rather than bright red. Fruit of the former is readily eaten by migrating birds and is not quite as persistent as fruit of *M. sieboldii* 'Calocarpa'. Loc. 47.

M. sieboldii (Regel) Rehder

Not an accepted name in this volume (see Chapter 10). Author proposes combining this taxon with *M. sieboldii* var. *arborescens* (Rehder) to form *M. toringo* Siebold ex De Vriese 1848 (Wijnands 1979). It is the author's view that *M. toringo* has yellow fruit, while *M. sieboldii* has red fruit. Over the years the two have hybridized in the wild resulting in yellow-fruited clones (e.g., *M.* 'Winter Gold') once called *M.* ×*zumi* (renamed *M. sieboldii* in the present volume).

M. sieboldii var. ***arborescens*** Rehder

Not an accepted name in this volume (see Chapter 10). Author proposes combining this subspecies with *M. sieboldii* (Regel) Rehder to form *M. toringo*, which see.

M. sieboldii var. ***zumi*** (Matsumura) Asami

Not an accepted name in this volume (see Chapter 10). Author proposes replacing it with *M. sieboldii* Fiala, which see.

M. sikkimensis (Hooker) Koehne

Plates 102, 103, 104

Trade name: Sikkim crabapple

A crabapple closely related to *M. baccata* and introduced from the Himalayan Mountains to England about 1849 but brought to the United States around 1895. Alfred Rehder described it thus:

> Brts. and leaves beneath tomentose; leaves ovate to ovate-oblong, 5–7 cm long, acuminate, sharply serrate; flowers single, pink in bud opening to white, 2.5 cm across; calyx pubescent; fruit obovoid, 1.5 cm long, red, dotted.

An alternate bearer, it is of no significance to ornamental horticulture. Its species standing is doubtful; it may well be a distant subspecies of *M. baccata*. No diseases (Nichols). Loc. 12, 24, 26, 31, 37, 81.

M.* ×*soulardii (L. H. Bailey) Britton

Parentage: *M. ioensis* × *M. pumila*

A group of hybrids with single, light pink flowers. Named after James G. Soulard, Galena, IL, who introduced the cross into cultivation in 1868. Upper side of leaves rugose (a characteristic not found in other clones of this hybrid); flowers single, pale pink; fruit abundant, yellow-green, to 2.1 in (5.5 cm) in diameter. Subject to mild scab and cedar-apple rust (Nichols). One form has been named *M.* 'Mercer'.

Malus ×*soulardii* is listed as a crabapple but because its fruit is over 2 in (5 cm) in diameter, it should be classified as an apple. It is not a tree of any great ornamental value. I have grown it at Falconskeape for 50 years and it remains a modestly, medium-sized tree, with heavy annual bloom and great quantities of messy fruit that falls quite early. I would not recommend it as far superior crabapples are available. As an apple, it could be carried by a large botanic collection merely to show it as a type of the cross. Loc. 10, 14, 18, 24, 31, 54, 79, 81.

***M.* ×*soulardii* 'Soulard'** Soulard 1868 Fig. 11.9

One of the named hybrids in the *M. soulardii* group. Named for James Soulard, Galena, IL,

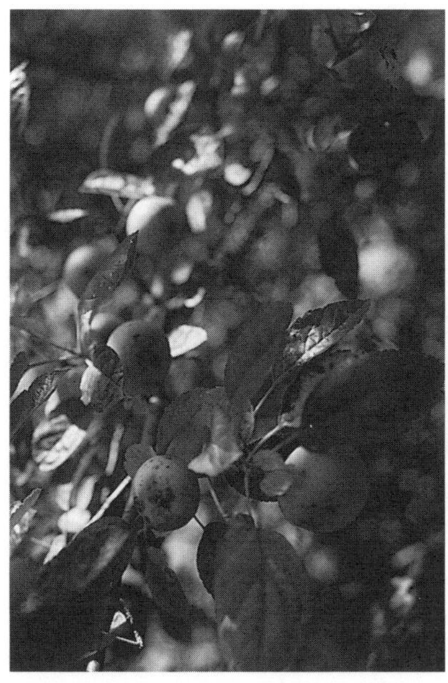

Figure 11.9. Because the yellow-green fruit of *M.* ×*soulardii* 'Soulard' is over 2 in (5 cm) in diameter, this tree should be classified as an apple.

who introduced it in 1868. Subject to severe scab and mild cedar-apple rust (Nichols). Loc. 26, 47, 54, 81.

M. spectabilis (Aiton) Borkhausen
Plates 105, 106

Trade name: Chinese flowering crabapple

Introduced before 1780 from China but not known in the wild. Most probably a hybrid, grown in England since 1750. One of the oldest and most handsome of the flowering crabapples. Subject to mild scab (Nichols). Alfred Rehder described it thus:

> Tree to 8 m of upright habit; young brts. sparingly pubescent, later red-brown; leaves elliptic to elliptic-oblong, 5–8 cm long, short acuminate, cuneate, appressed-serrate, lustrous and glabrous above, pubescent beneath when young, finally nearly glabrous, subchartaceous; petiole 1–3 cm long, pubescent; flowers deep rose-red in bud, fading to blush, 4–5 cm across, semi-double or sometimes single; pedicels 2–3 cm long like the calyx glabrous or slightly villous; sepals triangular-ovate, shorter than tube; fruit subglobose, about 2 cm across, yellowish, without cavity at base and stalk usually thickened at apex, sour.

Some confusion exists within the species as there is a single and a double form, which are almost identical; the latter, however, has double flowers and fruit with an occasional second whorl of carpels, a second core, which is easily recognized by the deformity of the fruit near the calyx end. This second core often contains seed that will germinate in addition to the seed of the regular core. Arie den Boer, the author, and other crabapple authorities point out that although *M. spectabilis*, which has never been found in the wild, is considered a species, its seedlings are a mixed lot, suggesting it is of hybrid parentage. Whatever its origin, it will probably never be known.

The single-flowering form, which Rehder listed as "single to semi-double flowering," is seldom found in collections. It is a smaller tree, growing in a natural vase form, almost fastigiate when young but spreading with age to a broader crown. "It is an ideal tree to be used as a single specimen, and, if given ample room will soon develop into one of the finest of ornamentals" (A. den Boer). Not only is it a magnificent specimen for single or group plantings, it is also an excellent plant for hybridizers. There remain many wonderful qualities, especially in the double-flowering form, that will produce outstanding new hybrids when combined with the best of the newest multibrids. The double form is by far the most attractive and should, alone, be used in landscaping. In this volume, *M. spectabilis* refers to the single form.

Malus spectabilis has been used to some extent by hybridizers with promising results. Although it seems to transmit the doubleness of flower and the vase form of the tree to its progeny, it also transmits the poor quality and yellow-brown fruit as well. With careful programs of hybridizing, a few of its progeny are receiving their fruit color from the alternate parent. Loc. 9, 12, 14, 15, 26, 31, 35, 61, 73.

Species crosses of *M. spectabilis* include the following:

- *M.* ×*magdeburgensis* (*M. spectabilis* × *M. pumila*)
- *M.* ×*micromalus* (*M. spectabilis* × ? *M. baccata*)

Progeny of *M. spectabilis* include *M.* 'Van Eseltine' New York Experiment Station—Geneva.

M. spectabilis var. ***grandiflora***

Synonym: *M.* 'Large Flesh Pink'

W. B. Clarke, San Jose, CA, listed a double-flowering, pink crabapple in 1918 under the name *M.* 'Large Flesh Pink', renaming it in 1929 *M. spectabilis* var. *grandiflora*. There remains considerable confusion as his introduction has about 15 petals and is certainly not the true *M. spectabilis* 'Riversii' (which see; also see *M. pumila* var. *sylvestris* 'Plena').

***M. spectabilis* 'Alba Plena'**
Most probably not a clone of *M. spectabilis*, but rather of *M. pumila* var. *translucens* (which see).

***M. spectabilis* 'Plena'** Plate 107
A name applied to any number of varied cultivars with double blossoms, including *M. spectabilis* var. *grandiflora* and *M. spectabilis* 'Rosea Plena'. Subject to mild scab and mildew (Nichols). Loc. 12, 31, 35, 37, 47.

***M. spectabilis* 'Riversii'** (Booth) Nash Plate 108
Synonym: *M. spectabilis* 'Rosea Plena'
Trade name: Rivers crabapple
Named for Thomas Rivers, a famous English nurseryman who introduced the clone in 1872. Introduced to the United States before 1883 by Parsons Nursery, Long Island, NY. One of the more widely grown forms. Has the largest double-pink flowers of any variety of *M. spectabilis*.
Flowers pink, double, with 9–20 petals, 1.8–2.4 in (4.5–6 cm) across; fruit yellow 1–1.4 in (2.5–3.5 cm) in diameter. Subject to mild scab. A very fine, showy clone.
It is all but very difficult to find the true *M. spectabilis* 'Riversii'. Many plants listed as *M. spectabilis* 'Riversii' in even the largest collections are in fact *M. spectabilis* 'Plena', and *M. ×scheideckeri* also has been confused for *M. spectabilis* 'Riversii'.
Of his introduction, Thomas Rivers stated, "a little disappointed at my failure in crossing." Arie den Boer and other horticulturists disagree with Rivers' assessment, proclaiming it an extremely beautiful plant. It should be far better known and carried by nurseries. Loc. 9, 11, 12, 18, 31, 32, 35, 37, 81.

***M. spectabilis* 'Rosea Plena'**
See *M. spectabilis* 'Riversii'.

M. ×sublobata (Zabel) Rehder Fig. 11.10
Synonym: *M.* 'Cashmere'
Trade name: Yellow autumn crabapple
Parentage: *M. toringo* (formerly *M. sieboldii*) × *M. prunifolia*
Introduced in 1892 by the Arnold Arboretum. Of unknown origin (according to Alfred Rehder), probably grown from seed brought by C. S. Sargent from Japan.
A pyramidal tree; leaves narrow-elliptic to elliptic-oblong, those of shoots broader, partly with 2 or only 1 short lobe, tomentose when young, pubescent beneath at maturity, 1.4–3.1 in (3.5–8 cm) long; buds rose-red, opening to masses of single, blush to white flowers 1.6 in (4 cm) across, very heavy flowering; pedicels and calyx villous; styles 4–5, rarely 3; fruit subglobose, 0.6–0.8 in (1.5–2 cm) in diameter, yellow, sometimes yellow and red, or orange, usually with calyx, sometimes without, persistent. Susceptible to severe scab (Nichols).

Figure 11.10. *Malus ×sublobata* in bloom.

This crabapple deserves to be better known. It is probably identical to the clone *M.* 'Cashmere', known at Aldenham House, England, before 1916. So far it has been listed only as a hybrid cross but all plants are not identical. Selected clones may be better than others. Since at maturity it is a rather good size tree, it is not recommended for smaller gardens, but it definitely has a place on larger estates, parks, and arboreta. It is quite showy in the abundance of its fruit. Loc. 11, 13, 14, 15, 16, 18, 24, 26, 31, 32, 35, 37, 79, 81, 87, 89.

M. sylvestris
See *M. pumila* var. *sylvestris*.

***M. sylvestris* 'Plena'**
See *M. pumila* var. *sylvestris* 'Plena'.

M. theifera Rehder
See *M. hupehensis*.

M. toringo (Siebold) Siebold ex De Vriese (Wijnands 1979) Plates 109, 110, 111
Synonyms: *M. sieboldii* (Regel) Rehder, *Pyrus sieboldii* Regel, *Pyrus toringo* Siebold, *M. toringo* var. *arborescens*, *M. toringo* 'Arborescens'
Trade name: Toringo crabapple
Malus toringo (formerly *M. sieboldii*) is a yellow-fruited species, whereas *M. sieboldii* (formerly *M. ×zumi*) is a red-fruited one. By natural hybridization and color mutations, *M. toringo* now has yellow-fruiting clones, but originally it was red. Since a great number of open-pollinated seeds have been collected in

the wild and in cultivation, there is considerable confusion as to identity of species and hybrids in both *M. toringo* and *M. sieboldii.*

Introduced to the United States in 1856 from Japan, where it is a cultivated dwarf mountain form. A natural quintaploid with 5*x* the number of chromosomes. Its greatest value lies in its late time of bloom and its low, bushlike form.

A small, shrublike tree; buds deep rose, opening to small light pink flowers that eventually turn nearly white, star-shaped, single, about 0.8 in (2 cm) across; fruit small, 0.25–0.3 in (0.6–0.8 cm) in diameter, globose, red or brown-yellow according to Alfred Rehder, or yellow according to Philipp von Siebold (see Chapter 10 for a discussion on the differences between the two descriptions). Subject to slight scab and fire blight (Nichols).

Rehder described it thus: "Leaves ovate or elliptic, acuminate, 2.5–6 cm long, sharply serrate, those of shoots broad-ovate, coarsely serrate and partly 3 or sometimes 5-lobed, pubescent on both sides, later glabrous or glabrescent above." He also referred to it as a "graceful and handsome tree." Not many horticulturists today would agree with him. Although it is a late and annual bearer, this crabapple is of inferior horticultural value and thus little seen except in many of the larger collections. I do not recommend it to as a single specimen in home gardens, although it has a place in larger collections and estates. It should be much more widely used by hybridizers for its shrublike form, its late blooming, its abundance of very small fruit, and its annual blooming. Loc. 9, 14, 18, 26, 31, 35, 47, 54, 61, 68, 79, 81.

Species crosses of *M. toringo* include the following:

- *M. ×atrosanguinea* (*M. toringo* × *M. halliana*)
- *M. sieboldii* (formerly *M. ×zumi*) (*M. toringo* × *M. baccata*)
- *M. ×sublobata* (*M. toringo* × *M. prunifolia*)

M. toringo **var.** ***arborescens*** Rehder

Synonyms: *M. toringo, M. toringo* 'Arborescens'

Trade name: Tree toringo

Malus toringo var. *arborescens*, which grows native in the mountains of Japan, has been determined by Yoshichi Asami to be identical to *M. toringo* Siebold ex De Vriese (Wijnands 1979). When it was introduced from seed collected by C. S. Sargent in 1882 for the Arnold Arboretum, this form was said to differ from the species. It is native to the mountains of Japan and the Island of Quelpart, Korea. Alfred Rehder wrote that it was "a smaller tree to 10 m; leaves larger, less deeply lobed and less pubescent." Buds pink, opening to single, white flowers 1.2 in (3 cm) across; fruit yellow, 0.3 in (0.8 cm) in diameter. Because the taxonomic characters of *M. toringo* var. *arborescens* as defined by Rehder have been documented by Asami as occurring also in the species, this variety is to be regarded as a synonym of *M. toringo*, not differing from the species.

***M. toringo 'Fuji'** 1968 Plates 112, 113, 114

Synonym: *M. sieboldii* 'Fuji'

Originally named *M. sieboldii* 'Fuji' but renamed *M. toringo* 'Fuji' (see Chapter 10). Introduced by the National Arboretum, Washington, DC, where for 26 years it was an unnamed crabapple. It had been received in 1942 from the USDA Plant Importation Station, Glenn Dale, MD—plant introduction No. 325256. The 40-year-old parent plant, whose origin is unknown, stands 28 ft (8.5 m) high with a spread of 46 ft (14 m).

An upright to spreading tree; expanding buds purple-red, opening to green-white flowers with occasional traces of purple-red, 1.5 in (3.8 cm) across, double, with 13–15 petals; fruit golden-orange, 0.5 in (1.2 cm) in diameter. Subject to moderate scab and powdery mildew (Nichols).

A prolific bearer, this unique tree probably has some hybrid origin. It is a very fine tree to contrast with a red- or pink-flowering clone in massed landscaping. Although it has gone unnoticed and unappreciated over the years, it is excellent for larger landscaping and should be used in hybridizing. Loc. 5, 16, 19, 26, 31, 35, 37, 47, 79, 81.

***M. toringoides** (Rehder) Hughes Fig. 11.11

Trade name: Cutleaf crabapple

Probably one of the most beautiful crabapples in fruit. Introduced in England by James Veitch & Sons, Chelsea, in 1904, and into the United States by the Arnold Arboretum in 1908, from seed collected by E. H. Wilson in western Szechwan, China, where it is native. The type plant at the Arnold Arboretum is No. 17475 grown from Wilson's No. 1285.

Malus toringoides is a small tree or shrub to 26 ft (8 m) high. Alfred Rehder described it thus:

> Brts. slightly villous at first, soon glabrous; leaves ovate to elliptic-oblong, 3–8 cm long, with usually 2 pairs of crenate-serrate lobes, occasionally undivided and lanceolate-oblong to lanceolate, at maturity pubescent only on the veins beneath; flowers single, 2–2.5 cm across, 3–6 in subsessile umbels; pedicels to 2 cm

Figure 11.11. *Malus toringoides* (Cutleaf crabapple), a little known species, is not very showy in bloom but has excellent, red fruit. There is considerable confusion in arboretum specimens as many do not have the cut leaves characteristic of the species.

> long, slightly villous; calyx tomentose, its lobes narrow-triangular; petals orbicular-obovate, hairy above; styles 4–5, rarely 3, glabrous; fruit globose-obovoid or obovoid-ellipsoid, 1–1.2 cm long, yellow, usually with red cheek. In fruit one of the most handsome of the crabapples.

The fruit is slightly pear-shaped, yellow with red on the sunny side. Arie den Boer wrote:

> It is among the last of the crabapples to open its blooms. These are small and pure white. Many consider the fruit the most beautiful of the entire group of crab-apples. In color they are apricot-yellow with a pink or rosy cheek, overlaid with a light bluish or purplish bloom. They are slightly longer than wide, sometimes pear-shaped, about one inch in diameter.

It is my opinion that the description by A. den Boer is the most accurate. A number of the specimens labeled *M. toringoides* in some of the largest collections do not appear to be authentic; many have leaves with no lobes at all. The species is subject to slight scab and fire blight (Nichols).

Certainly this crabapple should be more widely grown for its fruit alone. It is not a plant for the small garden, not because of its size, but rather because it puts on no great show in bloom and is an alternate bearer. On larger estates, in parks, and arboreta, planted in groups of three to five, it can make a very impressive autumn display. As it matures it looks more like a hawthorn with its spiny limbs and branches, which make it a haven for nesting birds. Although it has little been used in hybridizing, it should be used a great deal more because of its colorful small fruit. A few of its selected clones are described below. Loc. 3, 12, 15, 26, 31, 32, 35, 37, 69, 79, 81.

***M. toringoides* 'Bristol'** Fig. 11.12

A better form of the species with darker green leaves. Discovered in China in 1982. Seed brought back to Holden Arboretum by Peter Bristol and grown by the author at Falconskeape Gardens, Medina, OH. Selected and named in 1980 by the author and Lester Nichols to honor Bristol, a plant explorer for Holden Arboretum. Compared to the species this form has leaves that are incised much deeper and that are darker green; it is disease resistant and has better colored fruit. Nichols recommended it be named as he considered it the finest representative of *M. toringoides*. It was selected for hybridization at Falconskeape. Loc. 47.

Figure 11.12. The leaf shape of *M. toringoides* 'Bristol' is typical for the species.

***M. toringoides* 'Macrocarpa'** F. C. Stern 1933

Synonym: *M. macrocarpa*

Raised from seed collected at the Arnold Arboretum by F. C. Stern, Goring-by-the-Sea, Sussex, England. Introduced into the United States by the Arnold Arboretum from scions received in 1933 from Stern. This clone differs from the species by having larger fruit and leaves with less deeply cut lobes; expanding buds pink or pink-white, opening to white flowers about 1 in (2.5 cm) across; fruit orange, yellow, and red with a bluish bloom, 1 in (2.5 cm) in diameter. Subject to severe scab (Nichols). Loc. 9, 15, 26, 31, 54, 81.

M. transitoria (Batalin) Schneider Fig. 11.13

Trade name: Tibetan crabapple

Introduced into the United States by the Arnold Arboretum from seed collected in 1911 by William Purdom in Yenan-fu, Shensi, in

Figure 11.13. *Malus transitoria* (Tibetan crabapple), a species from northwestern China, is rarely seen today except in a few arboreta.

northwestern China, where it is native. Closely related to *M. toringoides*, but the tree form is somewhat smaller and more slender. Alfred Rehder described it thus: "Young brts. tomentose; leaves 2–3 cm long, more deeply lobed, with narrower lobes and more pubescent; flowers 1.5–2 cm across, single white; sepals shorter; petals broad-oblong; fruit 1.5 cm in diam., brown." Subject to severe scab (Nichols). It is not particularly ornamental and thus is rarely found, even in some of the larger collections, and has not been used by hybridizers who passed over it. Loc. 32.

M. trilobata (La Billardière) Schneider

Introduced into the United States from West Asia in 1880 by the Arnold Arboretum. An upright shrub or small tree to 19.7 ft (6 m) high; leaves handsome, lustrous. Rare in cultivation today, even in the largest collections. Alfred Rehder described it thus:

> Young bracts pubescent; leaves deeply 3-lobed and serrate, 5–8 cm long, the inner lobe with one or two smaller lobes on each side, the lateral lobes usually with a basal lobe, pubescent beneath when young, later nearly glabrous and light green, lustrous and bright green above; petioles slender, 3–7 cm long; flowers 6–8, single. white 3.5 cm across; pedicels about 2 cm long, villous; calyx tomentose; sepals lanceolate, longer than tube; fruit ellipsoid, red, 2 cm in diameter.

Because this species is rarely found in arboreta or in cultivation, it has been overlooked by hybridizers. Perhaps it should be found in more of the larger collections. It has no known hybrids or selected clones. Not particularly ornamental.

M. tschonoskii (Maximowicz) Schneider

Plates 115, 116, 117

This rather rare pyramidal crabapple was introduced by the Arnold Arboretum from seed collected in 1892 by C. S. Sargent in Nikko, Central Honshu, Japan, where it is wild. It has insignificant flowers and fruit, but its outstanding contribution is its white-silver (silvery-gray) leaves that turn orange-scarlet in the fall. Arie den Boer made some well-deserved remarks about it:

> This remarkable tree is very uncommon. It is surpassed in flower and fruit by almost every other species or variety of crabapple and one may well ask why it is worth having at all. The reason for mentioning it is that the foliage is so interesting that little else is needed to classify this tree as a desirable ornamental.

Alfred Rehder described it thus:

> Brts. tomentose; leaves elliptic-ovate to ovate-oblong, acuminate, rounded or subcordate at base, 7–12 cm long, irregularly serrate or doubly serrate, sometimes slightly lobulate, tomentose when young, finally glabrous above.

On young shoots the leaves appear almost white, covered with a fine silvery white, felty substance, but most of this silvery-white cover wears off as the leaves mature, except on the underside. In the fall no other crabapple surpasses this one in leaf color, which turns an amazing combination of purple, orange, bronze, yellow, and crimson. In some seasons this coloration is less noticeable or hardly noticeable at all. Crabapples with bright gold leaf color (e.g., *M.* 'Amberina' and *M.* 'Red Swan') or a multiple coloring (e.g., *M.* 'Satin Cloud') have the added distinction of brilliant crimson, abundant fruit, which is not found in *M. tschonoskii*.

A large, upright, pyramidal tree to 39.5 ft (12 m) high and 15 ft (4.6 m) wide; flowers single, white, 1.2 in (3 cm) across, not borne in great profusion; fruit globose, odd-shaped, 0.8–1.2 in (2–3 cm) in diameter, a brown-green or yellow-green, sometimes with a purple cheek, not especially attractive, with grit cells. Subject to slight scab and severe fire blight (Nichols).

Because this crabapple grows into a fairly large tree with a pyramidal head and neither flowers well nor produces good fruit, it is not recommended for the smaller garden (even though it has a silvery leaf color). There are better pyramidal crabapples. Furthermore, because it is plagued with several diseases, it is not recommended for ornamental landscaping in larger gardens. It is, however, suitable for a botanical collection. If all that one desires, however, is a silver-leafed, vase-shaped tree, this species has no equal. Placed next to the very deep purple foliage of *M.* 'Royalty', for example, it can be outstanding for its silvery leaf color and texture. It should be grown on larger estates, parks, and arboretums, if only for its gray-white foliage and fall coloring. It is not carried by many nurseries and is rarely seen outside of the largest collections. It has been little used by hybridizers, although someone should hybridize it in an attempt to get smaller, bright crimson fruit among the silver-gray foliage. Perhaps some outstanding hybrids could result. I know of no hybrids or selected named clones of *M. tschonoskii.* Loc. 5, 13, 24, 26, 28, 31, 35, 37, 46, 47, 54, 55, 69, 79, 80, 81, 86.

M. yunnanensis (Franchet) Schneider Plate 118
Trade name: Yunnan crabapple

This crabapple is different from all others in several ways. It was discovered by Pierre Delavay in Yunnan, China, and introduced into the United Sates by the Arnold Arboretum in 1909 through seed collected by E. H. Wilson in Ching-chi Hsien, China. Native in Hupei, Szechwan, and Yunnan provinces, this crabapple is little known and grown today. In 1979 seed was collected in China by the Arnold Arboretum, and several plants were grown giving some small variations. Two fine plants from this seed are now growing at Falconskeape Gardens, Medina, OH, and both show several variations: Clone No. AA-V-1 has smaller, more purple fruit. Since its native range is so large, one should expect a greater number of variations if seeds were collected at different areas of its range.

Malus yunnanensis is a pyramidal tree to 32.8 ft (10 m) high, narrow and upright. Older plants are more-or-less columnar and send up a number of long, very straight branches with a scattering of short laterals. Alfred Rehder described this species as follows:

> Young brts. tomentose; leaves ovate to oblong-ovate, rounded or subcordate at the base, short-acuminate, 6–12 cm long, sharply and doubly serrate, partly with 3–5 pairs of broad short lobes and partly or mostly without, tomentose beneath; petioles 2–3.5 cm long, tomentose; inflorescence many flowered, 4–5 cm across, rather dense; flowers single, white, 1.5 cm across; pedicels 1–2 cm long, like the calyx tomentose or villous; sepals triangular-ovate, acuminate, about as long as tube; petals suborbicular; styles 5, nearly glabrous; fruit subglobose, 1–1.5 cm across, red, punctate, calyx reflexed.

The description varies slightly from the one given by Arie den Boer, whose observations are most identical to my observations. The fruit does not appear to be "bright red" as Rehder stated but rather is a brown-purple. The leaves have a grayish cast and turn orange-scarlet in fall. It is disease free.

Malus yunnanensis should be planted much more, especially on larger estates, parks, and arboreta. Hybridizers have not used it, perhaps, because it is relatively unknown and unavailable, but I am certain some very worthwhile hybrids could be obtained if it were to be heavily used. It is not much of an ornamental, but hybridizers should appreciate it for fall foliage. No known existing hybrids. Loc. 10, 16, 31, 81.

***M. *yunnanensis* 'Veitchii'** Plates 119, 120

Selected from seedlings planted at Veitch Nursery, England. A narrow to upright tree 20 ft (6 m) high and 10 ft (3 m) wide; leaves heart-shaped, somewhat lobed, heavily textured, pubescent, green, with 6 or 7 pairs of small lobes, sometimes pointed but mostly rounded, scallops; buds yellowish, opening to single, creamy white flowers in dense hawthorne-like clusters (like the species), often containing up to 20 flowers per cluster; fruit brown-purple covered with gray-white or white dots (thus different from the species). Of the fruit, Arie den Boer wrote:

> This crabapple is also of interest for its peculiar fruits; these are held erect on stiff stems, brown-purple in color and covered with a grayish-white or white dots. They are about half an inch in diameter, slightly more in length. When they are fully ripe the calyx lobes are turned back, which makes the fruits look like small urns.

Subject to very severe fire blight but fairly resistant to other diseases. It forms a handsome tree with leaves turning orange-scarlet in the fall. A crabapple that as yet has not been used by hybridizers. Loc. 12, 18, 26, 31, 46, 47, 81, 86.

***M. *yunnanensis* 'Veitch's Scarlet'** Veitch before 1905

A selected seedling similar in all respects to the species but having red-brown fruit. Popular in England. An upright tree similar in form to *M. yunnanensis* 'Veitchii'; buds pink followed by single, white flowers borne in clusters, 1.4 in

(3.5 cm) across; fruit egg-shaped, bright red or brown-red, rather large, 1.8 in (4.5 cm), on erect stems, very interesting. Subject to mild scab and fire blight (Nichols). Should be of interest to any hybridizer, since this species has not, to my knowledge, ever been used in hybridizing. Not an ornamental tree. Loc. 10, 14, 26, 31, 35, 37, 54, 61, 81.

M. ×zumi* Rehder
Not an accepted name in this volume. Author's new name for this crabapple is *M. sieboldii* (Asami) Fiala. For a discussion of the reason for the name change, see "Proposed Change to Elevate *Malus sieboldii* var. *zumi* to Species Rank" in Chapter 10.

***M. ×zumi* 'Calocarpa'** Rehder
Not an accepted name in this volume. Author's new name for this crabapple is *M. sieboldii* 'Calocarpa' (Rehder) Fiala. For a discussion of the reason for the name change, see "Proposed Change to Elevate *Malus sieboldii* var. *zumi* to Species Rank" in Chapter 10.

***M. ×zumi* 'Wooster'** Rehder
Not an accepted name in this volume. Author's new name for this crabapple is *M. sieboldii* 'Wooster' (Rehder) Fiala. For a discussion of the reason for the name change, see "Proposed Change to Elevate *Malus sieboldii* var. *zumi* to Species Rank" in Chapter 10.

CHAPTER 12

Named Crabapples

In addition to the botanical species, varieties, hybrids, and named clones of documented authentic origin listed and described in Chapter 11, numerous crabapple clones and cultivars are known from sources that cannot be verified (e.g., from nursery catalogs or the personal notes of crabapple notables). For one reason or another, the true identity of these named crabapple introductions is not known. It is hoped, however, that with further research into crabapple relationships, many of these mysteries may be cleared up. In this chapter, most of the named clones are described, whatever their origin.

Newer Selections. Modern hybridizers and nurseries specializing in newer crabapples have done excellent work in selecting and introducing superior clones and in weeding out those that are inferior. One must admire the nursery professionals who go out on a limb to introduce good, new plants rather than remain content with the accustomed volume production and selling of older, inferior varieties.

In the past many crabapples were sold simply on the basis of a description, by a taxonomist or the introducer, of a single plant, species, hybrid, or clone, or merely by blossom color. Home landscaping value, disease resistance, colorful autumn fruit, and annual blooming were rarely mentioned. Many highly touted clones of the past, beautiful in springtime bloom only, are really inferior, disease-ridden clones that should long ago have been eliminated from the nursery trade. The late Professor Nichols courageously pointed out many clones that should be phased out because of disease problems and hopefully his work will be continued.

Included in the list of cultivars that follows are several very new crabapples not yet released for commercial propagation. Among them are the newest weeping crabapples, the low-growing multibrids, the mini-fruits, and the polyploids now being released by Charles Klehm & Sons Nursery, South Barrington, IL, and J. Frank Schmidt & Son Co., Boring, OR; the Round Table Series of genetically dwarf crabapples soon to be released by Lake County Nursery, Perry, OH; several newly named clones from Simpson Nursery, Vincennes, IN; and the most recently named clones from Falconskeape Gardens, Medina, OH.

To keep abreast with the most recent work of hybridizers and introducers, I have included new cultivars that have been tested (as of this writing) and that are soon to be released.

Plant Patents and Trade Mark Names. We have previously discussed the confusion in nomenclature between a clone and a cultivar (see "A Confusing Problem of Nomenclature" in Chapter 10). Adding to this confusion is the problem caused by some nurseries when they patent an already named crabapple. It appears another "cultivar name" is required so that the patented plant does not fall into the public domain from the previously, already registered name with the Plant Registrar after the time elapse of the plant patent. This additional name creates considerable confusion in knowing exactly which clone is being sold. Whenever known, I have included this name in the plant descriptions, but it is not to be understood as a new name, but rather a patent registration requirement. The original name as given by the hybridizer or introducer should always stand as the proper name for that particular clone. This is according to the rules of international nomenclature which specify that the first published name is the accepted name of any clone or cultivar. I sincerely hope nurseries will not replace the original names of plants with those names submitted to the patent office. Not only is it a violation of integrity to do so, but it bodes no good, except for future financial gain when the 17-year patent right expires. Furthermore, it causes endless confusion when plants are given several names: original names, trademark names, and patent names.

Availability of Named Crabapples. Some of the clones listed in the descriptions are unavailable from nurseries that are able to carry only a very limited number of crabapples. Many clones are found in only one arboretum or crabapple collection; others can be had only from the introducer. These clones need to be released for public dissemination if better crabapples are to be planted in our gardens and parks. Often, unless a plant is patented, arrangements can be made to obtain scionwood of the desired clone. As a hybridizer and introducer of new crabapples, I am well aware that many of my own introductions are not commercially available nor will they ever be sought by nurseries for propagation because they are too similar to other clones. They will, therefore, forever remain unknown, unless privately propagated. Hybridizers are often reluctant to release their plants hoping to obtain some measure of recompense for all the years of hybridizing needed to produce a superior plant. Nurseries are extremely reluctant to introduce newer clones unless they are able to control them by patenting. Arboreta are unwilling to place any clone in their collection unless it can be obtained from a nursery. The wheel goes around and around! Many excellent named clones die in their garden of origin. After a few attempts at introduction, many hybridizers give up and turn their horticultural skills to more profitable areas of nursery production or management. A few even write horticultural books.

Realistically, how many single, white-flowering, bright fruited, disease-resistant crabapples can the commercial market contain? How many will the general public want? Thankfully we now have a very wide selection from which to choose, yet there always remains room for greater improvement by hybridizers. The future will probably be in the development of the tetraploid and octoploid crabapples. Like most hybridizers working over a lifetime, I am certain I have named too many crabapples, but, be assured, I have discarded a hundred times more!

Misnamed Crabapples. In many years of evaluating crabapples for diseases, Professor Nichols traveled, perhaps more than anyone else, to private and public crabapple collections throughout North America. As an adjunct of his evaluation he also took pictures of most crabapples as they appeared in different collections. Looking at his slides, we often discussed the great variations a given clone showed in different locations, wondering which one was or was not the validly named plant. Trying to identify the authentic plant was not always easy: some plants are immediately seen as being incorrectly named; others are similar to the named clone but not identical.

Donald Wyman, Roland Jefferson, and others who have tried to identify specific crabapples have faced this same problem. Most large collections are reluctant to remove an older tree that has filled a place in their landscape design with beauty and aging dignity simply because it is not correctly named. These misnamed crabapples continue to hold their own in most collections. While misnamed crabapples should be appreciated for their beauty, they should not be propagated.

An example of misnamed crabapples is found in the many named clones of *Malus baccata*. When Professor Nichols studied these clones, their susceptibility to disease, and the number of "existing" trees that he observed, he listed the following that may have been misnamed:

M. 'Aurantiaca'	Severe scab	4 trees
M. baccata cutleaf	No disease	2 trees
M. baccata dwarf	No disease	2 trees
M. baccata hybrid	No disease	6 trees
M. baccata hybrid No. 28	No disease	7 trees
M. baccata hybrid scab immune No. 700-58	Mild scab	3 trees
M. baccata No. 107683	No disease	1 tree
M. baccata unusual dwarf	No disease	4 trees
M. 'Ceratocarpa'	Severe scab	1 tree
M. 'Cerasifera'	Severe scab	5 trees
M. cerasiformis	Mild scab	5 trees
M. 'Columnaris'	Severe scab	108 trees
M. costata	Moderate scab	4 trees
M. edulis	Mild scab	2 trees
M. 'Erecta'	No disease	2 trees
M. 'Flava'	No disease	1 tree
M. 'Fructu Flava'	Severe scab	4 trees
M. 'Flavescens'	Mild scab	4 trees
M. 'Gracilis'	Very severe scab	14 trees
M. himalaica	No disease	5 trees
M. 'Jackii'	No disease	66 trees
M. 'Illinois'	No disease	3 trees
M. macrocarpa	No disease	1 tree
M. 'Manchu'	No disease	2 trees
M. mandshurica	Mild scab	28 trees
M. mandshurica 'Odorata'	Severe scab	2 trees
M. mandshurica 'Midwest'	No disease	1 tree
M. microcarpa	No disease	1 tree
M. odorata	Severe scab	4 trees

M. oblonga	Moderate scab	2 trees
M. praecox	Mild scab	2 trees
M. 'Pyramidalis'	Mild scab	3 trees
M. striata	No disease	1 tree
M. 'Taliak'	No disease	2 trees

Some of these so-called named forms of *M. baccata* are undoubtedly the same (e.g., *M.* 'Columnaris', *M.* 'Erecta', and *M.* 'Pyramidalis' or *M.* 'Flava', *M.* 'Flavescens', and *M.* 'Fructu Flava'). Where only one tree exists, the question must be asked, is it really different from any other named specimens of *M. baccata*? Most are not worthy of being continued and thus their names should be phased out, while the remaining superior clones should be named and their distinguishing, specific character properly identified. The practice of naming or keeping every seedling should be strongly discouraged. Because a seedling has a name in Latin or any other language is no reason for placing it on a list of named and accepted crabapples. The practice of giving a fancy or local name to already named species or clones should be absolutely forbidden (e.g., *M. coronaria*, trade name: wild sweet crabapple). Furthermore, problems arise when clone names are Latinized; rather, the clone name should stand in the language in which it was first introduced. The multiplication of names for the same crabapple must be seriously discouraged. Since so many of the older, named clones of *M. baccata* have serious disease problems, the time has come for large arboreta and collections, where only one or two remain, to eliminate these older trees that would never be considered in the higher competition of today's market. They are neither historical nor good crabapples by today's standards! An inferior seedling always remains inferior and should not be kept in any collection.

Evaluation and Recommendations. Because there are hundreds of named crabapple clones, it is nearly impossible to evaluate each one, especially when many of them no longer exist or are grown only as a single plant in one arboretum collection. Thus, in the list of known flowering crabapples that follows, some clones are listed with no or only minimal description. Others, the better-known clones, are described and evaluated for beauty of bloom and autumn fruit. When known, a rating for disease resistance is included as are suggestions for landscape and/or hybridization value. If known, faults are noted—especially lack of disease resistance, overly large fruit size, and alternate blooming trait. The ratings used in the descriptions are as follows:

Excellent—superior in every way: flowering annually, good fruit color, and disease resistance

Recommended—superior for a special reason (e.g., double flowers, very rare, exceptional hybridizing value) or outstanding in bloom, fruiting, or autumn leaf color despite minor disease susceptibility

Good—satisfactory in flowering and fruit color but slightly susceptible to apple disease

Not recommended—having too many negative factors to be continued in commerce or for landscaping use

Should be phased out—too much disease

Name only—known in name only; no information available or very limited

Throughout the descriptions, "excellent" cultivars are marked with an asterisk (*) and "recommended" cultivars are marked with a plus sign (+).

There will be considerable difference of opinion as to the merits of individual plants. For example, at times a clone is designated "excellent" for a very special reason: it may be unusual in double flowers or very rare. It may have slightly larger fruit (making it excellent for highway planting since small fruit cannot be seen by fast-traveling vehicles), or so outstanding in bloom, fruiting, or autumn leaf color that it merits recommendation despite minor disease susceptibility. Some crabapples are recommended solely because they have outstanding hybridizing value. A few are so unique that one could build a whole new race of flowering crabapples using them as foundation breeders. Some of them are recommended because they are representative of advanced, induced polyploids that have only very recently been created and introduced.

A few clones designated "good" will be acceptable because of outstanding annual bloom, although they may have poor or no fruit (e.g., some of the double-flowering crabapples) or be slightly susceptible to minor diseases (e.g., may have some leaf spot but are not injured or defoliated by it). Considerable defoliation, subject to fire blight, large fruit, early fruit rot and alternate year blooming will place a plant on the "not recommended" list.

In recommending or evaluating the named clones I have combined the recommendations of many experts from the past and the present (they do not always agree in their opinions and evaluations). Included in this group are crabapple pioneers such as Arie den Boer, Roland Jefferson, Alfred Rehder, Charles Sargent, Wheelock Wilson, and Donald Wyman; crabapple authorities of today such as Robert Clark, John den Boer, Thomas Green, Ed Hasselkus, Robert Lyons, John Martens, Henry Ross, and John Sabuco; and crabapple hybridizers such as Donald Egolf, Carl Hansen, Niels Hansen, Isabella Preston, and Robert Simpson. Naturally I have also included my own observations over the past 50 years. In preparing this list I am particularly indebted to John den Boer, son of Arie; Thomas Green, Morton Arboretum; Ed Hasselkus, University of Wisconsin-Madison; and John Sabuco, Good Earth Publishers.

Disease Resistance. The ratings for disease resistance are taken mostly from the many annual reports published by the late Lester Nichols. Titled *Disease Resistant Crabapples*, his work is undoubtedly one of the monumental studies on the susceptibility to disease of various clones. Not only did Professor Nichols examine a large number of crabapples in many different locations, his study covered several years. The disease-resistance ratings of newer clones not rated by Nichols are based information supplied by the plant introducer and/or the nursery propagating them.

One must be aware that not all crabapples do well in every location. A concern that Professor Nichols and I often discussed was the variability of many clones that are completely disease resistant in the drier midwestern and eastern United States but show susceptibility to some diseases when planted in areas of greater moisture or heavy rainfalls. It would be wrong to list a clone as susceptible to some or all diseases simply because in one geographic area it does not perform well. To be fair to any given plant introduction, eventually crabapples will have to be rated by specific areas of the country. Until then, all ratings remain rather subjective and of limited use. They do, however, help weed out the most offending clones and point out those that appear to be superior. The performance of a crabapple in local arboretum collections, propagating nurseries, and large private plantings is the best indication for any area of the country as to the real disease susceptibility and general evaluation of that crabapple.

Where nursery ratings for disease are given, the question arises as to the validity of these ratings since spraying programs are a general rule because of the nursery's need to produce healthy stock. A crabapple's resistance or susceptibility to disease, under more or less sterile nursery conditions, cannot validly determine for the home owner, who never sprays ornamental landscaping, its real disease resistance. Professor Nichols often spoke to me of this continuing problem in rating crabapples. A few nurseries maintain a special "no spray" testing plot to determine the susceptibility of their plants to disease, but most nurseries use extensive, routine sprayings and are as disease sterile as a hospital ward because of fear of any contaminating diseases.

In addition to leaning very heavily on the studies of the late Lester Nichols, I have also relied on Charles Powell and on the judgment of crabapple growers and outstanding nursery professionals like Norbert Kinen, Roy and Sarah Klehm, Michael Scott, Keith Warren, Michael Yanny, and James Zampini. Their combined observations have been an education in evaluation, since they see flowering crabapples from so many different viewpoints.

I hope the reader will find that what follows is not a listing of sterile descriptions, but rather I hope the descriptions will come alive with the often overlooked observations of those who know, grow, hybridize, and love flowering crabapples.

***M.* 'Abondanza'**
See *M.* 'Abundance'.

***M.* 'Abundance'** Forest Nursery, Saskatchewan, Canada
Synonym: *M.* 'Abondanza'
An upright to spreading tree 20 ft (6 m) high and as wide; fruit medium-sized, deep dull red-purple. Loc. 12, 15, 31, 32, 54.

***M.* 'Adam'** Boughen
Parentage: Probably a seedling of *M. baccata*
Discovered in 1930 by W. S. Boughen, Manitoba, Canada. Introduced in 1935. Buds rose-red, opening to single, white flowers 1.7 in (4.3 cm) across. Some susceptibility to scab and fire blight. Loc. 15, 54.

***M.* 'Adams'** Adams Plate 121
Originated as a chance seedling circa 1947. Named after Walter Adams, president of Adams Nursery, Westfield, MA. A rounded, spreading tree to 20 ft (6 m) high; buds red, opening to deep pink flowers single, 1.6 in (4 cm) across; fruit dull carmine-red, 0.6 in (1.5 cm) in diameter, persistent, abundant, often mummifies. Subject to slight powdery mildew, very good disease resistance (Nichols). A crabapple that has been overlooked and could be more widely used especially in highway roadside plantings. For the home garden, the fruit color is not showy enough. Loc. 5, 10, 12, 24, 26, 31, 32, 35, 61, 69, 79, 81, 86, 100.

*+***M.* 'Adirondack'** Egolf 1987
Plates 122, 123, 124
Parentage: An open-pollinated seedling of *M. halliana* 'Koehne'
Selected and named by Donald Egolf, National Arboretum, Washington, DC, from 500 open-pollinated seedlings of *M. halliana* 'Koehne'. National Arboretum No. 54943, plant introduction No. 499828, inoculated with fire blight to determine disease resistance. A narrow, upright tree 12 ft (3.5 m) high and 6.6 ft (2 m) wide, with distinct obovate growth; branches upright, gray-brown, maroon tinged, maturing to dark gray with prominent lenticels; leaves leathery, dark green, 3.5–5.6 in (9–15 cm) long; buds dark carmine, opening to heavily textured, wide-spreading, white flowers with traces of red, 1.6–1.8 in (4–4.5 cm) across, single; fruit subglobose red, with half shaded to orange-red, 0.5–0.6 in (1.2–1.5 cm) wide and 0.6–0.7 in (1.5–1.8 cm) long, persistent until December. Completely disease resistant. One of the finest white, upright crabapples. Ideal for smaller landscapes and as a specimen crabapple. Loc. 35, 37, 47.

M.* ×*adstringens
See Chapter 11.

***M.* 'Akane'**
Name only. Probably a synonym of *M.* 'Akin'. Loc. 73.

M. 'Akin'
Synonyms: *M.* 'Aiken's Striped Winter', *M.* 'Akin's Winter'

M. 'Alberta' Preston
Parentage: A Rosybloom

M. 'Albion'
Name only.

M. 'Albright' CDA—Beaverlodge 1964
Parentage: An open-pollinated seedling of *M. baccata* and an unknown Rosybloom
Named after W. O. Albright, of the Canada Department of Agriculture (CDA), Beaverlodge, Alberta, who originally raised this seedling. An extremely hardy tree; buds pink, opening to single, pink flowers 2 in (5 cm) across; fruit dark purple with red flesh, fairly large, 0.8 in (2 cm) wide and 1.2 in (3 cm) long, persistent, color dull and too dark to be showy. An annual bearer. Disease resistant. Subject to very slight scab and fire blight (Nichols). A second-generation Rosybloom with large flowers. Better than most Rosyblooms. Loc. 10, 12, 31, 35.

M. 'Aldenham'
See *M.* ×*purpurea* 'Aldenhamensis' in Chapter 11.

M. 'Aldenham Purple'
Fruit almost twice the size of the fruit of *M.* ×*purpurea* 'Aldenhamensis'.

M. 'Alexander'
See *M. baccata* 'Alexander' in Chapter 11.

M. 'Alexis' N. E. Hansen 1919
Grown from seed of *M.* ×*robusta* collected in 1897 at the Imperial Botanical Gardens, St. Petersburg, Russia. Similar in every way to *M.* 'Dolgo'. Buds rose-pink, opening to single, white flowers 1.8 in (4.5 cm) across; fruit bright red to deep crimson with bluish bloom, 1.2 in (3 cm) in diameter. Not a very heavy fruiting clone, not showy. Very resistant to fire blight. A large-fruited clone that is as good or better than *M.* 'Dolgo' but does not rate as a good ornamental. Loc. 11, 12, 31, 54, 79, 81.

M. 'Algerienne'
Name only.

M. 'Alice Marie'
Name only. Good disease resistance (Nichols).

M. 'All Saints' Fiala 1967
Parentage: *M.* 'Van Eseltine' × *M.* 'Coralburst'
No. T67-6. An induced tetraploid. A small tree 10 ft (3 m) high; leaves very leathery, dark green; buds red, opening to large, single, white flowers; fruit small, 0.4 in (1 cm) in diameter, red. Disease resistant. A hybridizer's crabapple. Loc. 47.

M. 'Almata'
Synonym: *M. pumila* 'Niedzwetzkyana'
Named by Niels Hansen who brought the plant back from Turkestan. Today there are several seedlings of *M. pumila* 'Niedzwetzkyana' under the name of *M.* 'Almata'. Should be phased out—too much disease (Nichols). Because many of the Rosybloom crabapples are either open-pollinated or selfed *M. pumila* 'Niedzwetzkyana', hybridizers should evaluate them and select the best for breeding red-flowering crabapples. There is an advantage in using the best of the disease free Rosyblooms rather than going back to *M. pumila* 'Niedzwetzkyana'. Loc. 12, 79, 80, 81.

M. 'Almey' Leslie 1945 Fig. 5.3
Parentage: A Rosybloom
Morden No. 452. Developed by W. R. Leslie, Canada Department of Agriculture Experiment Station, Morden, Manitoba. Named for J. R. Almey, horticulturist of Canadian Pacific Railroad. It was very popular some decades ago for its very good, deep rose pink, springtime display. Leaves often defoliate in summer due to scab; flower has 5–7 soft red petals. Should be phased out—too much disease (Nichols). Loc. 5, 8, 9, 12, 18, 24, 31, 32, 35, 39, 40, 41, 43, 44, 68, 79, 80, 81, 89.

*__M. 'Aloise'__ Fiala 1960 Plate 125
Named to honor Aloise Fiala, mother of the introducer. A very graceful, weeping tree to 10 ft (3 m) high by 12 ft (3.5 m) wide; leaves red-green; buds dark red, opening to single, deep pink flowers; fruit small to 0.5 in (1.2 cm), purple-red, very dark unless placed next to a yellow-fruited clone. Subject to moderate scab. A very heavy, annual bloomer. Loc. 47.

M. 'Alred' Provincial Horticultural Station, Brooks, Alberta, Canada 1937
Parentage: An open-pollinated seedling of *M.* 'Hopa'
BF No. 6. An extremely hardy tree; flowers red, large. Disease free. Despite its good qualities, this Rosybloom is now considered obsolete.

***M.* 'Altagold'** Salamandyck
Parentage: An open-pollinated seedling of *M.* 'Rosilda'.
A second-generation hybrid of *M. baccata.*

***M. 'Ambergold'** Fiala 1989
Parentage: *M.* 'Satin Cloud' × *M.* 'Shinto Shrine'
No. N4-P6. A tetraploid. A small, rounded to upright tree to 10 ft (3 m) high and as wide; leaves very leathery, dark green, disease free; buds deep rose-pink, opening to large, single, white flowers in great abundance, blooming annually; fruit amber-gold, round, 0.25–0.4 in (0.6–1 cm) in diameter, very showy, persistent. Completely disease free. An outstanding smaller tree for the home landscape, patio, or as a focal point in large estates and parks. A newer introduction not yet discovered by nurseries, but one that should be outstanding. Loc. 47.

***+*M.* 'Amberina'** Fiala 1981 Plates 126, 127
Parentage: *M.* 'Christmas Holly' × (*M. sieboldii* No. 243 × *M. sieboldii* No. 768)
Introduced and patented by Klehm Nursery, South Barrington, IL. Named after the expensive, yellow-red glassware, which is made by mixing molten glass with gold. A small, upright to spreading tree to 12 ft (3.5 m) high and as wide, with very heavy annual blooming, strongly weeping in form; leaves deep green, turning bright yellow in fall; buds red, opening to creamy white, single flowers; fruit small, brilliant orange-red, 0.25–0.3 in (0.6–0.8 cm) in diameter, persistent. Completely disease resistant (Nichols). An outstanding crabapple in blossom and especially in brilliant, autumn fruit combined with bright yellow leaf color. An excellent parent for hybridizing. Has been involved in many of the multibrids developed at Falconskeape Gardens, Medina, OH. Loc. 47, 100.

***M.* 'Amedia'**
Name only.

***M.* 'American Beauty'** Flemmer 1970
Parentage: *M.* 'Katherine' × *M.* 'Almey'
Plant patent No. 2821. First flowered at Princeton Nurseries, Princeton, NJ. A very vigorous, upright-growing tree; leaves bronze-red when young, bronze-green with maturity; buds deep red-purple, flowers clear red, double, with 15 petals, 2–2.2 in (5–5.5 cm) across; fruit few, medium-sized, red, often scabby, not showy. Should be discontinued—highly susceptible to scab (Nichols). Loc. 2, 5, 20, 26, 46, 54, 61, 74, 79, 82, 85, 86, 90, 92.

***M.* 'American Masterpiece'** Zampini Plates 128, 129
Parentage: A seedling of *M.* 'Madonna'
Plant patent name "Amaszam". To be introduced by Lake County Nursery, Perry, OH, as one of the Round Table Series of dwarf crabapples developed by James Zampini. A somewhat upright tree to 25 ft (8 m) high and 18–20 ft (5.5–6 m) wide; leaves midnight maroon; flowers single, bright red, no bleaching; fruit medium-sized, pumpkin orange. Disease resistant. Appears to show great promise for landscaping, especially in narrow situations. The deep purple foliage makes it an attractive background throughout the summer, and the attractive orange-pumpkin fruit make it a welcome contrast in the autumn. Loc. 46.

***M.* 'American Spirit'** Baron 1989
Plant patent name "Amerspirzam." Introduced by Lake County Nursery, Perry, OH. A small, rounded tree 15–18 ft (4.6–5.5 m) high and as wide; leaves red-purple; flowers single, deep rose; fruit 0.5 in (1.2 cm) in diameter, red purple, persistent. Disease resistant. A new crabapple for any kind of landscaping need. Too new to be properly evaluated but appears to be an excellent introduction. Loc. 46.

***M.* 'Ames'** Iowa St. College before 1933
Parentage: *M.* 'Brier Sweet' × *M.* 'Mercer' (apple)
Buds pink, opening to single, white flowers 1.4 in (3.5 cm) across; fruit 1 in (2.5 cm) in diameter, red. Loc. 54.

***M.* 'Ames White'** Iowa State College
An upright to spreading tree to 25 ft (8 m) high and as wide; buds pink, opening to single pink and white flowers; fruit green-yellow, not as showy as most newer crabapples. Disease free (Nichols). Better-flowering and brighter-fruited clones are available today. Loc. 12, 89.

***M.* 'Amisk'** Preston 1920
Parentage: A Rosybloom
Named by Isabella Preston, CDA—Ottawa, in her Lake Series, for Amisk Lake, northeastern Saskatchewan, on the Manitoba border. Buds carmine, opening to pink, single flowers 2 in (5 cm) across; fruit red with yellow cheeks, 1.4 in (3.5 cm) in diameter. An alternate bloomer. Should be phased out—too much disease (Nichols). Loc. 24.

***M.* 'Ampla'**
Name only.

***M.* 'Amsib'**
See *M. ioensis* 'Amsib' in Chapter 11.

***M.* 'Amur'** N. E. Hansen 1912
Parentage: *M. ×robusta*
Grown from seed collected in 1897 at the Imperial Botanical Gardens, St. Petersburg, Russia. Severely susceptible to scab. Loc. 26, 32.

***M.* 'Anaros'** Wheeler before 1940
Parentage: A seedling of *M. pumila* 'Antonovka'
From Saskatchewan, Canada. Fruit yellow and red, 1.4 in (3.5 cm) in diameter. Susceptible to fire blight. Loc. 87.

M.* **'Angel Choir' Fiala 1962
Parentage: (*M. baccata* 'Alba' × *M. sieboldii*) × (*M. sieboldii* × *M.* 'Van Eseltine')
Introduced in 1981 by Klehm Nursery, South Barrington, IL. A sibling of *M.* 'Bridal Crown'. A small tree to 12 ft (3.5 m) high by 12 ft (4 m) wide, finely branched; buds pale pink, opening to clusters of small, double, white flowers that are very effective; fruit deep red, 0.4 in (1 cm) in diameter. A heavy annual bearer that blooms very heavily on spurs. Completely disease resistant (Nichols). A fine, delicate, double crabapple. Loc. 47, 100.

***M.* 'Angus'**
Name only. Originated at Central Experiment Farm, Ottawa, Canada. One of Saunders' crosses made in 1901 and named in 1913, but discarded later.

M. angustifolia
See *M. coronaria* var. *angustifolia* in Chapter 11.

***M. angustifolia* 'Pendula'** Harbison
See *M. coronaria* var. *angustifolia* 'Pendula' in Chapter 11.

***M. angustifolia* 'Plena'**
See *M. ioensis* 'Prince Georges' in Chapter 11.

M.* **'Anne E' Manbeck
Synonym: *M.* 'Manbeck Weeper' (former name)
Named for Anne E., an outstanding former worker in the propagation liner area of Manbeck Nurseries, New Knoxville, OH. A spreading weeper; bark distinctive in reddish color; flowers single, white; fruit small, cherry-red, persistent, with good color all winter, eaten by birds in midwinter. Good disease resistance. One of the better, older weepers that should be grown more. Loc. 100.

M.* **'Ann Marie' Fiala 1989
Parentage: *M.* 'Satin Cloud' × *M.* 'Tetragold'
No. NR3-P7. Named to honor a young horticulturist, Ann Marie Chanon, Maple Heights and Madison, OH. Introduced by Klehm Nursery, South Barrington, IL. An upright to somewhat vase-shaped tree to 12 ft (3.5 m) high and 10 ft (3 m) wide; leaves medium green, disease free; buds rose-pink, opening to large, single, pale pink flowers on long branches, like flowering wands, blooming when plant is young (often in nursery pots); fruit yellowish with orange blush, persistent, 0.7 in (1.8 cm) in diameter. A very heavy annual bloomer. Disease resistant. An excellent, very showy crabapple that should be of considerable interest to nurseries for its early blooming and excellent plant qualities. Suitable for all landscapes—smaller homes and patios as well as large estate or parks. Loc. 47, 100.

***M.* 'Ann Trio'** N. E. Hansen
Parentage: *M.* 'Tony' (apple) and *M.* 'Mercer' (apple)
One of the progeny of *M. baccata*.

M. apetela
See Chapter 11.

M.* **'Arch McKean' Fiala 1988
Plate 130, Fig. 2.3
Parentage: *M.* 'Joy' × *M.* 'My Bonnie'
NR3-P11-85. Named for a dear friend, plantsman, and horticulturist, Arch McKean, of Grand Beach, New Buffalo, MI, on his 94th birthday. Introduced by Klehm Nursery, South Barrington, IL, and Falconskeape Gardens, Medina, OH. A small, upright to fan-shaped tree to 12 ft (3.5 m) high by 10 ft (3 m) wide; leaves medium green, disease resistant; buds deep rose, opening to single, pale pink flowers; fruit deep red, 0.4 in (1 cm) in diameter, persistent. A heavy, annual bloomer with mini-fruit. Excellent disease resistance. A wonderful, very showy addition to any garden. Outstanding for small gardens and planter culture. Ideal wherever a small specimen plant is required. Still very new and unavailable, but will be an asset to the nursery professional, landscaper, and hybridizer. Loc. 47, 100.

***M.* 'Arctic Dawn'** Leslie 1952
Parentage: An open-pollinated seedling of *M. pumila* 'Niedzwetzkyana'
Selected by W. R. Leslie at Canada Department of Agriculture, Beaverlodge, Alberta.
A semiweeping tree; buds pink, opening to single, pale pink-white flowers 0.8 in (2 cm) across, with ruffled edges; fruit purple-red, 0.5 in (1.2 cm) in diameter, persistent into winter. Fairly good disease resistance; some moderate scab. Loc. 31, 81.

***M.* 'Arctic Red'**
Name only.

***M.* 'Argentea'**
An obsolete synonym for *M. baccata* 'Yellow Siberian'.

M. armeniacaefolia
An obsolete Latin name.

***M.* Arnold Arboretum No. 328-55-A**
See *M.* 'Red Barron'.

***M.* Arnold Arboretum No. 33340**
See *M. coronaria* 'Pink Pearl' in Chapter 11.

***M.* 'Arnold-Canada'**
See *M.* ×*robusta* 'Arnold-Canada' in Chapter 11.

***M.* 'Arnold-Canada No. 5'**
See *M.* ×*robusta* 'Arnold-Canada' in Chapter 11.

M.* ×*arnoldiana
See Chapter 11.

***M.* 'Arrow'** Preston 1920
Parentage: An open-pollinated seedling of *M. pumila* 'Niedzwetzkyana'
Buds deep purple-red, opening to purple-pink, single flowers 1.6 in (4 cm) across; fruit dull purple-red with heavy bluish bloom, 1 in (2.5 cm) in diameter. An annual bloomer. Should be phased out—too much disease (Nichols). May be as good as its parent in hybridizing. Loc. 10, 14, 24, 26, 31, 32, 54, 81, 89.

M. asiatica
See *M. prunifolia* 'Rinki' in Chapter 11.

***M.* 'Aspiration'**
See *M. baccata* 'Aspiration' in Chapter 11.

M.* ×*astracanica
See Chapter 11.

***M.* 'Astrachan'**
See *M.* ×*astracanica* in Chapter 11.

***M.* 'Athabasca'** Preston 1921
Parentage: A Rosybloom
Named by Isabella Preston, CDA—Ottawa, after the Athabasca glacier and ice field in the Canadian Rockies. Flowers pale purple-pink with white claw, 1.8 in (4.5 cm) across; fruit yellow-orange to red, 1.6 in (4 cm) in diameter. An alternate bloomer. Subject to scab, but otherwise has fair disease resistance. Loc. 15, 31, 32, 37, 54, 89.

M. atropurpurea
See *M.* 'Jay Darling'; see also *M.* ×*purpurea* 'Eleyi' in Chapter 11.

M.* ×*atrosanguinea
See Chapter 11.

***M.* 'Aurantiaca'**
See *M. baccata* 'Aurantiaca' in Chapter 11.

M. aurea
See *M. pumila* 'Aurea'.

***M.* 'Aurea'**
See *M. pumila* 'Aurea'.

***M.* 'Aurora'** Saunders 1904
Originated at the Central Experiment Farm, Ottawa, Canada, but discarded later.

***M.* 'Autumn Delight'** Halward
A Canadian hybrid from R. Halward, Royal Botanic Garden, Hamilton, Ontario, Canada. Very disease resistant.

***+*M.* 'Autumn Glory'** Fiala 1968 Plate 131
A new mini-fruited multibrid with heavy influence of *M. sieboldii* 'Wooster'. Introduced by Klehm Nursery, South Barrington, IL. A small, rounded to spreading tree 15 ft (4.6 m) high and as wide; leaves dark green, turning yellow in autumn; buds bright red, opening to single, blush and full white flowers that bloom very heavily on spurs; fruit bright orange-red, with a glossy finish, 0.25 in (0.6 cm) in diameter, coloring in late August, persistent until eaten by birds in November. An abundant, annual bearer. Very showy in spring and autumn. Completely disease resistant (Nichols). Ideal for smaller landscape designs. One of the best, small-fruited, newer crabapples. Loc. 32, 47, 100.

***M.* 'Autumn Gold'** Halward
A Canadian hybrid from Royal Botanic Gardens, Hamilton, Ontario, Canada. Fruit gold.

***M.* 'Autumn Treasure'** Fiala 1975
Parentage: *M.* 'Winter Gold' × *M.* 'Red Swan'
No. 85-1-3. Introduced by Klehm Nursery, South Barrington, IL. A small, graceful weeper 10 ft (3 m) high and as wide; leaves medium to dark green, disease resistant; buds red, opening to single, white flowers; fruit gold, very small, to 0.25 in (0.6 cm), coloring early, showy and persistent until hard freeze, relished by birds. An abundant, annual bearer. Disease resistant. Loc. 47, 100.

***M.* 'Babine'** Preston
Parentage: A cross or seedling of *M. baccata*
A discontinued Rosybloom.

M. baccata
See Chapter 11.

M. baccata* var. *himalaica
See Chapter 11.

M. baccata* var. *mandshurica
See Chapter 11.

***M. baccata* 'Alexander'**
See Chapter 11.

***M. baccata* 'Alexis'**
See Chapter 11.

***M. baccata* 'Aspiration'**
See Chapter 11.

***M. baccata* 'Aurantiaca'**
See Chapter 11.

***M. baccata* 'Cerasifera'**
See Chapter 11.

***M. baccata* 'Columnaris'**
See Chapter 11.

***M. baccata* 'Costata'**
See Chapter 11.

M. baccata flava
See *M. baccata* 'Flavescens' in Chapter 11.

***M. baccata* 'Flavescens'**
See Chapter 11.

***M. baccata* 'Flexilis'**
See Chapter 11.

***M. baccata* 'Fructu Flava'**
See *M. baccata* 'Flavescens' in Chapter 11.

***M. baccata* 'Gracilis'**
See Chapter 11.

***M. baccata* 'Halward'**
See Chapter 11.

***M. baccata* 'Jackii'**
See Chapter 11.

***M. baccata* 'Lady Northcliffe'**
See Chapter 11.

***M. baccata* 'Odorata'**
See Chapter 11.

***M. baccata* 'Spongberg'**
See Chapter 11.

***M. baccata* 'Taliak'**
See Chapter 11.

***M. baccata* 'Walters'**
See Chapter 11.

***M. baccata* 'Yellow Siberian'**
See Chapter 11.

***M.* 'Bailey'**
See *M.* 'Bailey's Crimson'.

***M.* 'Bailey's Crimson'**
Synonym: *M.* 'Bailey'
Name only.

****M.* 'Ballerina'** Fiala 1974
Parentage: *M.* 'Gemstone' × a tetraploid seedling of *M.* 'Silver Moon'
No. 85-4-6. An upright to fan-shaped tree 16 ft (5 m) high and 12 ft (3.5 m) wide; leaves glossy, dark green, disease free; buds pure white, opening to large, very cupped, white, single flowers, very showy; fruit 0.4–0.5 in (1–1.2 cm), bright yellow, persistent to hard freeze. Disease resistant. Excellent for narrow places. Should be grown commercially. Loc. 47.

***M.* 'Barbara Ann'** Wyman 1953 Fig. 12.1
Parentage: An open-pollinated seedling of *M.* 'Dorothea'
One of the progeny of *M.* ×*arnoldiana*. Named for youngest daughter of Donald Wyman, former horticulturist at the Arnold Arboretum. Flowers double, with 12–15 petals, deep purple-pink, fading to a lighter purple-pink, 1.8 in (4.5 cm) across; fruit purple-red,

Figure 12.1. *Malus* 'Barbara Ann'

about 0.5 in (1.2 cm) in diameter, not attractive. Should be discarded—too much scab (Nichols). Loc. 3, 8, 9, 11, 12, 15, 26, 31, 54, 61, 69, 79, 81, 89.

M. **'Barbier'**
Name only.

M. **'Bartletti'**
Name only. Probably *Pyrus* 'Bartletti', a pear.

M. **'Bartoni'**
Name only. Loc. 81.

M.* **'Baskatong' Preston before 1950
Parentage: *M.* 'Simcoe' × *M.* 'Meach'
A second-generation Rosybloom. Named by Isabella Preston, CDA—Ottawa, in her Lake Series, for a Canadian lake. A tree spreading to 25 ft (8 m) wide, with arching branches; buds dark purple, opening to red-purple flowers 1.75 in (4.4 cm) across, single; fruit dark purple-red, 1 in (2.5 cm) in diameter. Subject to minor scab, otherwise disease resistant (Nichols). A fine, larger tree with red blossoms, Good as a background tree. Loc. 10, 31, 61, 86.

M. **'Beauty'** N. E. Hansen 1919
Parentage: Probably a form of *M. baccata*
Grown from Russian seed. A tree of extremely fastigiate habit; leaves dark green; flowers white, single; fruit bright red, 1.25 in (3 cm) in diameter. Subject to moderate to severe scab, but very resistant to fire blight. Outstanding in fruit. Loc. 31, 32, 61, 77, 79, 80, 81.

M. **'Bechtel'**
See *M. ioensis* 'Plena' in Chapter 11.

M. **'Bedford'** Brandon Experiment Farm, Manitoba 1928
Resistant to fire blight but moderately susceptible to scab. Loc. 12, 31, 61, 81.

M. **'Behrens Crab'** Behrens
Synonym: *M.* 'L.B. No. 1'
Name only. No scab (Nichols). Loc. 32, 81.

M. **'Beverly'** Plate 132
An upright, spreading tree to 20 ft (6 m) high and as wide; buds pink, opening to white, single flowers; fruit excellent, small, bright red, 0.5–0.75 in (1.2–1.9 cm) in diameter, very showy but only in alternate years. Subject to severe fire blight on a regional basis only (Nichols). Not recommended because of alternate bearing. Loc. 5, 12, 18, 24, 26, 31, 35, 41, 46, 47, 54, 61, 69, 79, 80, 81, 86, 87, 89, 91, 100.

M. **'Big Red'**
Name only.

M. **'Big River'** P. H. Wright 1954
Parentage: *M. baccata* × *M.* 'Hopa'
A Rosybloom from Saskatoon, Saskatchewan, Canada. A pyramidal tree, very hardy; flowers deep rose. Disease resistant. Should be more popularly offered in the United States. Loc. 89.

M. **'Birdland'** Plate 133
A new introduction from Johnson's Nursery, Menomonee Falls, WI. Named by Lori Yanny because its fruit is so relished by birds, especially cedar waxwings and early robins, who finish off the persistent fruit. A rounded tree to 25 ft (8 m) high and 30 ft (9 m) wide; leaves glossy green; buds pink, opening to single, fragrant, white flowers; fruit 0.4–0.5 in (1–1.2 cm), yellow with red-orange blush, very persistent. An annual bearer. Good disease resistance, but moderate scab. An excellent newer clone with outstanding fruit. Should be grown more. Suitable for all landscaping needs. Loc. Johnson Nursery, Menomonee Falls, WI.

M. **'Bismer'**
Name only. Good disease resistance (Nichols).

M.* **'Blanche Ames' Sax 1939 Plate 134, Fig. 3.6
Parentage: An open-pollinated seedling of *M. spectabilis* 'Riversii'
Arnold Arboretum No. 6639. Named after Mrs. Oakes Ames, wife of a former professor of botany at Harvard University. A medium-sized, spreading to semiweeping tree to 20 ft (6 m) high and as wide; buds very pale pink, opening to semidouble, white flowers pro-

duced in great profusion annually, about 1.4 in (3.5 cm) across; fruit very small, yellow, 0.3 in (0.8 cm) in diameter. Moderate susceptibility to scab. One of the better flowering mini-fruited crabapples. Should be more widely grown. Ideal for smaller home landscapes. A semi-double-flowering crabapple that should be used more in hybridizing. Loc. 12, 13, 31, 81.

***M.* 'Bluebeard'** Ross circa 1960 Fig. 12.2

Parentage: A seedling of *M. ×purpurea* 'Lemoinei'

A small, rounded tree to 12 ft (3.5 m) high and as wide; leaves red-bronze with green; buds bright carmine to rose-red, opening to purple-red, single and semidouble flowers; fruit 0.5 in (1.2 cm) in diameter, purple-red with a definite blue bloom or blush, attractive. Subject to slight leaf spot and scab. Most interesting for its uniquely colored bluish fruit. Loc. 47.

Figure 12.2. *Malus* 'Bluebeard'

***M.* 'Bob F'**

Name only.

*__*M.* 'Bob White'__ Plates 135, 136, 137

Parentage: A chance seedling of unknown origin occurring in Massachusetts

Introduced by the Arnold Arboretum before 1876. A dense, rounded tree to 20 ft (6 m) high and 30 ft (9 m) wide; buds pink, opening to white, single flowers 1 in (2.5 cm) across; fruit yellow-green, often with brown on the shaded side, about 0.5 in (1.2 cm) in diameter, persistent to late winter. An alternate bearer in some areas of the country. Subject to moderate fire blight and some scab. This clone has been somewhat over-rated: its fruit is not a good gold color but rather a dull yellow-green with brown on the shaded side, and it bears in alternate years in some places. On the other hand, it has several good qualities: leaf color changes to bright gold each fall, which enhances the fruit; fruit color improves a bit after frosts; and fruit persists even to spring and thus is highly prized as a "bird feeder." It has been a popular crabapple, and rightfully so, even though there are many newer introductions that are far superior in fruit color (e.g., *M.* 'Winter Gold'), annual bearing, and disease resistance. Loc. 4, 10, 12, 13, 18, 20, 26, 31, 37, 39, 44, 61, 68, 69, 71, 79, 80, 81, 86, 87.

*__*M.* 'Bonfire'__ Fiala 1976

Parentage: *M.* 'Christmas Holly' × *M.* 'Amberina'

No. 85-1-8. A small, upright tree to 14 ft (4.3 m) high and 12 ft (3.5 m) wide; leaves medium to dark green, good; buds carmine-red, opening to single, white flowers, heavy, annual bloomer; fruit abundant, very small, 0.25 in (0.6 cm) in diameter, brilliant orange-red, very showy in color; persistent until eaten by birds. Disease resistant. An excellent crabapple for smaller landscapes or as a specimen tree. Loc. 47.

***M.* 'Boom'** Arrowwood

Name only.

***M.* 'Boone Park'**

See *M. ioensis* 'Boone Park' in Chapter 11.

M. bracteata

See *M. coronaria* var. *bracteata* in Chapter 11.

*__*M.* 'Brandywine'__ Simpson Plates 138, 139, 140

Synonym: *M. ioensis* 'Plena' Klehm's No. 8

Parentage: *M. ×purpurea* 'Lemoinei' × *M.* 'Klehm's Improved'

Plant patent name "Branzam." A rounded tree to 20 ft (6 m) high and as wide; leaves large, green with a wine-red overcast in spring; buds deep rose-red, opening to deep rose-pink, double, very fragrant flowers; fruit yellow-green, somewhat large (the one fault of this magnificent tree), 1 in (2.5 cm) in diameter, falling rather soon. Reasonably good disease resistance: mild scab, mildly subject to cedar-apple rust. In spring, this clone provides an outstanding display of deep rose-pink buds with the delightful crabapple fragrant and rose-like blossoms. No larger estate or park planting should be without it, but it should not be planted where the fallen fruit may cause a problem. One of the better new, double crabapples. Younger hybridizers would do well to use it and improve its disease resistance. Loc. 24, 31, 46, 61, 81, 82, 85, 86.

***M.* 'Brem'**
Name only.

M. brevipes
See Chapter 11.

*****M.* 'Bridal Crown'** Fiala 1962
Parentage: (*M. baccata* 'Plena Alba' × *M. sieboldii*) × (*M. sieboldii* × *M.* 'Van Eseltine')
A sibling of *M.* 'Angel Choir' and a *Zumi* hybrid. Introduced by Klehm Nursery, South Barrington, IL. An upright to spreading tree to 11 ft (3.4 m) high and 10 ft (3 m) wide; leaves dark green; buds pure white, opening to very double, white flowers in clusters, like a bride's corsage; spurs heavily fruited; fruit reddish, about 0.4 in (1 cm) in diameter, persistent. Disease resistant (Nichols). Small delicate tree with charming buds and blossoms. Should be good for hybridizing for double-flowering crabapples. Loc. 47, 100.

***M.* 'Brier'** Brier 1870
Parentage: A cross of *M. ×adstringens*
Flowers single, white, 1.8 in (4.5 cm) across; fruit 1.6 in (4 cm) in diameter, red and yellow. Should be phased out—too much disease (Nichols). Loc. 3, 10, 12, 31, 54, 61, 81.

***M.* 'Bright Angel'**
An upright to spreading tree to 12 ft (3.5 m) high by 15 ft (4.6 m) wide; buds rose, opening to single, white flowers; fruit bright red, 0.5 in (1.2 cm) in diameter; persistent to December. An annual bearer. Disease resistant. Loc. 47.

***M.* 'Brilliant'**
See *M.* 'Crimson Brilliant'

***M.* 'Bronx'**
Parentage: A clone of *M. ×soulardii*
Buds pale pink, opening to single, very attractive, somewhat cupped, white flowers with very rounded petals, exceedingly beautiful on close viewing. Subject to severe cedar-apple rust. Loc. 14 (but apparently no longer in existence).

***M.* Brook's No. 6**
See *M.* 'Jubilee'.

***M.* 'Buccaneer'** Fiala
A red-flowering descendant of *M. ×purpurea* 'Lemoinei'.

***M.* 'Buncombe'**
See *M. coronaria* var. *bracteata* in Chapter 11.

*+***M.* 'Burgandy'** Simpson 1980
Synonyms: *M.* 'Burgundy', *M.* 'Simpson 4-17'
A slender, vase-shaped tree to 18 ft (5.5 m) high and 6 ft (1.8 m) wide; leaves dark green with reddish cast; buds dark red, opening to single, rich dark red flowers with the fragrance of grapes (burgundy wine); fruit small, maroon, lost in the foliage. Subject to moderate scab (Nichols). An annual bloomer. Outstanding in bloom. One of the earliest, deep red flowering crabapples. Ideal for any landscaping. Loc. 5, 18, 26, 31, 47, 54, 61, 81.

***M.* 'Burgundy'**
See *M.* 'Burgandy'.

***M.* 'Burton'**
See *M.* 'Burton's Yellow Fruited'.

***M.* 'Burton's Yellow Fruited'**
Synonyms: *M.* 'Burton' Burton 1937, *M.* 'Yellow Fruited'
Parentage: A chance seedling.
Expanding buds pink, opening to white, single flowers; fruit yellow, somewhat large, rotting early and falling. Subject to mild scab (Nichols). Very showy in fall fruit for a month or so. Excellent for roadside plantings. Loc. 12, 15, 47, 61.

***M.* 'Butterball'**
Name only.

*****M.* 'Butterfly'** Fiala 1974
Parentage: *M.* 'Dorothea' × *M. floribunda*
A small tree or shrub to 8 ft (2.5 m) high and 10 ft (3 m) wide, with many slender branchlets; leaves medium green and slender; buds bright pink, opening to light pink flowers with narrow petals, giving the pleasing and effective appearance of a pink spray; fruit 0.4 in (1 cm) in diameter, bright red. Disease resistant. An excellent, low tree for the small garden. Rather unique in its fine-petaled bloom. Loc. 47.

*+***M.* 'Callaway'** Callaway Gardens, Pine Mountain, GA Plate 141
Synonyms: *M.* 'Calloway', *M.* 'Ida Cason'
Parentage: An open-pollinated seedling of *M. prunifolia*
An upright to rounded tree to 18 ft (5.5 m) high and 16 ft (5 m) wide, becoming semipendulous with age and heavy fruiting; buds light pink, opening to white, single flowers; fruit red, 0.75 in (1.9 cm) in diameter, persistent. Subject to very slight fire blight and cedar-apple rust (Nichols). A showy and heavily fruited clone

with somewhat larger fruit. An excellent ornamental. Performs very well in the middle South. According to Michael Dirr, "Perhaps one of the best white-flowered crabapples for southern gardens because of excellent disease resistance as well as an apparent minimal flower bud chilling requirement." This clone could well be a foundation plant for a much needed southern crabapple breeding program, which should be undertaken by the agriculture departments of southern states (e.g., Georgia, Florida, Louisiana, South Carolina, and Mississippi) and university researchers within these states. Loc. 5, 12, 26, 35, 79.

***M.* 'Calloway'**
See *M.* 'Callaway'.

***M.* 'Calros'** CDA—Rosthern
Parentage: A seedling of *M.* 'Blushed Calville'
Very susceptible to fire blight.

***M.* 'Cal Trio'** Hansen 1938
A large-fruited apple seedling. Moderate scab. Loc. 31.

****M.* 'Calvary'** Fiala 1970 Plates 142, 143
Parentage: *M.* 'Liset' × *M.* 'Redbird'
A small, upright to spreading tree to 12 ft (3.5 m) high by 12 ft (3.5 m) wide; leaves red-green to bronze-green; buds deep carmine rose, opening to medium crimson, single flowers that hold their color well; fruit small, bright red, to 0.6 in (1.5 cm) in diameter, persistent. An abundant and annual bloomer. Subject to very slight scab, otherwise disease resistant (Nichols). A dark red leafed crabapple with bright red fruit. Loc. 47.

***M.* 'Camelot'** Zampini Plate 144
Plant patent name "Camzam." To be introduced by Lake County Nursery, Perry, OH, as one of the Round Table Series of dwarf crabapples developed by James Zampini. A tree to 10 ft (3 m) high and 8 ft (2.5 m) wide; leaves dark green with burgundy overcast; flowers single, fuchsia-pink on white; fruit medium-sized, bright burgundy, persistent. Disease resistance not yet determined. Too new to be evaluated, but its small form should make it popular. Loc. 46.

****M.* 'Cameron'** Central Experiment Farm, Ottawa, Canada 1956
Parentage: *M.* 'Arrow' × *M.* 'Katherine'
Grown from seed. Named to honor D. F. Cameron, plant breeder, Canada Department of Agriculture, Ottawa. Introduced in 1973. A tall, oval-shaped tree; leaves lustrous bronze, turning dark green; flowers double, red, 1.8 in (4.5 cm) across; fruit small, 0.5 in (1.2 cm) in diameter, shiny purple. An exciting double, red-flowering crabapple that should be used in breeding and offered by more nurseries. Loc. 61.

***M.* 'Camille'**
Name only.

***M.* 'Canada Red'**
Name only. Subject to moderate scab (Nichols). Loc. 84.

***M.* 'Canadian Weeper'**
Name only. No diseases (Nichols). Loc. 28.

***M.* 'Canary'** Simpson
Parentage: A chance seedling.
Introduced by Robert Simpson. A medium-sized tree, somewhat open and spreading with age; flowers abundant, small, white, single; fruit very showy, tiny, canary yellow, in groups, on long stems.

****M.* 'Canarybird'** Fiala 1980
Parentage: *M.* 'Winter Gold' × *M.* 'Serenade'
No. SD-1. A small, upright to rounded tree to 15 ft (4.6 m) high and 10 ft (3 m) wide; leaves green, good; buds carmine, opening to single, white flowers in great abundance; fruit 0.5 in (1.2 cm) in diameter, deep gold, becoming a rich amber-gold after frost, persistent. Disease free. An annual bearer that appears to be extremely heavy fruited in alternate years. An excellent tree for fruit color next to bright red clones. Loc. 47.

***M.* 'Candied Apple'**
See *M.* 'Weeping Candied Apple'.

*+***M.* 'Candymint Sargent'** Simpson 1987
Parentage: A seedling of *M. sargentii*
Plant patent No. 6606. A small, picturesque tree with horizontal branching and vigorous growth; leaves purplish; buds carmine, opening to single, pink flowers with petals edged red. A very effective, abundant bloomer. Disease resistant. A very distinctive dwarf type tree for the landscape, smaller spaces, and patios. A new introduction of Robert Simpson that should be an excellent addition to the smaller crabapples.

****M.* 'Candy Pink'** Ross 1970
A small, upright to rounded tree to 10 ft

(3 m) high and as wide; leaves dark green; buds bright pink, opening to double, pink flowers; fruit yellowish, very small. Subject to very mild scab, otherwise disease resistant. A very fine crabapple that has been overlooked and should be better known. Loc. 47.

M. **'Canterbury'** Zampini

Plant patent name "Canterzam." To be introduced by Lake County Nursery, Perry, OH, as one of the Round Table Series of dwarf crabapples developed by James Zampini. A rounded tree to 10 ft (3 m) high and as wide; leaves dark green; buds deep rose, opening to single, pale pink to white flowers; fruit medium-sized, bright red, persistent. Disease resistant (per introducer); too new to be properly evaluated for disease resistance. Appears to be a welcome addition to the list of smaller, dwarf-type crabapples. Loc. 46.

M. **'Cape Cod'**

Name only. Subject to slight scab, but only known by one tree (Nichols).

M. **'Cap of Liberty'**

Name only. Disease resistant, but only known by one tree (Nichols).

M. **'Caputa'** N. E. Hansen

Name only.

M. **'Caramel'**

Synonym: *M.* 'Carmel' Hansen 1919

Buds light pink; flowers pink-white, 1.6 in (4 cm) across; fruit yellow-green to orange-yellow with red cheeks, 2 in (5 cm) in diameter. Disease resistant except for mild scab. Fruit too large for small gardens but could be a fine clone for highway plantings. Loc. 12, 37, 61, 89.

M. **'Cardinal'** Wellington

Parentage: One of the progeny of *M.* ×*arnoldiana*

Name only. Subject to moderate scab, otherwise the 26 trees tested were disease resistant (Nichols). Loc. 31, 32, 55, 61, 80, 81.

M. **'Cardinal King'**

Name only. Subject to severe scab, but only known by one tree (Nichols). Loc. 15.

M.* **'Cardinal's Robe' Fiala 1970

Plates 145, 146

Parentage: *M.* 'Liset' × *M.* 'Amberina'

No. E-84-1. Named to honor a friend, James Cardinal Hickey, Washington, DC. A small, rounded to spreading tree to 12 ft (3.5 m) high and as wide; bark unique, with stippling like cherry bark, very attractive in winter; leaves dark red-green, disease resistant; buds bright orange-red, opening to rose-red, single flowers produced in great profusion; fruit bright red, 0.4 in (1 cm) in diameter, firm, persistent, round. Disease resistant. An excellent tree for landscaping and hybridizing. Loc. 47, 86.

M. **'Carleton'** CDA—Ottawa

An obsolete Rosybloom crabapple.

M. **'Carmel'**

See *M.* 'Caramel'.

*+*M.* **'Carnival'** Fiala 1978

Parentage: *M.* 'Serenade' × *M.* 'Amberina'

No. 86-9-1. A small, rounded tree to 12 ft (3.5 m) high and 10 ft (3 m) wide; leaves dark green, very heavily textured; buds pink-red, opening to single, white flowers; fruit very small, 0.4 in (1 cm) in diameter, colors early, coloring is a combination of gold, orange, and red, very distinctive and showy, persistent until heavy freeze or eaten by birds. Disease resistant. An excellent, smaller tree for the home landscape or parks. Loc. 47.

M. **'Carol Ann'** Schwartze

Introduced by Chester D. Schwartze, Puyallup, WA, and named for his granddaughter, Carol Ann Morgan.

M.* **'Cascade' Fiala 1964

Name changed to *M.* 'Snow Ballerina' (which see) so as not to conflict with another weeper, *M.* 'White Cascade'.

M. **'Case Seedling'**

Disease free after 20 years of testing, but only 3 trees tested (Nichols). Loc. 8, 10, 13.

M. **'Cashmere'** Aldenham House, England

See *M.* ×*sublobata* in Chapter 11.

M. **'Cathay'** Hansen 1919

Parentage: A hybrid of *M. prunifolia*.

A good crabapple but not well known. Completely disease resistant in 17 years of testing (Nichols). Loc. 10, 31, 32, 35, 54, 81, 89.

M. **'Cathy'** Schwartze

Introduced by Chester D. Schwartze, Puyallup, WA, and named for his granddaughter, Cathy Gonsalves. Loc. 85.

M.* **'Centennial' University of Minnesota 1972

Fig. 2.5

A tree spreading to 25 ft (8 m) wide; flowers white, single, mildly fragrant; fruit bright red over yellow, 1.9 in (4.8 cm) in diameter, elongated. Disease resistant after 20 years of testing, with only an occasional mild scab (Nichols). Not an outstanding ornamental as the fruit is too large and messy, but a good jelly crabapple. Could well be used in place of *M.* 'Dolgo'. Loc. 5, 9, 12, 24, 31, 79, 89.

M.* **'Centurion' Simpson 1978 Plate 1
No. 11-57. Plant patent name "Centzam." Introduced by Simpson Nursery Co., Vincennes, IN. A columnar tree to 20 ft (6 m) high and 15 ft (4.6 m) wide; leaves dark green, glossy, good; flowers rose-red, single; fruit glossy, cherry-red, 0.6 in (1.5 cm) in diameter, effective for 2 months. Disease resistant (Nichols). Very fine newer crabapple. Loc. 5, 9, 12, 24, 26, 31, 35, 37, 46, 47, 55, 74, 79, 81.

M. cerasifera
An obsolete name for *M. baccata*.

***M.* 'Cerasifera'**
See *M. baccata* 'Cerasifera' in Chapter 11.

***M.* 'Charlottae'**
See *M. coronaria* var. *dasycalyx* 'Charlottae' in Chapter 11.

***M.* 'Cheal's Crimson'** Cheal 1919
Parentage: A clone of *M. prunifolia*.
Introduced by Joseph Cheal & Sons, Ltd., Crawley, Sussex, England. Buds pink, opening to single, white flowers; fruit bright red, 0.75 in (1.9 cm) in diameter, very persistent and showy. Subject to very severe scab. Loc. 15, 24, 31, 37, 54, 81.

***M.* 'Cheal's Golden Gem'** Cheal before 1929
Introduced by Joseph Cheal & Sons, Ltd., Crawley, Sussex, England. An upright to fan-shaped tree to 20 ft (6 m) high and 18 ft (5.5 m) wide; buds very pale pink, opening to single, white flowers; fruit 0.5 in (1.2 cm) in diameter, gold-colored. Subject to mild scab (Nichols). Loc. 2, 54.

***M.* 'Chestnut'** 1921
Minnesota No. 240. Named because it has the taste of the nut. Buds red; flowers single, white; fruit large, 2 in (5 cm) in diameter. Low susceptibility to scab, otherwise disease resistant after 20 years of testing (Nichols). A jelly crabapple with a unique, nutlike flavor. Loc. 12, 24.

***M.* 'Chilko'** Preston 1920
Parentage: An open-pollinated seedling of *M. pumila* 'Niedzwetzkyana'
A Rosybloom. Named by Isabella Preston, CDA—Ottawa, in 1930 for Chilko Lake, southwestern British Columbia. Flowers single, purple-pink, 2 in (5 cm) across; fruit bright red to crimson, very large, 2 in (5 cm) in diameter. Mildly susceptible to scab. An alternate bloomer. A possible substitute for *M.* 'Dolgo' as a canning apple. Loc. 15, 18, 26, 31, 32, 37, 54, 80, 81.

***M.* 'Chinook'** N. E. Hansen
Parentage: An open-pollinated seedling of *M. coronaria* 'Elk River'
One of a series of similar introductions by Niels E. Hansen. Named for the Chinook winds of the western prairies. Fair disease resistance.

***M.* 'Christmas Candles'**
See *M.* 'Golden Candles'.

+M.* **'Christmas Holly' Fiala 1969 Plate 147
Parentage: A multibrid
Introduced by Lake County Nursery, Perry, OH, and Klehm Nursery, South Barrington, IL. A small, rounded, spreading tree to 15 ft (4.6 m) high, completely covered in spring blossoms; buds bright red, opening to single, white flowers 1.5–1.6 in (3.8–4 cm) across; fruit very small, hollylike, bright red, 0.4 in (1 cm) in diameter, produced annually in abundance, persistent and very showy from September to December. Completely disease resistant (Nichols). A very heavy bloomer. One of the better, newer crabapples, very showy in blossom and fruit. Excellent for hybridizing. Loc. 5, 24, 26, 31, 35, 46, 47, 79, 81, 87, 100.

M.* **'Cinderella' Zampini
Plant patent name "Cinzam." Introduced in 1991 by Lake County Nursery, Perry, OH, as one of the Round Table Series of dwarf crabapples developed by James Zampini. A very small bush 6 ft (1.8 m) high and 4 ft (1.2 m) wide; leaves green; buds red, opening to single, white flowers; fruit small, with good gold color, persistent. Disease resistant (per introducer); too new to be properly evaluated for disease resistance. The extremely small form should make this clone a most desirable crabapple for small gardens, patios, or in other situations with limited space. Should be excellent in hybridizing newer small forms with gold fruit. Loc. 46.

M. 'Clark's Double Flowering'
Name only.

M. 'Clark's Dwarf'
Synonym: *M.* 'Malling No. 8.'
An understock for grafting.

M. 'Clausen' Clausen
Parentage: A natural seedling
Found by and named after a dentist in Alton, IL. Fruit orange, 0.4 in (1 cm) in diameter. Subject to heavy scab. Loc. 35, 61.

M. 'Clinton'
Name only.

M. 'Colonel Lee' Lee 1920
Introduced by Bay State Nursery. Named for Guy Lee, Chestnut Hill, MA. Name only. Loc. 61.

***+M. 'Color Parade'** Fiala 1976
Parentage: *M.* 'Serenade' × *M.* 'Coral Cascade'
No. 86-224. A refined semiweeping tree to 12 ft (3.5 m) high and as wide; leaves dark green, disease resistant; buds bright red, opening to single, white flowers; fruit 0.4–0.5 in (1–1.2 cm) in diameter, bright coral with red cheeks, coloring early, persistent until eaten by birds. A showy, heavy bloomer and annual bearer. Disease resistant. An excellent, smaller semiweeper with graceful branching. An outstanding springtime and autumn performer. Loc. 47.

M. 'Columbia' Saunders 1904
Parentage: *M. baccata* × *M.* 'Broad Green' (apple)
Subject to moderate scab (Nichols). Loc. 15, 31, 61, 81.

M. 'Columnaris'
See *M. baccata* 'Columnaris' in Chapter 11.

***+M. 'Copper King'** Fiala 1977 Plate 148
Parentage: *M.* 'Satin Cloud' × *M.* 'Shinto Shrine'
No. R2-85-N2. A second-generation octoploid. Introduced by Klehm Nursery, South Barrington, IL. A small, very tailored, round tree to 10 ft (3 m) high and as wide; leaves leathery, very dark green, turning yellow to orange in the fall, very disease resistant; buds white, opening to large, single, white flowers with spice fragrance; fruit 0.5 in (1.2 cm) in diameter, golden copper with reddish blush, very attractive. A heavy, annual bearer. Totally disease resistant. Increases in beauty each year. An excellent tree both for the landscaper and the hybridizer. Like *M.* 'Satin Cloud', a rare polyploid. Loc. 47, 86, 100.

***M. 'Coralburst'** Ross 1968
Plates 149, 150, 151, Fig. 6.5
Synonym: *M.* Ross's octoploid
Parentage: An open-pollinated seedling of *M. sieboldii*
Plant patent No. 2983. An octoploid and one of the very few polyploid crabapples. A hybridizer's dream plant from Henry Ross's fabulous Gardenview Horticultural Park, Strongsville, OH. A compact, dense, rounded tree 15 ft (4.6 m) high and as wide; buds coral pink, opening to double, rose-colored flowers; fruit bronze, 0.5 in (1.2 cm) in diameter. Excellent disease resistance. Very ornamental. An excellent specimen tree for the garden or patio. Loc. 3, 5, 12, 18, 19, 24, 26, 35, 46, 47, 54, 61, 68, 76, 79, 81, 86.

***+M. 'Coral Cascade'** Ross 1967 Plate 152
Parentage: An open-pollinated seedling of *M. toringo*
Patented. Henry Ross, Gardenview Horticultural Park, Strongsville, OH, has scored a winner with this fantastic clone! Introduced by Klehm Nursery, South Barrington, IL. A medium-sized tree to 15 ft (4.6 m) high, weeping with age; leaves deep green; buds deep coral-red, opening to blush white, single flowers; fruit pink-coral-orange, after frosts more copper-orange, 0.4 in (1 cm) in diameter, oval, fruiting heavily on spurs, persistent into January. Totally disease free after 20 years of testing (Nichols). One of the very best in its fruit color class, outstanding in blossom and especially in fruit. Heavily used in hybridizing programs at Falconskeape Gardens, Medina, OH. One parent of *M.* 'Coralene'. Loc. 47, 100.

***M. 'Coralene'** Fiala 1972 Plate 9
Parentage: *M.* 'Coral Cascade' × (*M.* 'Red Swan' × *M.* 'Coral Cascade')
No. 85-B5. A small, refined, rounded to spreading, almost semiweeping tree to 12 ft (3.5 m) high and as wide; leaves dark green, disease resistant; buds pink-red, opening to single, white flowers; fruit colors early, 0.25 in (0.6 cm) in diameter, a very showy coral and copper color, moderately persistent. An annual and heavy bloomer valued for its distinctive fruit color. Very fine but not quite as good as *M.* 'Coral Cascade'. Loc. 47.

M. 'Coralglow'
See *M. coronaria* 'Coralglow' in Chapter 11.

M. coronaria
See Chapter 11.

M. coronaria* var. *angustifolia
See Chapter 11.

M. coronaria* var. *bracteata
See Chapter 11.

M. coronaria* var. *dasycalyx
See Chapter 11.

***M. coronaria* var. *dasycalyx* 'Charlottae'**
See Chapter 11.

M. coronaria* var. *glabrata
See Chapter 11.

M. coronaria* var. *glaucescens
See Chapter 11.

***M. coronaria* var. *glaucescens* 'Dunbar'**
See Chapter 11.

M. coronaria* var. *lancifolia
See Chapter 11.

M. coronaria* var. *platycarpa
See Chapter 11.

***M. coronaria* var. *platycarpa* 'Hoopesii'**
See Chapter 11.

***M. coronaria* 'Aucubaefolia'**
See Chapter 11.

***M. coronaria* 'Coralglow'**
See Chapter 11.

***M. coronaria* 'Elk River'**
See Chapter 11.

***M. coronaria* 'Elongata'**
See Chapter 11.

***M. coronaria* 'Nieuwland'**
See Chapter 11.

***M. coronaria* 'Pink Pearl'**
See Chapter 11.

***M. coronaria* 'Thoms'**
See Chapter 11.

M. costata
An obsolete botanical name.

***M.* 'Costata'**
See *M. baccata* 'Costata' in Chapter 11.

****M.* 'Cotton Candy'** Ross 1979 Plate 25
Parentage: An open-pollinated seedling of *M.* 'Van Eseltine'
Another outstanding double-flowering crabapple from one of North America's most outstanding plantsmen, Henry Ross, Gardenview Horticultural Park, Strongsville, OH. A small, rounded tree to 12 ft (3.5 m) high by 10 ft (3 m) wide, somewhat slow growing; leaves deep green, heavy; buds deep pink, opening to semidouble, three-tiered flowers of deep pink to fully double, very showy; fruit deep yellow, 0.5 in (1.2 cm) in diameter, turning brown quickly and falling. Disease free (Nichols). One of the most attractive newer crabapples when in bloom, as yet little known. An ideal plant for hybridizers as well as landscapers. Loc. 47, 100.

***M.* 'Cowichan'** Preston 1920
Parentage: An open-pollinated seedling of *M. pumila* 'Niedzwetzkyana'
One of the original Rosyblooms. Named in 1930 by Isabella Preston, CDA—Ottawa, after Cowichan Lake, southwestern British Columbia. Buds pale rose-pink, opening to pale lavender flowers that are almost white, 1.8 in (4.5 cm) across; fruit dark red, 1.8 in (4.5 cm) in diameter. An annual bearer. Should be phased out—subject to severe scab (Nichols). Loc. 3, 9, 12, 24, 31, 32, 35, 54, 81.

***M.* 'Cowles House'**
See *M. ×robusta* 'Cowles House' in Chapter 11.

***M.* 'Cranberry'** Wodarz
Parentage: A seedling of *M. coronaria* 'Elk River', probably a cross between *M.* 'Redflesh' × *M.* 'Dolgo'
Name only.

*+***M.* 'Cranberry Lace'** Fiala 1989 Plate 153
Parentage: *M.* 'Liset' × *M.* 'Van Eseltine'
Introduced by Klehm Nursery, South Barrington, IL. An upright, columnar tree to 14 ft (4.3 m) high and 8 ft (2.5 m) wide, becoming slightly vase-shaped with age; leaves red-green, disease free; buds rose crimson, opening to semidouble to double flowers deep rose-carmine to deep pink mixed with pale pink, produced in abundance on spurs; fruit small, 0.4 in (1 cm) in diameter, deep red, round. An annual bearer. Disease resistant. A tree that fits perfectly into smaller areas and is both attractive in bloom and in fruit. One of the better

upright, double-flowering crabapples. Attractive in abundant red fruit; most double-flowering crabapples produce few fruits. Outstanding for landscapers and hybridizers. Loc. 47, 100.

***M.* 'Crimson Beauty'**
Name only. Only one tree known in 1965 (Nichols). Loc. 81.

***M.* 'Crimson Brilliant'** A. den Boer 1939
Synonym: *M.* 'Brilliant'
Parentage: An open-pollinated seedling of *M.* ×*purpurea* 'Eleyi'
Buds deep purple-red, opening to single and semidouble, bright rose-pink flowers with pale lavender star at base of petals, 1.6 in (4 cm) across; fruit dark purple-red, with russet marks, 0.8 in (2 cm) in diameter. An alternate bearer at Falconskeape Gardens, Medina, OH. Not a heavy bloomer. Should be phased out—too much disease (Nichols). Loc. 2, 8, 12, 18, 24, 26, 31, 35, 47, 54, 69, 79, 81.

*****M.* 'Crimson Comet'** Fiala 1986
Parentage: *M.* 'Serenade' × *M.* 'Amberina'
No. 86-302. A small, upright to spreading tree to 12 ft (3.5 m) high and as wide, dependable for bloom and fruit; buds crimson, opening to single, white flowers in abundant clusters; fruit very bright red, 0.6 in (1.5 cm) in diameter. An annual bloomer. Disease free. Creates an outstanding autumn show when used in massed groups of three next to yellow-fruited crabapples. Loc. 47.

***M.* 'Crimson Harvest'** Wayside Gardens 1973
Listed in the catalog of Wayside Gardens, Mentor, OH; probably now discontinued. Loc. 61.

***M.* 'Crittenden'**
Name only. One tree known in 1975 (Nichols).

***M.* 'Currant'**
An obsolete name for a clone of *M. baccata*. Origin unknown.

***M.* 'Custer'**
Name only. Very subject to fire blight (Nichols).

***M.* 'Dainty'** Kerr 1963
Parentage: Grown from open-pollinated seed of *M.* 'Royalty'
A small, pendulous bush form; leaves small, narrow, bronze, turning bronzy-red in autumn; flowers small, mauve-pink; fruit purple, 0.4 in (1 cm) in diameter, with corky skin, not showy. Subject to severe scab. A small form that offers very little horticulturally. Loc. 5, 24, 31, 35, 79.

*****M.* 'Dakota Beauty'** C. Hansen 1940
Parentage: A Rosybloom
Buds carmine, opening to dark red-purple, double flowers; fruit red fleshed, edible. Should be considered for hybridizing because of its double, deep red flowers. Not used as an ornamental because of sparse, larger fruit.

***M.* 'Dakota Pink Eye'**
See *M.* Pink Eye'.

***M.* 'Dana'**
Name only. Subject to moderate scab and cedar-apple rust (Nichols). Loc. 61.

*****M.* 'Dancing Elf'** Fiala/P. Murray
Parentage: *M.* 'Red Swan' × *M.* 'White Cascade'
No. B7WP. Developed at Falconskeape Gardens, Medina, OH. A very refined, fountain type, small weeper to 6 ft (1.8 m) high and as wide; buds pink, opening to single, white flowers; fruit 0.4 in (1 cm) in diameter, golden with reddish blush, showy, persistent. A very heavy, annual bloomer. Disease free. An excellent smaller weeper for container growing, patios, smaller gardens, garden walks, and wherever a smaller specimen plant is needed in the landscape. Loc. 47.

***M.* 'Dan Trio'** N. E. Hansen
Name only.

***M.* 'Darkest Red'**
Name only. Only one known tree (Nichols).

***M.* 'Dartmouth'** before 1883
Fruit large. Subject to severe scab. Loc. 9, 31, 32, 61, 81.

***M.* 'Dartt'**
Name only.

M. dasycalyx
See *M. coronaria* var. *dasycalyx* in Chapter 11.

M. dasyphylla
A clone of *M. baccata*. Discarded name.

***M.* 'Dauphin'** Preston 1920
Parentage: An open-pollinated seedling of *M. pumila* 'Niedzwetzkyana'
Not named by Isabella Preston, CDA—Ottawa, until 1930. May be a synonym of *M.* 'Dol-

phin' (which see). Buds deep purple-red, opening to single, purple-red flowers 1.8 in (4.5 cm) across; fruit 1.4 in (3.5 cm) in diameter, yellow streaked with red. Good disease resistance (Nichols). Loc. 10, 15, 24, 54, 79.

***M. 'David'** A. den Boer 1957 Plate 154, Fig. 3.1
Parentage: Unknown
Received by Arie den Boer from the Morton Arboretum in 1940. Named by the introducer for his grandson. A rounded, compact, small tree; leaves medium green, 2–3 in (5–8 cm) long, disease free; buds light pink, opening to single, pink-white flowers 1.5 in (3.8 cm) across; fruit scarlet red, 0.5 in (1.2 cm) in diameter, showy and persistent. An alternate bloomer. Excellent disease resistance (Nichols). Loc. 5, 9, 12, 18, 24, 26, 31, 35, 44, 54, 55, 61, 68, 79, 80, 81, 86, 89, 93.

M. 'David Nairn' H. R. Wright
Parentage: A clone of *M. baccata*

M. 'Dawson'
See *M.* ×*dawsoniana* in Chapter 11.

M.* ×*dawsoniana
See Chapter 11.

M. 'Debutante' Fiala/P. Murray
Parentage: *M.* 'Amberina' × *M.* 'Winter Gold' No. B11-89. A smaller, upright to fan-shaped tree 10 ft (3 m) high by 8 ft (2.5 m) wide; buds medium pink, opening to pale pink-white, single flowers produced in great profusion; fruit gold, 0.5 in (1.2 cm) in diameter, persistent. A very showy annual bloomer. A good, newer crabapple for smaller areas. Loc. 47.

M. 'Dekon Echtermeyer'
See *M.* 'Oekonomierat Echtermeyer'.

M. 'Delite' Broughen Nursery, Valley River, Manitoba, Canada
Buds pink, followed by single, white flowers 2 in (5 cm) across; fruit orange and red, 1.4 in (3.5 cm) in diameter. Loc. 54, 61, 81.

M. denticulata
An obsolete name. Subject to severe scab.

M. 'Des Moines'
Name only. Subject to moderate scab (Nichols). Loc. 32.

M. 'Diamond Jubilee'
See *M.* 'Pink Eye'.

M. diversifolia
An obsolete botanical name.

***M. 'Dolgo'** N. E. Hansen 1897
Grown from seed of *M.* ×*robusta* collected in 1897 at the Imperial Botanical Gardens, St. Petersburg, Russia. Introduced to the United States in 1917. Flowers single, white 1.75 in (4.4 cm) across; fruit bright red, 1.5 in (3.8 cm) in diameter, excellent for jelly, ripening quickly in August or becoming soft. Subject to slight scab and fire blight (Nichols). Loc. 8, 12, 13, 18, 24, 26, 31, 32, 35, 39, 41, 53, 55, 61, 77, 79, 81, 82, 86, 87, 89, 91, 93.
Progeny of *M.* 'Dolgo' include the following:
M. 'Centennial' University of Minnesota
M. 'Cranberry' Wodarz
M. 'Erl Trio' N. E. Hansen
M. 'Goolsbey' Wodarz
M. 'Heart River' Baird
M. 'Kerr' Kerr
M. 'Martha-Dolgo' CDA—Morden
M. 'Mecca-Dolgo' CDA—Ottawa
M. 'Northland' University of Minnesota
M. 'Red Heart' Porter
M. 'Red River' Yeager
M. 'Spring Snow' Porter

M. 'Dolphin'
May be a synonym of *M.* 'Dauphin'; not enough information available to make further distinction. Fruit red and dark red. Subject to moderate scab (Nichols).

M. 'Donald'
See *M. hupehensis* 'Donald' in Chapter 11.

M. 'Donald Wyman' Arnold Arboretum 1970
Parentage: A spontaneous seedling
Seedling first noticed at the Arnold Arboretum prior to 1950. Named after Donald Wyman, former horticulturist at the Arnold Arboretum. A rounded tree 20 ft (6 m) high and as wide; leaves dark green; buds pink, opening to white, single flowers 1.8 in (4.5 cm) across; fruit glossy, bright red, 0.4 in (1 cm) in diameter, persistent. An abundant, annual bearer. Subject to moderate scab and severe fire blight (Nichols). A fine clone that needs room to grow to perfection. Loc. 5, 8, 12, 13, 15, 18, 24, 26, 31, 35, 44, 46, 54, 55, 61, 69, 79, 80, 81, 86, 93, 100.

M. 'Dorothea' Wyman 1943
Parentage: Probably *M.* ×*arnoldiana* × *M. halliana* 'Parkmanii'; a chance seedling of doubtful parentage
Named for a daughter of Donald Wyman.

A small, upright to spreading tree 15 ft (4.6 m) high and as wide; leaves dark green; buds carmine, opening to semidouble (10–16 petals), rose-pink flowers that do not fade to white, 1.8 in (4.5 cm) across; fruit yellow, 0.5 in (1.2 cm) in diameter, not particularly showy. An annual bloomer. Not recommended—subject to severe scab and mild fire blight. In all other respects, a good, showy crabapple. Doomed to be phased out for lack of propagation and because of the development of newer clones. The fine, strong deep pink blossom color is suitable for any landscape. A clone with some possibilities for hybridizers if not for landscapers. Loc. 9, 11, 12, 13, 14, 15, 18, 19, 24, 26, 31, 35, 37, 38, 40, 41, 43, 47, 54, 55, 61, 68, 69, 79, 80, 81, 85.

Progeny with distant *M.* 'Dorothea' pedigree include the following:

- *M.* 'Barbara Ann' Wyman
- *M.* 'Grandmother Louise' (tetraploid) Fiala
- *M.* 'Mollie Ann' (octoploid) Fiala
- *M.* 'Satin Cloud' (octoploid) Fiala
- *M.* 'Spring Song' Fiala

***M. 'Dorothy Rowe'**

Named to honor a great plantswoman, Dorothy Rowe, Rowe Arboretum, Cincinnati, OH. Expanding buds pink, opening to white to cream, single and semidouble flowers; fruit shiny, bright red, a bit large, 1 in (2.5 cm) in diameter. Disease free (Nichols). A very fine crabapple that has not been popular with nurseries, or have they missed it? Loc. 26, 31.

***M. 'Dorsett Golden'**

Parentage: A cultivar of *M. pumila*, perhaps a seedling of variety *sylvestris*.

Brought into the United States from Nassau, Bahamas, by R. J. Knight, Plant Introduction Station, Miami, FL. Fruit yellow, with a 10-percent, slightly pink blush, 2–2.5 in (5–6.4 cm) in diameter, with sweet-tasting, firm flesh. Not recommended for its commercial value, but recommended for hybridizing with Asiatic and North American species. Because it requires very few hours of chilling to break dormancy, it could be useful in developing southern hybrids to extend the range of flowering crabapples into central Florida.

***+M. 'Doubloons'** Fiala 1988

Plates 155, 156, 157, 158

Plant patent no. 7216. Named after the Spanish doubloon, a gold coin no longer in use. Introduced and patented by J. Frank Schmidt & Sons Nursery, Boring, OR. A small, upright and spreading tree to 12 ft (3.5 m) high by 10 ft (3 m) wide; leaves deep green; buds rich carmine, opening to double and semidouble, white flowers; fruit bright lemon-yellow (RHS 13B to 15B), turning deeper lemon-gold after frost, 0.4 in (1 cm) in diameter, abundant, persistent to mid-November. A heavy bloomer. Disease resistant (Nichols). A smaller, excellent crabapple for any garden, and one that should be used in hybridizing. Loc. 47, 86.

***M. 'Dream River'** Fiala/P. Murray

Parentage: *M.* 'Luwick' × *M.* 'Red Jade'

No. NR7-P9-88. From the series of over 40 new, weeping crabapples developed at Falconskeape Gardens, Medina, OH, over the past 50 years. A heavily branched weeper to 10 ft (3 m) high and 12 ft (3.5 m) wide; buds pale pink to soft rose, opening to large, single, white flowers with pink reverse on fringed petals; fruit 0.5 in (1.2 cm) in diameter, bright red, persistent. Very attractive and showy in abundant, annual blossoming. Disease resistant. A new, relatively unknown weeper that is outstanding in blossom, fruit, and winter landscape form. Loc. 47.

M. 'Dr. Van Fleet'

Name only. Subject to mild scab (Nichols). Loc. 81.

M. 'Dunbar'

See *M. coronaria* var. *glaucescens* 'Dunbar' in Chapter 11.

M. 'Duncannon'

Name only.

M. 'Early Strawberry' U.S. before 1875

A large-fruited apple. Subject to mild scab (Nichols). Loc. 54.

M. 'Edith'

Name only. Disease resistant (Nichols). Loc. 2, 61.

M. 'Edna'

See *M.* 'Edna Mullins'.

M. 'Edna Mullins'

Synonym: *M.* 'Edna' Weston Nursery

Parentage: Unknown

Origin unknown. Named to honor Edna Mullins, former receptionist at Weston Nursery, Hopkinton, MA. Subject to mild scab and cedar-apple rust (Nichols). Loc. 5, 19, 69.

M. 'Edulis'

Parentage: A clone of *M. baccata*

***M. 'Egret'** Fiala 1980
Parentage: (*M.* 'Van Eseltine' × *M.* 'Serenade') × (*M. sieboldii* No. 768 × *M.* 'Red Jade')
An induced octoploid. Introduced by Klehm Nursery, South Barrington, IL. A graceful tree to 8 ft (2.5 m) high and 10 ft (3 m) wide, with long, thin, weeping branches to the ground; leaves very heavily textured, leathery, glossy, dark green, 2.5 in (6.4 cm) long and 0.75 in (1.9 cm) wide; buds deep rose pink, opening to semidouble, pink and white flowers with the outer side of petals a rose pink; fruit round, red, to 0.4 in (1 cm) in diameter. Completely disease resistant (Nichols). An unusual weeper that should be used in a program for hybrid polyploid weepers. Loc. 47, 100.

M. 'E. H. Wilson' Sim before 1931
Parentage: Unknown
Origin unknown. Named to honor E. H. Wilson, famous plant explorer, botanist, and author, who worked first for Veitch & Sons, England, and then for the Arnold Arboretum. Introduced by William Sim Nursery, Cliftondale, MA. Buds carmine to rose, opening to single, white flowers 1.9 in (4.8 cm) across; fruit orange-red to red, large, 1.2 in (3 cm) in diameter. Subject to severe scab and mild fire blight (Nichols). Loc. 12, 24, 32, 35, 37, 54, 81.

M. 'Eleyi'
See *M. ×purpurea* 'Eleyi' in Chapter 11.

***+M. 'Elfin Magic'** Fiala 1986 Fig. 2.2
Parentage: *M.* 'Christmas Holly' × *M.* 'Amberina'
No. 86-575. A small, upright to spreading tree to 12 ft (3.5 m) high by 10 ft (3 m) wide; leaves dark green, disease free; buds bright carmine red, opening to single, large white flowers; fruit brilliant orange-red, very attractive and abundant, 0.4–0.5 in (1–1.2 cm) in diameter, persistent to late winter, relished by smaller birds. An annual bearer. Completely disease resistant. An excellent mini-fruited crabapple that is extremely showy in autumn fruit color and fits into any landscape requiring a smaller specimen tree. Loc. 47.

M. 'Elijha' Fiala 1952
A discontinued clone; too similar to other red-flowering, red-fruited clones. A small tree 10 ft (3 m) high; leaves red-green; buds red, opening to single, red flowers; fruit dark red, 0.5 in (1.2 cm) in diameter. Subject to moderate scab. Loc. 46, 47.

***M. 'Eline'** Fiala Plate 159
No. NR7-R7-88. Named to honor Eline Kleiss, Ocala, FL, cousin of the introducer. A small, upright to vase-shaped tree to 12 ft (3.5 m) high and 8 ft (2.5 m) wide; buds rose-colored, opening to semidouble, white-mixed-with-pink flowers growing all along branches, wandlike; fruit copper-gold, persistent. A very heavy, annual bloomer. Disease free. A fine tree for smaller gardens, patios, and garden walks. New and as yet not well known. Loc. 47, 100.

M. 'Elise Rathke'
See *M. pumila* 'Pendula'.

M. 'Elk River'
See *M. coronaria* 'Elk River' in Chapter 11.

M. 'Ellen Gerhart' Simpson circa 1955
Parentage: *M. sieboldii* 'Calocarpa' × *M.* 'Van Eseltine'
No. 1413. Named by Robert Simpson for one of the first secretaries at his nursery. A medium-sized tree; leaves good, resembling those of *M. sieboldii*, scab resistant; flowers single and semidouble, pale pink; fruit glossy, brilliant red, 0.5–0.6 in (1.2–1.5 cm) in diameter, small, flattened with distinct conelike scar of rusty or golden color that adds to attractiveness, colors late, persistent. Subject to severe scab (Nichols). Loc. 5, 12, 18, 24, 26, 35, 37, 46, 47, 54, 55, 61, 79, 80, 81.

M. 'Ellwangeriana'
See *M. floribunda* 'Ellwangeriana' in Chapter 11.

M. 'Elongata'
See *M. coronaria* 'Elongata' in Chapter 11.

M. 'Elsa' CDA—Ottawa
Parentage: A Rosybloom
Now considered obsolete.

M. 'Elsie Burgess' H. R. Wright
Parentage: A seedling of *M.* 'Gorgeous'; a hybrid of *M. baccata*

M. 'Erie' Preston 1920 Plate 160
Parentage: An open-pollinated seedling of *M. pumila* 'Niedzwetzkyana'
Named in 1930 by Isabella Preston, CDA—Ottawa, in her Lake Series, for one of the Great Lakes between Canada and the United States. Buds purple-red, opening to rose-pink to lavender flowers with pale lavender claw, 2 in (5 cm) across; fruit dark red to orange, 0.9 in (2.3 cm) in diameter. An alternate bloomer. Subject to

severe scab. Like any member of the Lake Series, this clone might be slightly better for hybridizing newer Rosyblooms than *M. pumila* 'Niedzwetzkyana' itself. Loc. 31, 32, 79, 81.

***M.* 'Erl Trio'** N. E. Hansen
Parentage: A seedling of *M.* 'Dolgo'; a hybrid of *M. baccata*

****M.* 'Evelyn'** A. den Boer 1939
Synonym: *M. ioensis* 'Red Seedling No. 1'
Parentage: *M. ioensis* × *M.* ×*purpurea*
A hybrid selected by Arie den Boer from a large number of seedlings of *M. ioensis* at Waterworks Arboretum, Des Moines, IA. Named in 1953 by the introducer for a daughter-in-law, Evelyn, wife of son John. Buds deep rose-red, opening to single, rose-red to deep rose-red flowers 1.4 in (3.5 cm) across, single; fruit green-yellow and red, 1.4 in (3.5 cm) in diameter. An alternate bloomer. Should be phased out—subject to severe scab and very severe fire blight (Nichols). Loc. 12, 15, 18, 24, 31, 32, 35, 37, 54, 79, 80, 81.

***M.* 'Excalibur'** Zampini
Trade name: Excaliber
Plant patent name *M.* "Excazam". To be introduced by Lake County Nursery, Perry, OH, as one of the Round Table Series of dwarf crabapples developed by James Zampini. A small tree to 10 ft (3 m) high and 8 ft (2.5 m) wide; leaves green; buds red, opening to single, white flowers; fruit small, light gold, persistent. Good disease resistance (per introducer); too new to be properly evaluated for disease resistance. The small form should make this clone a welcome addition in smaller gardens, in front of larger trees, as a pot plant, and for all ornamental landscaping where a small tree or bush form in needed. Loc. 46.

***M.* 'Excelsior'**
Name only.

***M.* 'Exzellenz Thiel'**
See *M. floribunda* 'Exzellenz Thiel' in Chapter 11.

***M.* 'Fairy'** Jennings, England, 1870
Parentage: *M. baccata* × *M. pumila*.
Large-fruited. Loc. 54, 61.

****M.* 'Fairy Fire'** Fiala 1986
Parentage: *M.* 'Redbird' × *M.* 'Amberina'
No. 86-617. A small tree to 10 ft (3 m) high and as wide; leaves medium green, good, disease free; buds bright red, opening to single, white flowers produced in great abundance; fruit very small, 0.3 in (0.8 cm) in diameter, oblong, very brilliant, glossy, orange-red, very showy, persistent all winter, relished by small birds. An annual bloomer. Completely disease resistant. An excellent mini-fruited crabapple for the small home landscape, patio, or anywhere a specimen plant is needed. Outstanding when placed next to gold-fruited crabapples. A fine plant for hybridizing for mini-fruits. Loc. 47.

***M.* 'Fay Trio'** N. E. Hansen
Parentage: A hybrid of *M. baccata*

***M.* 'Ferguson's K-64'**
Name only. Subject to moderate scab. Loc. 31.

***M.* 'Ferrill's Crimson'** Ferrill before 1953
Parentage: An open-pollinated of unknown parentage
Leaves very red; flowers single, purple-red, 1.4 in (3.5 cm) across; fruit red, 0.6 in (1.5 cm) in diameter. Subject to severe scab. A clone that is practically unknown and yet has merits. Loc. 10, 15, 31, 61, 87.

****M.* 'Fiesta'** Fiala 1975
Parentage: *M.* 'Winter Gold' × *M.* 'Christmas Holly'
No. 82-1-1. A small to medium-sized semi-weeper to 15 ft (4.6 m) high and as wide, with slender, refined branches; leaves dark green; buds carmine red, opening to single, white flowers in cascades; fruit small, to 0.4 in (1 cm) in diameter, very attractive combination of colors on single fruit—bright burnt-coral to orange-gold, firm, persistent. A very heavy annual bearer. Fine disease resistance. An excellent weeper. Outstanding in form, blossom, and fruit. A showpiece in any garden or park. Loc. 47.

***M.* 'Fiona'**
Name only. Subject to severe scab. Loc. 61, 81.

***M.* 'Fiore's Improved Bechtel'** Fiore
Name only. Subject to severe scab. Loc. 89.

****M.* 'Firebelle'** Fiala 1975
Parentage: *M.* 'Christmas Holly' × *M.* 'Amberina'
No. 86-455. A small, rounded tree to 12 ft (3.5 m) high and 10 ft (3 m) wide; leaves dark green, disease resistant; buds red, opening to heavy clusters of single, white flowers; fruit very

small, 0.4 in (1 cm) in diameter, very bright red, round, glossy, firm, persistent into deep winter until eaten by birds. A very showy, heavy, annual bearer. Completely disease resistant. Excellent for smaller landscapes and as specimen lawn tree. Loc. 47.

M. 'Firebrand' Fiala 1982
Parentage: *M.* 'Redbird' × *M.* 'Amberina'
No. 86-5-25. A small, rounded tree to 14 ft (4.3 m) high and 10 ft (3 m) wide; leaves deep green, disease free; buds red, opening to single, white flowers; fruit very small, 0.3–0.4 in (0.8–1 cm) in diameter, brilliant orange-red, persistent to winter. An annual bearer. Fine disease resistance. An excellent plant for all landscapes. An extremely showy mini-fruited tree; as it matures, bearing on spurs increases. Loc. 47.

M. 'Fireburst' Fiala 1975
Parentage: *M.* 'Winter Gold' × *M.* 'Christmas Holly'
No. 82-1-2. A small, upright, slightly spreading tree to 15 ft (4.6 m) high and 12 ft (3.5 m) wide; leaves dark green, disease resistant; buds bright cherry-red, opening to single, white flowers; fruit small, 0.25 in (0.6 cm) in diameter, firm, very bright red, glossy and showy, persistent to deep freeze. An excellent crabapple in bloom and especially showy in fruit. Loc. 47.

M. 'Firecloud' Fiala 1984
Parentage: *M.* 'Red Jade' × *M.* 'Red Swan'
No. 86-616. A small semiweeper to 12 ft (3.5 m) high and as wide; leaves dark green, disease resistant; buds coral-rose, opening to single, white flowers produced in great abundance; fruit 0.25–0.4 in (0.6–1 cm) in diameter, bright red-orange, persistent until eaten by birds. An annual bearer. Very showy in bloom and fruit. An excellent tree for any landscape and a specimen tree. Loc. 47.

M. 'Firecracker' Fiala 1985
Parentage: *M.* 'Red Swan' × *M.* 'Amberina'
No. 86-461. A small weeper to 8 ft (2.5 m) high and 12 ft (3.5 m) wide; leaves dark green, good; buds rose-colored, opening to attractive, semidouble, pink-white flowers; fruit small, 0.6 in (1.5 cm) in diameter, bright red, persistent until eaten by birds. An annual bearer. Completely disease free. Showy in bloom and fruit. An ideal specimen for lawn planting. Loc. 47.

M. 'Firedance' Fiala 1969
Parentage: (*M. sieboldii* 'Wooster' × *M.* 'Red Jade') × *M.* 'Molten Lava'
A spreading weeper to 5 ft (1.5 m) high and 10 ft (3 m) wide, with horizontal branching; leaves medium green, subject to slight leaf spot; buds bright red, opening to single, white flowers; fruit bright red, 0.4 in (1 cm) in diameter, very showy. Good disease resistance; subject to mild scab that does not cause leaf drop. Loc. 46, 47, 100.

M. 'Firefly' Fiala 1964
A discontinued clone. An upright to spreading tree to 15 ft (4.6 m) high and 12 ft (3.5 m) wide; buds rose-red, opening to very pale pinkish, single flowers; fruit 0.4 in (1 cm) in diameter, bright red, persistent until eaten by birds. Subject to moderate scab. Loc. 47.

M. 'Fireglow' Fiala 1979
Parentage: *M.* 'Liset' × *M.* 'Amberina'
No. 6-223. A small, rounded tree to 10 ft (3 m) high and as wide; leaves red-green to bronze-green, disease free; buds rose-colored, opening to single, rose-pink flowers produced in great abundance; fruit 0.4–0.5 in (1–1.2 cm) in diameter, red, persistent to late winter. An annual bloomer. Completely disease resistant. An excellent rose-flowering crabapple with bright red fruit. An excellent all-purpose tree. Loc. 47.

*+***M. 'Fire Mountain'*** Fiala/P. Murray
No. UDM-T3-89. A small, upright to spreading tree 12 ft (3.5 m) high and 14 ft (4.3 m) wide; leaves red-bronze before turning to bronze-green, good disease resistance; buds deep rose-red, opening to single, deep rose-red flowers, fading to a medium rose; fruit 0.5 in (1.2 cm) in diameter, bright red, very showy and heavy, persistent to December. A very heavy, annual bloomer. Disease resistant. An outstanding rose-red flowering crabapple for all landscaping needs: the combination of red and rose flowers is very attractive in spring and the fall fruit is very effective. Should be one of the better small crabapples. Loc. 47. 100.

M. 'Flame' University of Minnesota 1920 Fig. 12.3
Parentage: An open-pollinated apple seedling
A hardy tree; buds pink, opening to single, white flowers; fruit bright red, 0.8 in (2 cm) in diameter. An alternate bearer. Subject to very severe scab and moderate fire blight. Loc. 13, 15, 24, 26, 31, 32, 35, 54, 55, 79, 80, 81, 87, 89, 91.

M. 'Flamingo' Fiala 1969
A small, graceful, fountain type weeper to 10 ft (3 m) high by 12 ft (3.5 m) wide; leaves

Figure 12.3. *Malus* 'Flame'

reddish; buds red, opening to magenta flowers; fruit red-purple, 0.5 in (1.2 cm) in diameter. An annual bloomer. Moderately resistant to scab. Fruit too dark purple to be showy. Loc. 47.

***M.* 'Flaming Star'** Fiala 1965
Parentage: *M.* ×*purpurea* 'Lemoinei' × *M.* 'Red Jade'
No. EFR-2. A graceful, fountain type weeper to 12 ft (3.5 m) high and as wide, with slender branches sweeping the ground; leaves green-red to bronze; buds deep red, opening to single, bright red flowers that fade to a medium rose; fruit 0.5 in (1.2 cm) in diameter, dull red. A heavy annual bloomer. Subject to mild scab that is not disfiguring. Grows into a very graceful weeper with age. Loc. 47.

***M.* 'Flava'**
See *M. baccata* 'Yellow Siberian' in Chapter 11.

***M.* 'Flavescens'**
See *M. baccata* 'Flavescens' in Chapter 11.

***M.* 'Flexilis'**
See *M. baccata* 'Flexilis' in Chapter 11.

***M.* 'Florence'** Gideon 1886
Fruit large. Subject to very severe scab (Nichols). Loc. 12, 54.

M. florentina
See Chapter 11.

***M.* 'Flore Plena'**
See *M. ioensis* 'Plena' in Chapter 11.

M. floribunda
See Chapter 11.

***M. floribunda* 'Ellwangeriana'**
See Chapter 11.

***M. floribunda* 'Exzellenz Thiel'**
See Chapter 11.

***M.* 'Fluke No. 10'** Fluke
Parentage: A selection of wild *M. ioensis*
Selected by N. K. Fluke, Davenport, IA.

***M. 'Fluke No. 29'** Fluke
Parentage: A selection of wild *M. ioensis*
Selected by N. K. Fluke, Davenport, IA.

M. formosana
See Chapter 11.

***M. 'Fountain'** Fiala 1950 Plate 161
An induced octoploid. A very low weeper to 4 ft (1.2 m) high and 6 ft (1.8 m) wide, very slow growing; leaves very small and misshapen because of ploidy, disease free, 0.5–0.75 in (1.2–1.9 cm) long and 0.4 in (1 cm) wide, with very small internodes; buds pink, opening to large flowers 2 in (5 cm) across, single, white; fruit dark red, 0.5 in (1.2 cm) in diameter, persistent. Subject to moderate scab but otherwise disease free, although leaves very oddly shaped (Nichols). Recommended for hybridizers and researchers. Could be a progenitor of a whole new race of polyploid, smaller weepers. Loc. 47.

***M.* 'Foxley'** Knight
Parentage: A hybrid of *M. baccata*

M. fragrans attenuata
See *M. coronaria* 'Elongata' in Chapter 11.

***M. 'Francis'** Fiala
Parentage: *M.* 'Amberina' × *M.* 'Winter Gold'
No. NR5-P15-89-515. Named to honor a friend and outstanding plant propagator and horticulturist, Francis Nock, Perry, OH. An upright, spreading tree to 15 ft (4.6 m) high and 20 ft (6 m) wide; buds rose-colored, opening to single, white flowers tinted pale pink, very fragrant; fruit 0.5 in (1.2 cm) in diameter, red with gold cheeks, extremely showy, persistent. An abundant, annual bloomer. Disease resistant. Very attractive when grown next to bright red fruiting clones. A showy tree for all landscaping needs, especially for bloom and fruit color. Loc. 47.

***M.* 'Franz Lipp'** Tures 1960
Named by Matt Tures Sons Nursery, Huntley, IL, for Franz Lipp, noted Chicago landscape architect. Name only.

***M.* 'Frau Luise Dittmann'** Henkel before 1909
From Germany in 1925. Identical with *M. spectabilis* 'Plena' (A. den Boer). An alternate bearer. Subject to moderate scab and mildew (Nichols). Loc. 12, 35, 37, 68, 87.

***M.* 'Frettingham's Victoria'**
An upright to round tree to 15 ft (4.6 m) high and 12 ft (3.5 m) wide; flowers single, white; fruit 0.5 in (1.2 cm) in diameter, green with reddish shaded side. Not particularly ornamental. Loc. 31.

***M. 'Fuji'**
See *M. toringo* 'Fuji' in Chapter 11.

***M. 'Full Sails'** Fiala/P. Murray
Parentage: *M.* 'Angel Choir' × *M.* 'Amberina'
No. 86-221. A small, upright to spreading tree 12 ft (3.5 m) high and 10 ft (3 m) wide; leaves green, good; buds pale pink, opening to semidouble, large, white flowers in great abundance; fruit 0.5 in (1.2 cm) in diameter, bright red, persistent to late November. An annual bloomer. Disease resistant. A fine, smaller tree for the average garden—showy in blossom and fruit. Loc. 47.

M. fusca
See Chapter 11.

M. fusca* var. *levipes
See Chapter 11.

***M. fusca* 'Wagener'**
See Chapter 11.

***M.* 'Gardenview-19'**
See *M.* 'GV-19'.

***M.* 'Garnet'** Broughen Nursery 1942
Parentage: Unknown
Introduced by Broughen Nurseries, Valley River, Manitoba, Canada. Flowers single, pink and white; fruit large (size of eating apples), red to purple-red, 2 in (5 cm) in diameter. Not well distributed and known. Some scionwood of what is now known as *M.* 'Gemstone' was released under the name *M.* 'Garnet' before the priority of names was determined. *Malus* 'Garnet' (Fiala) is now *M.* 'Gemstone' and in a few collections trees labeled *M.* 'Garnet' should be changed to *M.* 'Gemstone'.

***M.* 'Garry'** CDA—Morden 1962
Trade name: Garry crabapple
Parentage: An open-pollinated seedling of *M. pumila* 'Niedzwetzkyana'
MR-455. A Rosybloom. A tree with slender, arching form; buds maroon, opening to deep rose-red flowers; fruit crimson with heavy waxy bloom, 0.8 in (2 cm) in diameter, persistent all winter. Subject to moderate-to-severe scab (Nichols). One of the better red-leaf, red-flowering clones, although it is not well known and therefore not grown. In hybridizing it could be a substitute for *M. pumila* 'Niedzwetzkyana'. Loc. 12, 31, 54.

***M. 'Gemstone'** Fiala 1978
Parentage: *M. sieboldii* 'Wooster' × *M.* 'Christmas Holly'
Originally named *M.* 'Garnet', the name was changed so as not to conflict with a previous name. A small, upright to rounded and spreading tree 8 ft (2.5 m) high and as wide; leaves rich dark green, disease free; buds carmine red, opening to single, blush white flowers; fruit 0.4 in (1 cm) in diameter, deep garnet red, very glossy and attractive, firm, persistent to January. An annual bearer. Completely disease resistant (Nichols). An excellent tree, though fruit is a bit dark. Most effective when placed next to yellow-fruited clones. Loc. 46, 47, 100.

***M.* 'Geneva'** Preston 1920
Parentage: An open-pollinated seedling of *M. pumila* 'Niedzwetzkyana'
A Rosybloom selected by Isabella Preston, CDA—Ottawa. Named in 1930. Fruit large. Subject to very severe scab. Not particularly outstanding. Loc. 24, 54.

***M.* 'George Eden'**
Name only. Subject to mild scab and mild fire blight (Nichols). Loc. 54, 81.

***M.* 'Gertrude'**
Name only. Loc. 81.

***M.* 'Giant Wild'**
Parentage: A clone of *M. ×soulardii*
Name only. Subject to severe scab and moderate cedar-apple rust. Loc. 31, 54.

***M.* 'Gibb'** Peffer
Parentage: A hybrid of *M. baccata*
An upright, spreading tree to 18 ft (5.5 m) high and as wide; buds deep rose-colored, opening to single, pink flowers; fruit fairly large, green. Subject to very mild scab. Loc. 9, 15, 35, 37.

***M. 'Gibb's Golden Gage'** Aldenham House 1923
Parentage: A chance seedling

Introduced in the United States by the U.S. National Arboretum, Washington, DC. A small, rounded tree to 20 ft (6 m) high; buds pink, opening to single, white flowers; fruit gold, small, 1 in (2.5 cm) in diameter, persistent to February–March. According to Lester Nichols, "Disease free. A crabapple not carried by American nurseries but should be. It is a charming tree in its yellow-gold autumn fruit." A truly choice clone that has been overlooked. There is a great need for good yellow-fruiting crabapples. Loc. 31, 32, 35, 54, 79, 81.

M. **'Girard's Pendula Nana'**
See *M.* 'Girard's Weeping Dwarf'.

M. **'Girard's Weeping Dwarf'**
Synonym: *M.* 'Girard's Pendula Nana'
Girard Nursery, Geneva, OH
A small, fountain type weeper to 10 ft (3 m) high and 12 ft (3.5 m) wide; buds pale pink, opening to single, pure white flowers; fruit color not available. Subject to moderate scab (Nichols). Not much seen except at the Holden Arboretum, Mentor, OH. Loc. 26, 81.

M. glabrata
See *M. coronaria* var. *glabrata* in Chapter 11.

M. **'Gladwyne'** Henry 1939
Parentage: *M. angustifolia* × *M. ioensis* 'Plena' or an open-pollinated seedling
A cross made by Mrs. Norman Henry, Gladwyne, PA, although the cross is doubtful (because diploid crabapples do not cross well with tetraploids). Subject to severe cedar-apple rust and mild scab (Nichols). Not well known but could be a reasonably good clone. Loc. 12, 31, 68, 81.

M. glaucescens
See *M. coronaria* var. *glaucescens* in Chapter 11.

M. **'Glen Mills'** Moller's Nursery, Gresham, OR
A small to medium-sized, upright, spreading to rounded tree; flowers white, single; fruit red, very small, persistent. An annual bearer. Good disease resistance. Loc. Johnson's Nursery, Menomonee Falls, WI.

M. **'Gloriosa'**
See *M.* ×*gloriosa* in Chapter 11.

M.* ×*gloriosa
See Chapter 11.

M. **'Gold'** Buckman 1910
Probably *M.* 'Stark's Gold', which see.

M. **'Golden Anniversary'** Will 1931
Named to honor the 50th anniversary of the Oscar H. Will Co., Bismarck, ND. Flowers single, white; fruit yellow with red blush, 1 in (2.5 cm) in diameter. Subject to mild cedar-apple rust (Nichols). Loc. 10, 54.

M.* **'Golden Candles' Fiala 1971 Plate 7
Synonym: *M.* 'Christmas Candles'
Parentage: *Malus* 'Winter Gold' × *M. sieboldii* No. 768
An upright tree to 20 ft (6 m) high, becoming spreading to fan-shaped with age and the weight of very heavy annual fruiting; leaves dark green; disease free; buds deep carmine, opening to single white flowers that also bloom on spurs; fruit 0.4–0.5 in (1–1.2 cm) in diameter, chartreuse-bright lemon, firm, persistent to December or until eaten by birds. Subject to very slight, nondisfiguring scab, otherwise disease resistant (Nichols). An excellent, dependable crabapple. Very showy in fruit, particularly if beside a red-fruited clone. Loc. 31, 46, 47.
Progeny of *M.* 'Golden Candles' include *M.* 'Limelight' Fiala.

M.* **'Golden Dream' Fiala 1960
Parentage: *M.* 'Winter Gold' × *M. sieboldii* 'Wooster'
No. 85-12. Introduced by Klehm Nursery, South Barrington, IL. A small, rounded tree to no more than 12 ft (3.5 m) high and 10 ft (3 m) wide; leaves medium green, disease free; buds carmine pink, opening to single, white flowers produced in great abundance; fruit bright yellow-gold, 0.25–0.4 in (0.6–1 cm) in diameter, showy, firm and persistent until late winter, with a glossy, burnished-copper glow after freezing. An annual bearer. Totally disease resistant (Nichols). An excellent little tree that should be grown more; especially fine in small group plantings next to red-fruited clones. Outstanding for highway plantings. Loc. 46, 47, 100.

M.* **'Golden Galaxy' Fiala 1977 Plate 162
Parentage: *M.* 'Centurion' × *M.* 'Gypsy Gold'
No. 85-6-7, PP. Introduced by Klehm Nursery, South Barrington, IL. A small, rounded to slightly spreading tree to 12 ft (3.5 m) high and 10 ft (3 m) wide; leaves medium green, good, disease free; buds pale pink, opening to single, white flowers in great abundance; fruit rich gold, 0.6 in (1.5 cm) in diameter, persistent to

midwinter. An annual bloomer. Completely disease resistant (Nichols). An excellent gold-fruited tree that gives a showy autumn display. Fine for all landscapes. Deserves to be far more planted and known. Loc. 47, 100.

***M. 'Golden Gem'**
From Germany. USDA plant introduction No. 307500. Four different crabapples are named *M.* 'Golden Gem'—three at Morton Arboretum and one at Longwood: clones No. 755-58, No. GR601-62, plant introduction No. 307500, and No. PLT 788-58. The better one, plant introduction No. 307500, is an upright to spreading smaller tree; buds pink, opening to single, white flowers; fruit small, yellow. Disease free (Nichols). It may be that the German importation can be identified only by number and not by name. Specimens at Holden Arboretum, Mentor, OH, and elsewhere do not indicate which clone they are. Worthwhile clones should be named; GR601-62, with heavy scab infection, should be discarded. Loc. 2, 5, 26, 31.

***M.* 'Golden Harvest'** Wayside Gardens catalog 1973
Disease resistant (Nichols). Loc. 61.

***M.* 'Golden Hornet'** 1949
Parentage: A seedling of *M. toringo* (formerly *M. sieboldii*)
Of English origin. A small, upright tree to 15 ft (4.6 m) high and as wide, tending to be pendulous and spreading with age because of heavy fruiting; buds pale pink, opening to white, single flowers; fruit small, lime-yellow, 0.75 in (1.9 cm) in diameter, showy, persistent to early November, may russet and brown badly in the fall. A very heavy bearer. Subject to mild fire blight (Nichols). Loc. 5, 9, 11, 12, 15, 18, 24, 26, 31, 35, 46, 47, 54, 61, 68, 69, 79, 81, 87, 89.

***M.* 'Golden Noble'**
Name only.

***M.* 'Golden Spires'** Fiala 1971
An upright to fan-shaped tree; buds deep rose red, opening to white flowers; fruit small, 0.4 in (1 cm) in diameter, lemon-yellow. A heavy annual bloomer. Disease resistant (Nichols). Very similar to *M.* 'Golden Candles' but tree a bit more spreading and fruit a brighter shade of lemon. An excellent clone that tends to spread with age because of heavy fruiting. Excellent in smaller gardens as a background tree. Loc. 31, 46, 47.

***M.* 'Golden Wax'**
Name only. Subject to severe scab (Nichols). Loc. 61.

***M.* 'Golden Weeper'**
Name only.

***M. 'Goldfinch'** Lloyd/Swarthmore 1920
Parentage: A seedling of *M. baccata*
Raised from seed found under a tree at the Arnold Arboretum by Mrs. Horatio Gates Lloyd. Introduced by Swarthmore College in 1953. Flowers single, white, 1.4 in (3.5 cm) across; fruit yellow, small, 0.4 in (1 cm) in diameter. Subject to severe scab (Nichols). Not well known, therefore not grown. Loc. 4, 12, 26, 31, 54, 68, 81.

***M. 'Goldilocks'** Fiala 1976
Parentage: *M.* 'Tetragold' × *M.* 'Coral Cascade'
No. 85-6-9. An excellent, graceful semiweeper 15 ft (4.6 m) high and as wide, with long, slender branching, becoming a full weeper with maturity; leaves dark green, disease free; buds red, opening to single, white flowers produced in abundant cascades; fruit small, 0.25–0.4 in (0.6–1 cm) in diameter, bright yellow with gold blush on shaded side, beautiful in autumn with racemes of heavy fruit. A heavy, annual bloomer. Very minor trace of occasional scab, otherwise disease free. A tree for any focal point. Loc. 47, 86.

***M.* 'Golf Course'** M. Yanny Fig. 3.2
Parentage: Probably of older *M. sieboldii* background
Introduced by Johnson's Nursery, Menomonee Falls, WI. An upright to rounded tree with ascending branching; buds red-pink, opening to single, pure white flowers; fruit 0.25–0.4 in (0.6–1 cm) in diameter, a good red color, persistent throughout winter. A showy, annual bearer. Excellent disease resistance. Used by Lori and Michael Yanny extensively in hybridizing.

***M.* 'Goolsbey'** Wodarz
Parentage: A seedling of *M.* 'Dolgo'

***M. 'Gorgeous'** H. R. Wright 1925
Parentage: *M. sieboldii* × *M. halliana*
USDA plant introduction No. 64833. From Hayward Wright, Avondale, Auckland, New Zealand. A dense, rounded tree; expanding buds pink, opening to single, white flowers 1.3 in (3.2 cm) across; fruit crimson to orange-red, ovoid, 1 in (2.5 cm) in diameter. An annual

bearer. Subject to very mild scab and moderate mildew (Nichols). An excellent ornamental crabapple not as well known and planted as it deserves. Listed only in the collection at Swarthmore College, Swarthmore, PA, and grown by one or two nurseries. A crabapple of such merit should not be lost to the market but planted far more and offered by nurseries. Loc. 10, 15, 26, 31, 32, 37, 47, 54, 79, 81, 89.

Progeny of *M.* 'Gorgeous' include the following:

M. 'Bledisloe' H. R. Wright
M. 'Crimson Glory' H. R. Wright
M. 'Elsie Burgess' H. R. Wright
M. 'Jack Humm' D. Nairn
M. 'Sovereign' D. Nairn
M. 'Wright's Scarlet' H. R. Wright

***M.* 'Gracilis'**
See *M. baccata* 'Gracilis' in Chapter 11.

***M.* 'Grandmother Louise'** Fiala 1950
Parentage: An induced tetraploid seedling of *M.* 'Dorothea'

A discontinued clone because it grows too slowly for the commercial market. A small, rounded tree to 6 ft (1.8 m) high and 12 ft (3.5 m) wide, very slow growing; buds rose-colored, opening to deep rose-pink, semidouble flowers; fruit very few, if any. Loc. 46, 47.

***M.* 'Grant'**
Name only.

***M.* 'Greenbriar'**
Name only. Subject to some minor scab (Nichols). Loc. 12.

***M.* 'Guerney'**
See *M.* 'Guerney Sweet Harvest'.

***M.* 'Guerney Seedling'**
See *M.* 'Guerney Sweet Harvest'.

***M.* 'Guerney Sweet Harvest'**
Synonyms: *M.* 'Guerney Seedling', *M.* 'Guerney'

Name only. Subject to slight cedar-apple rust (Nichols). Loc. 54.

***M.* 'Guiding Star'**
Name only. Subject to mild scab, moderate mildew, and moderate-to-severe fire blight (Nichols). Loc. 31, 35, 54, 61, 81.

*****M.* 'Guinevere'** Zampini
Plant patent name "Guinzam." To be introduced by Lake County Nursery, Perry, OH, as one of the Round Table Series of dwarf crabapples developed by James Zampini. A very small, rounded tree or bush 8 ft (2.5 m) high and as wide; leaves becoming midnight wine in color with frost; buds deep carmine, opening to single, white flowers tinted mauve; fruit medium-sized, brilliant cherry red, persistent. Disease resistant (per introducer); too new to be properly evaluated for disease resistance. Appears to be a good addition to dwarf crabapples. Presents an excellent combination of leaves and white blossoms. Loc. 46.

+*M.* 'GV-19'** Ross Plate 163
Synonym: *M.* 'Gardenview-19' Ross 1968
Parentage: A seedling of *M.* 'Van Eseltine'

An outstanding crabapple from one of North America's foremost plantsmen, Henry Ross, Gardenview Horticultural Park, Strongsville, OH. An upright to spreading tree to 20 ft (6 m) high and 18 ft (5.5 m) wide; buds deep rose-colored, opening to very double, deep rose-pink flowers with inner petal layers of deep rose to pink to white; fruit sparse, gold-amber, insignificant. An extremely heavy, annual bloomer. Subject to slight scab, otherwise no diseases (Nichols). An excellent tree for spring show and beauty: it begins to bloom early and extends bloom over 2–3 weeks. Also, the multicolored flowers create an extremely pleasing effect. Suitable for any landscaping need except for the smaller, narrow places. Retains its rather upright form well. Should be far better known and grown. Loc. 47.

*****M.* 'Gwendolyn'** A. den Boer 1944
Parentage: A seedling of *M. floribunda*

Named after Gwendolyn Tobin, Des Moines, IA. Buds pink, opening to single, pink, very large flowers 1.6 in (4 cm) across; fruit red, 1 in (2.5 cm), heavy bearer. Totally disease resistant (Nichols). A crabapple that has been overlooked. Loc. 15, 18, 26, 31, 79, 81, 89.

*****M.* 'Gypsy Dancer'** Fiala 1976
Parentage: *M.* 'Gypsy Gold' × *M.* 'Amberina'

No. 86-441. A very graceful, somewhat spreading, upright tree to 14 ft (4.3 m) high and 12 ft (3.5 m) wide; leaves dark green, good, disease free; buds bright red, opening to single, white flowers in heavy clusters; fruit 0.4–0.5 in (1–1.2 cm) in diameter, a combination of brilliant colors of red, red-orange, yellow, and coral, very attractive, persistent until eaten by birds. An abundant, annual bloomer. Totally disease resistant. An excellent crabapple with a unique autumn color. Most effective when planted next to a clone with brilliant red or deep purple fruit. Loc. 47.

***M. 'Gypsy Gold'** Fiala 1970
Parentage: *M. baccata* × *M. baccata* 'Shaker Gold'
An upright to spreading tree to 14 ft (4.3 m) high and 12 ft (3.5 m) wide; leaves dark green; buds pink, opening to large, single white flowers; fruit bright yellow with orange cheek that turns to burnt orange after frost, 0.75 in (1.9 cm) in diameter, rounded, ribbed. A very heavy, annual bearer. Completely disease resistant (Nichols). Somewhat large-fruited for the home landscape but excellent elsewhere, especially as a roadside tree that can be seen in color from fast-moving vehicles. Loc. 46, 47, 100.

M. halliana
See Chapter 11.

M. halliana var. ***spontanea***
See Chapter 11.

***M. halliana* National Arboretum No. 127**
See Chapter 11.

***M. halliana* 'Parkmanii'**
See Chapter 11.

***M.* 'Halward'**
See *M. baccata* 'Halward' in Chapter 11.

***M.* 'Hamlet'** Zampini Plate 164
Plant patent name "Hamzam." To be introduced by Lake County Nursery, Perry, OH, as one of the Round Table Series of dwarf crabapples developed by James Zampini. A small, rounded tree or bush 10 ft (3 m) high and as wide; leaves green with a wine-red overcast; buds deep rose-pink, opening to single, rose-pink flowers; fruit red. Disease resistant (per introducer); too new to be properly evaluated for disease resistance. Another welcome addition to dwarf crabapples badly needed for city gardens, patios, sidewalk plantings, and other landscaping designs. Loc. 46.

***M.* 'Hampton's Siberian'** Hampton
Parentage: A hybrid of *M. baccata*

***M.* 'Hansen's Beauty'** Hansen
Parentage: A hybrid of *M. baccata*

***M.* 'Hansen's Red Leaf Crabapple'** N. E. Hansen
See *M.* 'Hopa'.

***M.* 'Hans Trio'** N. E. Hansen
Parentage: One of the progeny of *M. baccata* 'Yellow Siberian'

***M.* 'Harriman'**
Name only. Subject to moderate scab (Nichols). Loc. 35.

***M.* 'Hartman'**
Name only.

***M.* 'Hartwigi'**
See *M.* ×*hartwigii* in Chapter 11.

M.* ×*hartwigii
See Chapter 11.

***M. 'Harvest Gold'** Zampini 1987
Plant patent name "Hargozam." Introduced by Lake County Nursery, Perry, OH. Developed by James Zampini. An upright tree; flowers single, white; fruit gold, 0.7 in (1.8 cm) in diameter, abundant, persistent to late December. Very good disease resistance. An excellent new crabapple in the much needed gold-fruited class. Outstanding for street plantings, for small gardens, and to break the monotony of rounded tops along a garden walk. Also an excellent boundary crabapple. Should be planted against red-fruited clones. Loc. 46.

***M.* 'Hazel Wilson'** Wheelock Wilson
Name only. Reported to be an excellent crabapple. No known source.

***M.* 'Heart River'** Baird
A hybrid of *M. baccata*.

***M.* 'Hedwig'**
Name only. Disease resistant (Nichols). Loc. 31.

***M.* 'Hedwigiae'**
A Latinized name that should not be used for a clone. See *M.* 'Hedwig'.

***M.* 'Helen'** A. den Boer 1939
Parentage: An open-pollinated seedling of Rosybloom *M.* 'Jay Darling'
A poor sibling of *M.* 'Purple Wave'. Buds dark red, opening to large, red flowers 1.8 in (4.5 cm) across; fruit purple-red, 0.8 in (2 cm) in diameter. Subject to moderate scab (Nichols). Loc. 9, 15, 31, 54, 61, 81, 89.

***M. 'Henning'** Enterprise Nurseries, Wrightsville, PA
Synonym: *M.* 'Henningii' (a Latinized name that should not be used for a clone)
An upright to spreading tree to 25 ft (8 m) high; leaves shiny green; flowers single, white, very heavy blooming; fruit small, orange-red, 0.6 in (1.5 cm) in diameter. Disease free

(Nichols). An excellent crabapple of outstanding upright form. Loc. 5, 79, 81.

***M.* 'Henrietta Crosby'** Sax 1939
Parentage: *M.* ×*arnoldiana* × *M. pumila* 'Niedzwetzkyana'
Arnold Arboretum No. 19039. Introduced in 1947. Named by Karl Sax, Arnold Arboretum, for Henrietta Crosby, of Manchester, MA. Flowers single, pink, 1.8 in (4.5 cm) across; fruit dark red, 1 in (2.5 cm) in diameter, falling early. Should be phased out—too much disease (Nichols). Loc. 8, 9, 11, 12, 13, 18, 31, 54, 68, 81, 89.

***M.* 'Henry F. DuPont'** Sax 1946 Fig. 12.4
Parentage: An open-pollinated seedling of *M.* ×*arnoldiana* × *M.* ×*purpurea* 'Eleyi'
Named by Karl Sax, Arnold Arboretum, for industrialist Henry F. DuPont, Winterthur, DE. Buds purple-red, opening to purple-pink flowers that fade to pale magenta, 1.7 in (4.3 cm) across, single and semidouble, with 5–10 petals; fruit small, brown-red, 0.6 in (1.4 cm) in diameter. Subject to moderate scab (Nichols). Not popular because of the washed-out flower color and dull fruit. Loc. 3, 11, 12, 18, 24, 26, 31, 35, 37, 47, 54, 73, 79, 87.

Figure 12.4. *Malus* 'Henry F. DuPont'

***M.* 'Henry Kohankie'** Kohankie
Parentage: A seedling of *M. sieboldii*
Grown from seed received from Japan in 1933. Named and registered in 1965 by George Parmelee, Michigan State University, to honor the outstanding plantsman, Henry Kohankie, of Henry Kohankie Nurseries, Lake County, OH. A rounded tree to 20 ft (6 m) high and as wide; leaves large, dark green, lobed; expanding buds pink, opening to single, pink-white to white flowers 1.25–1.5 in (3–3.8 cm) across; fruit glossy red, ellipsoidal, about 1.25 in (3 cm) in diameter, edible, persistent through the winter, decorative after leaf fall. Disease free (Nichols). An excellent crabapple for the larger estates and park plantings, not for the small home garden. Loc. 5, 12, 31, 46, 61, 79, 81, 87.

***M.* 'Henry Ross'** Fiala
Parentage: *M.* 'Red Swan' × *M.* 'White Cascade'
No. B3-85. Named to honor a friend and one of North America's outstanding horticulturists and new plant introducers, Henry Ross, director and founder of Gardenview Horticultural Park, Strongsville, OH. A small, graceful, fountain type weeper 8 ft (2.5 m) high and 10 ft (3 m) wide; leaves dark green; buds light pink-rose, opening to single, white flowers; fruit 0.4 in (1.1 cm) in diameter, bright yellow-gold, persistent, very attractive. A heavy, annual bloomer. Disease free. From the long series of newer weeping crabapples developed in the past 50 years at Falconskeape Gardens, Medina, OH. An excellent fountain weeper for smaller gardens and as a focal point in any garden. Loc. 47.

M.* ×*heterophylla
See Chapter 11.

***M.* 'Hibernal'**
Name only.

***M.* 'Hilborn Pyramidal'**
Name only. Subject to moderate scab (Nichols). Loc. 54, 61.

M.* **'Hillier' Hillier 1928 Plate 22
Synonyms: *M.* 'Hillieri' (a Latinized name that should not be used for a clone), *M. floribunda* 'Hilleri'
Selected at Hillier & Sons Nursery, Winchester, England, from a group of plants obtained from an unknown European source. Introduced into the United States in 1928 by the Morton Arboretum, Lisle, IL. Named after the nursery of its origin. Thought to be a hybrid of *M. floribunda*. A spreading tree to 15–18 ft (4.6–5.5 m) high and 5 ft (1.5 m) wide; buds rose-red, opening to pink to pale pink flowers 1.3 in (3.2 cm) across, single and semidouble, with 5–9 petals; fruit yellow/orange, 0.7 in (1.7 cm) in diameter. Very showy in heavy, annual bloom. Subject to moderate scab (Nichols). Not particularly outstanding in fruit, but flowers sufficient to recommend it as a smaller ornamental. Loc. 4, 13, 15, 18, 24, 26, 31, 32, 35, 46, 54, 55, 68, 69, 79, 81, 89.

***M.* 'Hillier Dwarf'** Hillier
Name only. Subject to moderate scab (Nichols). Loc. 18.

M. 'Himalaica'
See *M. baccata* var. *himalaica* in Chapter 11.

M. 'Hollandia'
Name only. No diseases (Nichols). Loc. 61.

M. honanensis
See Chapter 11.

M. 'Honeywood No. 7'
Name only. Subject to moderate scab (Nichols). Loc. 12.

M. 'Honeywood No. 14'
Subject to mild scab (Nichols). Loc. 10, 12.

***M. 'Honor Guard'** Fiala/P. Murray
Parentage: (*M.* 'Liset' × *M.* 'Calvary') × (*M.* 'Ballerina' × *M.* 'Burgandy')
No. B11-88. An upright to columnar tree 18 ft (5.5 m) high and 10 ft (3 m) wide; new leaves red, turning to bronze-green; buds deep carmine-red, opening to small, bright red, single flowers produced in great abundance; fruit 0.5 in (1.2 cm), red, persistent. An annual bloomer. Disease free. A fine tree for narrower sites and where an accent, upright, red-flowering tree is needed. Loc. 47.

M. 'Hopa' N. E. Hansen 1920 Plates 165, 166
Synonyms: *M.* 'Hansen's Red Leaf Crabapple', *M.* 'Hoppa', *M.* 'Hoppi', *M.* 'Sunburst', *M.* 'Pink Sunburst'
Parentage: *M. pumila* 'Niedzwetzkyana' × *M. baccata*
A Rosybloom. Buds carmine, opening to carmine-pink, single flowers that fade to a lighter pink, 1.6–2 in (4–5 cm) across; fruit bright red, 0.8 in (2 cm) in diameter. Very susceptible to leaf diseases and apple scab. Should be phased out—too much disease (Nichols). In the past this clone was used extensively in hybridizing and for open-pollinated seedlings, but today its use should be discouraged as it transmits susceptibility to many apple diseases. Loc. 5, 8, 15, 18, 19, 24, 26, 31, 32, 35, 39, 40, 41, 43, 69, 74, 77, 79, 80.
Progeny of *M.* 'Hopa' include the following:
M. 'Big River' P. H. Wright
M. 'Mount Arbor Special' Welch
M. 'Patricia' A. den Boer
M. 'Radiant' Longley
M. 'Vanguard' Longley
M. 'White Fox River' P. H. Wright

M. 'Hopa Weeping'
Name only.

M. 'Hoppa'
See *M.* 'Hopa'.

M. 'Hoppi'
See *M.* 'Hopa'.

M. 'Hoser'
See *M.* ×*purpurea* 'Hoser'.

M. hupehensis
See Chapter 11.

***M. hupehensis* 'Donald'**
See Chapter 11.

***M. hupehensis* 'Rosea'**
See Chapter 11.

***M. hupehensis* 'Wayne Douglas'**
See Chapter 11.

M. 'Huron' Preston before 1930
Parentage: A Rosybloom
Named by Isabella Preston, CDA—Ottawa, in her Lake Series, for one of the Great Lakes between Canada and the United States. Buds purple-red, opening to single, amaranth-pink flowers with red anthers, strongly fragrant, large, 1.8 in (4.5 cm) across; fruit bright red, oval, bitter, somewhat large, 1.3 in (3.4 cm) in diameter.

M. hybrid No. 28
A hybrid of *M. baccata*.

M. hybrid scab immune GR 700-58
Flowers pink to white; fruit medium, light red. Disease resistant. Loc. 5, 31, 47.

M. 'Hyslop' before 1869
Origin unknown. Buds white; flowers single, white, 1.4 in (3.5 cm) across; fruit 1.6 in (4 cm) in diameter, yellow and green. Subject to severe fire blight. Once highly recommended, this clone should be phased out because of too many diseases, its pattern of alternate blooming, and its fruit that is too large, unless one is looking for a jelly crabapple.

M. 'Hyslop Sport'
Name only. Subject to severe scab (Nichols). Loc. 15.

M. 'Ida Cason'
See *M.* 'Callaway'.

M. 'Ida Red'
Name only.

***M.* 'Illinois'**
See *M. ioensis* 'Illinois'.

***M.* 'Imperial'**
Parentage: A selected clone of *M. spectabilis*

*+***M.* 'Indian Magic'** Simpson Plates 21, 167, 168, 169, 170
No. 11-63. A medium-sized to small tree to 15 ft (4.6 m) high and as wide; flowers showy rose-pink, single; fruit ellipsoid, glossy red, changing with frosts to orange, persistent until spring. A heavy bearer. Moderate disease susceptibility that does not affect foliage or fruit. There appear to be several clones, all not identical, some far superior to others. Lester Nichols thought that the trees at Falconskeape Gardens, Medina, OH, were superior to most others by the same name. Loc. 4, 5, 18, 20, 22, 24, 26, 31, 35, 46, 47, 53, 54, 55, 61, 71, 79, 80, 81, 86, 89.

****M.* 'Indian Summer'** Simpson Plate 171
No. 11-58. A rounded tree to 18 ft (5.5 m) high and 20 ft (6 m) wide; leaves bronze-green; flowers rose-red, single; fruit bright red, 0.6 in (1.5 cm) in diameter, persistent. Good disease resistance. A very fine crabapple. Loc. 5, 24, 26, 31, 54, 79, 81, 86, 93, 94, 95.

***M.* 'Inequalis'**
Parentage: A selected clone of *M. spectabilis*
Name only.

***M.* 'Inglis'**
See *M.* 'White Angel'.

M. ioensis
See Chapter 11.

M. ioensis* var. *texana
See Chapter 11.

***M. ioensis* 'Amsib'**
See Chapter 11.

***M. ioensis* 'Boone Park'**
See Chapter 11.

***M. ioensis* 'Fimbriata'**
See Chapter 11.

***M. ioensis* 'Fiore's Improved'**
See Chapter 11.

***M. ioensis* 'Illinois'**
CPS No. 825. Name only. Subject to mild scab, mild cedar-apple rust, and slight fire blight. Loc. 24.

***M. ioensis* 'Klehm's Improved Bechtel'**
See Chapter 11.

****M. ioensis* 'Marcy Road'** Johnson's Nursery 1990
Parentage: A selection of *M. ioensis*
Introduced by Johnson's Nursery, Menomonee Falls, WI. A medium-sized tree; leaves bright glabrous green; buds light rose, opening to double, pale pink flowers. One of the better, new selections of *M. ioensis*.

***M. ioensis* 'Nevis'**
See Chapter 11.

***M. ioensis* 'Nova'**
See Chapter 11.

***M. ioensis* 'Palmeri'**
See Chapter 11.

***M. ioensis* 'Plena'**
See Chapter 11.

***M. ioensis* 'Prairie Rose'**
See Chapter 11.

***M. ioensis* 'Prince Georges'**
See Chapter 11.

***M. ioensis* 'Red Seedling No. 1'** A. den Boer
See *M.* 'Evelyn'.

***M. ioensis* 'Spinosa'**
See Chapter 11.

***M. ioensis* 'Texana'**
See *M. ioensis* var. *texana* in Chapter 11.

***M.* 'Irene'** A. den Boer 1939
Parentage: *M.* 'Jay Darling' seedling No. 166
A poor blooming, dwarf tree. Should be phased out—too much disease (Nichols). Loc. 3, 9, 11, 15, 18, 26, 31, 35, 47, 54, 77, 79, 81.

***M.* 'Ivan'** N. E. Hansen 1916
Parentage: A seedling of *M. baccata*
Fruit red, large, 1.4 in (3.5 cm) in diameter. Loc. 54.

***M.* 'Ivanhoe'** Zampini
Plant patent name "Ivazam." To be introduced by Lake County Nursery, Perry, OH, as one of the Round Table Series of dwarf crabapples developed by James Zampini. A small, rounded tree to 10 ft (3 m) high and as wide; leaves burgundy-wine with frost; flowers single, scarlet-red; fruit scarlet-red. Disease resis-

tant (per introducer); too new to be properly evaluated for disease resistance. A welcomed, red-flowering dwarf clone. Could be used wherever a small tree is needed: city gardens, in front of larger plantings, as a potted tree, or massed for smaller landscaping design. Loc. 46.

***M.* 'Izo'**
Synonym: *M.* 'Izo Ames'
Name only.

***M.* 'Izo Ames'**
See *M.* 'Izo'.

***M.* 'Jack Humm'**
Name only. Subject to slight scab (Nichols). Loc. 61, 81.

***M.* 'Jackii'**
See *M. baccata* 'Jackii' in Chapter 11.

***M.* 'Janis'** Hollyhedge Nursery, Farmingdale, NJ, circa 1980
Parentage: An open-pollinated seedling of *M.* 'Selkirk'
A tree of weeping form; leaves purple, turning orange and red in autumn; flowers early, single, large, magenta; fruit bright red but not as shiny as fruit of *M.* 'Selkirk', falls early. Disease free.

***M.* 'Jan Kuperus'** Byland's Nursery, Kelowna, British Columbia, Canada 1985
Parentage: A Rosybloom
A newer crabapple with soft red flowers similar to those of *M.* 'Almey' but hardier. Too new to be evaluated.

***M.* 'Jay Darling'** A. den Boer
Synonym: *M. atropurpurea*
Parentage: *M. pumila* 'Niedzwetzkyana' × *M. baccata*
A Rosybloom crabapple. Named by Arie den Boer for Jay Darling, first president of the Des Moines Men's Garden Club. Flowers red; fruit purple, 1 in (2.5 cm) in diameter. Should be phased out—too much disease (Nichols). Some consider *M.* ×*purpurea* 'Eleyi' to be an unstable form of *M.* 'Jay Darling'. Arie den Boer, however, who made a lengthy study of the two, concluded they (i.e., *M.* ×*purpurea* 'Eleyi' and *M. atropurpurea*) were two different names for the same plant that grows differently in different locations. To avoid confusing the two, which were sold in the market interchangeably, the latter plant was renamed *M.* 'Jay Darling'. Loc. 3, 8, 24, 26, 31, 32, 54, 77, 79, 80, 81, 85, 89.

***M.* 'Jenison'** Arnold Arboretum 1940
Parentage: From a group of unnamed seedlings
Introduced by Michigan State University before 1966. The original tree was located near the main entrance of Jenison Gymnasium, Michigan State University, East Lansing, hence the name. Flowers single, white; fruit pyriform, bright red, 0.7 in (1.8 cm) in diameter, interesting. Loc. 10, 86, 89.

*+***M.* 'Jewelberry'** Simpson
Synonym: *M.* 'Simpson 7-62'
A dwarf, rounded bush to 8 ft (2.5 m) high and 12 ft (3.5 m) wide, densely branched; leaves green; flowers single, white with pink edges; fruit bright orange-red, 0.5 in (1.2 cm) in diameter, late in fall. Excellent disease resistance, although subject to slight scab and fire blight (Nichols). Blooms well as a young tree. Very showy in heavy fruiting. Should be more widely planted. Excellent for home landscapes or wherever a smaller crabapple is needed. A prime plant for hybridizers. Loc. 5, 31, 55, 79, 80, 81, 86, 93, 94.

***M.* 'Jewell'** CDA—Ottawa
Parentage: A hybrid of *M. baccata*
A discarded clone. Subject to slight scab and cedar-apple rust (Nichols). Loc. 35, 54.

***M.* 'J. L. Pierce'**
Discovered in 1955 by Milton Baron, Michigan State University, in the garden of Mr. and Mrs. J. L. Pierce, of Detroit. Subject to very mild fire blight (Nichols). Loc. 10, 81, 86, 89.

***M.* 'Joan'** Dunbar 1918
Named by John Dunbar, former propagator for the Rochester Parks System, Rochester, NY, to honor his granddaughter. Flowers single, white, 2 in (5 cm) across; fruit red, 1.4 in (3.5 cm) in diameter. An alternate bearer. Subject to moderate scab (Nichols). Loc. 12, 26, 32, 35, 81.

***M.* 'Joe Trio'** N. E. Hansen
Parentage: A hybrid of *M. baccata*

***M.* 'John Bowles'**
Name only. Subject to moderate scab. Loc. 31.

***M.* 'John Downie'** Holmes before 1891 Plate 20
Introduced into the United States in 1927. Named by E. Holmes to honor his friend, John Downie, a Scottish nurseryman and partner in the Handsworth Nurseries, Whittington, England. Buds pink, followed by single, white

flowers 2 in (5 cm) across; fruit large, 1.2 in (3 cm) in diameter, orange with red cheeks. An alternate bearer. Disease resistant (Nichols). Much better known in England than in North America. Loc. 12, 35, 54, 81.

***M.* 'John Edward'** Schwartze
Introduced by Chester D. Schwartze, Puyallup, WA, and named to honor his youngest grandson, John Edward Gonsalves. An upright to vase-shaped tree to 18 ft (5.5 m) high and 12 ft (3.5 m) wide; buds rose pink, opening to single, white flowers; fruit 0.8 in (2 cm) in diameter, pale apricot, turning to amber over red. Disease resistant (Nichols). Showy but overlooked due to large fruit. Loc. 5, 85.

***M.* 'John's Crab'**
Name only. Subject to severe scab (Nichols). Loc. 54.

***M.* 'Johnson's Walters'**
Parentage: A form of *M. toringo* or a hybrid
Fruit small, yellow. Sold by Johnson Nursery, Milwaukee, WI, under the name *M.* 'Walters' and obtained by them from Moller's Nursery, Gresham, OR. Since *M. baccata* 'Walters' has nomenclatural precedence, I am listing this clone as *M.* 'Johnson's Walters'.

M.* **'Joy' Fiala 1960 Plate 5
Parentage: *M.* 'Dorothea' × *M.* 'Liset'
No. 71-TD-8. An induced tetraploid. A small, rounded tree to 12 ft (3.5 m) high and as wide; leaves gray to pale purple, disease free; buds rose-purple, opening to single, coral-rose flowers produced in great abundance; fruit 0.4 in (1 cm) in diameter, medium purple, persistent, attractive only when next to a yellow-fruited clone. An alternate bloomer but outstanding when in bloom. Disease resistant (Nichols). Unique foliage color makes it excellent as background tree. Blossoms also unique in color. Excellent for hybridizers, but recommended only for its genetic tetraploid value. Loc. 47.
Progeny of *M.* 'Joy' include *M.* 'Arch McKean' Fiala.

***M.* 'Jubilee'** Provincial Horticultural Research Station, Brooks, Alberta, Canada, 1937
Trade name: *M.* Brooks No. 6
Parentage: A seedling of *M.* 'Hopa'
Originally introduced as Brooks No. 6, but renamed by the introducer in 1955. A Rosybloom with deep red blossoms. Some scab and mildly subject to fire blight. Should be phased out—too much disease (Nichols). Loc. 12, 31, 32, 61.

***M.* 'Judy'** Reynolds circa 1946
Parentage: *M. sieboldii*
Grown from seed received from Japan. Named to honor the sister of William D. Reynolds, Jr., of Hook's Nursery, Lake Zurich, IL. Buds pink, opening to single, white flowers; fruit yellow with blush cheek, 0.5 in (1.2 cm) in diameter, persistent, extremely abundant. A clone that has been overlooked and should be more planted.

***M.* 'Julian Potts Weeper'** Potts
Named for the owner of Julian Potts Nursery, Chesterland, OH, a world-renown propagator, horticulturist, and collector of very rare plants. Possibly a lost clone.

***M.* 'K & K'**
Name only. Loc. 81.

M. kansuensis
See Chapter 11.

M. kansuensis* var. *calva
See Chapter 11.

***M. kansuensis* 'Calva'**
See *M. kansuensis* var. *calva* in Chapter 11.

M.* **'Karen' Fiala 1989 Plate 14
Parentage: *M.* 'GV-19' × *M.* 'Van Eseltine'
No. NR4-P9. One of the newest clones. Named to honor Karen Tarpey Murray, a university professor, outstanding plantswoman, executive director of Falconskeape Gardens, Medina, OH, and executive director of Ameri-Hort Research, Medina, OH. An upright to vase-shaped tree 12 ft (3.5 m) high and 10 ft (3 m) wide; leaves medium green; buds deep carmine flushed with fuchsia-purple, opening to double, white flowers, with petals edged pink, very beautiful; fruit gold flushed reddish, 0.4 in (1 cm) in diameter. A heavy, annual bloomer. Excellent disease resistance. A fine double-flowering, smaller crabapple for any spot in the landscape. Excellent for hybridizing and should be well received when better known. Loc. 47, 100.

***M.* 'Kass'**
Name only. No diseases (Nichols). Loc. 9.

***M.* 'Katherine'** B. Slavin 1928
Parentage: Probably *M. halliana* × *M. baccata*
A chance seedling found in Durand-Eastman Park, Rochester, NY, by the park's superintendent Bernard Slavin. Named by Donald Wyman for Slavin's daughter-in-law, Catherine Clark

Slavin. Buds pink-white, flowers very large, double, with 15–24 petals, 2.1 in (5.4 cm) across; fruit yellowish with a red cheek, 0.4 in (1 cm) in diameter. Subject to moderate scab and mild fire blight (Nichols). A lovely, double-flowering white crabapple. Outstanding in bloom, but not recommended because of alternate blooming and lack of attractive fruit. Has great hybridizing potential; crossed with an annual bearer, the alternate-blooming habit is often recessive and some fine hybrids might be obtained. Loc. 4, 8, 10, 12, 13, 15, 18, 20, 24, 26, 32, 37, 38, 39, 40, 41, 43, 54, 68, 69, 71, 76, 79, 80, 81, 85, 87.

***M.* 'Katherine Seedling'**
Name only. Subject to moderate-to-severe scab (Nichols). Loc. 9.

***M.* 'Kay Street'**
Name only.

****M.* 'Kelsey'** CDA—Morden 1969 Plate 12
Parentage: A Rosybloom
Named for Henry Kelsey, an early explorer of Manitoba, Canada. Flowers semidouble to double, rose-red to purple-red with a white center. Subject to moderate scab (Nichols). Very little known as yet. Very beautiful in bloom. Semidouble Rosyblooms are rare. Loc. 5, 79, 82, 100.

***M.* 'Keo'** N. E. Hansen 1940
Parentage: A hybrid of *M. baccata*
Flowers pink-white, 2 in (5 cm) across; fruit very large, size of eating apples, carmine with yellow and green, 1.7 in (4.3 cm) in diameter. No disease (Nichols). Loc. 54.

***M.* 'Kerr'** Kerr (CDA—Morden) 1938
Parentage: *M.* 'Dolgo' × *M.* 'Haralson'
Morden 352. Flowers single, white; fruit large, yellow-red, to 1.6 in (4 cm) in diameter. No diseases (Nichols). Several of W. L. Kerr's introductions have been called *M.* 'Kerr' with the identifying numbers left off and some resulting confusion. Most are large-fruited. Loc. 12.

***M.* 'Kerr 63-6'**
Name only. No diseases (Nichols). Loc. 35, 37.

***M.* 'Kerr 63-7'**
Name only. No diseases (Nichols). Loc. 35.

***M.* 'Kerr 63-8'**
Name only. Subject to moderate scab (Nichols). Loc. 35.

***M.* 'Kess'**
Name only.

***M.* 'Kibele'** Clarice Hickox before 1949
Parentage: A chance seedling
No. 447-59. One of the smallest pink-flowering crabapples. This chance seedling was later moved to the home of Mr. and Mrs. R. R. Kibele, Springfield, IL. A small, upright to spreading, compact tree maturing at 8 ft (2.5 m) high; leaves purple-red, slightly glossy, 2–3 in (5–7.6 cm) long; buds dark red, opening to rose-pink flowers; fruit 0.5 in (1.2 cm) in diameter, dark burgundy red. Subject to very slight scab and moderate fire blight (Nichols). An excellent dwarf tree for smaller landscapes. Loc. 5, 31, 54, 79, 81, 88.

***M.* 'King Arthur'** Zampini Plates 172, 173
Plant patent name "Kinarzam." To be introduced by Lake County Nursery, Perry, OH, as one of the Round Table Series of dwarf crabapples developed by James Zampini. A small tree to 12 ft (3.5 m) high and 10 ft (3 m) wide; leaves dark green; buds rose pink, opening to single, white flowers; fruit bright red. Too new to determine final disease resistance. Landscapers will need to develop designs for this and other small crabapples to show off their full potential. Loc. 46.

***M.* 'Kingiton Black'**
Interesting name only.

***M.* 'King's'**
Name only. Subject to moderate scab (Nichols). Loc. 31.

***M.* 'Kingsmere'** Preston 1920
Parentage: *M. toringo* × *M. pumila* 'Niedzwezkyana'
A rare hybrid with reddish leaves and flowers. Named in 1930 by Isabella Preston, CDA—Ottawa, in her Lake Series, for Kingsmere Lake in Ontario, Canada. Buds deep carmine, opening to purple-pink, single flowers 2.2 in (5.5 cm) across; fruit crimson over purple-brown, shaded side green-brown, large, 1.2 in (3 cm) in diameter. An annual bearer. Subject to moderate scab. Discarded as inferior by a Central Experiment Farm horticulturist some years ago. Arie den Boer, an excellent judge of crabapples, considered it "one of the loveliest of all Canadian hybrids!" Although the fruit is somewhat dark and too large, this Rosybloom could be used in further hybridizing to improve the fruit. Loc. 4, 15, 18, 31, 32, 54, 81.

M. 'Kirghisorm'
Name only. Subject to moderate scab (Nichols). Loc. 12, 31.

***M. 'Kirk'** Fiala 1980
Parentage: *M. sieboldii* No. 243 × *M. sieboldii* No. 768
Named at Falconskeape Gardens, Medina, OH, by Lester Nichols who thought very highly of this clone. Introduced by Klehm Nursery, South Barrington, IL. Name sometimes misspelled "Kurt." A rounded, upright tree to 15 ft (4.6 m) high and as wide; leaves dark green, disease free; buds red, opening to white flowers borne in profusion; fruit rich red, produced in great abundance, about 0.6 in (1.6 cm) in diameter, persistent. An annual bloomer. Totally disease resistant (Nichols). A crabapple that can be counted upon each year for a splendid spring and fall display. Loc. 46, 47, 100.

M. 'Kit Trio' Hansen 1938
Parentage: *M.* 'Mercer' (apple) × *M.* 'Sweet Russet' (apple)
Introduced in 1938 by the South Dakota Agriculture Experiment Station, Brookings, SD. Buds pink; flowers single, white, 1.6 in (4 cm) across; fruit very large, size of eating apples, 1.6 in (4 cm) in diameter, yellow. No disease (Nichols). Not an ornamental. Loc. 54.

M. 'Kitty Pink'
Name only.

M. 'Klemi'
A Latinized name that should not be used for a clone. See *M. ioensis* 'Klehm's Improved Bechtel' in Chapter 11.

M. 'Klehm's Improved Bechtel'
See *M. ioensis* 'Klehm's Improved Bechtel' in Chapter 11.

M. 'Kobendza'
Name only for a clone of *M. ×purpurea*.

***M. 'Koi'** Fiala 1968
Parentage: *M. hupehensis* × *M.* 'Redbird'
No. 85-18. Named after *koi*, a scaleless Japanese goldfish, because the original tree was planted on the banks of Koi Pond, Falconskeape Gardens, Medina, OH. An upright, fan-shaped tree to 14 ft (4.3 m) high and 8 ft (2.5 m) wide; leaves medium green, disease free; buds deep pink, opening to single, white flowers on spurs; fruit bright orange-red, 0.4–0.5 in (1–1.2 cm) in diameter, very firm, persistent until February, very showy in winter landscape. Completely disease resistant (Nichols). The beauty of this clone increases with age. A smaller tree for any small space. Loc. 47.

***M. 'Kola'** Hansen 1922
Parentage: *M. coronaria* 'Elk River' × *M. pumila* 'Oldenburg'
One of the first tetraploid crosses. Has 68 chromosomes (B. Nebel). Named after the Sioux word for "friend." Buds rose to salmon pink, opening to single, pale pink flowers 1.6–2 in (4–5 cm) across; fruit large, green-yellow, fragrant, 1.8 in (4.6 cm) in diameter. Subject to mild scab and cedar-apple rust (Nichols). Arie den Boer considered this clone an excellent ornamental for large parks. It should be crossed with some of the newer polyploids (e.g., *M.* 'Satin Cloud') to enrich the small pool of polyploid crabapples. Recommended for its excellent breeding potential. Loc. 26, 31, 35, 37, 54, 73, 81.

M. 'Kornik'
See *M. ×purpurea* 'Kornicensis' in Chapter 11.

M. 'Kutanka'
Name only. Disease free (Nichols). Loc. 35.

M. 'Lady Ilgen' 1951
Of European origin. Received at Montreal Botanic Gardens. Fruit yellow, 1.4–2 in (3.5–5 cm). Subject to moderate scab (Nichols). Loc. 11, 12, 15, 31, 37, 81.

M. 'Lady Northcliffe'
See *M. baccata* 'Lady Northcliffe' in Chapter 11.

M. 'Lancelot' Zampini Plates 174, 175, 176
Plant patent name "Lanzam." To be introduced by Lake County Nursery, Perry, OH, as one of the Round Table Series of dwarf crabapples developed by James Zampini. A small tree or shrub to 10 ft (3 m) high and 8 ft (2.5 m) wide; leaves crisp green; buds rose pink, opening to single, white flowers; fruit light to medium gold, persistent. Disease resistant at introducing nursery; too new to be properly evaluated for disease resistance. One of the needed dwarf additions with gold fruit. Suitable wherever a smaller tree is desired. Loc. 46.

M. lancifolia
See *M. coronaria* var. *lancifolia* in Chapter 11.

M. 'Large Flesh Pink'
See *M. spectabilis* var. *grandiflora* in Chapter 11.

M. lasiostyla
M. baccata var. *lasiostyla*, an unacceptable botanical name.

M. laurifolia
An obsolete botanical name. Subject to mild scab and moderate fire blight (Nichols). Loc. 54.

***M.* 'Laxton's Red'** Laxton Bros. 1939
Parentage: *M. pumila* 'Niedzwetzkyana' × *M.* ×*scheideckeri*
A rare cross. Flowers red-purple, semi-double, fading to light mauve; fruit red-purple.

***M.* 'L.B. No. 1'**
See *M.* 'Behrens Crab'.

***M.* 'L. C. Chadwick'**
A yellow-fruited clone named after Professor Chadwick, Ohio State University. Subject to mild scab (Nichols). Loc. 47.

***M.* 'Leatherleaf'**
Name only.

***M.* 'Lee'** Fig. 12.5
A small weeper to 12 ft (3.5 m) high and 14 ft (4.3 m) wide; buds very pale pink, opening to double, white flowers, very showy; fruit insignificant. A fine weeper for a smaller garden or a focal point along a garden walk. Should be carried by more nurseries. Excellent for hybridizing. Loc. 32.

***M.* 'Lee Trio'** N. E. Hansen 1942
Parentage: A hybrid of *M. baccata*
Buds pink, opening to single, white flowers 1.6 in (4 cm) across; fruit 2 in (5 cm) in diameter, large, yellow-green-red. Disease free (Nichols).

***M.* 'Lemoinei'**
See *M.* ×*purpurea* 'Lemoinei' in Chapter 11.

Figure 12.5. *Malus* 'Lee'

***M.* 'Lennoxville'**
Buds pale pink, opening to single, white flowers; fruit pale apricot, flushed rose, 0.5 in (1.2 cm) in diameter.

****M.* 'Lenore'** Fiala/P. Murray
No. NR5-P5-503. Named to honor Elsie Lenore Meile, sister of Fr. J. Fiala. An upright to fan-shaped tree to 12 ft (3.5 m) high; buds rose-pink, opening to large, single, pale pink flowers produced in great abundance; fruit 0.5 in (1.2 cm) in diameter, dark red, persistent. An annual bloomer. Disease resistant. A fine pink-flowering tree for narrower places. Excellent next to white- or red-flowering crabapples. Loc. 47.

***M.* 'Leonard'**
Name only.

*+***M.* 'Leprechaun'** Fiala 1978 Plates 25, 177
Parentage: *M.* 'Christmas Holly' × (*M. sieboldii* No. 243 × *M. sieboldii* No. 768)
Introduced by Klehm Nursery, South Barrington, IL. A very heavily fruited, genetically small tree to 8 ft (2.5 m) high; leaves leathery, dark green, disease free; buds red, opening to an abundance of single, white flowers that bloom especially on spurs; fruit bright red, oval, 0.2–0.25 in (0.5–0.6 cm) in diameter, remaining firm and colorful into December. Completely disease resistant (Nichols). A very fine tree with very small colorful, abundant fruit. Should be grown more. Loc. 46, 47, 100.
Progeny of *M.* 'Leprechaun' include *M.* 'Little Troll' Fiala and *M.* 'Tiny Tim' Fiala.

***M.* 'Leslie'** Northwest Nursery, Valley City, ND 1945
Parentage: An open-pollinated Rosybloom
VC No. 3. Named in 1945 for William R. Leslie, Canada Department of Agriculture, Morden, Manitoba. Leaves purple-red to bronze; flowers single, deep purple-red; fruit dark red, 0.4–0.6 in (1–1.5 cm) in diameter. Should be phased out—too much disease (Nichols). Loc. 24, 81.

M. leucocarpa
See *M.* ×*robusta* 'Leucocarpa' in Chapter 11.

***M.* 'Limelight'** Fiala 1978
Parentage: (*M.* 'Winter Gold' × *M.* 'Golden Candles') × *M.* 'Golden Dream'
No. 86-N3-1. A rounded, somewhat upright tree to 14 ft (4.3 m) high and 10 ft (3 m) wide; leaves very heavily textured, leathery, dark green, disease free; buds light pink, opening to

single, white flowers; fruit ellipsoid, 0.5 in (1.2 cm) wide and 0.75 in (1.9 in) long, bright lime chartreuse, distinctive, attractive against the dark green foliage, persistent to October. An annual bearer. Subject to mild scab. Fruit may be a bit large, but is attractive nonetheless. Excellent next to a bright orange- or red-fruited crabapple. Loc. 47.

***M.* 'Linda'** A. den Boer

Parentage: A chance seedling from open-pollinated *M.* ×*arnoldiana*

Named in 1958 by Arie den Boer for his granddaughter. Buds rose-red to carmine, opening to single, pale pink flowers 1.8 in (4.5 cm) across; fruit bright to dark crimson, 1.1 in (2.8 cm) in diameter. Subject to severe scab (Nichols). A crabapple that is little known. Loc. 9, 31, 89.

***M.* 'Lings'**

Name only. Subject to moderate scab and mild cedar-apple rust (Nichols). Loc. 32, 79, 89.

***M.* 'Lisa'**

Parentage: A chance seedling of open-pollinated *M. ioensis* 'Seedling Red No. 2'

Very similar to *M.* 'Evelyn'. Selected by Arie den Boer and named after his granddaughter. A slow-growing, small tree; young leaves purplish; buds rose red to carmine, opening to single, rose-red to light carmine flowers 1.1 in (2.7 cm) across; fruit orange-yellow and carmine, 1 in (2.5 cm) in diameter. No disease (Nichols). A fine clone rarely seen except in the Morton Arboretum, Lisle, IL. Should be propagated and distributed. Recommended for hybridizers because of it its disease resistance. Loc. 31.

****M.* 'Liset'** Doorenbos Plates 18, 178, 179, 180

Parentage: *M.* ×*purpurea* 'Lemoinei' × *M. sieboldii*

Grown from a cross made in 1938 by S. G. A. Doorenbos, Department of Parks, The Hague, Netherlands (see Table 4 for parentage). Originally called *M.* 'Success', a name which had already been pre-empted, Doorenbos named it *M.* 'Liset' to honor his granddaughter. For many fanciers, this outstanding flowering crabapple surpasses *M.* ×*purpurea* 'Lemoinei' because of its bright crimson-red buds, which open to a rich rose-red or light crimson color.

A medium-sized tree to 15 ft (4.7 m) high and as wide, with a very open habit, lacking density; flowers single, about 1.5 in (3.8 cm) across; fruit dark crimson to maroon-red, glossy, 0.5 in (1.2 cm) in diameter, too dark to be showy. Begins to bloom as a young plant, blooming annually thereafter. New growth is red-maroon, then bronze green. It is more slender branched than *M.* ×*purpurea* 'Lemoinei' but presents a brighter crimson effect in full bloom; flowers fade only slightly. It is probably the brightest orange-red of all the crabapples in bloom and one of the showiest with good-to-excellent disease resistance. It is a clone that should be far more used in hybridizing, especially with double-flowering crabapples to produce rich red, double hybrids. Like its parent *M.* ×*purpurea* 'Lemoinei', it produces longitudinal cracks on some of the heavier branches but these cracks heal the same season they appear. It is a wonderful landscape tree for any garden, free of most diseases. When placed near white- or pink-flowering cultivars, it is a work of landscaping perfection, and the deep maroon fruit is especially effective when planted next to a yellow-fruited clone. Loc. 4, 5, 18, 24, 31, 37, 47, 54, 55, 73, 79, 86, 89.

Progeny of *M.* 'Liset' include the following:

- *M.* 'Calvary' Fiala
- *M.* 'Cardinal's Robe' Fiala
- *M.* 'Cranberry Lace' Fiala
- *M.* 'Fireglow' Fiala
- *M.* 'Honor Guard' Fiala/P. Murray
- *M.* 'Joy' Fiala
- *M.* 'Magic Flute' Fiala
- *M.* 'Maria' Fiala
- *M.* 'Orange Crush' Fiala
- *M.* 'Purple Wave' A. den Boer
- *M.* 'Wildfire' Fiala

****M.* 'Little Troll'** Fiala 1975

Parentage: *M.* 'Molten Lava' × *M.* 'Leprechaun'

No. 85-6-8. One of a series of new mini-fruits. A small, very refined and graceful weeper to 12 ft (3.5 m) high and as wide; leaves dark green, disease resistant; buds brilliant red, opening to single, white flowers produced in abundant cascades; fruit 0.25 in (0.6 cm) in diameter, bright orange-red, firm and persistent, relished by birds. Disease resistant. A wonderful addition to the very small mini-fruited crabapples. An excellent small weeper. A good crabapple for hybridizing weepers with mini-fruits. Loc. 47, 86.

***M.* 'Lonsdale'** Brand 1943

A group name for seedlings and hybrids of *M. baccata* propagated asexually from a large planting near Lonsdale, MN.

****M.* 'Louisa'** Hill 1962 Plates 181, 182, 183

Named by Polly Hill, Martha's Vineyard,

Table 4. Parentage of *M.* 'Liset'.

M. halliana	*M. atrosanguinea*			
M. sieboldii		*M. ×purpurea 'Lemoinei'*		
	M. pumila 'Niedzwetzkyana		*M.* 'Liset'	
		M. sieboldii		

MA, for her daughter Louisa Spotswood of Washington, DC. An umbrella-shaped weeper to 15 ft (4.6 m) high and as wide; leaves dark green, glossy; buds rose-colored, opening to beautiful, true pink flowers; fruit lemon-gold with small rose blush, 0.4 in (1 cm) in diameter. Excellent disease rating. One of the newer weepers that should be far better known and grown. An outstanding crabapple. Loc. 86.

***M.* 'Louise'**
Name only. No diseases (Nichols). Loc. 35, 37.

*****M.* 'Lullaby'** Fiala 1980 Plate 184
A smaller, more refined version of *M.* 'Red Jade' with yellow fruit. Introduced by Klehm Nursery, South Barrington, IL. A low weeper to 8 ft (2.5 m) high and 12 ft (3.5 m) wide, with graceful branches; buds red, opening to single, large, white flowers; fruit yellow, 0.25 in (0.6 cm) in diameter, oval, persistent. Totally disease free (Nichols). Loc. 47, 100.

*****M.* 'Luwick'** Fiala 1978 Plate 185
Parentage: A multibrid
Name is an affectionate Dutch nickname given by the hybridizer's family to his mother. Introduced by Klehm Nursery, South Barrington, IL. A graceful, refined weeper to about 6 ft (1.8 m) high and 10 ft (3 m) wide, with thin and very gracefully arching branches; leaves deep green, slightly tinged with rose; buds deep pink, opening to very light, soft pink flowers 1–1.2 in (2.5–3 cm) across; fruit rich red, about 0.25 in (0.6 cm) in diameter. Excellent disease resistance. A beautiful, graceful weeper that should be far better known and grown. Should be used by hybridizers for its excellent form. Loc. 46, 47,100.

***M.* 'Lyman Prolific'** H. M. Lyman, Excelsior, MN, before 1916
Buds pink, opening to single, white flowers 2.2 in (5.5 cm) across; fruit 1.2 in (3 cm) in diameter, orange. Subject to mild scab (Nichols). Loc. 89.

M. macrocarpa
See *M. toringoides* 'Macrocarpa' in Chapter 11.

*+***M.* 'Madonna'** Fiala 1979 Plate 186
Plant patent name "Mazam." Plant patent No. 6672. Named on a feast day to honor the Virgin Mary. Introduced and patented by Lake County Nursery, Perry, OH. A compact, upright tree 18–20 ft (5.5–6 m) high and 15–20 ft (4.6–6 m) wide that grows moderately and keeps it upright form for several years; buds white, opening to large, double, very attractive, white flowers resembling pure white roses, with a pleasant jasmine or gardenia fragrance; leaves dark green, disease resistant; fruit small brown-red, somewhat insignificant.. A heavy bloomer, it is one of the first crabapples to bloom, flowering over a long, 3.5-week period, and one of the last to go out of bloom. An excellent columnar tree. Ideal for narrow places, patios, street plantings, or as a focal point along a garden walk. A fine clone for hybridization programs seeking double-flowering crabapples. Loc. 24, 26, 31, 46, 47, 79.

***M.* 'Magdeburg'**
See *M. ×magdeburgensis* in Chapter 11.

M. ×magdeburgensis
See Chapter 11.

****M.* 'Magic Flute'** Fiala/P. Murray
Parentage: *M.* 'Van Eseltine' × *M.* 'Liset'
No. NR5-P2-502. A dwarf, upright tree to 8 ft (2.5 m) high; leaves green tinted reddish; buds purple, opening to single, light orchid flowers; fruit red, 0.6 in (1.4 cm) in diameter, persistent to November. An abundant, annual bloomer. Disease free. Very new. A slow grower suitable for smaller locations and foreground plantings. Blossom color very unique. Loc. 47.

*+***M.* 'Magic Mirror'** Fiala/P. Murray
Parentage: *M.* 'Burgandy' × *M.* 'GV-19'
No. NR7-P8-89. An excellent semidouble, red-flowering clone. A columnar to upright tree to 15 ft (4.6 m) high and 8 ft (2.5 m) wide; new leaves reddish, turning to bronze-green, good

disease resistance; buds deep rose-red, opening to large, semidouble, deep red flowers in great abundance; fruit 0.5 in (1.2 cm) in diameter, attractive, red, persistent. Very showy in annual spring bloom and fall fruit. An ideal companion to white-flowering *M.* 'Madonna'. Very new and relatively unknown. Loc. 47.

***M.* 'Magnus'** Saunders 1904
Parentage: *M. prunifolia* × *M.* 'Simbirsk No. 9'
Fruit pale yellow and scarlet, size of eating apples, 1.8 in (4.5 cm) in diameter. Subject to moderate scab (Nichols). Loc. 9.

*****M.* 'Makamik'** Preston 1921 Plate 187
Parentage: An open-pollinated seedling of *M. pumila* 'Niedzwetzkyana'
One of the best open-pollinated seedlings of *M. pumila* 'Niedzwetzkyana'. Named in 1933 by Isabella Preston, CDA—Ottawa, in her Lake Series, for Makamik Lake in western Quebec, Canada. An upright to rounded tree; leaves bronze-green to dark green; buds deep dark red, opening to large, single, purple-red flowers 1.9 in (4.8 cm) across, fading to a lighter tint, very showy in bloom; fruit red, somewhat large, from 0.75–1 in (1.9–2.5 cm) in diameter. An annual bearer. Very good disease resistance except for very mild scab. One of the few Rosyblooms that can be recommended, although the fruit is too large for sidewalk planting and close-in landscaping around building areas where fallen fruit would be objectionable. For backgrounds and larger estates and parks it makes an excellent bloomer, but it lacks any good fall display of fruit. Loc. 13, 15, 18, 24, 26, 31, 35, 54, 55, 79, 81, 87.

***M.* 'Makowieckiana'**
See *M.* ×*purpurea* 'Makowieckiama'.

M. malifolia
Latin for "poor foliage." A description, and thus worthless as a horticultural crabapple. Subject to severe scab. Loc. 15, 54.

***M.* 'Malling No. 8'**
See *M.* 'Clark's Dwarf'.

***M.* 'Manbeck Weeper'**
See *M.* 'Anne E'.

*****M.* 'Mandarin Magic'** Fiala 1974
Parentage: *M.* 'Shaker Gold' × *M.* 'Coral Cascade'
No. 86-526. A medium-sized, somewhat spreading tree to 15 ft (4.6 m) high and as wide; leaves very dark green, good disease resistance; buds red-pink, opening to large, single, white flowers; fruit late in coloring but very attractive changing colors, begins green with red cheeks, turning to orange with bright red and yellow cheeks, 0.5–0.75 in (1.2–1.9 cm) in diameter, very showy in late fall. Subject to very mild scab but mostly disease resistant. Excellent for landscape and background. A very heavy bearer, not suitable for small closed-in areas. Loc. 47.

***M.* 'Manita'**
Name only. Disease resistant. Loc. 10.

*****M.* 'Margaret'** Fenicchia
Parentage: A selected seedling of *M. coronaria*
Named by Richard Fenicchia to honor his wife, Margaret. A small to spreading tree to 15 ft (4.6 m) high and as wide; leaves dark green; buds rose-colored, on long pedicels, opening in cherrylike clusters to double, pink flowers that bloom late; fruit greenish. Disease free (Nichols). An excellent clone. Specimen in Highland Park, Rochester, NY.

+**M.* 'Maria'** Fiala 1978 Plate 188
Parentage: (*M.* ×*purpurea* 'Lemoinei' × *M.* 'Red Jade') × (*M.* 'Liset' × *M.* 'Red Jade')
Named on a feast day to honor the Virgin Mary. Introduced by Klehm Nursery, South Barrington, IL. An upright, spreading semiweeper to 12 ft (3.5 m) high and 15 ft (4.6 m) wide; new growth in spring is bright red, turning to bronze; leaves very glossy, heavily textured, leathery, attractive, narrow, four times as long as they are wide; buds deep orange-red, opening to single, large, bright red flowers that bloom on spurs; fruit 0.5 in (1.2 cm) in diameter, dark red-maroon, produced in great abundance, showy after leaf fall. Completely disease resistant (Nichols). A very fine bright red, semiweeper that is most attractive in bloom. With age, this very heavy annual bearer assumes a weeping form. Should be better known and widely grown. Loc. 46, 47, 100.

***M.* 'Maringo'**
Name only.

***M.* 'Marjoriensis Formosana'**
Trade name: Pretty Marjorie
Name only. Subject to severe scab (Nichols). Loc. 31.

***M.* 'Marshall Oyama'**
Introduced to the United States by Boyce-Thompson Arboretum in 1930 from Japan. A

narrow, upright tree; buds pink, opening to single, white flowers 1.4 in (3.5 cm) across; fruit 1 in (2.5 cm) in diameter, yellow with red cheeks. An annual bearer. Subject to moderate scab (Nichols). A good jelly crabapple. Loc. 12, 18, 24, 31, 35, 37, 54, 76, 77, 79, 81, 89.

***M.* 'Martha'** Gideon
Name only. Subject to severe scab (Nichols). Loc. 31, 54, 61.

***M.* 'Martha-Dolgo'** CDA—Morden 1943
Parentage: *M.* 'Martha' × *M.* 'Dolgo'
Flowers single, white; fruit yellow-red, 1.6 in (4 cm) in diameter, good eating. Subject to mild scab (Nichols). Loc. 81, 85.

***M.* 'Mary Currelly'** Macoun
Named to honor the wife of C. T. Currelly, curator, Royal Ontario Museum. Flowers pink, single, very large, 2.4 in (6 cm) across; fruit red, very large, 1.6 in (4 cm) in diameter. An alternate bloomer. Subject to moderate scab. A good jelly apple and a prospect for hybridizing as it has one of the largest flowers of all crabapples. Loc. 61, 89.

***M.* 'Mary Potter'** Sax 1939 Fig. 7.1
Parentage: *M. sargentii* 'Rosea' × *M.* ×*atrosanguinea*
Arnold Arboretum No. 17039. Introduced in 1947 by Karl Sax (his finest crabapple introduction), this hybrid is a triploid that tends to breed true from open-pollinated seed. It was named to honor a daughter of Charles Sargent, first director of the Arnold Arboretum. A lovely, low-growing tree to 6–8 ft (1.8–2.5 m) high, spreading to 18 ft (5.5 m) wide, producing very heavy blossoming and fruit; expanding buds pink, opening to white, single flowers 1.1 in (2.7 cm) across; fruit red, 0.5 in (1.2 cm) in diameter, persistent. May be an alternate bloomer. Subject to minor disease problems, including mild scab and fire blight. Deserves to be more widely grown as a specimen tree and especially on larger estates and arboreta where it can be displayed to perfection. Several beautiful, mature specimens grow at the Agriculture Experiment Station, Wooster, OH, where they are outstanding in the very large and well-landscaped collection. Clearly the pollen of this clone, where found fertile, should be used for hybridizing. Loc. 3, 5, 13, 18, 22, 24, 26, 31, 35, 54, 55, 61, 69, 71, 79, 80, 81, 86, 89, 100.

***M.* 'Masek'** Simpson Fig. 12.6
Parentage: A chance seedling
Discovered by Robert Simpson, Vincennes, IN, while attending a meeting of the Holly Society of America on a tour of the Missouri Botanical Garden, St. Louis, in late November. Named to honor John Masek, a nurseryman in St. Louis, MO. In a letter to Lester Nichols (dated 29 July 1983), Simpson wrote:

> A spot of color attracted me. In the middle of some shrubs was a slender volunteer crab with a few fruits still attractive. I asked John Masek, a local nurseryman, to send me some scion wood for budding the next summer. Years later I saw the same plant. The shrub was all gone and the tree had a six or eight inch trunk and was gorgeous with fruit. I felt the fruit was a bit large and it tended to bear heavily on alternate years.

Fruit 0.5–0.75 in (1.2–1.9 cm) in diameter, dark red, persistent. Subject to mild scab. Loc. 12, 24, 35, 37, 47.

Figure 12.6. *Malus* 'Masek'

***M. 'Matador'** Fiala 1974
Parentage: (*M.* 'Serenade' × *M.* 'Amberina') × (*M.* 'Coral Cascade' × *M.* 'Christmas Holly')
No. 84-1-4. A small, wide-spreading, upright tree to 14 ft (4.3 m) high and 16 ft (5 m) wide, very showy in bloom and fruit; leaves dark green, disease free; buds bright red, opening to single, white flowers; fruit very small, mini-fruited, brilliant red, firm, persistent, relished by birds. Good disease resistance. Loc. 47.

***M.* 'Mathews'** Downing 1873 Plate 189
Parentage: A clone of *M.* ×*heterophylla*
Buds and flowers single, pink, very large, 2.2 in (5.5 cm) across; fruit 2 in (5 cm) in diameter, yellow-green. An alternate bearer. Subject to severe scab and moderate cedar-apple rust. Loc. 31, 32, 35, 54, 81.

M. **'Maybride'** CDA—Ottawa 1956
Parentage: Unknown
A small, rounded tree to 12 ft (3.5 m) high and as wide; leaves green, good disease resistance; buds pale pink, opening to large, semidouble and double, white flowers 1 in (2.5 cm) across; fruit insignificant, reddish, 0.8 in (2 cm) in diameter. A very heavy and showy bloomer, although an alternate bloomer. Subject to moderate scab. Would be recommended if it were an annual bloomer and had some significant fruit. Loc. 47, 61.

******M.* **'Maysong'** Fiala 1975 Plate 190
Parentage: *M.* 'Silver Moon' × Seedling 68-12
No. 85-3-5. A very upright, narrow tree to 20 ft (6 m) high and 8 ft (2.5 m) wide, spreading to vase-shaped with age; leaves very heavily textured, deep green, disease resistant; buds pale pink-white, opening to large, single, white, cupped flowers, very showy, blooming on spurs; fruit 0.4–0.5 in (1–1.2 cm) in diameter, medium red, attractive. An annual bearer. An excellent crabapple for tight places or as an accent in the landscape. Loc. 47.

M. **'Maxima'**
Parentage: A clone of *M. baccata*

M. **'McPrince'** N. E. Hansen
Parentage: A hybrid of *M. baccata*

M. **'Meach'** Preston 1920
A Rosybloom clone, since discarded because it is inferior. Buds single; flowers purple-red, very large, to 2 in (5 cm) across; fruit red, 0.9 in (2.3 cm) in diameter. Progeny of *M.* 'Meach' include *M.* 'Baskatong' and *M.* 'Tomiko', both from the Canada Department of Agriculture, Ottawa, Ontario.

M. **'Mecca'** Saunders 1904
Parentage: *M. baccata* × *M.* 'Simbirsk No. 9'
Fruit red, 1.6 in (4 cm) in diameter.

M. **'Mecca-Dolgo'** CDA—Ottawa
Parentage: *M.* 'Mecca' × *M.* 'Dolgo'

M. **'Mercer'**
An apple. A form of *M.* ×*soulardii* found growing wild by Mr. Fluke in Mercer County, IN. Subject to very severe scab, cedar-apple rust, and frog-eye leaf spot (Nichols).

+M.* **'Michael'** Fiala 1978 Plate 191
Parentage: *M. sieboldii* 'Wooster' × *M.* 'Christmas Holly'
Named to honor Michael Scott, an outstanding plantsman, propagator, and friend. Introduced by Klehm Nursery, South Barrington, IL. A medium-sized, upright to vase-shaped, to spreading tree 14 ft (4.3 m) high and 10 ft (3 m) wide; leaves medium green, disease resistant; buds deep carmine, opening to single, blush pink-white flowers, very prolific in bloom once established, blooming on spurs; fruit brilliant orange-red, coloring in early September, firm, persistent to December, 0.4 in (1 cm) in diameter, extremely showy. According to Lester Nichols, it has "good disease resistance. An outstanding crabapple." An annual bearer, this should prove to be one of the finest new crabapple introductions. An excellent clone for any landscape. Loc. 47, 100.

M. **'Michigan 55-62-114'**
Name only. Disease free (Nichols). Loc. 81.

M. **'Michigan 55-74-02'**
Name only. Subject to severe scab (Nichols). Loc. 81.

M. ×***micromalus***
See Chapter 11.

M. **'Midnight'** P. H. Wright 1953
Parentage: An open-pollinated Rosybloom seedling
Leaves dark; buds and flowers carmine, fading to dull pink, 1.4 in (3.5 cm) across; fruit dark purple, very hardy to –55°F (–48°C). Subject to moderate scab. Considered obsolete in Canada. Loc. 12, 81.

M. **'Midwest'**
Synonyms: *M. baccata* var. *mandshurica* 'Midwest', *M. mandshurica* 'Midwest'
A strain (group), not a clone. Introduced by USDA Soil Conservation Service, Plant Materials Center, Bismarck, ND, from seed collected at Echo, Manchuria, by A. F. Woeikoff in the early 1920s.

> 'Midwest' is claimed to be disease resistant, winter hardy, and easy to propagate from seed. Plant Materials Center has been evaluating 'Midwest' since 1954, receiving the original seedlings from the Canada Dept. of Agri. Research Stat., Morden, Manitoba. Small amounts of seed and seedlings were made available to nurseries, organizations for testing or increase.

Because *M.* 'Midwest' is a cultivar (group) name and not a selected clone, there may be varying degrees of differences between plants of the same name. A medium-sized tree to 20 ft (6 m) high in 16 years, one of earliest to leaf out in spring, very hardy; flowers white, single; fruit 0.25 in (0.6 cm) in diameter.

M. 'Milliken'
Name only. Subject to very mild scab (Nichols). Loc. 12, 13, 61, 89.

M. 'Milo' N. E. Hansen 1942
Parentage: *M. baccata* × ?

M. 'Milton Baron No. 1'
See *M.* 'Sugar Tyme'.

***M. 'Milton Baron No. 2'**
Named for Milton Baron, a former landscape architect at Michigan State University. A rounded tree; flowers single, white; fruit bright red, 0.25–0.3 in (0.6–0.8 cm) in diameter, persistent. Completely disease free (Nichols). Roots readily from softwood cuttings. A good crabapple not well known. Loc. 46, 61, 89.

M. 'Milton Baron No. 3'
Name only. Subject to very slight scab (Nichols). Loc. 61.

M. 'Milton Baron No. 4'
Trade name: American spirit crab
Name only. Subject to slight scab (Nichols). Loc. 61.

M. 'Milton Kral'
Name only. Loc. 81.

M. 'Ming Dynasty' Fiala 1961
Parentage: *M. ×purpurea* 'Lemoinei' × *M.* 'Red Jade'
A tree spreading to semiweeper in form, 10 ft (3 m) high and 15 ft (4.6 m) wide; leaves rich red-bronze, disease free; buds deep rose-crimson, opening to large, single, mauve-rose pink flowers; fruit red-purple, 0.5–0.75 in (1.2–1.9 cm) in diameter, large, persistent. A heavy annual bloomer. Subject to slight scab, but otherwise disease resistant (Nichols). An excellent weeper but not recommended because of fruit size and slight scab. Large estates or parks could use this weeper for backgrounds. Very showy in bloom. Loc. 31, 47.

M. 'Minnesota No. 1492'
Disease free (Nichols). Loc. 12.

M. 'Minnesota 4-P'
Name only. Subject to severe scab (Nichols). Loc. 81.

M. 'Minnesota 11-AB'
Name only. Subject to severe scab (Nichols). Loc. 24, 81.

M. 'Minnesota 14-AB'
Name only. Subject to moderate scab (Nichols). Loc. 10, 12, 24, 35, 81.

M. 'Minnesota 15-C'
Name only. Subject to severe scab (Nichols). Loc. 35.

M. ×moerlandsii
See Chapter 11.

***M. 'Mollie Ann'** Fiala 1978
Parentage: (*M.* 'Dorothea' × *M. sieboldii*) × (*M.* 'Shinto Shrine' × *M.* 'Lullaby')
An induced octoploid. Named to honor a sister of the introducer, Mollie Ann Fiala Pesata, Medina, OH. Introduced by Klehm Nursery, South Barrington, IL. A unique semiweeper to 12 ft (3.5 m) high and 10 ft (3 m) wide, with thin branchlets in weeping, raceme-like clusters, unlike any other crabapple, assuming a semiweeping stage as the great number of racemes increases; leaves rich green, very heavily textured, leathery, very attractive even when tree is not in bloom; buds deep red, opening to finely petaled, single, white flowers in clusters; fruit deep red, about 0.4 in (1 cm) in diameter, not as abundant as flowers. According to Lester Nichols, this crabapple is completely disease resistant, "a unique tree as a polyploid and weeper." It certainly should be used by hybridizers, especially for its octoploid form and its unique racemelike branching. It should produce some outstanding and unique hybrids. Although interesting in its raceme form, it is primarily a hybridizer's clone. Loc. 47, 100.

*+**M. 'Molten Lava'** Fiala 1980 Plates 3, 192
A multibrid. Introduced by Klehm Nursery, South Barrington, IL, and Lake County Nursery, Perry, OH. An excellent broad weeper 12 ft (3.5 m) high and 15 ft (4.6 m) wide, with attractive yellow bark in winter; buds carmine-red, abundant, opening to white, single flowers; fruit brilliant orange-red fruit, flowing in cascades like lava and making a mature tree a showpiece in autumn, persistent. An annual bearer. Disease resistant (Nichols). One of the showiest weepers on the market today and among the best in heavy fruiting. An outstanding new crabapple for all purposes. Loc. 24, 26, 31, 46, 47, 79, 81, 100.
Progeny of *M.* 'Molten Lava' include *M.*

'Firedance', *M.* 'Little Troll', and *M.* 'Red Peacock'—all from Fiala.

M.* **'Moonglow' Fiala 1977
Parentage: *M.* 'Winter Gold' × *M.* 'Christmas Holly'
No. 86-1-12. A small, rounded tree to 12 ft (3.5 m) high and 10 ft (3 m) wide; leaves dark green, disease resistant; buds bright carmine, opening to masses of single, white flowers; fruit colors early, 0.4 in (1 cm) in diameter, lime-chartreuse with rosy cheeks, turning to pale lemon with rose-coral cheeks, firm, persistent. Disease free. Very attractive in blossom and unique colored fruit. An excellent disease-free crabapple. Loc. 47.

***M.* 'Montreal Beauty'** Cleghorn, Quebec, Canada, before 1833
Trade name: Montreal crab
Parentage: A clone of *M.* ×*adstringens*
Buds pink; flowers white, single, very large, 2 in (5 cm) across; fruit 1.6 in (4 cm) in diameter, green and red. Subject to severe scab (Nichols). Loc. 15, 35, 37, 68.

***M.* 'Morden 19-27'**
Disease free (Nichols). Loc. 37.

***M.* 'Morden 19-85'**
A small, upright tree; leaves purple-green; buds deep red, opening late to small, deep pink flowers; fruit small, maroon with heavy purplish bloom. Subject to mild scab (Nichols). Loc. 18, 31.

***M.* 'Morden 52-12'**
Name only. Disease free (Nichols). Loc. 24.

***M.* 'Morden 450'**
Name only. Subject to mild scab (Nichols). Loc. 54, 79, 81.

***M.* 'Morden 454'**
Name only. Subject to mild scab (Nichols). Loc. 31, 55, 81.

***M.* 'Morden 457'**
See *M.* 'Selkirk'.

***M.* 'Morden Rosybloom'**
Name only. Subject to very mild scab (Nichols). Loc. 15, 18, 31.

***M.* 'Morgansonne'**
Name only. May be identical with *M.* 'Morning Sun', though some find the calyx on *M.* 'Morgansonne' is persistent while the calyx of *M.* 'Morning Sun' is deciduous. Disease free (Nichols). Loc. 31.

M.* **'Morning Sun' Green Plates 193, 194
Parentage: A seedling of *M. sieboldii* 'Calocarpa'
Morton Arboretum No. 968-40. A yellow-fruited hybrid. Appears to be an outstanding clone soon to be released by the arboretum. Persistent fruit has excellent post-frost color. Loc. 31.

***M.* 'Morton'**
Synonym: *M.* 'Mortoni'
Parentage: A clone of *M. ioensis*
Subject to severe scab (Nichols). Loc. 31, 81.

***M.* 'Mortoni'**
See *M.* 'Morton'.

***M.* 'Mount Arbor'** Welch 1939
Parentage: *M.* 'Hopa' × *M.* 'Red Silver'
Probably same as *M.* 'Mount Arbor Special' (which see). Buds and single flowers carmine, fading to pink, 1 in (2.5 cm) across, blooming late but lasting 2 weeks; fruit red, 0.8 in (2 cm) in diameter, persistent to November. An abundant bloomer. Disease resistant. Loc. 15.

M.* **'Mount Arbor Special' Welch
Parentage: *M.* 'Hopa' × *M.* 'Red Silver'
A second-generation Rosybloom. A rounded tree to 20 ft (6 m) high; carmine buds and flowers, fading to dull pink; fruit red, 0.8 in (2 cm) in diameter. Disease free (Nichols). Fruit rather large but a fine crabapple that has been overlooked. Loc. 15, 81.

***M.* 'Mrs. Bayard Thayer'** Simpson 1931
Parentage: Doubtful
Flowers large, single, pink, 2.2 in (5.5 cm) across; fruit 1 in (2.5 cm), yellow-red. Subject to moderate scab (Nichols). Loc. 13, 15, 31, 35, 37, 54, 81.

***M.* 'Muskoka'** Preston 1920
Parentage: A Rosybloom
Named by Isabella Preston, CDA—Ottawa, in her Lake Series, for Muskoka Lake, Ontario, Canada. An alternate bearer. An inferior crabapple, now discarded.

***M.* 'My Bonnie'** Fiala 1965
An induced tetraploid. Name taken from one of the best-loved songs of the introducer's mother, Aloise Fiala, her children's cradle song. An upright to spreading tree 12 ft (3.5 m) high and as wide; buds rose-pink, opening to very

large, single, pale pink flowers; fruit red, 0.5–0.75 in (1.2–1.9 cm) in diameter, persistent to November. Disease resistant (Nichols). Suitable for planting at the edge of a wooded area. Fruit a bit dull and somewhat large by modern standards. Loc. 47.

***M.* 'Namew'** Preston 1921
Parentage: A Rosybloom
USDA plant introduction No. 148707. Named by Isabella Preston, CDA—Ottawa, in her Lake Series, for Namew Lake in Saskatchewan, Canada. Buds red-purple, opening to single, pink flowers 2 in (5 cm) across; fruit dark red, 1 in (2.5 cm) in diameter. Good for planting in large backgrounds. Today this crabapple is found only at Dominion Arboretum, Central Experiment Station, Ottawa, and at the Canada Department of Agriculture Experiment Farm, Morden, Manitoba. It does not appear in any U.S. collection. When crabapples are grown in only one or two collections, they easily become lost forever.

***M.* 'Nancy Townsend'**
Flowers single, pink, 1.6 in (4 cm) across; fruit 0.4 in (1 cm) in diameter, yellow and red. Subject to severe scab (Nichols). Loc. 12, 31, 54.

*+***M.* 'Naragansett'** Egolf 1986
Plates 195, 196, 197
Parentage: Hybrid No. 28 × *M.* 'Winter Gold'
USDA plant introduction No. 499829. Hybrid No. 28, an unnamed dwarf known as National Arboretum No. 3549, was originally procured from Michigan State University. The seedlings of this cross were inoculated with fire blight; only the disease-resistant seedlings were kept; after 10 years of field trial *M.* 'Naragansett' was selected and named. It is totally disease resistant.

A tree 13 ft (4 m) high after 12 years, with broad crown; bark gray-green; leaves dark green, leathery, dark velvety; buds carmine, turning bright red, showy for weeks, opening to single, white flowers with a pink tint, 1.2–1.6 in (3–4 cm) across; fruit glossy, subglobose, 0.4–0.6 in (1–1.5 cm) long and 0.6–0.8 in (1.5–2 cm) wide, cherry-red to red, underside a light orange-red, borne in clusters 1.2–2 in (3–5 cm) in diameter with 4–7 pendulous fruits on pedicels 0.8–1 in (2–2.5 cm) long, persistent to midwinter. A good annual bearer. Disease resistant, although in a few localities it is subject to severe but nondisfiguring apple scab (Nichols). A fine tree for small gardens, patios, as a focal point, or in massed plantings. An excellent crabapple released through the U.S. National Arboretum, Washington, DC. Needs to be better known and more available from nurseries. Would be a fine clone for hybridizing. Loc. U.S. National Arboretum in Washington, DC.

***M.* National Arboretum No. 127**
See *M. halliana* National Arboretum No. 127 in Chapter 11.

***M.* National Arboretum No. 40298**
Name only. Disease free (Nichols). Loc. 31, 47, 61.

***M.* 'Nebo'**
Name only. Subject to severe scab (Nichols). Loc. 31, 54.

***M.* 'Nertchinsk'** Hansen 1927
Name only. No disease (Nichols). Loc. 54.

***M.* 'Neville Copeman'** Copeman 1953
Parentage: A Rosybloom seedling of *M. ×purpurea* 'Eleyi'
Raised by and named for Neville S. Copeman, Royden Hall, Norfolk, England. Fruit larger than that of the parent, red, 1.2 in (3 cm) in diameter. Should be phased out—subject to very severe scab (Nichols). Loc. 26, 31, 37, 54, 81.

***M.* 'Nevis'**
See *M. ioensis* 'Nevis' in Chapter 11.

***M.* 'New York 11894'**
Name only. Subject to severe scab (Nichols). Loc. 61.

***M.* 'New York 11902'**
Name only. Subject to very mild scab (Nichols). Loc. 61.

***M.* 'New York 49-23'**
Name only. Subject to moderate scab (Nichols). Loc. 81.

***M.* 'New York 50-4'**
Name only. Subject to severe scab (Nichols). Loc. 81.

***M.* 'New York 58-22'**
Name only. Subject to moderate scab (Nichols). Loc. 61.

***M.* 'Nicholene'**
Name only.

M. 'Niedzwetzkyana'
See *M. pumila* 'Niedzwetzkyana' in Chapter 11.

M. 'Nieuwland'
See *M. coronaria* 'Nieuwland' in Chapter 11.

M. 'Nieuwlandiana'
See *M. coronaria* 'Nieuwland' in Chapter 11.

M. 'Nifong'
Name only.

M. 'Nipissing' Preston 1920
Parentage: A Rosybloom
Named in 1930 by Isabella Preston, CDA—Ottawa, in her Lake Series, for Nipissing Lake in southeastern-central Ontario, Canada. A very hardy tree; buds carmine red, opening to single, rose pink to pale lavender flowers 1.7 in (4.2 cm) across; fruit dark red with orange-yellow, shaded side is bronze-green, 1.4 in (3.5 cm) in diameter. An alternate bloomer. Subject to fire blight and severe scab (Nichols). Loc. 16, 32.

M. 'Northland' University of Minnesota No. 1423.

M. 'Nova'
See *M. ioensis* 'Nova' in Chapter 11.

M. 'Oakes' Oakes before 1950
Parentage: An open-pollinated seedling of M. 'Scugog'
Selected and introduced by William Oakes, Glenelm Nursery, Miami, Manitoba, Canada. It is not, as often listed, the same as Morden No. 450. Leaves purple; flowers dark red-mauve, single; fruit 1.6 in (4 cm) in diameter, purple-red. Should be phased out—subject to severe scab (Nichols) Loc. 12, 24, 31, 61.

M. obconoides
An obsolete clone name for *M. baccata*.

M. oblongata
Name only. Loc. 16.

M. 'Odorata'
See *M. baccata* 'Odorata' in Chapter 11.

M. 'Oekonomierat Echtermeyer' Späth 1914 Plate 198
Synonym: *M.* 'Dekon Echtermeyer'
Trade names: Echtermeyer crabapple, Pink weeper
Parentage: *M. floribunda* 'Exzellenz Thiel' × *M. pumila* 'Niedzwetzkyana'
A clone of *M. ×gloriosa*. A semiweeper; leaves bronze-green; flowers single, purple-red; fruit red, 1 in (2.5 cm); annual bearer. Should be phased out—subject to moderate scab (Nichols). Loc. 3, 8, 11, 13, 18, 24, 26, 31, 32, 35, 39, 46, 53, 54, 61, 69, 73, 76, 77, 79, 80, 81, 86, 87.

M. 'Olga' N. E. Hansen 1919
Parentage: *M. baccata* × *M. pumila* 'Duchess of Oldenburg'
Buds pink; flowers single, white, 2.2 in (5.5 cm) across; fruit bright red, 1.2 in (3 cm) in diameter. Subject to fire blight. Loc. 9, 31, 32, 37, 81.

M. 'Oporto'
From Europe. A member of the *M. ×purpurea* group. Not outstanding. Subject to very severe scab (Nichols). Loc. 12, 15, 31, 32, 35, 37, 54, 68.

M. 'Orange' before 1869
Of North American origin. Flowers pink and white, single, 1.4 in (3.5 cm) across; fruit 1.2–1.6 in (3–4 cm) in diameter, yellow and orange. Subject to very mild scab. Loc. 9, 31, 35.

***M. 'Orange Crush'** Fiala Plate 199
Parentage: *M.* 'Liset' × *M.* 'Red Swan'
Developed at Falconskeape Gardens, Medina, OH, by Fr. John L. Fiala in 1983 and introduced by Klehm Nursery, South Barrington, IL, in 1990. A medium-sized, spreading tree; leaves rich dark green-purple; buds bright orange-rose, opening to single, orange-crimson flowers about 1.4–1.5 in (3.5–3.9 cm) across; fruit deep maroon, oblong, to 0.6 in (1.6 cm) long and about 0.4 in (1 cm) wide, very attractive despite its deep color, in clusters of 3–5. The clone, which holds fruit well, is best displayed when flanked by a yellow-fruited clone. It is probably the brightest orange-crimson clone on the market today. Although very new, when available, it should be one of the finest in its color range as it is disease resistant and its somewhat slender branchlets tend to droop under the weight of the heavy crop of very small fruit. It should prove to be an excellent choice for further hybridization and could well be used with species of *M. coronaria* and *M. ioensis*.

M. 'Orchid'
Name only. Disease free. Loc. 31, 54, 81.

M. orientalis
See Chapter 11.

***M. 'Ormiston Roy'** Roy 1933

Introduced and named by Arie den Boer in 1954, for William Ormiston Roy, a landscape architect of Montreal, Canada. A broadly spreading tree to 20 ft (6 m) high and 25 ft (8 m) wide; leaves dark green; buds rose red, turning pale rose pink, opening to single, white flowers 1.6 in (4 cm) across; fruit 0.4 in (1 cm), yellow with pale orange blush, rather weak color, ripening very late, persistent all winter. An annual, prolific bearer. Excellent disease resistance (Nichols). Excellent for all-purpose landscaping. Loc. 4, 5, 15, 18, 24, 26, 31, 35, 37, 46, 54, 55, 68, 79, 80, 81, 86, 89.

***M.* 'Orna'**

Name only. Loc. 37.

***M.* 'O'Rourke'**

Name only. Subject to very severe scab (Nichols). Loc. 61.

M. orthocarpa

An obsolete botanical name. Subject to very severe scab (Nichols). Loc. 54.

***M.* 'Osman'** Saunders 1904

Parentage: *M. baccata* × *M.* 'Osimoe' (apple)

Named in 1911. Buds pink; flowers single, pink and white, 2 in (5 cm) across; fruit 1.4 in (3.5 cm) in diameter, orange to red. Subject to mild scab and slightly susceptible to fire blight. Loc. 15, 81, 87.

***M.* Ottawa 524**

A clone of *M. baccata*, formerly known as *M.* ×*robusta* No. 5 (see *M.* ×*robusta* 'Arnold-Canada' in Chapter 11). Subject to mild scab. Loc. 12.

****M.* 'Pagoda'** Fiala 1970

Parentage: *M.* 'Red Swan' × *M.* 'Autumn Glory'

No. 84-17. A small, rounded weeper to 10 ft (3 m) high and as wide; leaves dark green; buds bright carmine, opening to single, white flowers; fruit 0.4 in (1 cm) in diameter, coloring early to a brilliant orange-red, firm, persistent. Disease resistant. A very fine, tailored, mini-fruited weeper. Loc. 47, 100.

M. pallasiana

An obsolete botanical name for *M. baccata*.

***M.* 'Papal Guard'** Fiala/P. Murray

Parentage: *M.* 'Centurion' × *M.* 'Winter Gold'

No. B7W-89. An upright, columnar tree to 15 ft (4.6 m) high and 8 ft (2.5 m) wide; buds pink, opening to single, white flower; fruit small, 0.4 (1 cm) in diameter, lemon-yellow, persistent to November, then eaten by birds. An abundant, annual bloomer. Good disease resistance. Loc. 47.

***M.* 'Parent No. 1'**

Name only. Subject to moderate scab (Nichols). Loc. 61.

****M.* 'Park Centre'** Les Demaline, Willoway Nursery, Avon, OH, 1985

A vase-shaped to columnar tree of vigorous growth, with upright branching; leaves glossy green; flowers single, cotton candy pink, produced in abundance; fruit small, golden-yellow with pale red blush, dropping early. Appears to be completely disease resistant. Very new but could well be an excellent tree for smaller spaces and for columnar accent. Loc. 58.

***M.* 'Parkman'**

See *M. halliana* 'Parkmanii' in Chapter 11.

***M.* 'Parkmanii'**

See *M. halliana* 'Parkmanii' in Chapter 11.

***M.* 'Patricia'** A. den Boer 1953

Parentage: A chance seedling of *M.* 'Hopa' seedling No. 2.

A second-generation Rosybloom. Named by Arie den Boer for a daughter-in-law. Buds maroon-red, opening to single, deep purple-red flowers with a white claw, 2 in (5 cm) across; red fruit to 1 in (2.5 cm) in diameter. Should be phased out—subject to moderate scab (Nichols). Loc. 10, 15, 18, 26, 31, 32, 35, 37, 46, 54, 73, 81.

***M.* 'Pattie'**

Known at Morden. No diseases. Loc. 31, 54.

***M.* 'Paul Imperial'** Paul

Parentage: A hybrid of *M. baccata*

Introduced in the United States from England in 1888 by Ellwanger & Barry Nursery, Rochester, NY.

****M.* 'Pauline'** Fiala 1972

Parentage: *M. sieboldii* 'Calocarpa' × *M. sieboldii* 'Wooster'

No. KW-1. Named by the introducer for a sister-in-law, Pauline Policy Fiala, of Spencer, OH. An upright, spreading tree to 12 ft (3.5 m) high and as wide; leaves dark green; buds carmine, opening to masses of single, pure white flowers on many spurs; fruit claret-red,

0.5 in (1.2 cm) in diameter, very showy, persistent into late winter. A very heavy, annual bloomer. Totally disease resistant after many years of testing (Nichols). An excellent, dependable, landscaping crabapple of great springtime and autumn appeal. Excellent for all gardens. Loc. 47, 100.

*M. **'Peachblow'*** before 1930
Originated in United States. Possibly a hybrid of *M. floribunda*, but more upright. Flowers pinkish, single, 1.2 in (3 cm) across; fruit red, colors early, 0.4 in (1 cm) in diameter. An annual bearer. Subject to severe scab. Loc. 15, 31, 54.

M. 'Peter Murray' Fiala 1989 Plate 8
Parentage: *M.* 'Satin Cloud' × *M.* 'Tetragold'
No. NR4-P4. A second-generation tetraploid. Named to honor an outstanding garden superintendent, Peter Murray, superintendent of Falconskeape Gardens, Medina, OH, and president of Ameri-Hort Research, Medina, OH. A small, upright, spreading tree 10 ft (3 m) high and as wide; leaves dark green, leathery; buds pink, opening to large, single, white flowers, on spurs all along the branches; fruit 0.4 in (1 cm) in diameter, a combination of gold and burnished orange in color, very beautiful, persistent to midwinter. A very showy annual bloomer with heavy fruiting. Blooms when very young. Appears to be completely disease free. Outstanding for any place in the garden. Excellent for landscaping and hybridizing. Very new and yet not well known. Loc. 47.

*M. **'Peter Pan'** Fiala 1955
Parentage: *M. sieboldii* 'Wooster' × Seeding 48-75 (*M. sieboldii* × *M.* ×*micromalus*)
No. 60-4. A rounded tree to 14 ft (4.3 m) high and as wide; leaves medium green, disease resistant; buds bright red, opening to masses of single, white flowers; fruit small, 0.25 in (0.6 cm) in diameter, very bright red on spurs that increase with age, changing from red to an attractive copper-red with heavy frosts, persistent to March until eaten by birds, very showy. A very heavy annual bloomer and fruit bearer. Totally disease resistant (Nichols). Suitable for large estates and parks; excellent for roadside plantings. Loc. 47.

***M.* 'Pink Beauty'** CDA—Morden
Parentage: A hybrid of *M. baccata*
MR-451. Named by R. Simpson before 1958. A Rosybloom. Flowers single pink; fruit large, 0.9 in (2.3 cm) in diameter, red. Subject to very mild scab. Loc. 9, 24, 26, 31, 35, 55, 79, 80.

***M.* 'Pink Cascade'** Kerr 1920
Parentage: A Rosybloom seedling
No. 63-9. Selected in 1946 from Rosybloom seedlings at the Canada Department of Agriculture Experiment Station, Morden, Manitoba. Introduced and named in 1969 by Inter-State Nurseries, Hamburg, IA. A semiweeper 14 ft (4.3 m) high and 6–7 ft (1.8–2 m) wide, with branches hanging down perpendicularly; flowers abundant, single, pink; fruit bright red, 0.5 in (1.2 cm) in diameter, coloring in late summer and retaining color for many weeks. Subject to very mild scab, not defoliating. Loc. 10, 13, 24, 26, 34, 46, 54, 61, 76, 79, 85.

***M.* 'Pink Dawn'** Les Demaline, Willoway Nursery, Avon, OH
An upright to vase-shaped tree to 18 ft (5.5 m) high and 12 ft (3.5 m) wide; leaves red-green, disease free; buds rose-red, opening to single, clear pink flowers. Subject to very mild scab. Too new to be evaluated, but appears to be a good pink-blooming, upright tree. Loc. 5, 58.

***M.* 'Pink Eye'** Will before 1940
Synonyms: *M.* 'Dakota Pink Eye', *M.* 'Diamond Jubilee', *M.* 'Will's Pink Eye'
Buds pink-red, opening pink-white and white, with pale pink-white eye in center of flower; fruit red, 0.8 in (2 cm) in diameter. Not outstanding in bloom. Subject to moderate scab. Loc. 31, 61, 81.

***M.* 'Pink Feathers'**
A dwarf weeper; flowers pink, feathery, unique; fruit lemon-gold.

***M.* 'Pink Flame'**
Name only. Severe scab. Loc. 18.

*M. **'Pink Giant'** C. Hansen 1939
Parentage: Probably *M. baccata* × *M. pumila* 'Niedzwetzkyana'
Flowers single, pink-to-lavender, very large, 2 in (5 cm) across; fruit 0.4 in (1 cm) in diameter, orange to orange-red. Disease resistant (Nichols). Should be an outstanding crabapple. Some nursery should propagate it. Needs to be better known. Recommended for its very large flowers that could be a great asset for hybridizing, its orange fruit, and its disease resistance. Loc. 81, 89.

***M.* 'Pink Pearl'**
See *M. coronaria* 'Pink Pearl' in Chapter 11.

***M.* 'Pink Perfection'**
A small, upright to spreading tree to 12 ft (3.5 m) high and as wide; buds deep rose-colored, opening to double, pale pink and white flowers. Should be phased out—subject to very severe scab (Nichols). Loc. 5, 12, 20, 24, 39, 41, 46, 54, 61, 79, 85, 86, 92.

***M.* 'Pink Princess'**
A low-spreading, bushy tree to 8 ft (2.5 m) high and 12 ft (3.5 m) wide; leaves purple, turning bronze-green; flowers rose-pink; fruit deep red, 0.25 in (0.6 cm) in diameter. Fair-to-good disease rating. Should be carried by more collections and arboretums. Recommended for its low form, small fruit, good foliage, and disease resistance. Loc. 86.

*__*M.* 'Pink Satin'__ Simpson 1990
A medium-sized, upright to rounded tree with good leaf color; buds deep pink, opening to abundant clusters of single, pink flowers; fruit small, 0.4 in (1 cm), dark red, persistent. A very showy and heavy annual bloomer. Good disease resistance. Very showy tree in springtime bloom with a clear pink color not found in many crabapples. Very new. Loc. Simpson Nursery, Vincennes, IN.

***M.* 'Pink Spires'** Sutherland Tree Nursery, Saskatoon, Saskatchewan, Canada
A narrow, upright tree to 15 ft (4.6 m) high and 12 ft (3.5 m) wide; leaves maroon; flowers single, pink; fruit maroon, 0.5 in (1.2 cm) in diameter. Fair-to-good disease rating; subject to very mild scab and fire blight (Nichols). Loc. 5, 15, 24, 31, 54, 69, 74, 77, 79, 81, 84, 86.

***M.* 'Pink Stripe'**
Name only.

***M.* 'Pink Sunburst'**
See *M.* 'Hopa'.

***M.* 'Pioneer Scarlet'** Young before 1954
Parentage: A Rosybloom seedling
Subject to moderate scab (Nichols). Loc. 81.

***M.* 'Piotosh'** Saunders 1900
Parentage: *M.* 'Pioneer' (crabapple) × *M.* 'McIntosh' (apple)
A small, yellow and bright red apple. Named with the first and last syllables, respectively, of the parents. Loc. 12, 81.

***M.* 'Pixie'** A. den Boer 1940
Parentage: An open-pollinated seedling of *M.* 'Oekonomierat Echtermeyer'
Named by Arie den Boer in 1948. A semi-weeper; flowers single, white, 2 in (5 cm) across; fruit somewhat large, 1.6 in (4 cm) in diameter, red. Subject to mild scab. Loc. 31, 35, 54, 81.

M. ×platycarpa
See *M. coronaria* var. *platycarpa* in Chapter 11.

***M. ×platycarpa* 'Hoopesii'**
See *M. coronaria* var. *platycarpa* 'Hoopesii' in Chapter 11.

***M. ×platycarpa* 'Long Ashton'**
Name only. Subject to mild cedar-apple rust (Nichols). Loc. 73.

***M.* 'Ponass'**
Name only.

***M.* 'Prairie Gold'**
Name only. Disease free (Nichols). Loc. 31.

***M.* 'Prairie Maid'** Simpson 1956
Parentage: *M. sieboldii* 'Calocarpa' × *M.* 'Van Eseltine'
No. 8-29. A compact, rounded, medium-sized tree; flowers abundant, deep pink, blooming in midseason; fruit small, orange-red. Disease resistant. Simpson Nursery, Vincennes, IN.

***M.* 'Prairie Rose'**
See *M. ioensis* 'Prairie Rose' in Chapter 11.

*+__*M.* 'Prairifire'__ D. F. Dayton, Department of Horticulture, University of Illinois, Urbana, 1982 Plate 200
A moderately upright to rounded tree 20 ft (6 m) high and as wide; young leaves red-maroon, maturing to deep green; buds red-purple to crimson, opening to red-purple, single flowers 1.5–1.6 in (3.8–4 cm) across, pedicels 1.2–1.4 in (3–3.5 cm) long; fruit spheroid, 0.4–0.5 in (1–1.2 cm) in diameter, deep purple-red. Disease free (Nichols). A newer clone that should be far better known and grown for its very fine blossom color and fruit. An outstanding crabapple that needs room to develop but fits well into any landscape. Should be excellent in hybridizing. Loc. 24, 26, 31, 46, 79, 86, 100.

M. prattii
See Chapter 11.

***M.* 'Pretty Marjory'** Royal Moerheim Nursery—Holland
No. 294-58. Introduced by US Plant Intro-

duction Station, MD. Description not available. Subject to severe scab (Nichols). Loc. 9, 12, 13, 26, 31, 69, 72, 89.

***M.* 'Prince'** Saunders 1904
Parentage: *M. baccata* × *M. pumila* 'Tetofsky'
Named in 1911.

***M.* 'Prince Charming'**
Of Canadian origin. A small tree to 8 ft (2.5 m) high and 5 ft (1.5 m) wide; leaves red-green; buds carmine, opening to single, rose-red, very small flowers 0.6 in (1.4 cm) across; fruit very small, mini-fruited, 0.25 in (0.6 cm) in diameter, round, red. Subject to moderate scab. A slow growing tree, not a heavy bloomer, with dull fruit. Loc. 47.

***M.* 'Prince Georges'**
See *M. ioensis* 'Prince Georges' in Chapter 11.

***M.* 'Printosh'** Saunders 1905
Parentage: *M.* 'Prince' (crabapple) × *M.* 'McIntosh' (apple)
A second-generation cross of *M. baccata.* Named in 1920 with the first and last syllables, respectively, of the parents. Buds rose-pink, flowers single, white with touch of pink on back of petals, 1.7 in (4.2 cm) across; fruit pale orange and carmine, 2 in (5 cm) in diameter. Subject to fire blight. Fruit too large.

M.* **'Professor Sprenger' Doorenbos before 1950
Parentage: A clone of *M. sieboldii*
Named for Professor Sprenger, director of the Department of Horticulture, Wageningen, Netherlands. An upright, spreading tree 20 ft (6 m) high and as wide; buds deep rose-pink, opening to single, very fragrant, white flowers; fruit very showy, yellow-orange changing to orange-red with a pink blush, 0.4 in (1 cm) in diameter, persistent to January as the birds will not touch the fruit; an annual bearer. Disease free (Nichols). An excellent, showy crabapple for background planting. The name, like most crabapple names to honor men, adds sales resistance. Loc. 5, 24, 26, 31, 37, 81, 86, 87, 89, 100.

M.* **'Profusion' Doorenbos before 1938
Plates 201, 202
Parentage: *M. ×purpurea* 'Lemoinei' × *M. toringo* (formerly *M. sieboldii*)
A cross made before 1938 by S. G. A. Doorenbos, Department of Parks, The Hague, Netherlands. The name refers to the abundance of single flowers. This crabapple is similar to *M.* 'Liset', another clone of *M. ×purpurea* 'Lemoinei', except that its flower color is not as bright or as attractive as that of *M.* 'Liset'. An upright, spreading tree 20 ft (6 m) high and as wide; leaves purplish to bronze; buds deep red, expanding to purple-red, then fading to purple-pink; flowers single, deep rose-pink, 1.8 in (4.5 cm) across; fruit 0.6 in (1.5 cm) in diameter, maroon or blood-red. Very showy in bloom. Good disease rating. An excellent clone that should be planted more and used for hybridizing. A fine rose-blossoming tree to plant next to white-flowering crabapples. Loc. 12, 13, 24, 26, 31, 32, 35, 39, 40, 54, 79, 80, 81, 86, 87, 89, 91, 100.

***M.* 'Prolific'**
Name only.

M. prunifolia
See Chapter 11.

M. prunifolia* var. *rinki
See Chapter 11.

***M. prunifolia* 'Fastigata'**
See Chapter 11.

***M. prunifolia* 'Fructu Coccinea'**
Subject to mild scab (Nichols). Loc. 15.

***M. prunifolia* 'Kataika Saninskaa'**
Subject to moderate scab (Nichols). Loc. 87.

***M. prunifolia* 'Lutea'**
Name only. Subject to mild scab (Nichols). Loc. 54.

***M. prunifolia* 'Pendula'**
See Chapter 11.

***M. prunifolia* 'Xanthocarpa'**
Buds pink, opening to single, white flowers. Not an outstanding clone. Appears disease free (Nichols). Loc. 12, 13, 18, 32, 35, 79.

***M. prunifolia* 'Xanthocarpa Pendula'**
A weeping form of *M. prunifolia* 'Xanthocarpa'. Disease free (Nichols). Loc. 18.

M. pumila
See Chapter 11.

M. pumila* var. *sylvestris
See Chapter 11.

***M. pumila* var. *sylvestris* 'Flore Plena'**
See Chapter 11.

M. pumila var. ***sylvestris*** **'Plena'**
See Chapter 11.

M. pumila var. ***translucens***
See Chapter 11.

M. pumila **'Apetala'**
Subject to moderate scab. Loc. 14, 31.

M. pumila **'Aurea'**
Synonyms: *M.* 'Aurea', *M. aurea*
Name only. Subject to severe scab (Nichols). Loc. 81.

M. pumila **'Niedzwetzkyana'**
See Chapter 11.

M. pumila **'Paradisiaca'**
See Chapter 11.

M. pumila **'Paradisiaca Foleus Aureus'**
Subject to mild scab. Loc. 26, 54, 81.

M. pumila **'Paradisiaca Ruberrima'**
Subject to severe scab (Nichols). Loc. 31, 81.

M. pumila **'Pendula'**
See Chapter 11.

M. pumila **'Plena'**
See *M. pumila* var. *translucens* in Chapter 11.

M. pumila **'Translucens'**
See *M. pumila* var. *translucens*.

M. **'Purdom No. 179'**
Name only.

*+***M.*** **'Purple Prince'** Fiala 1970 Plates 203, 204
Parentage: *M.* 'Bluebeard' × *M.* 'Liset'
No. 85-20-R2. A small, rounded, tailored tree to 15 ft (4.6 m) high and as wide; leaves deep purple-green, disease resistant; buds bright carmine-red, opening to bright rose-red, single flowers that fade only slightly to a pleasing rose; fruit 0.4–0.5 in (1–1.2 cm) in diameter, blue-purple with a fine blue bloom, firm, persistent. Completely disease resistant (Nichols). A very heavy, annual bloomer with fine purple-green foliage and abundant, deep pink flowers. Excellent for any landscape. Fruit attractive and showy next to a gold- or orange-fruited crabapple. Loc. 47, 86.

M. **'Purple Wave'** A. den Boer 1951
Parentage: *M.* 'Jay Darling' seedling No. 3
Leaves dark purplish. Not a good bloomer. Should be phased out—too much disease (Nichols). Loc. 9, 15, 18, 24, 26, 31, 32, 37, 47, 55, 77, 79, 81.

M. **×*purpurea***
See Chapter 11.

M. **×*purpurea*** **'Aldenhamensis'**
See Chapter 11.

M. **×*purpurea*** **'Eleyi'**
See Chapter 11.

M. **×*purpurea*** **'Eleyi Compacta'**
See Chapter 11.

M. **×*purpurea*** **'Hoser'**
Should be phased out—subject to severe scab. Loc. 31.

M. **×*purpurea*** **'Kobendza'**
Should be phased out—subject to moderate scab. Loc. 31.

M. **×*purpurea*** **'Kornicensis'**
See Chapter 11.

M. **×*purpurea*** **'Lemoinei'**
See Chapter 11.

M. **×*purpurea*** **'Makowieckiana'**
Parentage: A clone of *M.* ×*purpurea*.
USDA plant introduction No. 256023. Subject to moderate scab (Nichols). Loc. 31.

M. **×*purpurea*** **'Szaferi'**
Synonym: *M.* 'Schaefer'
Name only. Subject to severe scab (Nichols). Loc. 31.

M. **×*purpurea*** **'Wierdakii'**
Name only. Subject to severe scab (Nichols). Loc. 31.

M. **'Pygmy'** Kerr Plate 205
No. 63-5. A small, almost perfectly rounded tree to 12 ft (3.5 m) high; leaves red-green; buds carmine-rose, opening to single, pink-mauve flowers. Subject to moderate scab. A genetic dwarf but not as decorative as others for home landscaping. Interesting genetic form. Loc. 5, 12, 31, 35, 61, 79, 81.

M. **'Pyramidalis'**
Parentage: A clone of *M. baccata*

M. **'Quaker Beauty'** before 1875
Buds pink, opening to single, pink-white flowers 2 in (5 cm) across; fruit green with red

cheeks, 1.6 in (4 cm) in diameter. Subject to mild scab and moderate cedar-apple rust (Nichols). Loc. 10, 15, 31, 54.

***M.* 'Quality'** Broughen before 1906
Parentage: Unknown
Introduced by Broughen Nurseries, Valley River, Manitoba, Canada Fruit red, 1.2 in (3 cm) in diameter. Extremely hardy. Subject to severe scab (Nichols). Loc. 12, 87.

***M.* 'Queen Mab'** Wheelock Wilson
Name only.

***M.* 'Queen's Choice'** before 1892
Parentage: A clone of *M.* ×*adstringens*
Buds white, opening to single, white flowers 1.8 in (4.5 cm) across; fruit yellow with red cheeks, 1.4 in (3.5 cm) diameter. Subject to mild scab (Nichols). Loc. 12, 14, 31, 32.

***M.* 'Quintuplet'**
Name only.

***M.* 'Radiant'** L. E. Longley, University of Minnesota, 1940 Plate 206
Parentage: A chance seedling; probably an open-pollinated seedling of *M.* 'Hopa'
University of Minnesota No. 6C, named in 1957. One of the best Rosyblooms. A broad, medium-sized tree to 25 ft (8 m) high and 20 ft (6 m) wide; leaves red-purple when young, fading to bronze; buds deep red, opening to single, deep pink flowers; fruit bright red, 0.5 in (1.2 cm) in diameter, coloring in midsummer. Tends to be an alternate bloomer. Subject to severe scab (Nichols). Very showy in bright deep red-pink blossoms. Loc. 4, 5, 10, 15, 18, 19, 24, 26, 35, 39, 40, 41, 43, 46, 47, 54, 55, 58, 71, 74, 77, 79, 80, 81, 86.

****M.* 'Ralph Shay'** Fig. 3.4
Parentage: *M.* 'Wolf River' × *M. sieboldii* 'Calocarpa'
Purdue University No. 15-56. Named to honor the late Ralph Shay, pathologist in charge of breeding programs, Purdue University, West Lafayette, IN. A vigorous, sturdy, horizontally branched tree that is broader than high; leaves an unusual dark green, disease free; buds red; flowers single, white; fruit 1.25 in (3 cm) in diameter, deep red from mid-September, persistent, not dropping until spring. Subject to mild scab (Nichols). Fruit a bit too large for smaller gardens, but excellent for highway plantings. Loc. 5, 24, 26, 31, 54, 61, 80, 81.

****M.* 'Red Barron'**
Synonyms: *M.* 'Simpson 328-AA', *M.* Arnold Arboretum No. 328-55-A
No. 624-73. Introduced and named by Simpson Nursery, Vincennes, IN. A medium-sized, compact, narrow tree with upright (columnar) growth, 18 ft (5.5 m) high to 8 ft (2.5 m) wide; leaves red-purple, turning to bronze-green, excellent in fall color; flowers single, dark red; fruit glossy, dark red, 0.5 in (1.2 cm) in diameter. Subject to mild scab (Nichols). An excellent tree for narrow places, street plantings, or for accent in a garden walk. Not to be confused with the apple clone *M.* 'Red Baron'; the crabapple has a double *r* in its name, while the apple clone has only one *r*. Loc. 5, 16, 24, 26, 46, 54, 55, 61, 81.

***+*M.* 'Redbird'** Fiala 1974 Plate 207
Plant patent name "Rebirzam". Introduced by Lake County Nursery, Perry, OH. Originally introduced by Klehm Nursery, South Barrington, IL. A small, upright, rounded tree to about 15 ft (4.6 m) high and 12 ft (3.5 m) wide; leaves dark green, disease resistant; buds brilliant red, opening to abundant, single, pure white flowers; fruit begins to color early in August, 0.4–0.6 in (1–1.5 in) in diameter, persistent into late November or until eaten by birds. Completely resistant to all disease (Nichols). An annual bloomer whose primary ornamental value lies in its brilliant crimson-red fruit; however, the combination of white flowers with unopened bright red buds in spring is also very ornamental. One of the finest of the early coloring crabapples that has been used for many years at Falconskeape Gardens, Medina, OH, in hybridizing. Ideal for all landscapes. Loc. 46, 47, 100.

***M.* 'Red Coat'**
Name only. Subject to severe scab (Nichols). Loc. 31, 35, 37.

***M.* 'Red Edinburgh'** Wayside Nursery catalog 1970
Subject to severe scab (Nichols). Loc. 26, 35.

***M.* 'Redfield'** New York State Experiment Station—Geneva 1924
Parentage: *M. pumila* 'Wolf River' (apple) × *M. pumila* 'Niedzwetzkyana'
A Rosybloom. Introduced in 1938. Carmine buds and single, red flowers fading to dull pink, 1.6 in (4 cm) across; fruit red, 1.4 in (3.5 cm) in diameter, red fleshed. Subject to severe scab (Nichols). Loc. 11, 18, 54, 81.

M. 'Redflesh' N. E. Hansen 1928
Parentage: *M. pumila* 'Niedzwetzkyana' × *M. coronaria* 'Elk River'
Buds carmine, opening to single, rose-pink flowers 1.8 in (4.5 cm) across, fragrant; fruit red with shaded side green-brown, red-fleshed, 1.9 in (4.7 cm) in diameter. An alternate bearer. Subject to severe scab (Nichols). An interesting crabapple that could be used in hybridization of *M. coronaria*. Loc. 14, 26, 32, 35, 54, 81.

M. 'Redford' New York State Experiment Station—Geneva 1921
Parentage: *M.* 'Wolf River' (apple) × *M. pumila* 'Niedzwetzkyana'
A Rosybloom similar to *M.* 'Redfield' except flowers not as dark, single, 2 in (5 cm) across; fruit 2 in (5 cm) in diameter, yellow and red. An alternate bloomer. Subject to mild scab (Nichols). Loc. 14, 31, 32, 35, 81.

M. 'Red Fruit'
Parentage: A clone of *M. spectabilis*

M. 'Redglobe'
Name only. Loc. 81.

M. 'Red Heart' Porter
Sometimes spelled as one word, *M.* 'Redheart'. Name only. No disease (Nichols). Loc. 31, 54.

M. 'Red Hill'
Name only.

*__M. 'Red Jade'__ Reed 1935 Plate 208, Fig. 6.2
Parentage: An open-pollinated chance seedling of *M. floribunda* 'Exzellenz Thiel'
Introduced and named in 1953. Patented in 1956, plant patent No. 1497. Found growing at the Brooklyn Botanic Garden, Brooklyn, NY, in 1935 by George M. Reed. A tree 10–12 ft (3–3.5 m) high and 20–30 ft (6–9 m) wide or even wider; leaves very attractive, glossy green; buds red, opening to single, white flowers 1.6 in (4 cm) across; fruit egg-shaped, 0.5 in (1.2 cm) in diameter, bright red, persistent through fall into winter. Subject to severe scab, fire blight, and powdery mildew in some areas (Nichols); in other areas (e.g., Ohio) it is little affected by any diseases. This clone well demonstrates how disease susceptibility can be a regional problem and not necessarily a universal one. It is an excellent, outstanding ornamental, the first really fine weeping crabapple. It has been used heavily by hybridizers. Because of its large spread (with age), it needs room to develop to perfection with its long, slender weeping branches. Suitable for larger estates, parks, and arboretum plantings but not smaller home gardens. Loc. 12, 18, 19, 20, 22, 24, 26, 28, 31, 32, 35, 37, 40, 46, 47, 55, 58, 61, 69, 71, 73, 76, 77, 79, 80, 81, 86, 100.

*__M. 'Red Jewel'__ Cole Nursery 1972
Plate 6, Fig. 3.3
Plant patent No. 3267. An upright, pyramidal tree to 18 ft (5.5 m) high and 12 ft (3.5 m) wide; leaves dark green, 2–3 in (5–7.6 cm) long; flowers single, white; fruit bright cherry red, 0.5 in (1.2 cm) in diameter, very attractive, persistent in color to December. Subject to very mild scab (Nichols). One of the better newer crabapples. A fine specimen plant. Suitable for planting in narrow places or as an accent to break a rounded landscaping line. Loc. 2, 5, 18, 19, 22, 26, 31, 35, 46, 54, 61, 69, 81, 86, 100.

M. 'Red Leaf'
Name only. Probably a synonym for *M. pumila* 'Niedzwetzkyana'.

M. 'Redman'
Name only. Subject to moderate scab (Nichols). Loc. 12, 54.

M. 'Red Mercer'
Name only. Subject to moderate scab (Nichols). Loc. 54.

*__M. 'Red Peacock'__ Fiala 1969 Plates 209, 210
Parentage: *M.* 'Molten Lava' × (*M.* 'Luwick' × *M. sieboldii* No. 243)
Introduced and patented by Klehm Nursery, South Barrington, IL. An upright semiweeper to 12 ft (3.5 m) high and 14 ft (4.3 m) wide; leaves dark green, disease resistant; buds bright red, opening to single, white flowers; fruit brilliant orange-red, 0.4–0.5 in (1–1.2 cm) in diameter, firm, persistent to December. A very heavy, annual bloomer. Very effective in heavy fruit on cascading branchlets, similar to a peacock's tail. Totally disease resistant (Nichols). A choice crabapple where there is space to appreciate its spreading form. Loc. 47, 100.

M. 'Red River' Yeager before 1938
Parentage: *M.* 'Dolgo' × *M.* 'Delicious' (apple)
Flowers single, pink and white, 2 in (5 cm) across; fruit 2 in (5 cm) in diameter, bright red. Subject to mild scab (Nichols). Loc. 5, 9, 54.

M. 'Red Ruby' Cole Nursery, Circleville, OH
Parentage: *M.* 'Van Eseltine' × *M.* 'Almey'
Plant patent No. 3052. A vigorous tree with

narrow to upright growth habit; leaves glossy, dark green; flowers double, cup-shaped, dark red, 2 in (5 cm) or more across, produced in great abundance; fruit almost sterile, but dark red and small when produced. Free of apple scab. A very showy springtime clone. Should be used more in landscaping and by hybridizers.

***M.* 'Red Siberian'**
See *M.* ×*robusta* 'Red Siberian' in Chapter 11.

***M.* 'Red Silver'** C. Hansen 1928
Parentage: A Rosybloom
Carmine buds and flowers fading to dull pink, 1.6 in (4 cm) across; fruit purple, 0.8 in (2 cm) in diameter. Slightly susceptible to scab; susceptible to fire blight. Wheeler Wilson lists it among his "best dozen crabapples." Fruit a bit too large to be recommended. Loc. 14, 24, 31, 35, 39, 40, 43, 54, 77, 79, 81.

***M.* 'Red Snow'**
Name of an older variety. Also the first name given to *M.* 'Red Swan' before a conflict in names was discovered. The *M.* 'Red Snow' that is mentioned in recent writings as an excellent weeper is a clone of *M.* 'Red Swan' (which see).

*****M.* 'Red Splendor'** Bergeson Nursery, Fertile, MN, 1948
Parentage: An open-pollinated seedling of *M.* 'Red Silver'
A Rosybloom selected in 1948. An open, graceful, upright, spreading tree 20 ft (6 m) high and as wide; leaves glossy red-green, turning red-purple in fall; buds rose-colored, opening to large, pink to rose-pink flowers 1.75 in (4.4 cm) across, with 5 petals; fruit 0.5 in (1.2 cm), dark red, persistent to December. Subject to mild scab and cedar-apple rust (Nichols). Loc. 2, 5, 12, 18, 24, 31, 35, 37, 39, 55, 72, 74, 79, 80, 81, 82, 86.

***M.* 'Red Star'**
Name only. Subject to severe scab (Nichols). Loc. 69.

*+***M.* 'Red Swan'** Fiala 1967
Plates 24, 211, 212, 213, 214, Fig. 3.5
Synonym: *M.* 'Red Snow'
Name changed from *M.* 'Red Snow' to *M.* 'Red Swan' to avoid conflict with an existing name. Introduced and patented by Klehm Nursery, South Barrington, IL. An excellent weeping, multibrid crabapple. A small to medium-sized tree 10 ft (3 m) high and 14 ft (4.3 m) wide, with long, graceful, arching, weeping branches and fine twigs; leaves fine, narrow, heavily textured, with very attractive gold colors in fall; buds elongated, pink-red, opening to single, pink-white flowers 1.5 in (3.8 cm) across; fruit oblong, 0.3 in (0.8 cm) in diameter, colors to bright orange-red, persistent through December and January. A very heavy, annual bloomer. Completely disease resistant (Nichols). The orange-red fruit and yellow-golden fall foliage are extremely attractive and make this one of the most attractive weeping crabapples, a showpiece as it matures. It should be displayed as a single specimen plant at a focal point in the garden landscape. It can fit into almost any landscaping design. With its cascades of brilliant orange-red fruit on long weeping branches, I would classify *M.* 'Red Swan', along with *M.* 'White Cascade', as the two very best weeping crabapples available today. Loc. 31, 35, 47, 100.
Progeny of *M.* 'Red Swan' include the following:

M. 'Autumn Treasure' Fiala
M. 'Coralene' Fiala
M. 'Dancing Elf' Fiala/P. Murray
M. 'Firecloud' Fiala
M. 'Firecracker' Fiala
M. 'Henry Ross' Fiala
M. 'Orange Crush' Fiala
M. 'Pagoda' Fiala
M. 'Rhapsody' Fiala
M. 'Royal Splendor' Fiala
M. 'Sinai Fire' Fiala
M. 'Spring Beauty' Fiala
M. 'Wildfire' Fiala

***M.* 'Red Tip'** N. E. Hansen 1919
Parentage: *M. coronaria* 'Elk River' × *M. pumila* 'Niedzwetzkyana'
Arie den Boer is probably correct when he doubts the presence of any *M. pumila* 'Niedzwetzkyana' in *M.* 'Red Tip'. Young leaves are red tipped; flowers single, pink, 1.6 in (4 cm) across; fruit very large, size of eating apples, 2 in (5 cm) in diameter, yellow-green. Subject to mild scab (Nichols); susceptible to fire blight. Loc. 12, 15, 54, 81.

***M.* 'Rehder Sweet'**
See *M. coronaria* 'Elongata' in Chapter 11.

***M.* 'Renee'** Schwartze
Named by Chester D. Schwartze, Puyallup, WA, for his eldest granddaughter, Renee Scheyer.

***M.* 'Renown'**
Name only.

M. 'Rescue' CDA—Scott 1936
A very hardy tree; flowers pink fading to whitish, 1 in (2.5 cm) across; fruit red, very large, 1.4 in (3.5 cm) in diameter. Resistant to fire blight but subject to moderate scab (Nichols). Loc. 15, 81.

M. 'Rhapsody' Fiala
Parentage: *M.* 'Red Swan' × *M.* 'Red Jade'
No. 85-D1-SPW. A refined, small semiweeper to 12 ft (3.5 m) high and 14 ft (4.3 m) wide; leaves dark green, disease free; buds carmine with pink, opening to large, single, white flowers produced in great abundance, very attractive; fruit bright, glossy, red, 0.4–0.5 in (1–1.2 cm) in diameter, persistent, showy. An annual bloomer. Completely disease free. An excellent weeper that could well surpass *M.* 'Red Jade' in popularity, especially in disease resistance; smaller, brighter fruit; and more refined plant habit. Outstanding for all garden landscaping needs—smaller home gardens, patios, or as a focal point in larger estates and parks. Massed in threes next to yellow-fruited crabapples, it is very showy. Unavailable as yet, too new. Loc. 47, 86.

M. 'Richard J. Eaton'
Name only.

M. 'Ringo'
Parentage: A clone of *M.* ×*sublobata*
Subject to mild scab (Nichols). Loc. 24, 80, 81.

M. 'Rival'
Name only.

M. 'Robert Nairn' H. R. Wright
Parentage: A hybrid of *M. baccata*
Flowers white; fruit small, orange-yellow. Subject to moderate scab (Nichols). Previously free of all diseases for over 10 years. An overlooked crabapple. Loc. 61.

M. 'Robin' Saunders 1904
Parentage: *M. baccata* × *M.* 'Simbirsk No. 9' (apple)
Buds rose-red, opening to single, white flowers, with petals showing a trace of pink along the edges, cupped, 1.6 cm (4 cm) across; fruit orange-yellow with pale red blush, evenly ribbed, large, 1.6 in (4 cm) in diameter. Extremely hardy. Subject to mild scab and cedar-apple rust (Nichols). Loc. 9, 11, 31.

M. 'Robin Hill Pink'
Name only.

M. 'Robin Jefferson'
Name only.

M. 'Robinson' Hobbs
Introduced by C. M. Hobbs Nursery, Indianapolis, IN. The original tree was located on adjacent property owned by James Robinson, for whom the crabapple is named. An upright, spreading tree 25 ft (8 m) high and as wide; leaves reddish, turning to bronze-green with maturity; buds crimson, opening to single, deep rose-mauve flowers that keep their color well; fruit 0.6 in (1.6 cm) in diameter, dark, glossy wine-red, hidden by foliage that persists. Excellent disease-free rating (Nichols). Loc. 5, 19, 24, 26, 31, 55, 61, 74, 81, 82, 86.

M. ×*robusta*
See Chapter 11.

M. ×*robusta* 'Arnold-Canada'
See Chapter 11.

M. ×*robusta* 'Costata'
See Chapter 11.

M. ×*robusta* 'Cowles House'
See Chapter 11.

M. ×*robusta* 'Erecta'
See Chapter 11.

M. ×*robusta* 'Gary's Choice'
See Chapter 11.

M. ×*robusta* 'J. L. Pierce'
See Chapter 11.

M. ×*robusta* 'Leucocarpa'
See Chapter 11.

M. ×*robusta* No. 5
See *M.* ×*robusta* 'Arnold-Canada' in Chapter 11.

M. ×*robusta* 'Persicifolia'
See Chapter 11.

M. ×*robusta* 'Red Siberian'
See Chapter 11.

M. ×*robusta* 'Yellow Fruited'
See Chapter 11.

M. ×*robusta* 'Yellow Siberian'
See Chapter 11.

***M.* ×*robusta* 'Xanthocarpa'**
See Chapter 11.

M. rockii
See Chapter 11.

***M.* 'Rockii'**
See *M. rockii* in Chapter 11.

***M.* 'Rocky Glenn'**
Name only.

***M.* 'Rodney'** Rodney F. Kelley, Kelley and Kelley, Long Lake, MN
Parentage: An open-pollinated seedling of *M.* 'Hopa'
A vigorously growing, very hardy tree; leaves thick, glossy, green, remaining on the tree after all other trees are bare; flowers single, white; fruit dark red, persistent into midwinter. Disease free (Nichols). Loc. 12.

***M.* 'Rondo'** CDA—Ottawa 1911
Parentage: A seedling of *M.* 'Salome'
A Rosybloom. Fruit yellow-red, persistent to December. Subject to moderate scab and mild cedar-apple rust (Nichols). Loc. 31, 35, 54, 61, 81.

***M.* 'Rosedale'**
Name only.

***M.* 'Roselow'**
See *M. sargentii* 'Roselow' in Chapter 11.

***M.* 'Rosilda'** Saunders 1905
Parentage: *M.* 'Prince' (crabapple) × *M.* 'McIntosh' (apple)
A second-generation hybrid of *M. baccata*. Named in 1920. Flowers single, pink, fading to white; fruit green-yellow, large, 1.9 in (4.8 cm) in diameter. Subject to severe scab (Nichols). Loc. 11.

******M.* 'Rosseau'** Preston 1920
Parentage: A Rosybloom
Named in 1930 by Isabella Preston, CDA—Ottawa, in her Lake Series, for Rosseau Lake in Ontario, Canada. A large, upright, spreading tree to 20 ft (6 m) high; buds maroon-red, flowers purplish to rose-red with white claw, fading to pink, 1.8 in (4.5 cm) across; fruit carmine to light jasper red, 1 in (2.5 cm) in diameter. A good annual bearer. Subject to scab. Disease resistant (Nichols). One of the better Rosyblooms. Recommended, as so many of the Rosyblooms are subject to crabapple diseases. Loc. 2, 9, 15, 24, 31, 81.

*+***M.* 'Ross's Double Red'** Ross Plate 215
Parentage: *M.* 'Van Eseltine' × *M.* ×*purpurea* 'Lemoinei'
An outstanding introduction of Henry Ross, director and founder of Gardenview Horticultural Park, Strongsville, OH. A rounded to spreading tree to 12 ft (3.5 m) high and 16 ft (5 m) wide, with beautiful branches from the ground; leaves reddish, turning bronze-green; buds bright rose-carmine, opening to clusters of large, double, rose-pink flowers that come late and remain for a long period of time; fruit insignificant (as in most double-flowering crabapples), dark red-purple, 0.5 in (1.2 cm) in diameter. An annual bloomer. Very good disease resistance, except very mild leaf scab that does not harm the foliage (Nichols). Should be far better known and propagated by nurseries. Its flowers have three colors—deep rose pink, layered with medium pink, and pale pink interior petals—making a very pleasing effect as buds open and flowers fade. It is excellent as a showpiece center of any garden, despite the lack of fall fruit, and a hybridizer's special. Loc. 47.

***M.* Ross's Octoploid**
See *M.* 'Coralburst'.

***M.* 'Royal Ruby'** Simpson 1971
Plant patent No. 3052. A narrow to upright tree; flowers double, cup-shaped, dark red, about 2 in (5 cm) across; fruit small and dark red (when produced), otherwise almost sterile. Subject to moderate scab, slight powdery mildew and fire blight (Nichols). An annual bloomer, we have found it a fine crabapple when in bloom but it lacks any show of autumn fruit and it is not a heavy bloomer. Loc. 2, 5, 18, 19, 22, 26, 31, 35, 47, 54, 55, 61, 71, 79.

******M.* 'Royal Scepter'** Zampini Plates 216, 217
Parentage: A seedling of *M.* 'Madonna'
Plant patent name "Royscezam." To be introduced by Lake County Nursery, Perry, OH, as one of the Round Table Series of dwarf crabapples developed by James Zampini. An upright, columnar tree to 18 ft (5.5 m) high and 6 ft (1.8 m) wide; leaves wine-red, turning bronze green; buds deep bright red, opening to double, rose-pink and white flowers; fruit bright red, very abundant and showy. Disease resistant (per introducer). An excellent double-flowering, red-fruiting crabapple suitable for all gardens. Too new to be properly evaluated but it appears to be a clone with a future. Could well be used in any narrow space, as a street tree, or to break the monotony of straight plantings. Loc. 46.

*M. **'Royal Splendor'** Fiala 1975
Parentage: M. 'Red Swan' × M. 'Autumn Glory'
No. 85-19B. A tree to 10 ft (3 m) high and 12–14 ft (4–4.3 m) wide; leaves green, good, disease resistant; buds red-pink, opening to single, white flowers in heavy cascades, increasing in beauty with age, on blossom spurs; fruit small, 0.4–0.5 in (1–1.2 cm) in diameter, brilliant red, very showy, firm, persistent into midwinter then eaten by birds. A heavy, annual bearer. Completely disease resistant. An excellent, smaller, spreading weeper for smaller areas or as a specimen tree. Ideal for Japanese gardens. One of the finer, new weepers. Loc. 47.

*M. **'Royalty'** Kerr 1958 Plate 10
Parentage: An open-pollinated Rosybloom seedling
Sutherland No. 2. Similar to sibling M. 'Thunderchild'. A dense, moundlike, crowned tree to 15 ft (4.6 m) high and as wide; leaves dark purple; flowers single, crimson to almost purple, not showing up well against the dark purple leaves; fruit dark red, about 0.6 in (1.6 m) in diameter. Subject to severe scab and fire blight (Nichols). One of the very best trees for dark purple foliage color (far superior to the purple leaf plum). Makes a handsome color contrast when grown next to the silvery-white leafed *M. tschonoskii*. Guardedly recommended only for its rich leaf color since it is highly subject to fire blight. Loc. 4, 5, 19, 22, 24, 26, 31, 35, 37, 46, 54, 55, 58, 71, 74, 76, 77, 79, 80, 81, 82, 86, 100.
Progeny of M. 'Royalty' include M. 'Dainty' Kerr.

***M.* 'RRW'**
Name only.

***M.* 'Ruby Luster'**
Name only. Loc. 81.

***M.* 'Rudolph'** F. L. Skinner 1954
Parentage: Possibly *M. baccata* × ? Rosybloom
A Canadian Rosybloom. Flowers single, pink, to 2 in (5 cm) across; fruit 0.5 in (1.2 cm), red-purple. Subject to moderate scab and mild fire blight (Nichols). Too much disease. Loc. 12, 24, 31, 81.

*M. **'Ruth Ann'** Simpson
No. 4-28. A vase-shaped tree; leaves good; flowers showy, semidouble, deep pink, produced in great abundance; fruit small, not effective (most semidouble- and double-flowering crabapples do not have abundant fruit). Subject to very mild scab (Nichols). Outstanding in bloom. Named by Robert Simpson, Vincennes, IN, for one of the members of his office staff. Loc. 5, 61, 81.

*M. **'Ryan'** Fiala 1989
No. NR6-P3-603-89. Named to honor Ryan Murray, son of Peter and Karen Murray, Falconskeape Gardens, Medina, OH. A dwarf but spreading tree to 8 ft (2.5 m) high and as wide; buds deep purple-red, opening to single, pale-pink flowers with reverse of petals purple; fruit 0.6 in (1.4 cm) in diameter, red, persistent. A very showy annual bloomer. Disease resistant. An excellent low-growing shrub-tree for smaller gardens, foreground plantings, or as a focal point—wherever a dwarf tree is needed. New and as yet relatively unknown. Loc. 47.

***M.* 'Santa Mary Weeper'**
Name only.

***M.* 'Sapina'** N. E. Hansen
A Rosybloom hybrid of *M. baccata*.

*+M. **'Sarah'** Fiala 1990 Plate 218
Parentage: M. 'Autumn Glory' × M. 'Angel Choir'
Named to honor an outstanding plantswoman, Sarah Klehm, of South Barrington, IL. An upright to rounded tree to 15 ft (4.6 m) high and as wide; leaves dark green; buds pale rose pink, opening to semidouble and double, pure white flowers in abundant clusters; fruit orange-red, 0.4 in (1 cm) in diameter, showy, persistent. Produces a very showy annual display of both blossoms and fruit. Disease free. Too new to be completely evaluated. Excellent for any landscape use. The large, semidouble blossoms add to the mass flower effect. Loc. 47, 100.

M. sargentii
See Chapter 11.

***M. sargentii* 'Illinois'**
Name only.

***M. sargentii* 'Rosea'**
See Chapter 11.

***M. sargentii* 'Roselow'**
See Chapter 11.

***M. sargentii* 'Scanlon's Rancho Ruby'**
XP 177. Probably the same as M. 'Rosea'. Loc. 81.

***M. sargentii* 'Seedling'** Polly Hill
Similar to the species but with pink buds and pink and white flowers. No disease (Nichols). Loc. 28, 35, 38.

***M. sargentii* 'Tina'**
See Chapter 11.

***M. sargentii* 'Upright Form'**
Name only. Disease free (Nichols). Loc. 31.

M. sargentii* × *M.* ×*astracanica
Name only. Subject to mild scab (Nichols). Loc. 12, 13.

M. sargentii* × *M.* ×*atrosanguinea
Sax seedling No. 335-44. Loc. 16.

***M.* 'Saska'** Wheeler 1938
Parentage: A seedling of *M. baccata*
Fruit 1.2 in (3 cm), bright red. Disease free (Nichols). Loc. 54.

***M.* 'Saskatchewan 406'**
Name only.

*+***M.* 'Satin Cloud'** Fiala 1970
Plates 219, 220, 221
Parentage: (*M.* 'Coralburst' × a tetraploid form of *M. sieboldii*) × (a tetraploid seedling of *M.* 'Dorothea' × a tetraploid form of *M. sieboldii*)
No. T-61. Named for its appearance in bloom—as a rounded satin cloud. Introduced and patented by Klehm Nursery, South Barrington, IL. One of only three known octoploids. Developed by colchicine treatment. A very rounded (as if sheared) tree to 10 ft (3 m) high and as wide, with very fine branches; leaves very heavily textured, like leather, rich deep green during the summer, turning to brilliant shades of orange-red and purple in the autumn; leaf bud internodes very close, often 5 per inch, making it difficult for budding; abundant buds are pale, faintly pink-white, opening to large, single, pure white flowers that have a delightful cinnamon-clove fragrance (very strong on older trees), produced abundantly on spurs; fruit small, 0.4 in (1 cm) in diameter, turning from green-yellow to amber-yellow, hard, persistent. Entirely disease resistant over a period of many years (Nichols). One of the finest new crabapples. Challenges hybridizers to develop a whole new race of polyploid crabapples. Slow growing, but outstanding in bloom, fragrance, fruit, and autumn foliage. Excellent for the small home garden and for any focal point in the landscape. Loc. 47, 100.

At Falconskeape Gardens, Medina, OH, Fr. John Fiala and Peter Murray developed a series of polyploid crabapples (No. B9-90) using *M.* 'Satin Cloud' as one parent and *M.* 'Shinto Shrine' or *M.* 'Copper King' as the other. Named in 1990, the progeny include *M.* 'Satinglow', *M.* 'Satin Lace', *M.* 'Satin Rose', *M.* 'Satin Sheen', *M.* 'Satin Silver', and *M.* 'Satin Splendor'. All are small, rounded trees with heavily textured, leathery leaves; bud and blossom colors vary, although they are mostly white; and fruit colors are excellent. The trees are completely disease resistant. They are not yet completely evaluated, as they are too new to be described individually and marketed, but they should be available in a few years. Along with the polyploids already released by Falconskeape Gardens, Medina, OH, these new crabapples are the beginning of a new race of flowering crabapples. Not only are they outstanding landscaping material but they are especially intended for polyploid hybridizing in the future. Loc. 47.

*+***M.* 'Satinglow'** Fiala/P. Murray 1990
Progeny of *M.* 'Satin Cloud' (which see).

*+***M.* 'Satin Lace'** Fiala/P. Murray 1990
Progeny of *M.* 'Satin Cloud' (which see).

*+***M.* 'Satin Rose'** Fiala/P. Murray 1990
Progeny of *M.* 'Satin Cloud' (which see).

*+***M.* 'Satin Sheen'** Fiala/P. Murray 1990
Progeny of *M.* 'Satin Cloud' (which see).

*+***M.* 'Satin Silver'** Fiala/P. Murray 1990
Progeny of *M.* 'Satin Cloud' (which see).

*+***M.* 'Satin Splendor'** Fiala/P. Murray 1990
Progeny of *M.* 'Satin Cloud' (which see).

***M.* 'Scanlon's Pink Bud Sargent'**
See *M. sargentii* 'Rosea' in Chapter 11.

***M.* 'Schaefer'**
See *M.* ×*purpurea* 'Szaferi'.

M.* ×*scheideckeri
See Chapter 11.

***M.* ×*scheideckeri* 'Aspect'**
Name only. Disease free (Nichols). Loc. 54.

***M.* 'Scott No. 1'** Tyler Arboretum
Name only. Subject to very mild cedar-apple rust (Nichols). Loc. 68.

***M.* 'Scugog'** Preston 1920 Plate 222
Parentage: An open-pollinated seedling of *M. pumila* 'Niedzwetzkyana'
A Rosybloom. Named in 1930 by Isabella Preston, CDA—Ottawa, in her Lake Series, for Scugog Lake, southeastern Ontario, Canada. Buds dark purple-red, opening to single, purple-red flowers with a white claw, 1.8 in (4.5 cm) across; fruit dark crimson to oxblood red, 1.8 in (4.5 cm) in diameter. An alternate bearer. Should be phased out—too much disease, including moderate scab (Nichols). Loc. 12, 24, 26, 32, 35, 37, 61, 79, 81.

***M.* 'Seafoam'** A. den Boer 1939
Parentage: Seedling No. 1 of *M.* 'Oekonomierat Echtermeyer'
A semiweeper; flowers single, pink, to 1.8–2 in (4.5–5 cm) across; fruit yellow, 0.4 in (1 cm) in diameter. Subject to moderate-to-severe scab (Nichols). Loc. 31, 35, 54, 61.

*****M.* 'Selkirk'** CDA—Morden 1962 Plates 223, 224
Synonym: *M.* 'Morden 457'
Parentage: *M. baccata* × *M. pumila* 'Niedzwetzkyana'
A Rosybloom hybrid resembling *M.* 'Hopa' but smaller and of medium vigor. A rounded tree to 20 ft (6 m) high and 25 ft (8 m) wide; leaves glossy red-green, turning to green-bronze, very attractive; buds bright rose-colored, opening to deep purple-pink flowers; fruit one of the glossiest, brightest red fruit of any crabapple, 0.75 in (1.9 cm) in diameter, coloring early (in August), persistent into October, like 'Bing' cherries. A profuse bloomer when young. May be an alternate bloomer in some locations, but it has never been alternate for us in Ohio. Subject to slight scab, slight fire blight, and moderate powdery mildew (Nichols); disease free at Falconskeape for 50 years. Very attractive although somewhat large. An excellent crabapple, very showy in blossom and especially in its early display of brilliant, cherrylike fruit. Loc. 5, 15, 18, 20, 22, 24, 26, 31, 32, 39, 40, 44, 46, 47, 54, 55, 61, 71, 79, 80, 81, 86, 100.

*+***M.* 'Sensation'** Fiala 1976
Parentage: *M.* 'Serenade' × *M.* 'Amberina'
No. 86-301. A graceful, small, semiweeper to 12 ft (3.5 m) high and as wide; leaves dark green, disease resistant; buds carmine-red, opening to single, white flowers; fruit on spurs, 0.5 in (1.2 cm) in diameter, bright orange with red cheek, firm, very showy, persistent until December–January. A very heavy, annual bloomer and fruit bearer. Totally disease resistant. Excellent for any landscape. Loc. 47.

*****M.* 'Sentinel'** Simpson Plate 225
Synonym: *M.* 'Simpson 12-27'
A narrow, upright tree 20 ft (6 m) high and 12 ft (3.5 m) wide; leaves glossy, dark green; buds rose-colored, opening to single, pale pink to whitish flowers; fruit small 0.5 in (1.2 cm) in diameter, bright red, persistent. Excellent disease resistance, although subject to slight scab and fire blight (Nichols). Another very fine crabapple from Robert Simpson, Vincennes, IN. Should be far better known and grown. Loc. 5, 18, 24, 26, 31, 37, 46, 47, 54, 55, 61, 81, 86, 100.

***M.* 'September'** Gideon before 1888
Yellow-red apple.

*+***M.* 'Serenade'** Fiala 1968 Plates 226, 227, 228, 229
A multibrid. Introduced and patented by Klehm Nursery, South Barrington, IL. A graceful, semiweeper to 12 ft (3.5 m) high and as wide, with very fine, arching branches (heavy annual fruiting make it almost weeping with age); leaves dark green, heavily textured, disease free; buds deep pink, opening to pale, blush white, single flowers; fruit exceptionally colorful, beginning pale coral, becoming deep coral-orange with amber highlights, finally turning pale orange-gold to deep burnt orange with frosts, elliptic but rounded at base, 0.5 in (1.2 cm) wide to 0.6 in (1.5 cm) long, persistent, very showy. A heavy annual bearer. Completely disease resistant (Nichols). One of the showiest crabapples in fruit. Next to a red-fruited clone it is a work of landscaping art! Loc. 47, 100.

***M.* 'Severn'** Boughen 1906
Fruit yellow, to 1.4 in (3.5 cm). Loc. 81.

*****M.* 'Shaker Gold'** Ross 1960
Parentage: Probably a seedling of *M. baccata*
Discovered by Henry Ross, Gardenview Horticultural Park, Strongsville, OH, growing at Shaker Lake, Shaker Heights, OH. Subsequently grown and named at Falconskeape Gardens, Medina, OH. A medium-sized, rounded to spreading tree to 15 ft (4.6 m) high and 12 ft (3.5 m) wide; leaves dark green, disease free; buds carmine-pink, opening to single, white flowers; fruit 0.75 in (1.9 cm) in diameter, yellow-orange with bright orange-red cheek, very heavy and effective in fruit, persistent. Completely disease resistant (Nichols). On rare occasions, after an unusually heavy fruiting

season, it may be alternate fruiting the next year. An excellent, showy background tree for the larger garden and parks. Loc. 31, 47, 86, 100.

***M.* 'Shakespeare'** Scanlon
Similar to *M.* ×*atrosanguinea*, except grafted on high standards. The Scanlon Nursery, Olmsted Falls, OH, was wont to rename older clones when they were grafted on higher standards that changed the tree form, and this often caused considerable confusion. Loc. 100.

***M.* 'Sheila'** Fiala 1989
Parentage: *M.* 'GV-19' × *M.* 'Serenade'
No. 86-211. Named to honor Sheila Murray, daughter of Peter and Karen Murray, Falconskeape Gardens, Medina, OH. A small, upright to spreading tree 12 ft (3.5 m) high and 10 ft (3 m) wide; leaves bright green, disease free; buds rose-pink, opening to double, pink flowers; fruit red, 0.6 in (1.6 cm) in diameter, persistent. A very attractive, heavy, annual bloomer. Disease free. An outstanding, newer crabapple for smaller gardens and for all landscaping needs. One of only a few double-flowering crabapples with excellent red fruit. Loc. 47.

***M.* 'Shelley'** P. H. Wright 1978
Parentage: A Rosybloom
With deep pink flowers. Now considered obsolete.

***M.* 'Sherwood Park'** Machin 1987
Parentage: A Rosybloom
A new crabapple now under test in Canada. Flowers rose-cupped, in clusters; leaves small, dark, shiny. Loc. Devonian Botanic Garden and Canada Department of Agriculture, Morden, Canada.

***M.* 'Shields'**
Name only. Severe scab (Nichols). Loc. 54.

***M.* 'Shinto Shrine'** Fiala 1965
An induced octoploid. A rounded tree to 12 ft (3.5 m) high and as wide; leaves small, very leathery, dark green, with numerous leaf buds, 6 per inch (2.5 per cm); buds red, opening to clusters of single, white flowers; fruit small, 0.4 in (1 cm) in diameter, yellow, persistent. Subject to mild scab, but otherwise disease free. Not formally introduced; reserved as a hybridizer's crabapple. Loc. 47.

***M.* 'Shoko'** N. E. Hansen
Parentage: A seedling of *M. coronaria* 'Elk River'

***M.* 'Showboat'** Fiala/P. Murray
No. NR6-Pl-89. A small, vase-shaped to spreading tree; leaves green, good; buds rose-colored, opening to large, semidouble, pink-white flowers; fruit 0.5 in (1.2 cm) in diameter, copper-gold, showy for a semidouble flowering crabapple. An abundant, annual bloomer. Disease resistant. An excellent addition to the semidouble-flowering crabapples, and the smaller size makes it a tree for all gardens and landscape needs. Loc. 47.

M. sieboldii
See *M. sieboldii* (Rehder) Fiala and *M. sieboldii* (Regel) Rehder in Chapter 11.

***M. sieboldii* 'Calocarpa'**
See Chapter 11.

***M. sieboldii* 'Fuji'**
See *M. toringo* 'Fuji' in Chapter 11.

***M. sieboldii* No. 243**
Formerly *M.* ×*zumi* No. 243. Involved in the parentage of *M.* 'Amberina', *M.* 'Kirk', *M.* 'Leprechaun', and *M.* 'Red Peacock'.

***M. sieboldii* No. 768**
Formerly *M.* ×*zumi* No. 768. Involved in the parentage of *M.* 'Amberina', *M.* 'Egret', *M.* 'Golden Candles', *M.* 'Kirk', and *M.* 'Leprechaun'.

***M. sieboldii* 'Wooster'**
See Chapter 11.

M. sikkimensis
See Chapter 11.

***M.* 'Silver Cloud'** Fiala/P. Murray
Parentage: *M.* 'Satin Cloud' × *M.* 'Shinto Shrine'
No. NR9-P3-89. One of the Satin Series of polyploid crabapples from Falconskeape Gardens. Medina, OH (see *M.* 'Satin Cloud' above). An octoploid. A small, rounded tree to 10 ft (3 m) high; leaves green, leathery, excellent; buds pale pink-white, opening to large, single, fragrant, white flowers; fruit golden to copper, to copper-orange with frosts. An abundant, annual bloomer. Disease resistant. Very new, showy, and excellent for all landscaping needs requiring smaller trees. Loc. 47.

***M.* 'Silver Drift'** Simpson 1987
Synonyms: *M.* 'Vincennes University' (formerly)

Parentage: Unknown

Introduced by Simpson Nursery, Vincennes, IN. Resembles *M.* 'Snowdrift' except fruit is small, red, with good color into December. Disease resistant. Loc. Simpson Nursery.

***+*M.* 'Silver Moon'** Simpson 1968 Plates 27, 230, 231, 232

Parentage: Probably *M. baccata*

No. S-1. Another outstanding crabapple selected by Robert Simpson, Vincennes, IN. A strongly oval to upright tree to 20 ft (6 m) high and 15 ft (4.6 m) wide, somewhat heavily spurred; leaves green; flowers and buds pure white, single, produced on terminals after tree is in full leaf; fruit 0.5 in (1.2 cm), red, persistent. A late, but heavy, annual bloomer. Subject to moderate scab and moderate fire blight (Nichols); entirely disease free at Falconskeape. Because it blooms 10 days after all other crabapples have faded, it is an excellent addition for extending bloom time. Loc. 5, 24, 26, 31, 35, 37, 47, 54, 55, 61, 79, 80, 81, 86. Progeny of *M.* 'Silver Moon' include *M.* 'Ballerina' Fiala and *M.* 'Maysong' Fiala.

***M.* 'Silver Mound'**

Name only. Subject to very severe scab (Nichols). Loc. 61.

***M.* 'Silvia'** Saunders 1904

Parentage: *M. baccata* × *M. pumila*

Susceptible to scab and fire blight. Loc. 9, 12, 81.

***M.* 'Simcoe'** Preston 1928

Parentage: *M. baccata* × *M. pumila* 'Niedzwetzkyana'

A Rosybloom. Named in 1930 by Isabella Preston, CDA—Ottawa, in her Lake Series, for Simcoe Lake, 40 miles (60 km) north of Toronto, Ontario, Canada. Buds dark red, opening to light purple-red flowers 1.8 in (4.5 cm) across; fruit carmine and orange, 1 in (2.5 cm) in diameter. An alternate bloomer. Loc. 24.

****M.* 'Simpson 4-17'** Simpson

Renamed *M.* 'Burgandy', which see.

****M.* 'Simpson 7-62'** Simpson

Renamed *M.* 'Jewelberry', which see.

***M.* 'Simpson 12-69'** Simpson

****M.* 'Simpson 12-77'** Simpson

Renamed *M.* 'Sentinel', which see.

****M.* 'Simpson 328-AA'** Simpson

Renamed *M.* 'Red Barron', which see.

***+*M.* 'Sinai Fire'** Fiala 1974 Plate 233

Parentage: *M.* 'Red Swan' × *M.* 'Amberina'

No. 84-101. Introduced and patented by J. Frank Schmidt & Sons Nursery, Boring, OR. A weeper 15 ft (4.6 m) high and as wide, with somewhat unique, downward branching; leaves large, glossy, dark green, leathery, disease resistant; buds brilliant red, opening to large, single, white flowers that cascade in abundance; fruit colors early, bright orange-red, with a waxy sheen, 0.4–0.5 (1–1.3 cm) in diameter, attractive, persistent to November. Excellent disease rating (Nichols). A very fine weeper for the landscape. Loc. 47, 86.

***M.* 'Sinai Sunset'** Fiala 1990

Parentage: *M.* 'Amberina' × *M.* 'Aloise'

No. B-3. An upright to spreading tree to 15 ft (4.6 m) high and 12 ft (3.5 m) wide, with somewhat pendulous branching; leaves red-green, disease free; buds deep carmine, opening to single, rose-red flowers 1 in (2.5 cm) across; fruit dark red, 0.6 in (1.5 cm) in diameter. A good background tree for spring color and early autumn colored fruit. Disease free. Loc. 47.

***M.* 'Sir Galahad'** Zampini Plate 234

Plant patent name "Sirgazam." To be introduced by Lake County Nursery, Perry, OH, in the Round Table Series of dwarf crabapples developed by James Zampini. An upright to vase-shaped tree 10 ft (3 m) high and 8 ft (2.5 m) wide; leaves deep lustrous green, leathery; buds pink, opening to single, white flowers; fruit gold, turning bright red. Disease resistant. Too new to be properly evaluated. Loc. 46.

***M.* 'Sissipuk'** Preston 1920

Parentage: *M. pumila* 'Niedzwetzkyana' × *M. baccata*

One of the best red-flowered Rosyblooms, the deepest red of them all. Named in 1930 by Isabella Preston, CDA—Ottawa, in her Lake Series, for Sissipuk Lake, British Columbia, Canada. Buds deep carmine, opening to rose-red, fading to deep pink flowers 1.2 in (3 cm) across; fruit dark maroon purple to oxblood red, 1.1 in (2.7 cm) in diameter. Disease resistant (Nichols). A late bloomer. Should be used by hybridizers to capture the deep red flower color. Loc. 16, 18, 24, 26, 31, 35, 37, 81.

***M.* 'Slansky's Red Fruited'**
See *M.* ×*sieboldii* 'Wooster' in Chapter 11.

***M.* 'Slocan'**
Discarded by Isabella Preston. Subject to severe scab (Nichols). Loc. 54, 81.

***M.* 'Smith'**
Name only. Loc. 81.

***M.* 'Snead's Crab'**
Name only. Subject to mild cedar-apple rust (Nichols). Loc. 73.

*****M.* 'Snow Ballerina'** Fiala 1964 Plate 235
Synonym: *M.* 'Cascade'
Name changed from *M.* 'Cascade' to *M.* 'Snow Ballerina' to avoid conflict with *M.* 'White Cascade'. An excellent small, fountain type weeper to 10 ft (3 m) high and 15 ft (4.6 m) wide; leaves green, good; buds deep rose-pink, opening to large, single, white flowers produced in great profusion in showy cascades; fruit 0.6 in (1.5 cm) in diameter, bright red, persistent, showy for 2 months. An annual bloomer. Disease resistant, but subject to moderate nondefoliating scab. An excellent weeper that can be headed low and will not exceed 4 ft (1.2 m) high. Excellent for rock gardens, small spaces, and home gardens. Original tree at 26 years old is only 5 ft (1.5 m) high and 10 ft (3 m) wide. Loc. 31, 46, 47, 100.

***M.* 'Snowbank'** H. P. Kelsey 1934
Parentage: A seedling or hybrid of *M. floribunda*
Buds pink, opening to single, white flowers 1.2 in (3 cm) across; fruit yellow, 0.4 in (1 cm) in diameter. An alternate bearer. Subject to moderate-to-severe scab (Nichols). Loc. 13, 15, 26, 31, 32.

****M.* 'Snowcap'** CDA—Alberta 1941
Received as *M. baccata siberica* No. 3201. Flowers glistening white, single, 0.5 in (1.2 cm) across; fruit 0.25 in (0.6 cm), bright red, persistent to winter. An annual bearer. Subject to mild scab (Nichols). Very hardy and should be far better known. Loc. 5, 24, 31, 35, 61, 69, 79, 81.

***M.* 'Snowcloud'**
Should be phased out—too much disease (Nichols). Loc. 2, 5, 10, 12, 24, 26, 39, 54, 61, 79, 81.

****M.* 'Snowdrift'** Cole 1965
Plate 236, Figs. 5.3, 8.2
Parentage: A chance seedling of unknown parentage
NDBT. A rounded to oval, densely branching tree to 20 ft (6 m) high and as wide; leaves attractive, glossy green; buds pink, opening to single, white flowers; fruit orange-red 0.4 in (1 cm) in diameter. Subject to slight scab and moderate fire blight (Nichols). Outstanding in bloom. Recommended despite fire blight, which can be regional. Loc. 2, 4, 5, 12, 18, 19, 20, 22, 24, 26, 31, 37, 43, 44, 46, 54, 55, 61, 68, 69, 71, 74, 81, 83, 86, 100.

***M.* 'Snow Flake'**
Name only.

****M.* 'Snow Magic'** Les Demaline, Willow Way Nursery, Avon, OH
Plant patent No. 4815. A rounded tree to 15 ft (4.6 m) high; leaves dark green; buds pink, opening to abundant single, white flowers; fruit small, red, persistent. Slightly susceptible to scab. A good ornamental. Not as yet well known. Loc. 47, 58, 100.

***M.* 'Snyder'**
Name only.

M.* ×*soulardii
See Chapter 11.

***M.* ×*soulardii* 'Soulard'**
See Chapter 11.

***M.* 'South Dakota Ben'** N. E. Hansen
Parentage: A hybrid of *M. baccata*
Subject to severe fire blight (Nichols). Loc. 54.

***M.* 'South Dakota Bison'** N. E. Hansen
Parentage: A hybrid of *M. baccata*
Loc. 54.

***M.* 'South Dakota Bona'** N. E. Hansen
Parentage: A hybrid of *M. baccata*

***M.* 'South Dakota Eda'** N. E. Hansen
Parentage: A hybrid of *M. baccata*

***M.* 'South Dakota Jonsib'** N. E. Hansen
Parentage: A hybrid of *M. baccata*

***M.* 'South Dakota Macata'** N. E. Hansen
Parentage: *M.* 'McIntosh' (apple) × *M. baccata*

***M.* 'Sovereign'**
Name only. No disease (Nichols). Loc. 61.

***M.* 'Sparkler'** University of Minnesota Fruit Breeding Farm 1945
Parentage: An open-pollinated seedling of *M.* 'Hopa'
A Rosybloom crabapple selected in 1947. Commercial introduction 1969. A small, flat-topped tree to 12–15 ft (4–4.6 m) high, with horizontal branching; leaves broadly ovate, acuminate, serrate, 1.5–2 in (3.8–5 cm) long, reddish in spring, turning dark green thereafter; flowers single, rose-red, 2 in (5 cm) across; fruit dark red, 0.25–0.6 in (0.6–1.6 cm) in diameter. Severely subject to scab. Another of the severely disease ridden seedlings of *M.* 'Hopa'. Loc. 5, 16, 24, 26, 31, 32, 46, 54, 61, 69, 76, 77, 79.

M. spectabilis
See Chapter 11.

M. spectabilis* var. *grandiflora
See Chapter 11.

***M. spectabilis* 'Alba Plena'**
See Chapter 11.

***M. spectabilis* 'Clark's Flowering'**
Name only. Disease free (Nichols). Loc. 35.

***M. spectabilis* 'Imperialis'**
Name only. Subject to mild scab and leaf spot. Loc. 54.

***M. spectabilis* 'Plena'**
See Chapter 11.

***M. spectabilis* 'Riversii'**
See Chapter 11.

***M. spectabilis* 'Rosea Plena'**
See *M. spectabilis* 'Riversii' in Chapter 11.

***M.* 'Spinosa'**
See *M. ioensis* 'Spinosa' in Chapter 11.

***M.* 'Spongberg'**
See *M. baccata* 'Spongberg' in Chapter 11.

M.* **'Spring Beauty' Fiala 1988
Parentage: *M.* 'Red Swan' × *M.* 'My Bonnie'
No. NR3-P3. A small, graceful and charming semiweeper to 10 ft (3 m) high and 12 ft (3.5 m) wide; buds rose-pink, opening to single, pale pink flowers in great abundance; fruit 0.5 in (1.2 cm) in diameter, red, showy, persistent. Disease-free. Loc. 47.

***M.* 'Spring Glory'** CDA—Morden
No. 454. Loc. 81.

***M.* 'Spring Snow'** Porter, Inter-State Nurseries, 1967
Plant patent No. 2667. A rounded tree to 25 ft (8 m) high and 22 ft (6.5 m) wide; leaves bright green; flowers fragrant, single, white; fruit none, almost sterile. Subject to slight scab and mild fire blight (Nichols). A springtime only crabapple, but there are better white-flowering crabapples. Loc. 4, 5, 12, 24, 31, 35, 37, 46, 54, 55, 61, 69, 74, 76, 77, 79, 81, 82, 83, 84, 86.

+M.* **'Spring Song' Fiala 1979 Plate 237
Parentage: (*M.* 'My Bonnie' × *M. sieboldii*) × (*M.* 'Dorothea' × *M.* 'Winter Gold')
Introduced and patented by Klehm Nursery, South Barrington, IL. A genetically small, upright to vase-shaped tree to 10 ft (3 m) high and 7 ft (2 m) wide; leaves of good texture, medium green; buds deep pink, opening to very large, single, light pink flowers about 1.5–2 in (3.8–5 cm) across; fruit yellow-amber, about 0.5 in (1.2 cm) in diameter. A heavy, annual bloomer. Disease resistant (Nichols). A fine pink-blooming, small crabapple that fits into all landscape needs. Excellent for smaller spaces. Loc. 47, 100.

***M.* 'Springtime'** Fiala 1962
Parentage: *M. ×atrosanguinea* × *M.* 'Oekonomierat Echtermeyer'
No. BBE. A small, fountain type weeper to 8 ft (2.5 m) high and 10 ft (3 m) wide, with long, slender branches; leaves red-bronze; buds deep rose-orchid, opening to single, medium to light lavender-orchid flowers 1–1.2 in (2.5–3 cm) across, very striking; fruit dull red-purple, 0.5 in (1.2 cm) in diameter, not showy. A very heavy annual bloomer. Highly susceptible to apple scab and thus not recommended for general introduction, though it might be of some use to hybridizers for the unique orchid flower color. Loc. 47.

M.* **'Starburst' Fiala 1987
Parentage: *M.* 'Van Eseltine' × *M.* 'Maria'
No. NR3-P14. An upright to vase-shaped or fan-shaped tree to 15 ft (4.6 m) high and 10 ft (3 m) wide; leaves red-green; bud deep rose-red, opening to double, rose to pink flowers produced in abundance, very showy; fruit 0.5 in (1.2 cm) in diameter, red, persistent. Disease free. A fine tree for narrower places, for smaller gardens, as a break in the landscape, or in a garden walk. Planted next to white-flowering crabapples it is very attractive. Rather new and yet fairly unknown. Loc. 47.

***M.* 'Stark's Gold'**
Name only. Subject to severe scab (Nichols). Loc. 54, 61, 81.

*+***M.* 'Starlight'** Fiala 1980 Plate 238
No. BF-2W. A small, upright to rounded tree to 15 ft (4.6 m) high and as wide; leaves dark green, good; buds pale pink, opening to abundant clusters of large, single, white, starlike flowers with prominent yellow anther centers, very showy; fruit 0.4 in (1 cm) in diameter, red, attractive, persistent. A very heavy, annual bloomer and fruit bearer. Appears disease resistant. Suitable for any need in smaller landscapes. New and not yet well known. Loc. 47.

***M.* 'Strathmore'** W. R. Leslie, Alberta Horticulture Research Station, Brooks, Alberta, Canada, 1949
Parentage: A Rosybloom
A narrow, upright tree; leaves fine, reddish, turning scarlet in autumn; flowers dark pink; fruit 0.8 in (2 cm), purple. Should be phased out—too much disease (Nichols). Loc. 3, 12, 18, 24, 26, 31, 32, 35, 37, 69, 79, 81.

***M.* 'Strawberry Parfait'** Flemmer, Princeton Nurseries, Princeton, NJ
Plant patent No. 4632. A vase-shaped, spreading tree 18 ft (5.5 m) high and 20 ft (6 m) wide; leaves red-purple, turning green with maturity; buds red, opening to single, pink flowers in clusters; fruit yellow with red blush, 0.4 in (1 cm) in diameter. Excellent disease rating but not rated for fire blight. Not very ornamental. Loc. 81, 86.

*__*M.* 'Striped Beauty'__ H. R. Wright 1930
USDA plant identification No. 88577. Obtained from H. R. Wright, Auckland, New Zealand. Flowers single, white, 0.8–1 in (2–2.5 cm) across; fruit striped yellow and red, 1 in (2.5 cm) in diameter, showy. Disease free (Nichols). Loc. 31, 35, 61, 81.

M.* ×*sublobata
See Chapter 11.

***M.* 'Sugar Crab'** Hansen 1919
Fruit larger, yellow-green.

*__*M.* 'Sugar Tyme'__ Baron Plate 239
In the summer 1986 issue of *Malus*, Lester Nichols identified *M.* 'Sugar Tyme' as the same as 'Milton Baron No. 2', but a year later (summer 1987) he identified it as the same as 'Milton Baron No. 1'. Plant patent No. 7674, plant patent name "Sutyzam." First named for Milton Baron, a former landscape architect at Michigan State University. An upright, oval tree 18 ft (5.5 m) high and 15 ft (4.6 m) wide; leaves green; buds pale pink, opening to white, fragrant, single flowers; fruit red, 0.5 in (1.2 cm) in diameter, persistent into January. Mostly disease resistant. A good showy tree. Loc. 24, 26, 31, 46, 79, 81, 86, 100.

***M.* 'Sunburst'**
See *M.* 'Hopa'.

*__*M.* 'Sundog'__ W. R. Leslie, Canada Department of Agriculture, Morden, Manitoba, 1947
Parentage: A Rosybloom
Morden No. 453. Named after a type of rainbow that occurs on the prairie in winter—actually a colored refraction of sunlight on snow and ice that is called *parhelion* or, more popularly, *sundog*. A columnar tree; buds rose-colored, opening to single, rose-pink flowers 1.4 in (3.5 cm) across; fruit dark red, 1–1.2 in (2.5–3 cm) in diameter. An annual, persistent bearer. Subject to very mild scab, but resistant to fire blight. A fine crabapple that has certainly been overlooked. Loc. 9, 15, 24, 32, 35, 38, 54, 79, 81.

***M.* 'Sunset'** Fiala 1979
A small, upright tree to 10 ft (3 m) high and as wide; leaves reddish; buds orange-red, opening to bright red-mauve, single flowers that fade very little; fruit deep claret, 0.5 in (1.2 cm) in diameter. Very good disease resistance. Fruit too dark to make a good showing. Discarded. Loc. 47.

***M.* 'Susan'** Lied's Nursery, Sussex, WI
A vase-shaped tree; flowers single, white. Subject to slight scab (Nichols). Loc. 31, 79, 81.

***M.* 'Sutherland'** CDA—Sutherland 1955
Parentage: A Rosybloom
Leaves dark; flowers small, purple-red. Subject to mild scab (Nichols). Loc. 10, 12, 31, 32, 81.

M. sylvestris
See *M. pumila* var. *sylvestris* in Chapter 11.

***M. sylvestris* 'Plena'**
See *M. pumila* var. *sylvestris* 'Plena' in Chapter 11.

***M.* 'Sylvia'**
See *M.* 'Silvia'.

***M.* 'Szaferi'**
See *M.* ×*purpurea* 'Szaferi'.

M. 'Taliak'
See *M. baccata* 'Taliak' in Chapter 11.

M. 'Tanner' Tanner before 1931
Parentage: Probably a clone or hybrid of *M. baccata*
Flowers single, creamy-white, 1.6 in (4 cm) across; fruit 0.6 in (1.5 cm), red, persistent throughout winter, very showy. Subject to severe scab and mild fire blight (Nichols). An excellent crabapple for any landscape. Next to a pure white crabapple, the flowers are a definite creamy yellow. This crabapple also looks good next to a pink- or red-flowering crabapple. Loc. 4, 12, 18, 24, 26, 54, 61, 77, 79, 81.

M. 'Tayshnoe'
Sometimes spelled *M.* 'Tayeshnoie'. Name only.

M. 'Teatime' Fiala 1965
Parentage: A selection of *M. hupehensis*
No. 85-17. A tetraploid. An upright, vase-shaped tree; leaves deep green, good; buds pale pink, opening to single, white flowers; fruit differs from species in color, lime-chartreuse with a red cheek, firm, persistent, otherwise same as species. Excellent disease resistance (Nichols). Loc. 47.

M. 'Teobel'
Name only.

M. 'Tetragold' Fiala 1950
Parentage: *M.* 'Winter Gold' × *M. sieboldii* 'Wooster'
An induced tetraploid. An upright, spreading tree to 15 ft (4.6 m) high and 12 ft (3.5 m) wide; leaves dark green, very leathery; buds bright carmine, opening to large, single, white flowers; fruit bright gold, 0.6 in (1.5 cm) in diameter, persistent. Totally disease resistant. A hybridizer's crabapple. Discontinued in 1975. Loc. 47.

M. 'Thomas Roland' Sim 1931
Parentage: Doubtful
Introduced by William Sim Nursery, Cliftondale, MA. Buds pink, opening to very large, white flowers 2.2 in (5.5 cm) across; fruit very large, 0.8–1 in (2–2.5 cm) in diameter, red. Subject to severe scab (Nichols). Loc. 12, 35, 54.

M. 'Thoms'
See *M. coronaria* 'Thoms' in Chapter 11.

M. 'Thor'
Name only.

*+**M. 'Thumbelina'** Fiala/P. Murray
No. NR9-P1-89. An octoploid, dwarf crabapple. A slow-growing tree 6 ft (1.8 m) high and as wide; leaves red to bronze-red, small; buds deep red, opening to single, red flowers; fruit red, small, 0.5 in (1.2 cm) in diameter. A showy, annual bloomer. Disease resistant. Excellent for smaller gardens and foreground planting along a garden walk. Should be an outstanding addition for polyploid hybridizing. Very new. Loc. 47.

*__M. 'Thunderchild'__ P. H. Wright 1978
Parentage: An open-pollinated seedling of *M.* 'Sutherland'
A Rosybloom clone similar to sibling *M.* 'Royalty', except that it has short internodes which make it a denser, more compact form. Leaves dark purple-red, redder than those of *M.* 'Royalty'; flowers bright pink-red, single; fruit 0.4 in (1 cm) in diameter, dark purple-red, not showy. Moderately susceptible to scab but very resistant to fire blight—far superior in resistance than *M.* 'Royalty'. A good Rosybloom with prospects for further hybridization. Outstanding leaf color.

M. 'Timiskaming' Preston 1920 Plate 240
Parentage: A Rosybloom
Named by Isabella Preston, CDA—Ottawa, in her Lake Series, for Lake Timiskaming, in southwestern Quebec, Canada. Buds deep carmine red, opening to single, rose-red flowers fading to pink, with a white star, 1.8 in (4.5 cm) across; fruit dark purple-red, 0.9 in (2.3 cm) in diameter. An alternate bearer. Subject to moderate scab and mild fire blight (Nichols). Loc. 14, 54, 61.

*+**M. 'Tiny Tim'** Fiala 1989
Parentage: *M.* 'Leprechaun' × *M.* 'Winter Gold'
No. 89-NR4. A small, upright to slightly spreading tree to 10 ft (3 m) high and as wide; leaves dark green, disease free; buds carmine, opening to single, white flowers; fruit small, 0.25 in (0.6 cm) in diameter, very glossy, round, brilliant red flushed deep orange, outstanding in fruit color, persistent until eaten by birds. A very abundant, annual bloomer. Very disease resistant. An excellent mini-fruited hybrid for smaller home gardens, patios, or as a focal point in larger estates and parks. Begins to bloom when very young, often in nursery pots. A fine addition to the hybridizer seeking to increase mini-fruited crabapples. Loc. 47, 86.

***M.* 'Tipi'** N. E. Hansen 1922
Parentage: One of the progeny of *M. coronaria* 'Elk River'
A natural tetraploid.

***M.* 'Toba'** CDA—Morden
Parentage: A hybrid of *M. baccata*

***M.* 'Tolsteme'** N. E. Hansen
Parentage: A seedling of *M. baccata*
A seedling given to Niels E. Hansen in 1934 by Ivan Mitchurin of Russia. Introduced by South Dakota Agriculture Experiment Station, Brookings, SD, in 1943. Bears freely when only 5 ft (1.5 m) high. Buds rose-pink, opening to single, white flowers 1.4 in (3.5 cm) across; fruit large, dark red to oxblood red, orange-red on shaded side, 1.2 in (3 cm) in diameter. Disease free (Nichols). Loc. 12, 81.

***M.* 'Tomiko'** CDA—Ottawa before 1935
Parentage: *M.* 'Meach' × *M.* ×*purpurea* 'Eleyi'
A second-generation Rosybloom known for its foliage. Named by Isabella Preston, CDA—Ottawa, in her Lake Series, for Tomiko Lake in the Nipissing area of Ontario, Canada. Leaves rich purplish; buds dark maroon, opening to single, red-purple flowers 1.75 in (4.4 cm) across. A poor bloomer. Disease free (Nichols). Loc. 10, 12, 31, 81.

***M.* 'Tops-In-Bloom'**
An upright to spreading tree to 20 ft (6 m) high and 18 ft (5.5 m) wide; leaves red-green; buds deep red, opening to single, red flowers; fruit purple, medium-sized. Subject to moderate scab (Nichols). Loc. 10, 12, 13, 31, 35, 61.

***M.* 'Torch River'** P. H. Wright 1978
A Rosybloom crabapple with rich pink flowers. Now considered obsolete.

M. toringo
See Chapter 11.

M. toringo* var. *arborescens
See Chapter 11.

***M. toringo* 'Arborescens'**
See *M. toringo* var. *arborescens* in Chapter 11.

***M. toringo* 'Fuji'**
See Chapter 11.

M. toringoides
See Chapter 11.

***M. toringoides* 'Bristol'**
See Chapter 11.

***M. toringoides* 'Macrocarpa'**
See Chapter 11.

***M.* 'Toshprince'** Saunders 1905
Parentage: *M.* 'McIntosh' (apple) × *M.* 'Prince' (apple)
Flowers single, white; fruit red. Name is a combination of the first and last syllables, respectively, of the parents. Loc. 81.

***M.* 'Trail'** Saunders 1904
A very hardy tree; buds pink, opening to single, white flowers 1.6 in (4 cm) across; fruit 1.6 in (4 cm) in diameter, orange. Totally disease resistant (Nichols). Fruit too large. Loc. 16, 25, 54, 81.

***M.* 'Transcendent'**
A European apple introduced before 1844. Subject to severe fire blight. Loc. 54.

M. transitoria
See Chapter 11.

***M.* 'Tres'**
Parentage: A clone of *M. ioensis*

M. trilobata
See Chapter 11.

***M.* 'Trio'**
Name only.

M.* **'True Love' Fiala/P. Murray
No. 86-233. A fine-leafed, graceful, fountain type weeper to 8 ft (2.5 m) high and as wide; buds rose-pink, opening to single, white flowers produced in great abundance; fruit bright red, persistent until eaten by birds. An annual bloomer. Disease free. A very showy and refined tree for smaller gardens, patios, or as a specimen plant. Loc. 47.

M. tschonoskii
See Chapter 11.

***M.* 'Turesi'** Matt Tures Sons Nursery
A spreading tree to 18 ft (5.5 m) high and 15 ft (4.6 m) wide; leaves dark green; buds pink, opening to single, white flowers; fruit 0.8 in (2 cm) in diameter, yellow, rots early. Should be discarded—too much disease. Loc. 12, 18, 24, 26, 35, 37, 47, 54, 73, 79, 80, 81.

***M.* 'Turkmenorum'**
Name only. Subject to leaf spot (Nichols). Loc. 31.

*M. **'Twosome'** Fiala/P. Murray
No. 82-221. An upright to vase-shaped tree 15 ft (4.6 m) high and 8 ft (2.5 m) wide; buds deep carmine, opening to large, semidouble, white flowers with pink on reverse side of petals, attractive; fruit 0.4 in (1 cm) in diameter, bright red, showy, persistent. A very showy, annual bloomer. Disease resistant. An excellent tree for smaller gardens and limited spaces. Loc. 47.

M. 'University' Brand 1943
Parentage: A clone of *M. baccata*
One of a large group of seedlings growing near Lonsdale, MN. Fruit too large—1.8 in (4.5 cm). Subject to mild scab (Nichols). Loc. 31, 54, 81.

M. 'University of Michigan'
Name only.

M. 'Upsaliensis'
Name only. No disease (Nichols). Loc. 54.

M. 'Upton Pyne'
Name only. No disease (Nichols). Loc. 9.

M. 'Valley City'
Name only. No disease (Nichols). Loc. 24.

*M. **'Van Eseltine'** New York Experiment Station, Geneva Plate 11
Parentage: *M. ×arnoldiana × M. spectabilis*
Crossed by Glen P. Van Eseltine in 1930 and initially called *M.* 'Geneva', after the New York Agriculture Experiment Station, Geneva, NY, where the cross was first made. Named in 1942 after the originator. A very fine, narrow, vase-shaped tree to 15 ft (4.6 m) high and 10 ft (3 m) wide, slow growing; buds deep rose-red to rose-pink, opening to pink flowers fading to pale rose, 2 in (5 cm) across, very heavily double, with 13–19 pale pink and white petals; fruit rots early, yellow with brown or reddish cheeks, 0.7 in (1.8 cm) in diameter. Very showy in bloom; fruit has no ornamental value. Subject to moderate scab and fire blight (Nichols). At Falconskeape Gardens, Medina, OH, this crabapple is not affected by fire blight, although others claim their trees are severely affected by it. Recommended despite fire blight susceptibility because of its elegant form and beautiful, abundant, double flowers. An important parent in hybridizing double-flowering crabapples. Loc. 4, 9, 15, 18, 19, 20, 24, 26, 31, 35, 37, 39, 40, 41, 47, 54, 61, 68, 69, 71, 79, 80, 81.
Progeny of *M.* 'Van Eseltine' include the following:

M. 'All Saints' Fiala
M. 'Angel Choir' Fiala
M. 'Bridal Crown' Fiala
M. 'Cotton Candy' Ross
M. 'Cranberry Lace' Fiala
M. 'Egret' Fiala
M. 'Ellen Gerhart' Simpson
M. 'GV-19' Ross
M. 'Karen' Fiala
M. 'Magic Flute' Fiala/P. Murray
M. 'Prairie Maid' Simpson
M. 'Red Ruby' Cole Nursery
M. 'Ross's Double Red' Ross
M. 'Starburst' Fiala

M. 'Vanguard' L. E. Longley, University of Minnesota, 1940
Parentage: A chance seedling of *M.* 'Hopa'
No. 11AA. Introduced in 1963. A Rosybloom. Flowers single, rose-pink, 2 in (5 cm) across; fruit red, 0.8 in (2 cm) in diameter. Should be phased out—too much disease, especially very severe scab (Nichols). Loc. 12, 24, 31, 35, 40, 54, 79, 80, 81.

M. 'Van Houttei'
Of Dutch origin. Introduced but no longer carried by Notcutt, Ltd., Suffolk, England, as *M.* 'Golden Hornet' replaced it and today *M.* 'Winter Gold', which is far superior to *M.* 'Golden Hornet', has replaced it. Flowers single, white; fruit pale yellow, turning deeper yellow. Subject to mild cedar-apple rust (Nichols). Loc. 10, 12, 31, 61.

M. 'VC-4' Northwest Nursery Co., Valley City, ND
A vigorous, medium-sized tree; leaves small, narrow, with purple cast all seasons (resembling purple leaf plum), better than that of *M.* 'Red Silver'; flowers bright pink, contrasting with expanding foliage, more effective in bloom than *M.* 'Red Silver'; fruit small, maroon. Subject to mild scab (Nichols). Loc. 18, 32, 35.

M. 'VC-5'
Name only. Disease free (Nichols). Loc. 35, 37.

M. 'Veitchii'
See *M. yunnanensis* 'Veitchii' in Chapter 11.

M. 'Veitch's Scarlet'
See *M. yunnanensis* 'Veitch's Scarlet' in Chapter 11.

*M. **'Velvet Pillar'** Simpson
No. 68-67; Cole No. 71-10; plant patent No. 4758. An upright tree to 20 ft (6 m) high and 14

ft (4.3 m) wide; leaves purple; flowers single, pink; fruit sparse, reddish, 0.5 in (1.2 cm) in diameter. Fair-to-good disease resistance (Nichols). Suitable as a hedge row tree or a single specimen plant. May be trimmed to any height as a hedge. Loc. 24, 26, 31, 35, 46, 81, 86, 100.

***M.* 'Victorian'** Zampini
Plant patent name "Viczam." To be introduced by Lake County Nursery, Perry, OH. Developed by James Zampini. A small, spreading tree 12 ft (3.5 m) high and 15 ft (4.6 m) wide; leaves crisp green; buds mauve, opening to double, white flowers; fruit red. Too new to be properly evaluated but good double-flowering crabapples are always in demand. Its smaller size makes it a fine tree for landscaping. Loc. 46.

***M.* 'Vikla's Ornamental'** Vikla
Parentage: A chance seedling
Found in Vikla's Nursery, Lonsdale, MN.

***M.* 'Virginia'**
See *M.* 'Virginia Seedless'.

***M.* 'Virginia Seedless'**
Synonyms: *M.* 'Virginia', *M.* 'Virginica'
A horticultural oddity of no value. Subject to mild scab (Nichols). Loc. 54, 81.

***M.* 'Virginica'**
See *M.* 'Virginia Seedless'.

***M.* 'Voikles'**
Name only. No disease (Nichols). Loc. 46.

***M.* 'Volcano'** Fiala 1961
A medium-sized, rounded tree to 18 ft (5.5 m) high; leaves dark green; buds pink, opening to white, large, single flowers; fruit red, 0.5 in (1.2 cm) in diameter, persistent. Disease resistant; subject to mild scab (Nichols). Very heavily fruited in alternate years, but a discontinued clone because it appears to be an alternate bloomer. Loc. 47.

***M.* 'Wabiskaw'** Preston 1920
Parentage: *M. pumila* 'Niedzwetzkyana' × *M. baccata*
A Rosybloom. Named in 1930 by Isabella Preston, CDA—Ottawa. An upright tree; leaves turn red in autumn; buds deep rose-red, opening to single, purple-red flowers 1.8 in (4.5 cm) across; fruit few, carmine-red, yellow-brown to green-brown on shaded side, 1.2 in (3 cm) in diameter. An annual bearer. Should be phased out—too much disease, including very severe scab (Nichols). Branches tend to break badly in storms. Loc. 14, 18, 24, 31, 54, 61, 81.

***M.* 'Wakonda'** N. E. Hansen
Parentage: A seedling of *M. ioensis* 'Nevis'

***M.* 'Wakpala'** or ***M.* 'Walpala'** N. E. Hansen 1928
Parentage: A Rosybloom.
Buds pink, opening to single, white flowers 2.1 in (5.3 cm) across; fruit yellow and red, 2–2.4 in (5–6 cm) in diameter. An annual bearer.

***M.* 'Walters'**
See *M. baccata* 'Walters' in Chapter 11; see also *M.* 'Johnson's Walters' above.

***M.* 'Walter's Upright'**
Name only.

***M.* 'Waltztime'** Fiala/P. Murray
No. 86-234. A heavy weeper to 6 ft (1.8 m) high and 10 ft (3 m) wide; leaves large, green; buds carmine, opening to single, white flowers; fruit 0.4 in (1 cm) in diameter, orange-red, with good color and persistence until eaten by birds. A showy, annual bloomer. Disease free. A tree for any limited space. Loc. 47.

'Wamdesa' Hansen 1938
Parentage: *M. coronaria* 'Elk River' × *M.* 'Jonathan' (apple)
Sometimes spelled *M.* 'Wamdeza'. Buds pink, opening to single, white flowers 1.4 in (3.5 cm) across; fruit red, 2 in (5 cm) in diameter, keeps all year. A very interesting cross of *M. coronaria*. A hybrid of the type *M.* ×*soulardii* 'Soulard'.

***M.* 'Wanblee'**
Name only.

***M.* 'Wanda'**
Name only. Subject to very severe scab (Nichols). Loc. 79.

***M.* 'Wanew'**
Name only.

***M.* 'Waubay'** Hansen 1933
Parentage: An open-pollinated seedling of *M.* 'Grimes Golden' (apple)
Fruit red, 1.4 in (3.5 cm) in diameter.

***M.* 'Wayne Douglas'**
See *M. hupehensis* 'Wayne Douglas' in Chapter 11.

M. 'Wecota' N. E. Hansen
Parentage: A seedling of *M. ioensis* 'Nevis'

***M. 'Weeping Candied Apple'** Zampini
Synonym: *M.* 'Candied Apple'
Plant patent name "Weepcanzam"; plant patent No. 4038. Developed by James Zampini of Lake County Nursery, Perry, OH. A tree 10–15 ft (3–4.6 m) high and as wide, with horizontal to pendulous branches, irregular in form but very artistic and picturesque; leaves heavily textured, dark green with red overcast; buds deep rose-pink; flowers single, with outer side of petals deep pink and inner petal whitish edged pink—a pleasing contrast that causes the tree, when viewed from a distance, to appear pink in bloom; fruit bright cherry-red, 0.5 in (1.2 cm) in diameter, persistent to December. Subject to very slight scab but otherwise disease resistant (Nichols). An excellent semi-weeper for all landscapes. Loc. 46, 81, 86, 100.

M. 'Weiser'
See *M.* 'Weiser Park'.

M. 'Weiser Park'
Synonym: *M.* 'Weiser'
Flowers purple-red; fruit large, purple-red. Subject to very severe scab (Nichols). Loc. 5.

M. 'Wellington Bloomless'
Name only. Subject to mild-to-moderate scab (Nichols). Loc. 15, 54.

M. 'Weston No. 474'
Name only. No disease (Nichols). Loc. 54.

M. 'Wetonka' N. E. Hansen
Parentage: A seedling of *M. ioensis* 'Nevis'

***M. 'White Angel'** Inglis 1947
Synonym: *M.* 'Inglis'
Parentage: A chance seedling of unknown parentage
Introduced by Beno's Nursery in 1962. Originated at the Inglis Nursery. A compact, vase-shaped tree to 20 ft (6 m) high and as wide; leaves dark green, glossy; buds pink, opening to single, white flowers 1 in (2.6 cm) across; fruit glossy, red-scarlet, about 0.6 in (1.5 cm) in diameter. Subject to very slight scab, cedar-apple rust, and fire blight (Nichols). A good, dependable blooming and fruiting crabapple. One of the fine white-flowering crabapples. Loc. 2, 3, 5, 12, 18, 20, 24, 26, 28, 47, 54, 55, 61, 69, 79, 81, 82, 85, 86.

***M. 'White Candle'** Simpson Plate 13
No. 6-15. An upright, compact tree to 15–18 ft (4.6–5.5 m) high; leaves dense dark green; flowers semidouble, pink and white; fruit sparse (which is not uncommon with semidouble- and double-flowering crabapples). Subject to mild scab and very mild fire blight (Nichols). Recommended as there are too few semidouble- and double-flowering crabapples. Loc. 5, 10, 24, 35, 37, 46, 54, 55, 61, 71, 76, 77, 81.

*+**M. 'White Cascade'** Ross 1974
Plates 241, 242, 243, Fig. 6.4
Plant patent No. 3644. Developed by Henry Ross at Gardenview Horticultural Park, Strongsville, OH. An excellent, graceful weeper 15 ft (4.6 m) high and as wide, with fine branches; leaves green; buds pink, opening to single, white flowers; fruit green-yellow, 0.4 in (1 cm) in diameter. An abundant, annual bloomer. Excellent disease resistance; only the mildest touch of scab (Nichols). One of the finest and most graceful weepers on the market today. Ideal for small landscapes, patios, or as a focal point. A choice crabapple for landscapers and hybridizers. Loc. 5, 19, 22, 47, 79, 81, 86.

M. 'White Dawn'
Name only.

M. 'White Fox River' P. H. Wright 1954
Synonym: *M.* 'White River'
Parentage: Probably *M. baccata* × *M.* 'Hopa'
Developed at Moose Range, Saskatchewan, Canada. A Rosybloom. Buds deep carmine-rose, opening to single, purple-red flowers 1.8 in (4.5 cm) across; fruit 2.4 in (6 cm) in diameter. Very hardy to –67°F (–55°C).

M. 'White Gold'
Expanding buds deep carmine, opening to white, single flowers; fruit yellow, about 0.5 in (1.2 cm) in diameter. Moderate disease resistance (Nichols).

M. 'White River'
See *M.* 'White Fox River'.

M. 'Whitney' Whitney before 1869
A European commercial crabapple. Flowers single, pink and white, 2.2 in (5.5 cm) across; fruit yellow with red stripes, 2 in (5 cm) in diameter. Susceptible to cedar-apple rust and mild fire blight (Nichols). Loc. 12, 15.

M. 'Wickson'
An apple, not a crabapple. Subject to moderate scab (Nichols). Loc. 26, 61.

M. 'Wierdakii'
See *M.* ×*purpurea* 'Wierdakii'.

***M.* 'Wies'**

An upright tree; leaves purplish; flowers single, pink; fruit very dark red to purple, 0.5–0.6 in (1.2–1.6 cm) in diameter. "Totally resistant to all diseases but fruit color may be too dark to be attractive" (Nichols). If placed next to yellow-fruited crabapples, the fruit becomes more appealing, particularly after leaf fall. A crabapple that may have been overlooked by landscapers and hybridizers as well. Loc. 31.

***M.* 'Wijcik'** Wijcik Nursery, Kelowna, British Columbia, Canada

Not a wild apple, but a mutation discovered in 1964 by Don Fisher of the Summerland Research Station, British Columbia. Fisher found it in a commercial orchard (at Wijcik Nursery) as a single-shoot mutation emerged below the point at which a branch had been pruned near the top of a 50-year-old *M.* 'Summerland McIntosh' tree. A very narrow, upright-growing mutation of *M. pumila* 'McIntosh' with short lateral spurs and very few short branches. Because it is polelike in growth, trees can be grown a foot apart in the row, just like a row of corn.

Wijcik has planted rows of this upright form (also some upright seedlings). Stark Bros. Nursery, Louisiana, MO, has sold a tree called *M.* 'Wijcik McIntosh', which they have also renamed *M.* 'Starkspur Compact McIntosh'. When *M.* 'Wijcik McIntosh' is hybridized with other apple cultivars, the columnar growth habit is inherited by some of the offspring.

About one-half of the offspring are columnar at the East Malling Agricultural Station, England, where research scientists have hybridized it in an attempt to obtain a very upright apple tree. Four named clones of a series called the Ballerina Trees have been named and marketed: *M.* 'Bolero', *M.* 'Polka', *M.* 'Waltz', and *M.* 'Maypole'. The fruit of the first three are edible but *M.* 'Maypole' is a May-flowering ornamental crabapple. Since it is the most upright, polelike of all the *Malus* clones discovered so far, hybridizers using it may produce crabapples of considerable horticultural value that are even more upright in form. It would probably require a few generations to obtain the best polelike crabapple with small enough, abundant, colorful, and attractive fruit that would be superior to many of the excellent columnar types already being commercially grown. Serendipity produces strange results! Who would have judged that the Siberian *M. pumila* 'Niedzwetzkyana' would be the progenitor of so many excellent, red-flowering crabapples of today? Its third-generation progeny have many outstanding clones! *Malus* 'Wijcik' could be a "serendipity clone" with considerable, hidden genetic potential already being demonstrated. Roger D. Way, professor emeritus of pomology at New York State Agriculture Experiment Station, Cornell University, has researched *M.* 'Wijcik McIntosh' and provided much of the information for its description. Loc. University of Washington; New York Agriculture Experiment Station, Geneva; Stark Bros. Nursery, Louisiana, MO.

*+***M.* 'Wildfire'** Fiala 1975 Plate 244

Parentage: (*M.* 'Coral Cascade' × *M.* 'Liset') × *M.* 'Red Swan'

No. 85-455. A small, attractive semiweeper to 14 ft (4.3 m) high and as wide; leaves dark red-green, disease free; buds bright red, opening to pink, single flowers; fruit small, 0.25–0.5 in (0.6–1.2 cm) in diameter, brilliant red, firm, persistent, showy among the dark foliage. Disease resistant. Fine for any landscape or garden as well as for hybridizers. Loc. 47.

***M.* 'Wild Red'**

Parentage: A clone of *M. ×soulardii*

Subject to very mild scab and cedar-apple rust (Nichols). Loc. 32, 35, 54, 61.

***M.* 'William Anderson'** Sim 1931

Parentage: A chance seedling of unknown parentage

Originated at William Sim Nursery, Cliftondale, MA, and named for the caretaker of the Massachusetts estate of Mrs. Bayard Thayer. Buds rose red, opening to single, light pink to pink-white flowers flushed with rose, 1.4 in (3.5 cm) across; fruit 0.8 in (2 cm) in diameter, green and red. Subject to severe scab (Nichols). Loc. 10, 13, 15, 31, 61, 81.

***M.* 'William Sim'** Sim 1931

Parentage: Doubtful

Originated at William Sim Nursery, Cliftondale, MA. Buds carmine, opening to single, pale pink flowers, with back of petals flushed deeper pink, 2.2 in (5.5 cm) across; fruit carmine, yellow to green-yellow on shaded side, pointed, decorative, 1–1.2 in (2.5–3 cm) in diameter. Subject to moderate scab and mild fire blight (Nichols). A crabapple with odd-shaped fruit, slightly large yet effective. Loc. 9, 15, 31, 32, 54, 81.

***M.* 'Will's Pink Eye'**

See *M.* 'Pink Eye'.

*+***M. 'Winter Gold'*** Doorenbos before 1947 Plate 4

Parentage: *Malus ×moerlandsii*; possibly a seedling selection of *M. toringo* or a hybrid of it with *M. sieboldii*

Introduced by S. G. A. Doorenbos. A somewhat rounded, vase-shaped to oval tree 25 ft (8 m) high and 20 ft (6 m) wide; leaves green; buds carmine, opening to white, single flowers 1.25 in (3 cm) across; fruit bright lemon-yellow, about 0.4 in (1 cm) in diameter, keeping its color even after frosts, persistent until January–February. Subject to mild scab and, in some limited localities, very mild fire blight and slight powdery mildew (Nichols). One of the very best yellow-fruited crabapples. Outstanding in fruit and blossom. Lester Nichols, who found several differing clones with this name, reported: "The finest for color are the plants at Falconskeape Gardens, Medina, Ohio, the Morton Arboretum and the National Arboretum. This clone should be designated as the 'true' *M.* 'Winter Gold'." Loc. 5, 9, 15, 18, 24, 26, 31, 35, 41, 47, 79, 80, 81, 86.

Progeny of *M.* 'Winter Gold' include the following:

M. 'Autumn Treasure' Fiala
M. 'Canarybird' Fiala
M. 'Debutante' Fiala/P. Murray
M. 'Fiesta' Fiala
M. 'Fireburst' Fiala
M. 'Golden Candles' Fiala
M. 'Golden Dream' Fiala
M. 'Limelight' Fiala
M. 'Moonglow' Fiala
M. 'Naragansett' Egolf
M. 'Papal Guard' Fiala/P. Murray
M. 'Spring Song' Fiala
M. 'Tetragold' Fiala
M. 'Tiny Tim' Fiala
M. 'Woven Gold' Fiala

M. 'Winter Green' or ***M. 'Wintergreen'***
Name only.

M. 'Wisley' Royal Horticulture Gardens, Wisley 1924

A crabapple of English origin, not much grown in the United States. Flowers single, purple, 2 in (5 cm) across; fruit red. Subject to very mild scab (Nichols). If the flowers are the size claimed, these outstanding blossoms should be incorporated in hybridization programs. Loc. 31, 35.

M. 'Wiyuta' N. E. Hansen

Parentage: A seedling of *M. ioensis* 'Nevis'

One of a series selected and introduced by Niels Hansen, a skillful, observing hybridizer of excellent reputation whose introductions have been mostly overlooked. The series should be propagated and offered by some nursery. Because the series is superior to the species, it should be found in many more of the larger collections and offered for estate planting.

M. 'Wooster'
See *M. sieboldii* 'Wooster' in Chapter 11.

M. 'Wotanda' N. E. Hansen

Parentage: A seedling of *M. ioensis* 'Nevis'

****M. 'Woven Gold'*** Fiala 1975 Plate 2

Parentage: *M.* 'Winter Gold' × (*M.* 'White Cascade' × *M.* 'Peter Pan')

No. 84-2. A small semiweeper to 12 ft (3.5 m) high and as wide; leaves dark green, disease resistant; buds carmine-red, opening to single, pure white flowers; fruit small, to 0.4 in (1 cm) in diameter, on spur clusters, bright yellow-gold in showy cascades, firm, persistent. Subject to very mild scab (Nichols). More abundantly fruiting as it matures. Very attractive if placed next to a red-, purple-, or orange-fruited crabapple. Loc. 47, 86.

M. 'Wynema'

Parentage: A clone of *M. ×soulardii*

Found near Oskaloosa, IA, in 1920. A dwarf crabapple; flowers single, pink, 1.6 in (4 cm) across; fruit 2 in (5 cm) in diameter, yellow gold. A heavy bearer in alternate years. Subject to moderate scab and cedar-apple rust (Nichols). Loc. 12, 31, 37, 81.

M. 'Yaeger's Sweet'
Name only. No disease (Nichols). Loc. 54.

M. 'Yankee Doodle' Fiala/P. Murray

No. 85-7-10. An upright to fan-shaped tree to 18 ft (5.5 m) high and 10 ft (3 m) wide; buds medium rose-colored, opening to single, pale pink and white flowers borne in great profusion on fruiting spurs all along the branches; fruit 0.5 in (1.2 cm) in diameter, yellow with orange to reddish cheeks, sometimes orange-reddish. An annual bloomer. Disease resistant. Very showy in the landscape. Loc. 47.

M. 'Yellow Dwarf'
Name only.

M. 'Yellow Fruited'
See *M.* 'Burton's Yellow Fruited'.

M. 'Yellow Fruited'
See *M.* ×*robusta* 'Yellow Fruited'.

M. 'Yellow Jewel' Simpson
No. 4-53. No information available, but as an introduction of Robert Simpson, Vincennes, IN, it should be a superior crabapple. Loc. 81.

M. 'Yellow Siberian'
See *M. baccata* 'Yellow Siberian' in Chapter 11.

M. 'Yellow Siberian'
See *M.* ×*robusta* 'Yellow Siberian' in Chapter 11.

M. 'Yellow Weeper'
Name only. Subject to moderate scab (Nichols). Loc. 28.

M. 'Yephory's Chernosus'
Name only. No disease (Nichols). Loc. 35.

M. 'Young America'
An apple. Should be phased out—too much disease, especially severe scab (Nichols). Loc. 15, 81.

*+**M. 'Yuletide'** Fiala Plate 245
Parentage: *M.* 'Tiny Tim' × *M.* 'Dancing Elf'
No. HE-85. A dwarf, upright to moderately spreading tree or bush to 8 ft (2.5 m) high and 6 ft (1.8 m) wide; leaves dark green, somewhat glossy, excellent; buds carmine-red, opening to single, white flowers borne in great profusion, mildly fragrant; fruit excellent, brilliant red, 0.3–0.4 in (0.8–1 cm) in diameter, very showy, persistent. An annual bearer; blossoms very young, often on second-year growth. Disease resistant. One of the finest mini-fruited trees for very small gardens, container culture, or for the smaller landscapes of rock or Japanese gardens. Ideal for foreground plantings. A newcomer in the dwarf, mini-fruits that should gain rapid popularity with landscapers for its spring bloom, fall fruit, and small size. Loc. 47, 86, 100.

M. yunnanensis
See Chapter 11.

***M. yunnanensis* 'Veitchii'**
See Chapter 11.

***M. yunnanensis* 'Veitch's Scarlet'**
See Chapter 11.

M. 'Zapata' N. E. Hansen
An apple.

M. 'Zaza' N. E. Hansen 1933
A clone related to the Rosybloom group. Buds carmine; flowers single, red, fading to dull pink; fruit red-fleshed, 1.2 in (3 cm) in diameter.

M. 'Zelma' N. E. Hansen
Parentage: A hybrid of *M. baccata*

M. 'Zita' N. E. Hansen 1933
Similar to *M.* 'Zaza'. Related to the Rosyblooms with red flesh. Buds carmine, single; flowers red, fading to dull mauve, 1.8 in (4.5 cm) across; fruit red, 1.6 in (4 cm) in diameter.

*__M. 'Zumarang'__
An upright, broadly pyramidal to rounded tree; leaves glossy green; flowers white; fruit red, 0.4 in (1 cm) in diameter. Good disease resistance; somewhat subject to fire blight but not enough to not recommend it.

M. ×*zumi*
See *M. sieboldii* in Chapter 11.

M. ×*zumi* 'Calocarpa'
See *M. sieboldii* 'Calocarpa' in Chapter 11.

M. ×*zumi* 'Wooster'
See *M. sieboldii* 'Wooster' in Chapter 11.

Appendices

APPENDIX 1

List of the Best Flowering Crabapples

With the hundreds of crabapples available today, it would be difficult to choose the very best for any given location. Performance, disease resistance, and reliability of bloom and fruiting vary to some degree from place to place across the land. Some crabapples are best for landscaping needs, others for close viewing, color, fragrance, or another desired trait. The lists could be very extensive, yet when one has spent a lifetime with flowering crabapples, some varieties stand out above all the rest. Not many—perhaps only three dozen—are "nearly perfect" crabapples. While they differ considerably from one another, the instant response these crabapples elicit from viewers is almost always, "This one is magnificent!"

My list of best crabapples is further divided into two categories: the best all-around crabapples for planting and the best crabapples for future hybridizing research. I shall give you both my lists. You are certain to have your own, which you will defend, even more than I. In the beginning I admit that I am extremely prejudiced in favor of many of my own introductions. Having nurtured them from generation to generation, I know them better than any others. But that is the nature of all hybridizers: we would not introduce anything unless we truly felt it was better or was some great improvement over what already exists. Bulldog-like, we defend our own to the very last.

Each person has his or her certain favorites based on fragrance, flower color, single or double blossoms, fruit color, or tree form. Here are some astonishing crabapples that will steal your heart. They already have enslaved mine many, many years ago.

THE BEST ALL-AROUND CRABAPPLES FOR LARGE OR SMALL GARDENS

The Best Botanical Species

M. ×*atrosanguinea*—excellent form, buds, and blossoms
M. baccata 'Alexander'—very heavy bloomer, excellent in fruit
M. baccata 'Halward'—excellent all around, smaller red fruit
M. baccata 'Jackii'—outstanding white bloom and red fruit

M. coronaria var. *dasycalyx* 'Charlottae'—fragrant beauty, with fire blight
M. coronaria 'Coralglow'—unique flower color, late bloom
M. floribunda—excellent bloom time
M. halliana 'Parkmanii'—pink double blossoms, rarely fruits
M. ioensis 'Klehm's Improved Bechtel'—double blossoms
M. ioensis 'Prairie Rose'—fragrance and rosebuds
M. ioensis 'Prince Georges'—double pink, fragrant
M. 'Liset'—top-of-the-list orange-red flowering
M. 'Orange Crush'—outstanding, new orange-red flowers
M. ×*purpurea* 'Lemoinei'—outstanding bright red blossoms
M. 'Red Splendor'—excellent bloom, Rosybloom
M. ×*scheideckeri*—double loveliness
M. 'Selkirk'—early red "cherry" fruit, Rosybloom
M. sieboldii 'Calocarpa'—one of the finest
M. sieboldii 'Wooster'—excellent, early coloring
M. spectabilis—excellent
M. spectabilis 'Riversii'—very fine
M. 'Van Eseltine'—shades of pink doubleness

The Best Named Introductions

M. 'Adams'—clear red bloom
M. 'Adirondack'—upright to rounded tree, excellent in bloom
M. 'Amberina'—small rounded tree, fantastic fruit, leaf color
M. 'Anne E'—good, refined weeper, excellent smaller fruit
M. 'Autumn Glory'—small rounded tree, outstanding red mini-fruit
M. 'Ballerina'—upright to columnar, cupped blossoms
M. 'Baskatong'—a fine Rosybloom, good disease resistance
M. 'Blanche Ames'—semidouble, pink-white, excellent in bloom
M. 'Brandywine'—little pink roses, very fragrant
M. 'Burgandy'—upright to vase-shaped, red-flowering, fragrant, early
M. 'Callaway'—single, white flowering, a southern crabapple
M. 'Cardinal's Robe'—rounded tree, deep pink flowers, fine winter bark
M. 'Carnival'—small, rounded tree, wonderful, tri-colored fruit
M. 'Centurion'—upright, columnar, heavy bloomer
M. 'Christmas Holly'—small, rounded tree, wonderful fruit and bloom
M. 'Copper King'—new polyploid, gold-copper fruit, very showy
M. 'Coralburst'—excellent octoploid, a crab for any place
M. 'Coral Cascade'—unique colored fruit, semiweeper, outstanding
M. 'Cotton Candy'—masses of double, pale pink blossoms
M. 'Cranberry Lace'—semidouble, pink-red flowering, upright
M. 'Doubloons'—double, white flowers, gold fruit, small tree
M. 'Elfin Magic'—fantastic orange-red mini-fruit
M. 'Eline'—pale pink, semidouble blossoms
M. 'Fiesta'—small, semiweeper, multi-colored fruit, excellent
M. 'GV-19'—double, pink blossoms
M. 'Golden Candles'—upright, yellow fruit
M. 'Golden Dream'—small, rounded tree, gold fruit
M. 'Golden Galaxy'—small tree, heavy white spring bloom, golden autumn fruit

M. 'Gypsy Dancer'—semi to full weeper, tri-colored fruit
M. 'Henry Ross'—elegant smaller, refined weeper with yellow fruit, very showy
M. 'Hillier'—mounds of pink blossoms, yellow-orange fruit
M. 'Indian Magic'—wonderful fruit and autumn leaf color
M. 'Jewelberry'—elegance supreme in fruit, dwarf bushlike
M. 'Karen'—new double with orchid tones, small, upright tree
M. 'Lemoinei'—red-flowering excellence once tree reaches blooming age
M. 'Lenore'—sheer pink elegance, single blossoms, heavy bloomer
M. 'Leprechaun'—small tree, red mini-fruit
M. 'Liset'—a wonder of orange-red bloom
M. 'Louisa'—excellent pink weeper
M. 'Luwick'—pale pink fountain weeper
M. 'Madonna'—perfection in double, white blossoms
M. 'Maria'—small semiweeper, fantastic red-copper leaves
M. 'Michael'—oval form, brilliant fruit
M. 'Molten Lava'—fantastic in cascading orange-red fruit
M. 'Naragansett'—upright excellence
M. 'Peter Murray'—polyploid excellence
M. 'Prairie Rose'—pink rosebuds, fragrant, very late to bloom
M. 'Prairifire'—excellent fall fruit
M. 'Purple Prince'—abundant, purple fruit, dark rose blossoms
M. 'Redbird'—outstanding orange-red fruit
M. 'Red Jade'—classic red-fruited weeper, fire blights
M. 'Red Jewel'—upright form, brilliant red fruit
M. 'Red Peacock'—semiweeping, fire-red fruit
M. 'Red Swan'—finest red-fruited, delicate weeper, magnificent
M. 'Ross's Double Red'—flowering elegance
M. 'Royalty'—deepest purple foliage
M. 'Sarah'—excellent semidouble, white flowers, showy in fruit
M. 'Satin Cloud'—rounded, clipped, octoploid, sheer elegance
M. 'Selkirk'—early red fruited
M. 'Serenade'—orange-fruited semiweeper
M. 'Silver Moon'—late white flowering, upright form
M. 'Sinai Fire'—red-fruited weeper
M. 'Snowdrift'—rounded form, white abundance
M. 'Spring Song'—small tree, with large, showy, pink blossoms
M. 'Tiny Tim'—delightful mini-fruited
M. 'Van Eseltine'—shades of pinks, double
M. 'White Cascade'—one of the finest weepers, truly outstanding
M. 'Winter Gold'—one of the finest bright yellow fruited

There are several other crabapples that could have, and perhaps should have, been added to the above list. But the list is a starting point for anyone who is looking for a certain trait—whether tree form, color, or something else.

Is it mere coincidence? I would recommend this same list to those seeking to hybridize yet even better crabapples—with but a few additions.

THE BEST CRABAPPLES FOR HYBRIDIZING IN THE FUTURE

Weepers and Semiweepers

M. 'Anne E'
M. 'Blanche Ames'
M. 'Color Parade'
M. 'Coral Cascade'
M. 'Dancing Elf'
M. 'Fiesta'
M. 'Goldilocks'
M. 'Henry Ross'
M. 'Little Troll'
M. 'Louisa'
M. 'Luwick'
M. 'Maria'
M. 'Mollie Ann'
M. 'Molten Lava'
M. 'Pink Cascade'
M. 'Red Peacock'
M. 'Red Swan' (formerly *M.* 'Red Snow')
M. 'Serenade'
M. 'Showboat'
M. 'Sinai Fire'
M. 'Spring Beauty'
M. 'True Love'
M. 'White Cascade'
M. 'Wildfire'
M. 'Woven Gold'

Rounded or Spreading Form

M. 'Amberina'
M. 'Autumn Glory'
M. 'Birdland'
M. 'Christmas Holly'
M. 'Copper King'
M. 'Elfin Magic'
M. 'Fire Mountain'
M. 'Francis'
M. 'Golden Galaxy'
M. 'Indian Magic'
M. 'Indian Summer'
M. 'Jewelberry'
M. 'Lemoinei'
M. 'Liset'
M. 'Morning Sun'
M. 'Orange Crush'
M. 'Peter Murray'
M. 'Pink Giant'
M. 'Prairifire'
M. 'Profusion'
M. 'Purple Prince'
M. 'Redbird'
M. 'Ryan'
M. 'Satin Cloud'
M. 'Selkirk'
M. 'Shaker Gold'
M. 'Silver Moon'
M. 'Snowcap'
M. 'Snowdrift'
M. 'Spring Song'
M. 'Starlight'
M. 'Sugar Tyme'
M. 'Winter Gold'

Upright to Columnar Form

M. 'Adirondack'
M. 'Arch McKean'
M. 'Ballerina'
M. 'Burgandy'
M. 'Centurion'
M. 'Cranberry Lace'
M. 'Lenore'
M. 'Madonna'
M. 'Maysong'
M. 'Park Center'
M. 'Red Jewel'
M. 'Robert Clark'
M. 'Royal Scepter'
M. 'Sentinel'
M. 'Sheila'
M. 'Sundog'
M. tschonoskii
M. 'Velvet Pillar'

Semidouble and Double Flowers

M. 'Brandywine'
M. 'Bridal Crown'
M. 'Cameron'
M. coronaria 'Nieuwland'

M. 'Cotton Candy'
M. 'Cranberry Lace'
M. 'Doubloons'
M. 'Eline'
M. halliana 'Parkmanii'
M. ioensis 'Klehm's Improved Bechtel'
M. ioensis 'Nova'
M. ioensis 'Prairie Rose'
M. ioensis 'Prince Georges'
M. 'Karen'
M. 'Kelsey'
M. 'Madonna'
M. 'Magic Mirror'
M. 'Margaret'
M. 'Maria'
M. 'Ross's Double Red'
M. 'Ruth Ann'
M. 'Sarah'
M. 'Showboat'
M. 'Starburst'
M. toringo 'Fuji'
M. 'Van Eseltine'
M. 'White Candle'

New Polyploids—Tetraploids and Octoploids

M. 'Ann Marie'
M. 'Copper King'
M. 'Coralburst'
M. 'Fountain'
M. 'Kola'
M. 'Mollie Ann'
M. 'Peter Murray'
M. 'Satin Cloud'
M. 'Satin Lace'
M. 'Silver Cloud'
M. 'Thumbelina'
M. 'Tipi'

Dwarf or Shrublike Crabapples

M. 'Camelot'
M. 'Cinderella'
M. 'Excalibur'
M. 'Jewelberry'
M. 'Kibele'
M. 'Naragansett'
M. 'Pygmy'
M. 'Ryan'
M. 'Thumbelina'
M. 'Tiny Tim'
M. 'Yuletide'

Crabapples with Unusual Foliage

M. 'Joy'—lavender dappled silver-gray
M. 'Maria'—very rich, leathery red-burgundy on new foliage, slightly bronzed by late summer
M. 'Royalty'—rich royal, deep purple
M. 'Satin Cloud'—deep green, very leathery foliage, turning brilliant gold, orange, red, and deep purple in autumn
M. tschonoskii—pale gray-green with silvery pubescent underside
M. 'Velvet Pillar'—deep purple

MY FAVORITE TWO DOZEN CRABAPPLES

Many of the newer crabapples would have to be included here, but I cannot list them all.

M. 'Amberina'
M. 'Arch McKean'
M. 'Blanche Ames'
M. 'Christmas Holly'
M. 'Copper King'
M. 'Coral Cascade'
M. 'Doubloons'
M. 'Eline'
M. 'Indian Magic'
M. 'Karen'
M. 'Liset'
M. 'Molten Lava'
M. 'Orange Crush'
M. 'Prairie Rose'
M. 'Red Swan'
M. 'Ross's Double Red'
M. 'Sarah'
M. 'Satin Cloud'
M. 'Serenade'
M. 'Showboat'
M. sieboldii 'Calocarpa'
M. 'Spring Boat'
M. 'White Cascade'
M. 'Winter Gold'

APPENDIX 2

Nurseries and Notables Active in Crabapple Research and Development

---

NURSERIES

Ameri-Hort Research, Inc., Medina, OH 44256
Arborville Farm Nursery, Larry Rawton, Holt, MO 55369
Bald Eagle Nursery, Garry Kopf, Fulton, IL 61252
Billings Nursery, Robert Marble, Billings, MT 59101
Biringer Nursery, Josef Biringer, Marysville, WA 98270
Bonners Ferry Nursery, E. P. Copp, Bonners Ferry, ID 83805
Boyer Nursery, Martha Lower, Biglerville, PA 17307
Brotzman's Nursery, Timothy Brotzman, Madison, OH 44057
Carlton Plants, David Cox, Dayton, OR 97114
Carroll Nurseries, David Carroll, Cochranton, PA 16314
Chagrin Valley Nursery, Victor Mastrangelo, Gates Mills, OH 44040
Clayton Nursery Co., William Clayton, Nampa, ID 83653
Colombine Nursery, Charles H. Grant, Littleton, CO 80123
The Cottage Gardens, Ted Meyer, Lansing, MI 48910
Crow-Hassan Nursery, Thomas Hoverson, Rogers, MN 55374
Deeter Nursery, Dave Deeter, Clayton, OH 45315
Dixie View Nursery, Jerome Biedenharn, Florence, KY 41042
Downham Nursery, Frank Kearney, Strathroy, Ontario, Canada
Eastside Nursery, Richard Wilson, Groveport, OH 43125
Eder Nursery, Kathy Eder, Fransville, WI 53126
Egyptian Nursery, Terry Vogel, Farina, IL 62838
Fermite Nursery, Aurora, OR 97002
Flint Farm Nursery, Larry Flint, Burghill, OH 44404
Four Seasons Landscaping, George Brenn, Chesterton, IN 46304
Gooding's Nursery, Richard Gooding, Sherrodsville, OH 44675

Goodyear Nursery, Alfred Goodyear, Morton, IL 61550
Green Thumbers, Frank Paaske, Davenport, IA 52803
Halka Nursery, Chester Halka, Englishtown, NJ 07726
Hansen Nursery, Richard Hansen, Sassamanville, PA 19472
Hawks Nursery, John Orton, Wauwatosa, WI 53226
Hidden Lake Gardens, Thomas Wolf, Tipton, MI 49287
Hillenmeyer Nursery, Chris Hillenmeyer, Lexington KY 40511
Hillerman Nursery, Bernard Hillerman, Washington, MO 63090
Hollyhedge Nursery, Thomas Palver, Farmington, NJ 07727
Holly Hollow Nursery, Donald Wilcenski, Peconic, NY 11958
Holmlund Nursery, John Holmlund, Gresham, OR 97030
Johnson's Nursery, Wayne Johnson, Menomonee Falls, WI 53051
Judkins & Son Nursery, Ben Davis, Smithville, TN 37166
Kankakee Nursery, Robert Worth, Aroma Park, IL 60910
King Nursery, James King, Montgomery, IL 60538
Klehm Nursery, Roy C. Klehm, S. Barrington, IL 60010
Kluck Nursery, James Kluck, Rogers, NE 68659
Kridler Gardens, Barrie Kridler, Mt. Pleasant, TX 75455
Lafayette Home Nursery, Roger Ingels, Lafayette, IL 61449
Law's Nursery, Tim Power, Hastings, MN 55033
Tom Lett Nursery, Thomas Lett, Cape Girardeau, MO 63701
Lincoln Nurseries, Grand Rapids, MI 49504
London Grove Nursery, J. P. Kauffman, Avondale, PA 19311
Manbeck Nursery, Alfred Manbeck, New Knoxville, OH 45871
A McGill & Son, A. McGill, Fairview, OR 97024
McGinty Bros., Pat McEntree, Long Grove, IL 60047
McKay Nursery Co., Bernard Fourrier, Waterloo, WI 53594
McLaren Nursery, John McLaren, Shenandoah, IA 51601
Millane Nursery, Michael Millane, Cromwell CT 06416
Moller's Nursery, Gary Moller, Gresham, OR 97030
Moon Nursery, John Punsell, Yardley, PA 19067
Mosquito Creek Nursery, Mark Damery, Blue Mound, IL 62513
Nappe & Son Nursery, Curtis Nappe, Boring, OR 97009
North Hills Nursery, Robert Danik, Jr., Valencia, PA 16059
Onarga Nursery, Shane Cultra, Onarga IL 60955
Paul Tree Farm, Thomas Paul, Ludington, MI 49431
Plesant Cove Nursery, John Collier, Jr., Rock Island, TN 38581
Princeton Nurseries, William Flemmer III, Allentown, NJ 08540
Quail Creek Landscaping, Iowa City, IA 52240
Ridge Road Nursery, E. W. Coffman, Bellevue, IA 52031
Roaring Brook Nursery, Dorothy Glazier, Monmouth, ME 04259
Scarff's Nursery, New Carlisle, OH 45344
Schichtel's Nursery, Ronald Walkowiak, Orchard Park, NY 14127
J. Frank Schmidt & Son Nursery, J. Frank Schmidt, Jr., Boring, OR 97009
Scioto Nursery, James Wolford, Circleville OH 43112
Seely Nursery, Richard Seely, Red Creek, NY 13143
Shadow Nursery, Don Shadow, Winchester, TN 37398
Shady Park Nursery, Dean Miller, Columbia City, IN 46725
Sheridan Nurseries, Oakville, Ontario, Canada L6J 4Z2

Simpson Nursery, Robert Simpson, Vincennes, IN 47591
Speer & Sons Nursery, Patrick Speer, Hillsboro, OR 97123
Stark Bro. Nursery, Joseph Preczewski, Louisiana, MO 63353
Stonegate Nursery, George and Sue Schuman, Poplar Grove, IL 61065
Sunleaf Nursery, Robert Lyons, Madison, OH 44057
Sunny Fields Nursery, Bill Horman, Detroit, MI 48215
Sylvan Green Nursery, David Nelson, Downers Grove, IL 60525
Thornapple Nursery, Ralph Little, Geneva, IL 60134
Trees for Everyone, Gloria Bilotta, Salamaca, NY 14779
Valley Pines Nursery, Warren Molko, Gering, NE 69341
Wade & Gatton Nursery, Brian Wade, Bellville, OH 44813
Weston Nursery, Mrs. Edmund Mezitt, Hipkinton, MA 01748
Williamdale Nursery, Duane Hombs, Columbia, MO 65203
Willoway Nursery, Inc., Lester Demaline, Avon, OH 44011
Wilson Nursery, Roger Fick, Hampshire, IL 60140

NOTABLES

Bickelhaupt, M/M Robert, Bickelhaupt Arboretum, Clinton, IA 52732
Bristol, Peter, Holden Arboretum, Mentor, OH 44060
Brooklyn Botanic Gardens, Brooklyn, NY 11225
Bubelis, Walter, Horticulture Department, Edmonds Community College, Lynwood, WA 98036
Carpenter, Edwin, University of Connecticut, Storrs, CT 062525
Chadwick, L. C., Columbus, OH 43214
Clark, Professor Robert B., Birchwood Gardens, Meredith, NH 03253
Cochran, Kenneth, Secrest Arboretum, OARDC, Wooster, OH 44691
Collins, William, Columbus, OH 43213
Cook, Alan, Dawes Arboretum, Newark, OH 43055
Cummins, James N., New York State Agriculture Experiment Station, Geneva, NY 14456
den Boer, John, Killen, AL 35645
Egolf, Donald, National Arboretum, Washington, DC; and Marlboro, MD 20772
Flemmer, William, Princeton Nurseries, Allentown, NJ 08540
Flint, Harrison, Department of Horticulture, Purdue University, W. Lafayette, IN 47901
Foote, Ronald, Michigan State University, East Lansing, MI 48824
Gleason, Mark, Iowa State University, Ames, IA 50011
Green, James, Department of Horticulture, Oregon State University, Corvallis, OR 97331
Green, Thomas L., Morton Arboretum, Lisle, IL 60532
Hartman, Ronald, Department of Plant Pathology, University of Kentucky, Lexington, KY 40546
Hasselkus, Edward, University of Wisconsin, Madison, WI 53706
Herold, Glenn, Central College, Creve Coeur, IL 61611
Hill, Joseph, Clinton, IA 52732
Hill, Mrs. Julian, Wilmington, DE 19805
Holloway, Patricia, University of Alaska, Fairbanks, AK 99775
Huckins, Charles, Mt. Vernon, VA 22121
Hyland, Robert, Longwood Gardens, Kennett Square, PA 19348
Jardin Botanique, Montreal, Quebec, Canada PQ H1X 2B2

Kinen, Norbert, J. Frank Schmidt & Son, Boring, OR 97009
Klehm, Roy, Klehm Nursery, S. Barrington, IL 60010
Klett, James, Colorado State University, Ft. Collins, CO 80523
Liles, W. B., Monroe, LA 71201
Lyons, Robert, Sunleaf Nursery, Madison, OH 44057
Martens, John, Naperville, IL 60540
McCoy, Miles, Oregon Association of Nurserymen, Milwaukie, OR 97222
Meyers, Elmer, University of Michigan, Ann Arbor, MI 48105
Mower, Robert, Cornell University, Ithaca, NY 14853
Murray, Karen, Ameri-Hort Research, Inc.; and Falconskeape Gardens, Medina, OH 44256
Murray, Peter, Superintendent, Falconskeape Gardens, Medina, OH 44256
Nebraska Statewide Arboretum, University of Nebraska, Lincoln, NE 68583
Paine, C. W. Eliot, Holden Arboretum, Mentor, OH 44060
Pair, John, Kansas State University, Wichita, KS 67233
Radler, William, Boerner Botanic Garden, Hales Corner, WI 53130
Robinson, Helen, Hyde Hall, Rettendon, Clemsford, Essex, England CM3 5ET
Ross, Henry, Gardenview Horticultural Park, Strongsville, OH 44136
Sabuco, John, Plantsmen's Publication, Flossmoor, IL 60422
Schmidt, J. Frank, J. Frank Schmidt & Son, Boring, OR 97009
Scott, Michael, Portland, OR
Simpson, Robert C., Simpson Nursery, Vincennes, IN 47591
Smith, Elton, Ohio State University, Worthington, OH 43085
Stover, Bryan, University of Arkansas, Fayetteville, AR 72701
Suk, Carl, Tyler Arboretum, Lima, PA 19037
Thomas, Leonard, Spring Grove Cemetery, Cincinnati, OH 45232
Tobitt, Kenneth, Fruit Breeding Department, East Malling, Research Station, Maidstone, Kent, England ME19 6BJ
University of Alberta, Department of Horticulture, Edmonton, Alberta, Canada T6G 2M7
Warren, Keith, J. Frank Schmidt & Son, Boring, OR 97009
Way, Roger, New York Experiment Station, Geneva, NY 14456
Yanny, Michael & Lori, Milwaukee, WI 53225
Zuk, Judy, Swarthmore College, Swarthmore, PA 19081

APPENDIX 3

Landscape Architects Specializing in Flowering Crabapples

Aube, Donald, Aube Landscape, Inc., Bloomfield Hills, MI 48013
Brewster, Robert, Hidden Lane Landscaping, Oakton, VA 22124
Calvia, D. & K., Earthworks, River Falls, WI 54022
Danik, Robert, North Hills Landscape, Valencia, PA 16059
Dimenn, Alan A., Lincoln Landscaping, Harvard, IL 60033
Finger, Mark, Landscape Architect, Hickory Hills, IL 60457
Fullmer, L., Landscaping Inc., Dayton, OH 45427
Gilmore, Gary, Gilmore Design Land., Cortland, OH 44410
Hill, Pat, Hill Landscape Designs, Elgin, IL 60120
Hoy, George, Hoy Landscaping, Northbrook, IL 60062
Hund, Walter, Classic Landscape Ltd., Addison, IL 60101
Lingren, Mark, Band Landscape, St. Charles, IL 60174
Melka, James, Melka Landscaping, Orland Park, IL 60462
Migdal, Fern, Garden Consultants, Highland Park, IL 60035
Miller, Ken, Horticulture Consultants, St. Louis, MO 63122
Morby, Karen, Classic Landscaping, Evanston, IL 60202
Palmer, Barbara, Landscape Designs, Chicago, IL 60625
Paxton, William, Earthforms Landscape Design, Greensburg, PA 15601
Roalstad, Ronald, Midwest Landscape, Maple Grove MN 55369
Sabuco, John, Good Earth Publication, Flossmoor, IL 60422
Scheibe, Marshall, Scheibe Landscape, Brookfield, WI 53005
Somalski, Richard, Bay Landscaping, Essexville, MI 48732
Strider, John, Landscape & Design, Brighton, CO 80601
Van Scoy, Douglas, Landscape, Loves Park, IL 61132
Wilbrant, Douglas, CBO Landscaping, Crystal Lake, IL 60014

APPENDIX 4

Hybridizers, Introducers, and Originators of Crabapple Progeny

As many of the leading introducers, originators, or hybridizers of crabapples are long deceased, the place of their work is listed rather than a home address. For living contemporaries, a residence is listed, if known.

Adams Nursery, Westfield, MA
Aldenham House Gardens, Elstree, Hertfordshire, England
Andrews, Charles, Marengo, IL
Arrowwood, James, Navis Trail Breeding Station, Park Rapids, MN
Baird, W. P., U.S. Northern Great Plains Field Station, Mandan, ND
Barbier Nursery, Orleans, France
Baron, Professor Milton, Michigan State University, Lansing, MI
Bay State Nurseries, Farmingham, MA
Bechtel, E. A., Staunton, IL
Bergeson (Berguson) Nursery, Fertile, MN
Boughen Nursery, Valley River, Manitoba, Canada
Boyce Thompson Arboretum, Yonkers, NY
Brand, A. M., Brand Peony Farm, Faribault, MN
Brandon Experiment Farm, Manitoba, Canada
Brier, B. B., Baraboo, WI
Brooklyn Botanic Garden and Arboretum, Brooklyn, NY
Buckman, Benjamin, IL
Canada Department of Agriculture, Beaverlodge, Alberta
Canada Department of Agriculture, Morden, Manitoba
Canada Department of Agriculture, Ottawa, Ontario
Canada Department of Agriculture, Rosthern, Saskatchewan
Canada Department of Agriculture, Scott, Saskatchewan
Canada Department of Agriculture, Sutherland, Saskatchewan

Cheal, J., & Sons, Ltd., Crawley, Sussex, England
Clarke, Walter Bosworth, San Jose, CA
Cleghorn, Robert, Montreal, Quebec, Canada
Copeman, T. N. S., Roydon Hall, Diss. Norfolk, England
Currelly, C. T., Royal Ontario Museum, Ontario, Canada
den Boer, Arie, Des Moines Water Works, Des Moines, IA
De Wilde, Roland, Shiloh, NJ
De Wolf, Charlotte, Waukegan, IL
Dieck, George, Zoeschen, Germany
Doorenbos, S. G. A., Department of Parks, The Hague, Netherlands
Dunbar, John, Monroe County Parks System, Rochester, NY
Egolf, Donald, U.S. National Arboretum, Washington, DC, and Upper Marlboro, MD
Eley, Charles, East Bergholt, Suffolk, England
Ellwanger & Barry, Rochester, NY
Etter, Albert, Ettersburg, CA
Fenicchia, Richard, Monroe County Parks Department, Rochester, NY
Ferrill's Nursery, Salem, OR
Fiala, Fr. John Lee, Falconskeape Gardens, Medina OH
Fothergill, John, Carr End, Yorkshire, England
Gideon, Peter M., Excelsior, MN
Hampton, William C., Hardin County, OH
Hansen, Carl A., Hansen Nurseries, Brookings, SD
Hansen, Niels E., Agricultural Experiment Station, Brookings, SD
Harbison, T. G., Asheville, NC
Heard, Clyde, 4727 Beaver Ave., Des Moines, IA
Henkel, Heinrich H., Germany
Hill, Polly, Martha's Vineyard, MA
Iowa State College, Ames, IA
Jack, J. G., Arnold Arboretum, Jamaica Plain, MA
Jennings Nursery, Shipston-on-Stour, S. Warwick, England
Kelsey-Highlands Nursery, East Boxford, MA
Kerr, W. L., Forestry Farm Park, Sutherland, Saskatoon, Saskatchewan, Canada
Klehm, Roy and Sarah, Charles Klehm & Sons Nursery, South Barrington, IL
Knight, Thomas A., Elton, Hertfordshire, England
Kornik Arboretum, Kornik, Poland
Laxton Brothers, Bedford, England
Lemoine, Emil, Victor Lemoine & Fils, Nancy, France
Lemoine, Victor, Victor Lemoine & Fils, Nancy, France
Leslie, W. R., Canada Department of Agriculture, Morden, Manitoba
Lyman, H. M., Excelsior, MN
Machin, Thomas, Devonian Botanic Garden, Sherwood Park, Alberta, Canada
Macoun, W. T., Canada Department of Agriculture, Ottawa, Ontario
Mathews, B. A., Knoxville, KY
Minnesota, University of, State Fruit Farm, Excelsior, MN
Montreal Botanic Gardens, Sherbrooke St. East, Montreal, Quebec, Canada
Morton Arboretum, Lisle, IL
Murray, Karen and Peter, Falconskeape Gardens, Medina, OH
New York State Agricultural Experiment Station, Geneva, NY
Nairn, Robert, Nairn's Nurseries Ltd., Christchurch, New Zealand

Nock, Francis, 4826 Middle Ridge Rd., Perry, OH
Oakes, William, Glenelm Nursery, Miami, Manitoba, Canada
Parsons, S. B. & Sons, Flushing, Long Island, NY
Paul, Paul & Son, Cheshunt, England
Peffer, George P., Pewaukee, WI
Porter, A. J., Parkside, Saskatchewan, Canada
Potts, Julian, Julian Potts Nursery, Chesterland, OH
Preston, Isabella, Canada Department of Agriculture, Ottawa, Ontario
Provincial Horticultural Station, Brooks, Alberta, Canada
Reed, George M., Brooklyn Botanic Garden, Brooklyn, NY
Rivers, Thomas, Rivers Nursery, Sawbridgeworth, England
Ross, Henry, Gardenview Horticultural Park, Strongsville, OH
Royal Botanical Gardens, Hamilton, Ontario, Canada
Royal Botanic Gardens, Kew, England
Royal Horticultural Society Gardens, Wisley, Surrey, England
Salamandyck, William, Red Deer, Alberta, Canada
Sargent, Charles S., Arnold Arboretum, Jamaica Plain, MA
Saunders, William, Canada Department of Agriculture, Ottawa, Ontario
Sax, Karl, Bussey Institute and Arnold Arboretum, Jamaica Plain, MA
Scheidecker Nursery, Munich, Germany
Siebenthaler Nursery, Dayton, OH
Sim, William, Cliftondale, MA
Simpson, Robert C., Simpson Orchard Co., Inc., Vincennes, IN
Skinner, Frank Leith, Dropmore, Manitoba, Canada
Slavin, Bernard H., Monroe County Parks, Rochester, NY
Soulard, James G., Galena, IL
Späth, Ludwig, Späth Nurseries, Berlin, Germany
Stern, Major F. C., Goring-by-the-Sea, Sussex, England
Swarthmore College, Swarthmore, PA
Tanner, J. A., Palo, IA
University of Minnesota, St. Paul, MN
USDA, Division of Plant Exploration and Introduction, Bureau of Plant Industry, Washington, DC
Van Eseltine, G. P., New York State Experiment Station, Geneva, NY
Veitch, James & Sons, Ltd., Chelsea, England
Waterer, John & Sons, Bagshot, Surrey, England
Wayside Gardens, 1 Garden Lane, Hodges, SC
Welch, E. S., Mount Arbor Nurseries, Shenandoah, IA
Wellington, Richard, Geneva, NY
Wheeler, Seager, Canada Department of Agriculture, Rosthern, Saskatchewan
Whitney, A. E., Franklin Grove, IL
Will, Oscar H., & Co., Bismarck, ND
Wilson, E. H., Arnold Arboretum, Jamaica Plain, MA
Wilson, Wheelock, Minnesota State Arboretum, Excelsior, MN
Wodarz, R. L., Wyndmere, ND
Wood, A., Barrie, Canada
Wright, Hayward R., Auckland, New Zealand
Wright, Percy H., Moose Range, Saskatchewan, Canada

Wyman, Donald, Arnold Arboretum, Jamaica Plain, MA
Yanny, Michael and Lori, Johnson's Nursery, Milwaukee, WI
Yeager, A. F., Agricultural Experiment Station, Fargo, ND
Young, A. L., Bonnie Brooks Farms, Brooks, Alberta, Canada
Zampini, James, Lake County Nursery, Perry, OH

APPENDIX 5

Key to Crabapple Locations

Many descriptions of species and cultivars in this volume include numbers corresponding to locations where specimen trees can be found. The numbers for these locations are identical to those numbers used by Lester P. Nichols in his monumental work covering the disease ratings for flowering crabapples. Numbers omitted from the following list refer to locations eventually dropped by Nichols from the study for various reasons.

2 Longwood Gardens Nursery, Kennett Square, PA
3 Longwood Gardens, Kennett Square, PA
4 Swarthmore College, Swarthmore, PA
5 Rock Springs Test Plot, Rock Springs, PA
8 Case Estates, Arnold Arboretum, Weston, MA—street trees
9 Case Estates, Arnold Arboretum, Weston, MA—fields
10 Case Estates, Arnold Arboretum, Weston, MA—nursery
11 Case Estates, Arnold Arboretum, Weston, MA—Ash Street
12 Arnold Arboretum, Jamaica Plain, MA—Peter's Hill
13 Arnold Arboretum, Jamaica Plain, MA—hillside
14 Arnold Arboretum, Jamaica Plain, MA—Bussey Street
15 Arnold Arboretum, Jamaica Plain, MA—along Ry Road
16 Arnold Arboretum, Jamaica Plain, MA—listing
18 Dawes Arboretum, Newark, OH
19 Cole Nursery, Circleville, OH
20 Studebaker Nursery, New Carlisle, OH
22 Deeter Nursery, Clayton, OH
24 Secrest Arboretum, Ohio Agriculture Experiment Station, Wooster, OH
26 Holden Arboretum, Mentor-Kirtland, Mentor, OH
28 Dugan Nursery, Perry, OH
30 Busch Nursery, Pittsburgh, PA
31 Morton Arboretum, Lisle, IL—East
32 Morton Arboretum, Lisle, IL—West

35 U.S. National Arboretum, Washington, DC—main collection
36 U.S. Plant Introduction Station, Glenn Dale, MD
37 U.S. National Arboretum, Washington, DC—Bladenburg Road
38 Lester Nichols Residence
39 Eisler Nursery, Butler, PA—Rt. 528 East
40 Eisler Nursery, Butler, PA—Rt. 528 West
41 Eisler Nursery, Butler, PA—Rt. 528 N.E.
43 Eisler Nursery, Butler, PA—Rt. 528, back of barn
44 Eisler Nursery, Butler, PA—back of greenhouse
46 Lake County Nursery, Perry, OH
47 Falconskeape Gardens, Medina, OH
49 Adams Nursery, Westfield, MA
53 Snipes Garden Center, Morrisville, PA
54 Arie den Boer Arboretum, Water Works Park, Des Moines, IA
55 Purdue Horticultural Park, West Lafayette, IN
58 Willoway Nursery, Avon, OH
61 Michigan State University, Beaumont Nursery, East Lansing, MI
68 Tyler Arboretum, Media, PA
69 Weston Nursery, Hopkinton, MA
70 London Grove Nursery, West Grove, PA
71 Manbeck Nursery, New Knoxville, OH
72 Arnold Arboretum Nursery, Jamaica Plain, MA
73 Research Fruit Farm, Pennsylvania State University, Biglerville, PA
74 Campbell's Nursery and Garden Center, Lincoln, NE—Pinelake Road
75 Campbell's Nursery and Garden Center, Lincoln, NE
76 Nebraska Nurseries, Inc., Lincoln, NE
77 Marshall Nursery, Arlington, NE
78 Prusha Nursery Inc., Omaha, NE
79 University of Wisconsin Arboretum, Madison, WI
80 Municipality of Delavan, Delavan, WI
81 Boerner Botanical Gardens, Hales Corner, WI
82 Pioneer Gardens & Nursery, Pioneer St., Lincoln, NE
83 Hendrick's Sodding & Landscaping, Lincoln, NE
84 Westside Nursery, Omaha, NE
85 Chester Schwartze Nursery, Puyallup, WA
86 J. Frank Schmidt & Son Nursery, Boring, OR
87 University of Washington Arboretum, Seattle, WA
88 Hoffman Nursery, Stoystown, PA
89 Michigan State University, Campus, East Lansing, MI
91 Stonegate Farm Nursery, Poplar Grove, IL
93 John Peplinski residence, Fairbrook, PA
94 Win and K. Hock residence, Boalsburg, PA
95 Ted Kaufmann residence, Panorama Village, PA
100 Klehm Nursery, S. Barrington, IL

Glossary

Clone. A plant identical in all its parts to the original plant. A plant specially selected for certain unique characteristics that can be reproduced only by asexual propagation (e.g., by tissue culture, budding, cuttings, or grafting) whether that plant originated in the wild (i.e., as a species) or in cultivation.

Cultivar. A cultivated plant. Any unselected cultivated seedling, whether a member of a group of unnamed seedlings or a member of a group of similar seedlings of the same hybrid background (e.g., Rosyblooms).

Deccabrid. A plant resulting from the cross of ten species.

EMLA. A series of virus-free rootstocks from the Paradise apple stocks of Europe. The series is named for the *E*ast *M*alling and *L*ong *A*shton research stations in England, which introduced these dwarfing rootstocks.

Hybrid. A plant resulting from the cross of two species.

Mini-fruit. Any miniature crabapple whose fruit has a diameter less than 0.25 in (0.6 cm).

Multibrid. A plant with many species in its makeup. Multibrids are so intercrossed it is impossible to determine their progenitors.

Nonobrid. A plant resulting from the cross of nine species.

Octobrid. A plant resulting from the cross of eight species.

Quatrobrid. A plant resulting from the cross of four species.

Quintobrid. A plant resulting from the cross of five species.

Rosyblooms. A group of open-pollinated seedlings of *Malus pumila* 'Niedzwetzkyana' or crosses of *M. pumila* 'Niedzwetzkyana' × *M. baccata*. Rosybloom crabapples are characterized by red leaves, red buds, red flowers, and red fruit. All are outstanding in deep rose-red, pink, rose with lavender or magenta tones of springtime bloom. Their fruit is rather large and a dull red-purple. Their great fault is that most are leafless or heavily defoliated by mid-summer with apple scab. As a group they are rather large trees often reaching 35–40 ft (10.8–12.2 m) high and as wide.

Septobrid. A plant resulting from the cross of seven species.

Sextobrid. A plant resulting from the cross of six species.

Strain. A seedling group.

Tribrid. A plant resulting from the cross of three species.

Bibliography

Anderson, Edgar. 1949. *Introgressive Hybridization*. New York: John Wiley.

Anderson, Edward. 1935. "Oriental Crabapples." *Bulletin of the Arnold Arboretum* 8 (Dec.): 18–20. Reprinted in *Garden Digest* 8 (Feb. 1936): 18–20.

Arnold Arboretum. 1990. Computer Listing of all Flowering Crabapples at the Arboretum, Jamaica Plain, MA.

Asami, Yoshichi. 1927. *The Crabapples and Nectarines of Japan*. Tokyo: Marquis Nabeshima. 1–55, 78–86.

Bickelhaupt, Robert. 1986. "Typar Solves Weed and Root Sprout Problems." *Malus* (IOCS Bulletin) 2 (1): 16–17.

Boom, B. K. 1965. *Nederlandse Dendrologie*. Vol. 1. Wageningen: H. Veenam & Zonen N.V. 275–280.

Brewer, James E. 1977. "Crabapple Trees Offer Seasonal Ornamentation." *Science in Agriculture* 24: 2.

Brewer, James E., Lester P. Nichols, Charles C. Powell, and Elton M. Smith. 1980. *The Flowering Crabapple: A Tree for All Seasons*. The Cooperative Extension Service of the Northeast States. 1–38.

Browicz, K. 1970. "*Malus florentina*: Its History, Systematic Position and Geographical Distribution." *Fragm. Flor. et Geobot.* 16 (1): 61–83.

———. 1972. "*Malus* × *Malosorbus*." *Erilobus in Flora of Turkey* 4: 157–160.

Chadwick, L. C. 1963. "Flowering Trees, Crabapples." *Brooklyn Botanic Garden, Special Handbook of Plants & Gardens* 19 (1): 4–10.

Challice, J. S., and A. H. Williams. 1970. "A Comparative Biochemical Study of Phenolase Specificity in *Malus*, *Pyrus* and Other Plants." *Phytochemistry* 9: 1261–1269.

Chapman, D. J. 1978. "Crab Apples Can Be Both Beautiful and Tough Weeds." *Trees and Turf* 27, 30.

Cummings, James N. 1988. "Further Notes on the Oregon Crabapple, *Malus fusca*, Which Were Featured in *MALUS* 1985." *Malus* 2 (1): 3.

Darlington, C. D., and A. P. Wylie. 1961. *Chromosome Atlas*. 2nd ed. London: George Allen & Unwin; New York: Hafner Publishing Co.

den Boer, Arie F. 1958. "Some Outstanding Old and New Varieties of Flowering Crabapples." *Iowa State Horticulture Society Proceedings, 1956–57* 91: 56–59.

———. 1959. *Flowering Crabapples.* American Association of Nurserymen.
———. 1938–1962. Letters to author.
Dirr, Michael A. 1977. *Manual of Woody Landscape Plants: Their Identification, Ornamental Characteristics, Culture, Propagation and Uses.* Champaign, IL: Stipes Publishing Co. 438–458.
Donner, Henry E. 1963. "Crabapples." *Popular Gardens* (April): 39 ff.
Eickhorst, Walter, Ray Schulenberg, and Floyd Swink. 1972. *Woody Plants of the Morton Arboretum.* Lisle, IL: Morton Arboretum.
Ellenwood, C. W. 1929. "Fruit Varieties in Ohio. IV. Crab Apples." *Ohio Agriculture Experiment Station Bulletin* 434.
Evans, Thomas H. 1985. "Design Aspects of Crabs in Architecture." *Malus* (IOCS Bulletin) 1 (2): 24–26.
Falconskeape Gardens. 1990. Computer Listing of all Flowering Crabapples at Falconskeape, Medina, OH.
Ford, John E. 1973. "Flowering Crabapples." *Secrest Arboretum Notes.* 1–2.
Goble, H. W. 1971. "Insects and Mites of Ornamental Trees and Shrubs." Department of Environmental Biology, Ontario Agriculture College, University of Guelph. Ontario Department of Agriculture and Food Publication 93.
Graham, T. O. 1975. "The Possible Significance of Present Interest in Crosses Between *Amelanchier, Aronia, Cotoneaster, Crataegus, Malus, Pyracantha, Pyrus,* and *Sorbus.*" *American and Canadian Society of Horticultural Science Bulletin* (August). University of Guelph, Ontario, Canada.
Green, Jim. 1988. "The Most Popular Shade and Flowering Trees." *Malus* (IOCS Bulletin) 3 (2): 12–15.
Green, Thomas. 1985. "Evaluating Crabapples for Aesthetic Qualities." *Malus* (IOCS Bulletin) 1 (2): 19–20.
———. 1988a. "The Allegheny Crab." *Malus* (IOCS Bulletin) 3 (1): 21–22.
———. 1988b. "Meritorious *Malus*: *Malus* ×*zumi* and *Malus* ×*zumi* var. *calocarpa.*" *Malus* (IOCS Bulletin) 3 (2): 17–20.
———. 1990a. "Crabs You Should Know." *Malus* (IOCS Bulletin) 4 (2): 4–6.
———. 1990b. "Crabs You Should Know: *Malus* 'Professor Sprenger'." *Malus* (IOCS Bulletin) 4 (2): 4–6.
———. 1990c. "*Malus coronaria* var. *dasycalyx.*" *Malus* (IOCS Bulletin) 4 (2): 7–8.
———. N.d. National Crabapple Evaluation Program, Morton Arboretum. Mimeo.
Green, Thomas K., Garry Watson, and Kris R. Bachtell. 1989. "Tree Planting Recommendations." *Malus* (IOCS Bulletin) 4 (1): 8–9, 13–17.
Hansen, N. E. 1927. "Plant Introductions." *South Dakota Agriculture Experiment Station Bulletin* 224: 6–17.
———. 1929. "Experiments in Plant Heredity." *South Dakota Agriculture Experiment Station Bulletin* 237.
———. 1931. "The Ornamental Trees of South Dakota." *South Dakota Agriculture Experiment Station Bulletin* 260: 28–38.
———. 1937. "Fruits, Old and New, and Northern Plant Novelties." *South Dakota Agriculture Experiment Station Bulletin* 309: 7–9.
———. 1940. "New Hardy Fruits for the Northwest." *South Dakota Agriculture Experiment Station Bulletin* 339.
———. 1944. "Fifty Years Work as Agricultural Explorer and Plant Breeder." *Iowa State Horticulture Society Trans.* 79: 43–47.
Hasselkus, Edward R. 1986. "Rootstock Suckering: A Common Maintenance Problem." *Malus* (IOCS Bulletin) 2 (1): 14–15.
Henning, W. 1947. "Morphologisch-Systematische und Genetische Undersuchungen an Arten und Artbastarden der Gattung *Malus.*" *Der Züchter* 17–18 (10–12): 289–349.

Hill, Polly. 1988. "Crabs You Should Know: *Malus* 'Louisa'." *Malus* (IOCS Bulletin) 3 (1): 17.

Holtz, Ann E. 1989. "*Malus obscurus—Malus angustifolia.*" *Malus* (IOCS Bulletin) 4 (1): 18–20.

Huckins, C. A. 1968. "Flower and Fruit Keys to the Ornamental Crabapples Cultivated in the United States." *Baileya* 15 (4): 129–164.

———. 1972. "A Revision of the Sections of the Genus *Malus*." *Diss. Abstract Int. B.* 33 (3): 1031.

Hyslop, Craig Alan. 1988. "*Malus* 'Obscurus'—*Malus* 'Hyslop'." *Malus* (IOCS Bulletin) 3 (2): 1–2.

Janick, Jules. 1987. "The Apple-Pear Pickle—The Name of the Apple." *Malus* (IOCS Bulletin) 2 (2): 3–5.

Jarrett, J. M., and A. H. Williams. 1971. "Chemo-Taxonomy of *Malus* Species: The Fruit of *Malus* Species and Hybrids." *Long Ashton Research Station Report 1970.*

Jefferson, Roland M. 1968. "'Fuji'—A New Crabapple—and Other Doubles." *Horticulture* 47 (1): 22–25.

———. 1970. *History, Progeny, and Locations of Crabapples of Documented Authentic Origin.* National Arboretum Contribution No. 2. Washington, DC: Agricultural Research Service, U.S. Department of Agriculture.

Kinnen, Norbert. 1986. "The Work of the Late Professor Lester P. Nichols." *Malus* (IOCS Bulletin) 2 (1): 6–8.

Klehm, Roy. 1990. Wholesale Catalog—Descriptive Listing of New Ornamental Crabapples: Extensive Descriptions of Newly Patented Clones and Originators. South Barrington, IL: Klehm Nursery. 14–21.

Koidzumi, G. 1934. "A Synopsis of the Genus *Malus*." *Acta Phytotax. et Geobot.* 3 (4): 179–196.

Krüssmann, G. 1962. *Handbuch der Laubgeholze*. Vol. 2. Berlin. 110–125.

Lape, Fred. 1965. *A Garden of Trees and Shrubs: Practical Hints for Planning and Planting an Arboretum.* Ithaca, NY: Comstock Publishing Association, Cornell University Press. 80 ff.

———. 1979. *Apples and Man*. New York: Van Nostrand Reinhold, Litton Educational Publishing. 160.

Leslie, W. R. 1946. "Tree Fruits Grown in Prairie Orchards." *Farmers' Bulletin* (Canada Department of Agriculture, Morden, Manitoba): 135.

———. 1949. "Plant Introductions." *Progress Report 1938–1946* (Canada Department of Agriculture, Dominion Experiment Station, Morden, Manitoba): 11–13.

Liberty Hyde Bailey Hortorium. 1978. *Hortus Third: A Concise Dictionary of Plants Cultivated in the United States and Canada*. 3rd ed. New York: Macmillan. 699–701.

Likhonos, F. D. 1974. "A Survey of the Species in the Genus *Malus* Mill." *Trudy Prikl. Bot. Genet. Sel.* 52 (3): 16–34.

Mackey, Elizabeth. 1988. "Crabs You Should Know—*Malus* 'Madonna'." *Malus* (IOCS Bulletin) 3 (2): 23–26.

Martens, John. 1985a. "*Malus obscurus—M. fusca.*" *Malus* (IOCS Bulletin) 1 (1): 8–9.

———. 1985b. "*Malus obscurus—M. ioensis.*" *Malus* (IOCS Bulletin) 1 (2): 27–28.

———. 1986. "*Malus obscurus—M. formosana.*" *Malus* (IOCS Bulletin) 2 (1): 22–25.

———. 1987a. "*Malus obscurus—M. florentina.*" *Malus* (IOCS Bulletin) 2 (2): 3–5.

———. 1987b. "*Malus obscurus—M. tschonoskii.*" *Malus* (IOCS Bulletin) 2 (3): 23–24.

Martens, John, and Thomas Green. 1988. "*Malus obscurus—Malus sieboldii.*" *Malus* (IOCS Bulletin) 3 (1): 26–28.

National Arboretum. 1990. Computer Listing of all Flowering Crabapples at the National Arboretum, Washington, DC.

Nichols, Lester P. 1950–1986. Letters to Fr. John L. Fiala.

———. 1967. "Selecting Disease-Free Flowering Crab Apples for 1967." Pennsylvania State University, Plant Pathology Extension Service.
———. 1968. "Selecting Disease Resistant Crabapples. Pennsylvania State University, College of Agriculture and Home Economics, Extension Service.
———. 1973. "Disease-Resistant Crabapples—1973." Pennsylvania State University, Plant Pathology Extension Service.
———. 1974. "Disease Resistant Crabapples—1974." Pennsylvania State University, Plant Pathology Extension Service.
———. 1978. "Disease Resistant Crabapples—Results of 1977 Survey." Pennsylvania State University, Plant Pathology Contribution No. 1020.
———. 1979a. "Disease Resistant Crabapples—Results of 1978 Survey." Pennsylvania State University, Plant Pathology Contribution No. 1057.
———. 1979b. "Disease Resistant Crabapples—Results of 1979 Survey." Pennsylvania State University, Plant Pathology Contribution No. 1159.
———. 1981. "Disease Resistant Crabapples—Results of 1980 Survey." Pennsylvania State University, Plant Pathology Contribution No. 1244.
———. 1983. "Disease Resistant Crabapples—Results of 1981–1982 Survey." Pennsylvania State University, Plant Pathology Contribution No. 1401.
———. 1984a. "Disease Resistant Crabapples—Results of 1983 Survey." Pennsylvania State University, Plant Pathology Contribution No. 1447.
———. 1984b. "Fragrance in Crabapples." Letter to Nancy Ernst. 27 January.
———. 1985a. "Disease Resistant Crabapples—Results of 1984 Survey." Pennsylvania State University, Plant Pathology Contribution No. 1502.
———. 1985b. "The Origin of the International Ornamental Crabapple Society." *Malus* (IOCS Bulletin) 1 (1): 5–6.
———. 1986a. "Disease Resistant Crabapples—Results of 1985 Survey." Pennsylvania State University, Plant Pathology Contribution No. 1558.
———. 1986b. "Fragrance of Flowering Crabapples." *Malus* (IOCS Bulletin) 2 (1): 12–13.
———. 1986c. "List of Crabapple Code Numbers and Current Accepted Names for Three Crabapples." *Malus* (IOCS Bulletin) 2 (1): 9–11.
———. 1987a. "Flowering Crabapples Named for People, Flowering Crabapples Named for Places, Miscellaneous Names of Flowering Crabapples." *Malus* (IOCS Bulletin) 2 (3): 12–20.
———. 1987b. "A List of the Common Names of Crabapples." *Malus* (IOCS Bulletin) 2 (3): 9–11.
Nichols, L. P., and J. E. Brewer. 1972. "Evaluation of Selected Crabapple Cultivars—Disease Resistance and Growth Characteristics—1972." Pennsylvania State University, College of Agriculture and Home Economics, Extension Service.
———. 1974. "Evaluation of Selected Crabapple Cultivars—Disease Resistance and Growth Characteristics—1973." Pennsylvania State University Cooperative Extension Service.
———. 1977. "Flowering Crabapples in Central Pennsylvania." Pennsylvania State University, Plant Pathology Contribution No. 1019, Horticulture Mimeo Series II-71.
———. 1979. "Flowering Crabapples in Pennsylvania—1978." Pennsylvania State University, Plant Pathology Contribution No. 1066, Horticulture Mimeo, Series II-75.
———. 1985a. "Crabapple Diseases and Their Prevention." *Malus* (IOCS Bulletin) 1 (2): 9–18.
———. 1985b. "National Crabapple Evaluation Program." *Malus* (IOCS Bulletin) 1 (2): 1–2.
Nichols, L. P., and Gordon DeWolf. 1976. "The Best Flowering Crabapples." *Horticulture* 54 (9): 17–19.
Norton, R. A., and J. King. 1990. "Ornamental Crabapple Trials." Washington State

University, Research & Extension Unit, Mount Vernon, WA. *Malus* (IOCS Bulletin) 4 (2): 10–13.

Ohwi, Jisaburo. 1965. *Flora of Japan*. Washington, DC. 548–549.

Pair, John C. 1988. "Inhibition of Crabapple Suckers." *Malus* (IOCS Bulletin) 3 (1): 23–25.

Palven, Jan. 1988. "Ornamental Crabapple Trees in Monmouth County, New Jersey." *Malus* (IOCS Bulletin) 3 (2): 4–11.

Pellett, Harold, and Ken Vogel. 1990. "Research Activities (Fruit Persistence and Quality)." *Malus* (IOCS Bulletin) 4 (2): 23–29.

Ponomarenko, V. V. 1974. "The Taxonomy and Geography of Some Species in the Genus *Malus*." *Bot. Genet. Sel.* 52 (3): 35–47.

Powell, Betty. 1988. "A Perfect Crab—*M.* × 'Naragansett'." *Malus* (IOCS Bulletin) 3 (1): 18–20.

Preston, Isabella. 1941. "Rosybloom Crabapples." *Canada Horticulture and Home Magazine* 64: 93, 102.

———. 1944. "Rosybloom Crabapples for Northern Gardens." *New York Botanical Garden Journal* 45: 169–174.

Rehder, Alfred. 1920. "New Species, Varieties and Combinations from the Herbarium and the Collections of the Arnold Arboretum." *Arnold Arboretum Journal* 2: 47–58.

———. 1926. "New Species, Varieties and Combinations from the Herbarium and the Collection of the Arnold Arboretum." *Arnold Arboretum Journal* 7: 24–28.

———. 1937. *Manual of Cultivated Trees and Shrubs*. 1st ed. New York: Macmillan. 391–400.

———. 1949. *Bibliography of Cultivated Trees and Shrubs*. Jamaica Plain, MA: Arnold Arboretum. 267–276.

———. 1958. *Manual of Cultivated Trees and Shrubs*. 2nd ed. New York: Macmillan. 389–399.

———. N.d. Personal File Cards—Genus *Malus*: Notes on All Known Names, Citations and Evaluations of Crabapples.

Ross, Henry. 1988. "A Clone by Any Other Name . . . Is Not a Clone." *American Nurseryman* (December): 47 ff.

Sabuco, John J. 1987. "True Confessions of a Crabby Landscape Architect." *Malus* (IOCS Bulletin) 2 (3): 25–31.

———. 1989. "Crabs You Should Know: *Malus* 'Indian Magic'." *Malus* (IOCS Bulletin) 4 (1): 10–12.

Sargent, C. S. 1926. *Manual of the Trees of North America*. 2nd ed. Boston and New York. 379–389.

Saunders, William. 1911. "Progress in the Breeding of Hardy Apples." *Canada Central Experiment Farm Bulletin* 68.

Scanlon, Edward H. 1965. "Classic Trees for Urban Gardens and Streets." *New York Botanical Garden Journal* 15 (5): 186–189, 210.

Schmidt, H. 1974. "The Inheritance of Apomixis in Polyploid *Malus* Rootstock Material." *Proceedings XIX International Horticulture Congress* 1a: 345.

Schmidt, J. Frank, & Son Co., 1990–91. Catalog—Descriptive Listing and Charts of Named Newer Clones of Flowering Crabapples. Boring, OR. 40–55.

Simpson Nursery Co. 1982. "Descriptive Listing." Mimeo.

Simpson, Robert. N.d. "The Flowering Crabapples—A Descriptive List." Vincennes, IN: Simpson Orchard Co. 1–7.

Skirm, G. W. 1939. "Breeding New Varieties of Ornamental Crabapples at the Arnold Arboretum." *Bulletin of Popular Information* (Arnold Arboretum) 7: 65–67.

Slavin, A. D. 1931. "Notes on New Forms of *Malus* and *Crataegus*." *American Midland Naturalist* 12: 363–364.

Snyder, L. C., A. G. Johnson, and R. J. Stadtherr. 1957. "New Ornamentals for 1958."

Minnesota Agriculture Experiment Station Misc. Report 29.

Snyder, L. C., R. A. Phillips, and A. G. Johnson. "A New Flowering Crabapple." *Minnesota Agriculture Experiment Station Misc. Report* 51.

South Dakota Agriculture Experiment Station. 1939. *Northern Plant Novelties for 1939.* Brookings, SD.

———. 1940. *Northern Plant Novelties for 1940.* Brookings, SD.

———. 1941. *Northern Plant Novelties for 1941.* Brookings, SD.

Van der Hoeven, Gus A., and John C. Pair. 1988. "Flowering Crabapples." *Malus* (IOCS Bulletin) 3 (1): 5–10.

Van Eseltine, G. P. 1933. "Notes on the Species of Apples. II. The Japanese Flowering Crabapples of the Sieboldii Group and Their Hybrids." *New York State Agriculture Experiment Station Technical Bulletin* 214.

———. 1934. "Ornamental Apples and Crabapples." *New York State Agriculture Experiment Station Circular* 139.

Vick, Roger. 1990. "The Rosybloom Story." *Malus* 4 (2): 14–18.

Wang, Chi-wu. 1961. "The Forests of China with a Survey of Grassland and Desert Vegetation." Maria Moors Cabot Foundation, Publication No. 5, Harvard University, Cambridge, MA. 72–77, 82, 99, 106, 114, 128, 183, 240.

Warren, Keith. 1985. "Propagation and Production of Ornamental Crabapples." *Malus* (IOCS Bulletin) 1 (2): 21–23.

———. 1987. "Crabapple Bloom Sequence." *Malus* (IOCS Bulletin) 2 (2): 7–8.

———. 1989. "Perfecting the Crab." *Malus* (IOCS Bulletin) 4 (1): 4–7.

Wijnands, D. O. 1978–1979. "De Systematiek Van Het Geslacht *Malus.*" *Botanische Tuinen te Wageningen, Vakgroep Plantensystematiek en-geografie der Landbouwhogeschool.* Wageningen: Groen. 403–409. (Reprint from *Dendrologendag* 5 October 1978.)

Wijnands, D. O., and J. Belder. 1979. *De Appel Van Von Siebold, Vakgroep Plantensystematiek en-geografie.* Wageningen: Groen.

Wilson, Ernest H. 1928. *More Aristocrats of the Garden: The American Crabapples.* Boston: Stratford Company. 238–247.

Wilson, Wheelock. N.d. "The Evaluation of Crabapples." Special mimeo publication, Men's Garden Clubs of America.

Wister, John. 1951. "The Best in Flowering Crabapples." *Arborist's News* 16: 25–28.

———. 1955–56. *Swarthmore Plant Notes.* Vol. 1, part 1. Swarthmore, PA. 107–121.

Wyman, Donald E. 1939. "Flowering Crabapples for Spring and Fall." *Bulletin of Popular Information* (Arnold Arboretum) 7: 25–31.

———. 1948. "New or Rare Ornamental Plants Recently Distributed to Commercial Nurserymen by the Arnold Arboretum." *Arnoldia* 8: 54–56.

———. 1955. *Crabapples for America.* American Association of Botanical Gardens and Arboretums.

———. 1956. "Crabapples for Ornamental Fruit." *Arnoldia* 16: 29–32.

———. 1958. "Where Some of the Crab-Apples Come From." *New York Botanical Garden Journal* 8: 122–124.

———. 1959. "Crabapples of Merit." *Arnoldia* 19: 15–22.

———. 1965. *Trees for American Gardens.* New York: Macmillan. 294–319, 483–486.

Yanny, Michael D., and Lori K. Yanny. 1988. "The Boerner Crabapple Collection." *Malus* (IOCS Bulletin) 3 (1): 11–15.

———. 1990. "The Ornamental Crabapple: A Tree with an Image Problem." *Malus* (IOCS Bulletin) 4 (2): 19–22.

Yu, Te-tsun, and Chen-lung Yen. 1956. "Study of the Chinese Species of Genus *Malus.*" *Acta Phytotax. Sinica* 5 (2): 108–110, fig. VIII, t/m XXI.

Zampini, James W. 1990. Catalog—Descriptive Listing of New Crabapples. Perry, OH: Lake County Nursery. 72–82.

General Index

Index of Crabapple Names

Boldfaced numbers indicate main entries.